Household War

un CIVIL WARS

Household War

*How Americans Lived and
Fought the Civil War*

EDITED BY **LISA TENDRICH FRANK**
AND **LEEANN WHITES**

The University of Georgia Press *Athens*

Designed by
Set in Adobe Caslon Pro by Classic City Composition LLC, Athens, Georgia

Most University of Georgia Press titles are
available from popular e-book vendors.

Printed digitally

Library of Congress Cataloging-in-Publication Data

Names: Frank, Lisa Tendrich, editor. | Whites, LeeAnn, editor.
Title: Household war : how Americans lived and fought the Civil War / edited by
   Lisa Tendrich Frank and LeeAnn Whites.
Description: Athens : The University of Georgia Press, [2019] | Series: Uncivil wars |
   Includes bibliographical references and index.
Identifiers: LCCN 2019020515 | ISBN 9780820356310 (hardcover) | ISBN 9780820356341 (paperback) |
   ISBN 9780820356303 (ebook)
Subjects: LCSH: Families—United States—History—19th century. | Households—United
   States—History—19th century. | United States—History—Civil War, 1861–1865—
   Social aspects. | United States—Social conditions—To 1865.
Classification: LCC E468.9 .H805 2019 | DDC 973.7/1—dc23
LC record available at https://lccn.loc.gov/2019020515

CONTENTS

Household War

The Civil War as a Household War

LISA TENDRICH FRANK AND LEEANN WHITES

This volume is based on a simple but important premise: that the Civil War can be read as a household war, a conflict rooted in, fought by, and waged against households. As a physical place and an ideological construct, households were the guiding principle behind many of the war's causes as well as the impetus for wartime strategies pursued by the individuals, polities, and militaries involved. In the war's aftermath, the reconstruction of households now free of slavery and the establishment of autonomous households by the formerly enslaved both constituted critical centers of continued resistance and conflict. The importance of households to the Civil War and to the era as a whole should not come as a surprise. After all, many scholars have demonstrated the ways that households served as the basis of the social order for preindustrial societies across the globe. In the United States, slaveholding and nonslaveholding communities, rural and urban communities, Northern and Southern communities, as well as native-born Americans, immigrants, and members of Native American tribes all operated in a world centered around the household. As a result, even with cultural and regional differences, the household served as the basic building block for American politics, economics, and social relations. The household structured democratic representation as well as labor and guided how individuals engaged with one another and formed communities. The Confederacy and the Union necessarily relied on the support and mobilization of these households, which in turn shaped their nations in their image. Consequently, in terms of the long social trajectory, the Civil War is best framed as the most revolutionary moment in the transformation of the nation's household order. The war itself was a household war.[1]

Indeed, the Civil War itself should be understood as a military struggle that was made necessary by the difficulties inherent in the transformation of an American household order grounded in the enslavement of African Americans. Prior to the war, political tensions were exacerbated by the structural divergence of households. In the South, democratic rights were consolidated in the hands of a small community of predominately rural white male heads of households with an increasingly widespread and entrenched system of slaveholding. This Southern household structure contrasted with developments in the North where the growing market economy and a growing dedication to separate spheres took work out of the household and expanded political power to a growing population of white male workers, while contributing to the rise of the status of women and domesticity. The wealthiest and most politically empowered households were often white slaveholding Southern households, and the contradictions between these household forms became increasingly pointed. Westward expansion, in particular, highlighted the growing differences between free Northern and slaveholding Southern households. At the same time, it brought them together in what is commonly recognized as the military root of the Civil War, the border war of Missouri and Kansas.[2]

Commentary on these disparate household forms came to the forefront of the national debate over the expansion of slavery. That discussion also bled into the nation's popular culture, most notably in the form of Harriet Beecher Stowe's *Uncle Tom's Cabin*. The novel struck a chord with American readers, in part because its appeal to antislavery sentiment was based on the way that slavery as an institution undermined familial ties for all members of slaveholding households. In particular, Stowe's novel drew attention to the ways in which those people rendered as property by the law were bought and sold in the market as it benefited the economic viability of the white household, while the system simultaneously broke apart African American households as slaveholders sold enslaved mothers away from their children and husbands away from their wives. For white slaveholding household members, rendering black people as property without even the legal right to their own bodies created, as South Carolina diarist Mary Boykin Chesnut noted, enslaved children who resembled their white slaveholders: "the mulattoes one sees in every family exactly resemble the white children." In her account of a conversation among slaveholding women who had read Stowe's book, she noted the irony of the situation. After all, she wrote, "every lady tells you who is the father of all the mulatto children in everybody's household, but those in her own she seems to think drop from the clouds, or pretends so to think." Although banned in the

South for its attack on the "peculiar institution," Stowe's domestic call to arms resonated with Northerners. Its focus on the way slaveholding violated the integrity of familial relations and household structures reflected a rising respect and recognition that accompanied the rapid growth of the capitalist market order and the emergence of the family increasingly distanced from class relations in the North.[3]

The focus in this volume on the Civil War era household is, then, quite different from the common way that Civil War households are generally discussed. Collectively, these essays demonstrate that the war actually revolved around the homefront and, specifically, the household and household relations rather than the other way around. The essays explore the household as both a physical place and a set of social ideals. This approach differs from other scholarly conceptualizations of the wartime household. Most stories of divided families and households, where one brother fought for the Confederacy and another for the Union, illuminate and personalize the national tragedy and otherwise liven up the descriptions of battles and the familial struggles of individual soldiers. Moving beyond the household as the encumbrance or the inspiration of individual soldiers and reframing our understanding of the war as a household war both allows and compels us to grapple with the reality that households were both the sites of war as well as the basic social structures that underlay the Confederate and Union armies, polities, and economies. These essays show some of the ways in which the war itself was fought primarily in, through, or as an extension of the household and household relations. Viewing the war from the location of the household itself allows us to consider the role that all members played in the conflict, men and women, enslaved and free.[4]

Following Stephanie McCurry's observation that even the poorest white man in the South who was a head of his own household was nonetheless considered a free man and a "master" in the household economy, we can understand how men on both sides of the war fought for what they considered to be their standing as free men in the household order as well as in the larger social order. The decision to fight, remain in the army, or desert were all household decisions that were both made by families and felt by families. In both the Union and the Confederacy, households were mobilized and were deployed in order to wage war, and armies waged war on households in order to undermine their willingness and ability to support the war. Soldiers went to the battlefield to protect their own households, and they survived on the war front because of the supplies sent to them from their distant households. Some soldiers left their units, often temporarily, to protect personally their households, and others stayed on the battlefield because of encouragement from their households. In all cases, household relations determined how soldiers thought about and fought the war. As J. Matthew Gallman has noted about men's service in the Union, communities understood that men's military service was contingent on the situation of their households.[5]

Acknowledging the importance of the household to the making of war, some commanders brought the war directly to households, invading the physical spaces that defined it. In various ways, households transformed into battlefields. Farmlands and backyards filled with military encampments and became locations of battles. Enemy forces besieged towns and ransacked homes filled with civilians. In all cases, the lines between battlefield and homefront became blurred and households increasingly had to deal with the realities of wartime including deprivation, destruction, and invasion. Individuals on both sides of the war redefined and reestablished households as they voluntarily moved from place to place or were forced to evacuate their own homes.[6]

Conceptualizing the war as a household war similarly highlights the ways in which men and women experienced the Civil War in a unified rather than segregated manner and allows a closer look at how women influenced the war. This interpretation contrasts with most histories that have considered the household, women, and gender relations as auxiliary to the formal field of battle. In this conventional approach, battles and armies shaped the basic contours of the separate homefront. Women and households were important in a narrowly defined way for what they could do for men at the front. In framing the battlefield as central and the household as secondary, these works miss the ways in which women's wartime contributions—whether in the household, the waged labor force, or on the military front—were part of a larger transformation of the social order into the modern form of the household, the family, where women were recognized for their critical contribution to the grounding of household relations in affective relations.[7]

Household developments during the Civil War are most easily discerned by considering emancipation, which offers the most obvious connection between the war and the transformation of the household, one that continued long after the closing of the military conflict. This change went beyond transforming the household economies and separating black and white households in the postwar South. A study of emancipation necessarily includes the ways that Union military campaigns addressed the Southern household as a site of confrontation and liberation as well as the ways that families of enslaved men and women took their own households (within households) into account during wartime. It also includes the Northern households that favored or feared the implications of African Americans altering their financial and cultural futures. Centering households in discussions of wartime emancipation highlights the interconnectedness between the experiences of free African Americans, military officials, and households across the nation.[8]

Reframing the war to consider the household as an originating point in the war, rather than as an auxiliary to it, allows us to see "occupation" as integral to the war. The focus on the traditional field of battle obscures the ways in which much of the war is about invading the South and occupying the captured areas, including private residences. Consequently, occupation was a driving force of Union and Confederate war strategies. Women and households were not "the hapless victims or collateral damage of Union occupation" but were instead the "critical bottom rail of the war of occupation." The spaces that people occupied during the war were in part dictated by family and in part governed by necessity. Households shifted throughout the war to deal with missing household members or additional ones and to adapt to wartime conditions. Households also extended to incorporate friends and family who boarded together often out of necessity and for reasons including safety, support, and loneliness. Households also relocated throughout the war, sometimes because they were forced to do so and sometimes out of choice. As enemy troops occupied towns, the residents found themselves looking for ways to adapt their households as well as to move them.[9]

Recent work in guerrilla studies has especially explored the interconnectedness between fighting men and their households. Following in the wake of the assumed dissociation of the formal field of battle from the homefront, guerrilla war during the Civil War has been understood as an aberration, a violation of the properly separate fields of the household and the battlefield. However, as Joseph M. Beilein Jr. has demonstrated, guerrilla war was, in fact, a form of warfare fought out of households, supplied by households, and pursued in the defense of household interests. In some places, white men fought from the outset as guerrillas, especially in the slaveholding border states that the Union moved first to occupy. Their war has not been counted either literally or figuratively. Historians who assess the loyalty or disloyalty of these regions based on the numbers of men who fought for the Confederacy or the United States fail to consider the men who fought as household warriors. When traditional military historians have considered guerrilla warfare and its relationship to households, they have characterized it as random or little more than robbery; rather than seeing it as a household war, they instead judge it as a war against households. However, new research in the field indicates that guerrilla warfare was not a random war of violence against households, but that it was primarily aimed against occupying Union forces—it was household warfare.[10]

This approach to household war builds on our own past work in *Occupied Women*, but also follows the way that the field has been advanced along similar lines. If the Civil War was a household war, it became one because of the centrality of households in antebellum America. In her now classic work, *Within the Plantation Household*, Elizabeth Fox-Genovese made the most convincing argument for the slaveholding household as the primary defining quality and organizational structure of the South. In fact, she argues, it was the Southern household's grounding in slavery and the attendant political empowerment of the slaveholding class and the slaveholding household as a social structural form that created the biggest roadblock to the emergence of a modern social order in the United States. As a result, the South's focus on the slaveholding household led first to a sectional crisis over the expansion of slavery in new territories and next to the secession of the slaveholding South. Finally, it led to a bloody war that ended slavery and, on the face of it, established all households as free. This process was a giant step in the direction of reconfiguring the household for the entire United States as a home centered on kin relations, while at the same time rendering free labor the baseline in the labor market. As a result, the Civil War can be seen as firmly rooted in the household because of "the deep ideological differences between northern and southern households [which] resulted primarily from the different social systems in which they were embedded."[11]

Building on Fox-Genovese, other scholars have expanded this view of the household and shown its close connection to the war. Tellingly, one of the early seminal works on gender and the Civil War was entitled *Divided Houses*. Furthermore, regardless of region, households played an important role in antebellum America because "the root of commonality was the household itself, at once an economic, familial, and political unit." The household, therefore, encompassed family and community, sometimes black and white. As a result, in both regions the head of the household was equally important. Other scholars have noted that the rise of the Republican Party was in part due to the changes occurring in Northern households. These households remained important throughout the war and emerged altered from the conflict. Postwar elite households "were in flux," because "the loss of fathers, brothers, husbands, suitors, and friends created temporary alterations, some of which became permanent. Shifts in position and wealth also made a difference in the kinds of kin and non-kin who resided and visited in the white household." Consequently, the wartime necessity of living together with relatives and long-term visitors had lasting effects on the resulting Southern household. Furthermore, the Civil War "quite literally turned the household inside out" and "laid bare to public view and public significance the role of gender in the social order." If we ignore the fact that it was "a war of divided households," we cannot truly understand the motivations, repercussions, and implications of the Civil War as a whole.[12]

Exploring the Civil War from the household vantage point allows us to revisit some familiar fronts from a new angle. In this volume we have purposefully put the homefront as the center of our narrative and left the formal field of battle as an extension of it. This inversion of focus follows from recent claims as to the widespread nature of guerrilla or irregular war, the household base of this type of combat, and the predominance of the skirmish, rather than the formal battle as the primary military form. The essays in this volume push off of this work of military historians as well as new work by historians of women and gender relations concerning the extent to which the formal field of battle itself is also dependent on the domestic supply line and the way in which soldiers' behavior is in fact structured by their household status or their understanding of the connection between masculinity and battlefield performance.[13]

All of the essays in this volume build on scholarship that understands the Civil War as an era rather than as an event limited to the four years on the formal field of battle. This momentous era includes the shifting ground that led to the war as well as the decades after the war in which the struggle continued in more dispersed and localized ways. The long Civil War era included economic, social, cultural, and political changes as well as a military conflict. This longer and more inclusive approach to the study of the Civil War can be employed to reveal the ways in which the restructuring of households was a process that began prior to the war and continued long after the military hostilities concluded. As earlier scholars have noted, Reconstruction was not a finite event but rather a long-term process. So, too, was the restructuring of American households. Consequently, this volume also addresses how the war flowed from, required, and often resulted in the restructuring of the household. In essence, it interweaves the military conflict with the transformation of households that occurred nationwide.

Furthermore, the essays in the volume explore how the reconstruction of households continued long after the military conflict officially ended.[14]

This anthology opens with three critical Civil War figures, Mary Todd Lincoln, Robert E. Lee, and Ulysses S. Grant, and the ways that their actions during the war can be understood through the lens of the histories of the households of origin that formed them. As the First Lady of the United States, Mary Todd Lincoln was responsible for the First Household and faced much criticism for the way that she ran it—both while she was in the White House and in the years since then. In her essay, "The Material World of Mary Todd Lincoln: Her Households in Peace and War," Joan Cashin reconsiders Mary Todd Lincoln's much discussed failure to rise to the task of First Lady during the Civil War. In Cashin's essay, Mary Todd Lincoln's inability to govern effectively the first household during the Civil War is read as the consequence of her longer household history. Cashin suggests that Mary Lincoln suffered early trauma in her life, especially in the death of her mother in her early years that left her without critical household management skills. She eventually righted herself as an adult and by the time of her husband's election as president, she had put together a viable household. The demands of running the first household in times of the war, however, stressed her along deeply ingrained fissures and she was unable to cope with a household that was as much a public site as a private one, much less the first household in what was in fact a household war.

In "Householder and General: Lee's War as a Household War," Joseph M. Beilein Jr. considers the weight of Lee's household history upon his wartime military decisions. Like Mary Todd Lincoln, Lee carried the marks of the household relations through which he was formed as a man and head of household. Beilein focuses on the role that Lee's father, Henry Lee, a hero of the Revolutionary War, played in Lee's early years. Rising to fame as a guerrilla fighter during the American Revolution, after the war "Light-Horse Harry" went on to become a rather erratic head of household. When he died, he left his oldest son Robert to deal with the responsibility of caring for his infirm mother. By the time of the Civil War, Lee, like Mary Lincoln, had plastered over the legacy of a parent that he lost too soon and had matured into the head of a viable household. However, the war would weigh on him and remind him of this past, and he too would make decisions—in particular about the wisdom of guerrilla warfare and his concession to the Union—that can be read through the lens of his childhood experiences in his particular household.

Brooks D. Simpson, in "The Divided Houses of Ulysses S. Grant," demonstrates that Grant, too, was strongly influenced by his household and his family relationships. His public and private struggles overlapped and governed his behavior as a father, husband, son, son-in-law, and general. Primarily Grant was driven by the desire to provide for his family. He was the son of an antislavery Whig and was married to a slaveholder's daughter, and his complicated family relationships impacted his behavior. Household concerns—especially tensions over slavery between his in-laws, his wife, and his father, as well as rumors about his secessionist wife and her slave—shaped Grant's behavior. In the end, Grant's military success allowed him to redeem his household reputation, support his family, and sever his dependence on his father. Grant's household continued to hold sway over him after Appomattox, when family members took advantage of his reputation and his administration suffered from charges of nepotism. Even when family fortunes waned again, Grant was able to provide for his household by penning his memoirs, which he finished a few days before he died from cancer.

While the first section of the book considers the ways in which household relations were formative in the development and behavior of leading wartime figures, the second section of the book moves on to how household relations and structures played out in the war itself. In "The Soldier's Dream of Home," Jonathan White highlights the ties to home and households that are revealed in soldiers' dreams. Although physically separated from their loved ones, soldiers continually visited home and their household relations in their dreams and then wrote to their loved ones about those dreams. While physically at the formal military front, White concludes, soldiers were in spirit within their households, if only in their dreams. On the other hand, Julie Mujic, in "'Now I Can Bear My Ills Patiently': The Expanding Realm of Wisconsin Households during the Civil War," considers how women expanded their households' reach to meet their fathers', husbands', and sons' dreams in reality. These women sent letters to state officials demanding better conditions for their fighting men, provided direct material support to their fighting men, and visited the field of battle and the hospitals when loved ones on the front were ill or wounded. Like the dreams of their men, Wisconsin women saw no line of division between themselves and their men; instead, they saw the need to extend their roles within the household to create a new merger between their men in the field and their households. The essays in this section work together then to destabilize the common understanding of a bifurcated relationship between the homefront and battlefield and replace it with what LeeAnn Whites refers to as a "relational war." As do all of the essays in this volume, Whites's essay, "Written on the Heart: Soldiers' Letters, the Household Supply Line, and the Relational War," suggests that the Civil War is best understood in relation to households rather than as physically separated from them. Her essay suggests that it is through the relational politics of the household that critical material supplies as well as emotional supplies for the troops were provided. To a much greater extent than those approaches that emphasize the separate and ancillary relationship of the household to the formal field of battle, all the articles in this section emphasize the way that individual households, through their continued contact with their men, supplied the emotional and physical need of their kinsmen on the warfront.

The third section of the book considers the household as the site of war. The first two essays explore how the Union military utilized a household strategy and made war on Confederate households. In "A 'Fearful Family Quarrel': The Union Assault on Southern Households as Battle Strategy," Lisa Tendrich Frank highlights the way in which we have misread military tactics, in this case Sherman's "evacuation" of Atlanta, based on the preconceived notions of a disconnected, apolitical, and at most "auxiliary" role of the homefront in the waging of the Civil War. Frank suggests that rather than understanding the evacuation of Atlanta as an effort on Sherman's part to protect a helpless civilian population, as Sherman publicly claimed, it is important to see it as a military action and an eviction of an enemy population. The recognition that the households of Atlanta played a critical role in the relational war reveals that this removal order was not a fatherly evacuation or an attempt to protect defenseless women and children but rather an eviction of enemies, a critical disabling of Atlanta's households to resist and undermine the Union war effort from within.

Margaret Storey carries on this line of discussion in "War's Domestic Corollary: Union Occupation Households in the Civil War South." Like Frank, Storey suggests that we need to read the homefront, in particular the occupied Confederate homefront, as a "domestic corollary" to the formal field of battle. Storey highlights the importance of women's roles in this domestic corollary through the sequestering of Confederate homes in occupied areas by the wives of Union officers. She demonstrates that as Union women set up households in occupied areas, they simultaneously upended secessionist households, an effective way to make war on the Confederacy through particularly feminine channels. Consequently, we need to understand Union wives' establishment of households in Confederate homes as a pointed form of warfare against their Southern enemies.

Households in other areas similarly became sites of war. In "Creek and

Seminole Households on the Trail of Blood on Ice," Andrew K. Frank looks at an event in the Civil War West that has most frequently been described as a military one and shows how it was actually grounded in Native American households. Native American households were, from the start, intrinsically involved in the war and all that it meant. From the beginning, Creek and Seminole Indians stated that their goal was to protect their homes. Native homes were targeted by the enemy and protected by members of the community. Concern for their households guided Native behavior even after those households were displaced, and Union concern for the household shaped commanders' military decisions. Consequently, as Frank stresses, Union and Native American policy in this theater of war were similarly structured by concerns for Native households, instead of focused directly only on soldiers.

Lorien Foote's "Aid and Comfort to the Enemy: Escaped Prisoners and the Home as Site of War" details how thousands of Southern households actively undermined the Confederacy by aiding escaped prisoners of war. Households became the sites of battle in the Carolinas, as escaped Union prisoners of war streamed into the area. Individual households as well as groups of households working together shaped the course of the war by giving these Union soldiers supplies and directions as well as by hiding them. Aid to Union soldiers was not restricted to the men of these Southern households. All members of the family, adult and child, male and female, took part in these subversive actions. These escaped prisoners resulted in fewer prisoners in custody for the Confederacy to use as collateral against the Union. As a result, Southern households' aid to escaping Union men not only personally helped the enemy soldiers, but also hampered the ways in which the Confederacy could conduct its war effort. The 2,800 soldiers who escaped were equal to an army brigade and were vital soldiers lost to the Confederacy and returned to the Union forces.

The final section continues the discussion of the central role of the household into the reconstruction of the new social order, especially in the South where slavery was no more. In "Disordered Households: Reconstruction, Klan Terror, and the Law," Victoria E. Bynum discusses how the emancipation of the enslaved gave them nothing but freedom from the status of being legally defined as property. African Americans still had to construct a positive freedom for themselves by waging a war for the integrity and very existence of their own households. As white households lost enslaved workers and status, black men and their dependents gained the ability to carve out a modicum of domestic space. In many ways, the war underwrote the ability of the enslaved to escape their position in white households and to claim a new status in relation to their enslavers.

White Southern households, too, had to redefine and reorder themselves as a result of the changes stemming from the Civil War. As Angela Esco Elder reveals in "Dead Husband, Dead Son: Widows, Mothers-in-Law, and Mourning in the Confederacy," the household war not only transformed the position of the enslaved into free men and free women but it also entailed the alteration of white household relations from bottom to top. Elder's focus on widows and their mothers-in-law brings into stark relief some of the complicated household relations exacerbated by the war. With the absence of men, women continued to fight, sometimes on their own and sometimes together. Even though the men had died, they were still present in spirit, both as a touchstone to bring the women together and as a lightning rod that caused friction.

The returning veterans similarly had to reconstruct their households and their places in them. Their insertion back into the household brought the war home. The process of reconstructing the household, which began prior to the war, continued with a postwar reconstruction of the Southern household order. Brian Craig Miller's "Stand by Your Manhood: The United Confederate Veterans and the Rehabilitation of the Southern Household" explores the difficulties Confederate veterans faced in reestablishing their status as heads of household as a result of defeat and Southern women's wartime independence. Furthermore, veterans' defeat on the battlefield and their physical scars were constant reminders of failed Southern masculinity. Veterans were often forced to turn to their governments for help in supporting their households, and they felt undermined by this dependency. The United Confederate Veterans organization formed, in part, to give the veterans a larger household that would reaffirm their manhood, and it played a major role in reasserting and redefining manhood and household in the postwar South.

The Civil War resulted from and otherwise shaped the transformation of the American household. As all of these essays demonstrate, viewing the war through the lens of the household illuminates a new and fuller understanding of the war. Households influenced the onset of war, the course of the war, and the postwar era. We cannot truly understand the war without understanding the history of the household. Prior to the war, households had begun to shift their focus and their format, but the Civil War sped up these slow and regionally based adjustments. The transformation of households was of long duration and wide geographic scope, of which the experience of the United States offers only one possible trajectory, a trajectory that was arguably unique for the way that it fused widespread democratic rights for rural white male producers with a widespread and entrenched system of slaveholding, most notably by the time of the Civil War, the Southern slaveholding farm or plantation. It took a civil war to move this process forward, and what it took to fight the war was part and parcel of how the household form was or was not transformed.

NOTES

1. Eric Foner, *Nothing but Freedom: Emancipation and Its Legacy* (Baton Rouge: Louisiana State University Press, 1983); James M. McPherson, *Battle Cry of Freedom: The Civil War Era* (New York: Oxford University Press, 1988); Elizabeth Fox-Genovese, *Within the Plantation Household: Black and White Women of the Old South* (Chapel Hill: University of North Carolina Press, 1988); Stephanie McCurry, *Masters of Small Worlds: Yeoman Households, Gender Relations, and the Political Culture of the Antebellum South Carolina Low Country* (New York: Oxford University Press, 1995); Victoria E. Bynum, *The Free State of Jones: Mississippi's Longest Civil War* (Chapel Hill: University of North Carolina Press, 2001); James L. Roark, *Masters without Slaves: Southern Planters in the Civil War and Reconstruction* (New York: W. W. Norton, 1977); Peter W. Bardaglio, *Reconstructing the Household: Families, Sex, and the Law in the Nineteenth-Century South* (Chapel Hill: University of North Carolina Press, 1995).

2. On the household, see Fox-Genovese, *Within the Plantation Household*; Drew Gilpin Faust, *Mothers of Invention: Women of the Slaveholding South in the American Civil War* (Chapel Hill: University of North Carolina, 1996); Kirsten E. Wood, *Masterful Women: Slaveholding Widows from the American Revolution through the Civil War* (Chapel Hill: University of North Carolina Press, 2004); Stephanie E. Jones-Rogers, *They Were Her Property: White Women and Slave Owners in the American South* (New Haven: Yale University Press, 2019); Nancy C. Bercaw, *Gendered Freedoms: Race, Rights, and the Politics of Household in the Delta, 1861–1875* (Gainesville: University Press of Florida, 2003); Victoria E. Bynum, *Unruly Women: The Politics of Social and Sexual Control in the Old South* (Chapel Hill: University of North Carolina Press, 1992); LeeAnn Whites, *The Civil War as a Crisis in Gender: Augusta, Georgia, 1860–1890* (Athens: University of Georgia Press, 1995); Nina Silber, *Gender and the Sectional Conflict* (Chapel Hill: University of North Carolina Press, 2009); McCurry, *Masters of Small Worlds*; Mary P. Ryan, *Cradle of the Middle Class: The Family in Oneida County, New York, 1790–1865* (New York: Cambridge University Press, 1981). On the border war, see Kristen Tegtmeier Oertel, *Bleeding Borders: Race, Gender, and Violence in Pre–Civil War Kansas* (Baton Rouge: Louisiana University Press, 2009); Nicole Etcheson, *Bleeding Kansas: Contested Liberty in the Civil War Era* (Lawrence: University Press of Kansas, 2004).

3. Mary Boykin Chesnut, March 18, 1861, *Mary Chesnut's Civil War*, ed. C. Vann Woodward (New Haven: Yale University Press, 1981), 29.

4. On the homefront, see Joan E. Cashin, ed., *The War Was You and Me: Civilians in the American Civil War* (Princeton: Princeton University Press, 2002), especially the essays by George C. Rable, "Hearth, Home, and Family in the Fredericksburg Campaign," 85–111, Cashin, "Deserters, Civilians, and Draft Resistance in the North," 262–85, and Amy E. Murrell, "Union Father, Rebel Son: Families and the Question of Civil War Loyalty," 358–91; Whites, *Civil War as a Crisis in Gender*; Judith Giesberg, *Army at Home: Women and the Civil War on the Northern Home Front* (Chapel Hill: University of North Carolina Press, 2009); Nina Silber, *Daughters of the Union: Northern Women Fight the Civil War* (Cambridge: Harvard University Press, 2005); Lisa Tendrich Frank, "War Comes Home: Confederate Women and Union Soldiers," in *Virginia's Civil War*, ed. Peter Wallenstein and Bertram Wyatt-Brown (Charlottesville: University of Virginia Press, 2005), 123–36.

5. McCurry, *Masters of Small Worlds*; Wood, *Masterful Women*; J. Matthew Gallman, *Defining Duty in the Civil War: Personal Choice, Popular Culture, and the Union Homefront* (Chapel Hill: University of North Carolina Press, 2015); James Marten, *The Children's Civil War* (Chapel Hill: University of North Carolina Press, 1998), esp. 68–100; Silber, *Gender and the Sectional Conflict*; Laura F. Edwards, *Gendered Strife and Confusion: The Political Culture of Reconstruction* (Chicago: University of Illinois Press, 1997); Aaron Sheehan-Dean, *Why Confederates Fought: Family and Nation in Civil War Virginia* (Chapel Hill: University of North Carolina Press, 2007); Stephanie McCurry, *Confederate Reckoning: Power and Politics in the Civil War South* (Cambridge: Harvard University Press, 2010), esp. 94–100.

6. On war being waged on households, see Lisa Tendrich Frank, *The Civilian War: Confederate Women and Union Soldiers during Sherman's March* (Baton Rouge: Louisiana State University Press, 2015); Joseph M. Beilein Jr., *Bushwhackers: Guerrilla Warfare, Manhood, and the Household in Civil War Missouri* (Kent, Ohio: Kent State University Press, 2016). On soldiers going to the battlefield to protect their households, see Bertram Wyatt-Brown, *The Shaping of Southern Culture: Honor, Grace, and War, 1760s–1880s* (Chapel Hill: University of North Carolina Press, 2001), esp. 194–202; James M. McPherson, *For Cause and Comrades: Why Men Fought in the Civil War* (New York: Oxford University Press, 1997), esp. 131–47.

7. On separate spheres, see Jeanne Boydston, *Home and Work: Housework, Wages, and the Ideology of Labor in the Early Republic* (New York: Oxford University Press, 1994); Ryan, *Cradle of the Middle Class*; Amy Dru Stanley, *From Bondage to Contract: Wage Labor, Marriage, and the Market in the Age of Slave Emancipation* (New York: Cambridge University Press, 1998); Nancy F. Cott, *The Bonds of Womanhood: "Women's Sphere" in New England, 1780–1835* (New Haven: Yale University Press, 1977); Barbara Welter, "The Cult of True Womanhood, 1820–1860," *American Quarterly* 18 (Summer 1966): 151–74.

8. Leslie Schwalm, *A Hard Fight for We: Women's Transition from Slavery to Freedom in South Carolina* (Urbana: University of Illinois Press, 1997); Manisha Sinha, *The Slave's Cause: A History of Abolition* (New Haven: Yale University Press, 2016); Chandra Manning, *Troubled Refuge: Struggling for Freedom in the Civil War* (New

York: Knopf, 2016); Elizabeth Regosin, *Freedom's Promise: Ex-Slave Families and Citizenship in the Age of Emancipation* (Charlottesville: University Press of Virginia, 2002).

9. LeeAnn Whites and Alecia P. Long, eds., *Occupied Women: Gender, Military Occupation, and the American Civil War* (Baton Rouge: Louisiana State University Press, 2009), 6; David Silkenat, *Driven from Home: North Carolina's Civil War Refugee Crisis* (Chapel Hill: University of North Carolina Press, 2016). Other works on occupation include Judkin Browning, *Shifting Loyalties: The Union Occupation of Eastern North Carolina* (Chapel Hill: University of North Carolina Press, 2011); Alecia P. Long, "(Mis)Remembering General Order No. 28: Benjamin Butler, The Woman Order, and Historical Memory," in *Occupied Women*, ed. Whites and Long, 17–32; Stephen V. Ash, *When the Yankees Came: Conflict and Chaos in the Occupied South, 1861–1865* (Chapel Hill: University of North Carolina Press, 1995); Chester G. Hearn, *When the Devil Came Down to Dixie: Ben Butler in New Orleans* (Baton Rouge: Louisiana State University Press, 1997); Margaret Storey, *Loyalty and Loss: Alabama's Unionists in the Civil War and Reconstruction* (Baton Rouge: Louisiana State University Press, 2004), esp. 87–132.

10. On guerrilla war as household destruction, see Michael Fellman, *Inside War: The Guerrilla Conflict in Missouri during the Civil War* (New York: Oxford University Press, 1989); Daniel Sutherland, *A Savage Conflict: The Decisive Role of Guerrillas in the American Civil War* (Chapel Hill: University of North Carolina Press, 2009). For new explorations of guerrilla warfare as rooted in the household, see Beilein, *Bushwhackers*; Brian D. McKnight and Barton A. Myers, eds., *The Guerrilla Hunters: Irregular Conflicts during the Civil War* (Baton Rouge: Louisiana State University Press, 2017); Matthew Christopher Hulbert, *The Ghosts of Guerrilla Memory: How Civil War Bushwhackers Became Gunslingers in the American West* (Athens: University of Georgia Press, 2016); Joseph M. Beilein Jr. and Matthew C. Hulbert, eds., *The Civil War Guerrilla: Unfolding the Black Flag in History, Memory, and Myth* (Lexington: University Press of Kentucky, 2015), especially the essays by Andrew William Fialka, "Controlled Chaos: Spatiotemporal Patterns within Missouri's Irregular Civil War," 43–69, and Joseph M. Beilein Jr., "'Nothing but Truth Is History': William E. Connelley, William H. Gregg, and the Pillaging of Guerrilla History," 207–30; Matthew M. Stith, *Extreme Civil War: Guerrilla Warfare, Environment, and Race on the Trans-Mississippi Frontier* (Baton Rouge: Louisiana State University Press, 2016); LeeAnn Whites, "Forty Shirts and a Wagonload of Wheat: Women, the Domestic Supply Line, and the Civil War on the Western Border," *Journal of the Civil War Era* 1, no. 1 (March 2011), 56–78.

11. Fox-Genovese, *Within the Plantation Household*, 67. Jean V. Berlin asserted that "the fact that the South's society was based on the household became a part of its downfall." Berlin, "Did Confederate Women Lose the War? Deprivation, Destruction, and Despair on the Home Front," in *The Collapse of the Confederacy*, ed. Mark Grimsley and Brooks D. Simpson (Lincoln: University of Nebraska Press, 2001), 187. Other discussions of the Southern household and its organization

around slavery include Catherine Clinton, *The Plantation Mistress: Woman's World in the Old South* (New York: Random House, 1982); Anya Jabour, *Scarlett's Sisters: Young Women in the Old South* (Chapel Hill: University of North Carolina Press, 2007); Marli F. Weiner, *Mistresses and Slaves: Plantation Women in South Carolina, 1830–80* (Urbana: University of Illinois Press, 1998); Brenda F. Stevenson, *Life in Black and White: Family and Community in the Slave South* (New York: Oxford University Press, 1996); Jones-Rogers, *They Were Her Property*.

12. Catherine Clinton and Nina Silber, eds., *Divided Houses: Gender and the Civil War* (New York: Oxford University Press, 1992); Orville Vernon Burton, *The Age of Lincoln* (New York: Hill and Wang, 2007), 13; Michael D. Pierson, *Free Hearts and Free Homes: Gender and American Antislavery Politics* (Chapel Hill: University of North Carolina Press, 2003); Jane Turner Censer, *The Reconstruction of White Southern Womanhood, 1865–1895* (Baton Rouge: Louisiana State University Press, 2003), 51; Whites, *Civil War as a Crisis in Gender*; LeeAnn Whites, *Gender Matters: Civil War, Reconstruction, and the Making of the New South* (New York: Palgrave Macmillan, 2005), 5, 6.

13. For examples, see Frank, *Civilian War*; and Beilein, *Bushwhackers*.

14. Eric Foner, *Reconstruction: America's Unfinished Revolution, 1863–1877* (New York: Harper & Row, 2014); Gregory P. Downs, *After Appomattox: Military Occupation and the Ends of War* (Cambridge: Harvard University Press, 2015); Ira Berlin, *The Long Emancipation: The Demise of Slavery in the United States* (Cambridge: Harvard University Press, 2015). On the restructuring of households in the border states, see Amy Murrell Taylor, *The Divided Family in Civil War America* (Chapel Hill: University of North Carolina Press, 2005); Margaret Creighton, *The Colors of Courage: Gettysburg's Forgotten History, Immigrants, Women, and African Americans in the Civil War's Defining Battle* (New York: Basic Books, 2005).

PART 1

The Importance of the Household to Civil War Behavior

The Material World of Mary Todd Lincoln

Her Households in Peace and War

JOAN E. CASHIN

The American Civil War reached into almost every household in the country between 1861 and 1865, including of course the First Household, the White House. This building has been the epicenter of cultural and political struggles over many issues, and some of them involved the controversial First Lady, Mary Todd Lincoln. Her travails had a lot to do with the house itself and, more broadly, with her attitudes toward material objects and the consumer culture of her day. The building at 1600 Pennsylvania Avenue has much to recommend it as a public monument, for it is spacious and grand. The house has been described as a living museum, the chief symbol of the U.S. government, and one of the most recognizable buildings in the world. In keeping with its significance, the structure's history is well documented.[1]

Actually living in the White House is a different matter. The building's dual nature as a public showcase and family home has challenged many of its occupants. Mr. J. B. West, the chief usher between the administrations of Franklin Roosevelt and Lyndon Johnson, remarked that someone is always watching the First Lady. Some of these closely observed women have enjoyed living there, and some have not. The public-private duality bedeviled Mary Todd Lincoln during her four years of residence there. Irish architect James Hoban, who designed the building in the 1790s, envisioned the White House as a European country house with its quasi-public character.[2]

Hoban's building, first occupied by the Adams family in 1800, had thirty-one rooms on two floors. After the British burned the White House during the War of 1812, the replica, completed in 1817, became the home of

President James Monroe and his family. Monroe took an eager interest in replacing the furniture and ordering many items directly from France, and he brought in some attractive pieces he owned before he became president. The other furnishings were rather ordinary, purchased by his staff at estate sales. After 1817, the building was still a work in progress, as subsequent presidents made changes to the exterior. Andrew Jackson, for instance, constructed the north portico that faces Pennsylvania Avenue. The house retained something of its Old World inspiration. In 1840, a visitor said it resembled the country estate of an English nobleman, with a few excellent rooms and a lot of shabby furniture, and much like those estates, a kind of permanent "open house" prevailed.[3]

Mary Todd Lincoln lived there at the most difficult time, when the country was breaking apart, and she was under microscopic scrutiny. She was controversial from the start because of her birthplace, Kentucky, and because some of her relatives supported the Confederacy. Beyond that, she was much criticized for her management of the White House. As First Lady of the United States, that was one of her chief responsibilities, according to public belief, her husband's views, and her own assumptions. The Lincolns had a simple division of labor along traditional gender lines: he ran the country, and she ran the house. Her approach to the material culture of the household, before, during, and after the war, is the subject of this article. No one has explored this aspect of her story. The chief argument is that Mary Lincoln, making decisions about the White House on her own, with little guidance, did not understand that the bloody conflict changed many assumptions about material culture. The wartime context called for public austerity and self-denial, and the First Lady, a product of the antebellum era, wanted lavish display.[4]

Mary Lincoln's early life did not prepare her for the duties of running a large semipublic establishment in times of peace or war. Her childhood homes were bigger and finer than the log cabins that most white families inhabited during the early nineteenth century, but no one taught her how to run them. She was born in 1818 in a two-story, nine-room house on Short Street in Lexington, Kentucky, the daughter of Robert S. Todd, a lawyer, politician, and merchant. Her mother, Eliza Parker Todd, also hailed from a prominent Kentucky family. A few house slaves assisted Mary's mother, but she seems to have felt overwhelmed by her duties, for she once confided that she had no idea that housekeeping was so much trouble. The home was full of small children—Mary had five siblings—and none of the Todd offspring seem to have gotten much attention from their mother. After Eliza Todd died in 1825, Robert Todd quickly remarried. He and his new wife, Elizabeth Humphreys, eventually had eight children together.[5]

Mary Todd was only six when her mother died, too young to learn much from her about running a house, and she seems to have absorbed little or nothing from her stepmother, whom she disliked intensely. In 1832, her father purchased a more impressive two-story brick house of fourteen rooms, surrounded by slave quarters, a kitchen, a smokehouse, and other outbuildings. The interior of the house, located on Main Street in Lexington, had some nice furniture and expensive paintings. Ten enslaved African Americans worked in this building. The house was crowded with the Todd children, occasional overnight guests, and a private tutor who resided there. The place may have provided an emotional haven for some of the Todds, but Mary said she never felt at home there.[6]

The next significant house in Mary's life, and the only one she would ever be able to shape to reflect her own sensibilities, was the home she shared with her husband. Not long after she completed her education in Lexington, she departed for Springfield, Illinois, the state capital, where two of her older sisters had settled. After she married Abraham Lincoln in 1842, they lived briefly in a local tavern and then in a small rented house; in 1844, they moved to a one-and-a-half story residence on Jackson and Eighth Streets. The dwelling, which originally had five rooms, cost $1,200. The Lincolns resided here, except for during Abraham's term in the U.S. Congress, until they left in 1861 for Washington, D.C. In 1856, the Lincolns added a full second story, which Mary evidently designed with the help of some local carpenters. By the late 1850s, the house had nine rooms. The wooden exterior was painted a light brown with green shutters. The façade had an appealing Georgian symmetry, with the front door placed in the center of the building and an equal number of windows arrayed on each side.[7]

This house was about the same size as Mary's childhood home on Short Street, but it was much more private, with a small number of people in the same physical space, and it was predominantly her own house. In most societies in the modern world, gender matters in the organization of domestic space, and Abraham let his wife manage their home, telling her to buy what she wanted. She proved to be good at running this household. His income rose steadily in the 1840s and 1850s—as high as $5,000 in one prosperous year—so they had plenty of money. Mary purchased some of her furniture from local merchants on credit under easy terms, yet she kept within the couple's budget, choosing carpets and articles of furniture they could afford. She loved fine clothes, as most people know, and she loved attractive household objects as well. Many human beings get some pleasure from beautiful objects, but she seems to have derived a particularly acute enjoyment from such things, especially beautiful *new* things. This behavior may have been an attempt to compensate for her childhood losses, as her biographers have speculated, but it was not just a matter of individual psychology. Society at large exhorted married white women with disposable income to buy decorative objects for the home. They were in the vanguard of antebellum consumer culture.[8]

As she ran her household, Mary consulted Eliza Leslie's best-selling advice volume, the *House Book*, published in 1845, as well as Leslie's cookbook, both of which she purchased in Springfield. In her *House Book* Leslie reassured her audience that every middle-class white woman could learn how to run a household competently, quoting the adage, "'Where there is a will there is a way.'" Leslie offered detailed information on many aspects of household management, from how to do laundry to how to hang a picture. She made practical suggestions, pointing out that marble-top tables were durable and easy to clean, and she criticized green venetian blinds because the color faded quickly. Leslie advised her readers that married men prized a "neat and well-conducted house," thus connecting the state of the household to marital happiness. Like her contemporary Catherine Beecher, Leslie portrayed the home as a place where small numbers of people—parents and children—focused lovingly on each other. These ideas saturated American society before 1861.[9]

Mary Lincoln worked hard at putting her household together, and she excelled at the task. Like many white women of her generation, she saw the home as the physical manifestation of her role as a wife and mother. In the late 1850s, the floor spaces were carefully differentiated, as was common in a prosperous home, divided into a front parlor, a rear parlor, a sitting room, a dining room, a guest bedroom, and a maid's room. The house's furnishings are also well documented. Decorating required more than applying preexisting motifs to an interior—it required a modicum of artistic ability, and she had some genuine, inborn talent. In furnishing the house, she drew on a variety of styles, such as late Empire, Gothic, and Rococo Revival. One of the bedrooms had a Marseilles quilt, which was much admired, according to Eliza Leslie, for its filigreed surface. The house had a private library as well as other objects that signaled cultivation, such as a chess set, and affluence, such as a champagne basket. Mary Lincoln seems to have focused on texture, color, and ornamentation in choosing her household objects.[10]

The Lincolns did not live in a palace. Their house did not feature the most expensive objects available or the most stylish. The windows sported cotton drapes, not the more costly silk, and some green blinds, possibly faded as the expert Eliza Leslie predicted they would be. The side chairs in the front parlor were constructed of mahogany veneer, rather than the more expensive walnut. Some of the furniture seems to have been handmade. The Lincoln home was nonetheless an inviting place with a pleas-ing lack of clutter. The house reflected Mary's good taste, her niece recalled, and it made a favorable impression on less biased observers. In the late antebellum era, visitors portrayed the household as "orderly and refined," the home of a gentleman, not an aristocrat. One journalist from the *Utica Morning Herald* complimented Mary as "a true type of American lady."[11]

The home was clean, too, largely because of the labor of house servants. In the 1840s and 1850s, Mary employed several black women, one Portu-guese woman, and several Irish women who helped her with washing, iron-ing, and cooking. Typically Mary employed one or two workers at a time. Writer Catherine Beecher counseled white women to be patient with diffi-cult servants and guide them to do better, but Mary had a mixed record on this score. One of the servants portrayed her as hard to please, while others recalled her as a good employer. When they left, sometimes she fired them, and sometimes they just quit. Such tensions between mistresses and ser-vants were common in antebellum America, but it was a private matter to hire and fire servants in Springfield. If the neighbors gossiped, that did not seriously harm Abraham's legal career or political prospects.[12]

The Springfield house also provided a reasonably happy haven for the Lincoln family. Abraham and Mary had different temperaments: he was quiet, abstract, and methodical, while she was lively, particular, and impul-sive. They had their share of quarrels, as their biographers have noted, but they learned how to live with their conflicts. They seem to have loved each other, and they adored their four sons, born between 1843 and 1853. If it is true, as Carl Sandburg suggests, that the chief purpose of marriage is to run a household together, then the Lincolns succeeded. Moreover, the Lincolns felt secure enough as a couple to invite numerous guests over for dinner parties and receptions, which helped facilitate Abraham's political career. Most guests agreed that the Lincolns provided them with a hearty welcome and superb fare at the table. All in all, the Lincolns occupied a comfortable home appropriate for an upper-middle-class white family in any town in the antebellum era. By the standards of the day, Mary Lincoln succeeded as a housekeeper in her years in Springfield.[13]

In 1860, Abraham Lincoln's growing fame began to transform the household in several practical respects. That year, Mary hired a black man named William Johnson to answer the door because her spouse drew more and more journalists, politicians, and curious strangers to the Springfield home. Even with a doorman in place, visitors besieged the Lincolns before and after the presidential election. Mary enjoyed most of the attention, and she was thrilled at her husband's triumph. As they prepared to move to the nation's capital, the couple decided to leave some of their furniture in Springfield. Other pieces they sold or put into storage, and a few they took with them to Washington. The house itself, they rented to another family.[14]

When the Lincolns arrived in Washington in early 1861, they moved into a house that was far bigger than any place either one of them had ever lived. The East Room on the ground floor was the same size as their entire house in Springfield. The other public salons were located on the ground floor, with offices and private living quarters on the second floor. The Pierce administration did the last major redecoration in the early 1850s, and the house and its contents had been allowed to deteriorate. In some rooms, the wallpaper was peeling off the walls. Because of the constant foot traffic, the place was nearly impossible to keep clean, and the atmosphere was impersonal. William Stoddard, who later worked as Mary Lincoln's secretary, said that much of the house was worn and dirty like an old, unsuccessful hotel.[15]

The mansion's furnishings included some pieces that would later be designated as heirlooms, such as the original lock on the front door, which survived the fire in 1814, and a mahogany-and-morocco chair that had belonged to Andrew Jackson. But the historic preservation movement did not gain momentum until the twentieth century, and most White House residents in the nineteenth century took a rather utilitarian view of its objects. For decades, the furniture had been reupholstered, replaced, and sold. During the Buchanan administration, pieces of the Monroe furniture were auctioned off to the public. In 1861, some of the desks upstairs were sagging, and at least one of the bed frames was broken. President Lincoln became angry in late 1861 about his wife's lavish spending, and he fumed that the White House was better furnished than any place they had ever lived, but that was not quite true. In terms of cleanliness, privacy, and comfort, the Springfield house was superior.[16]

When the Lincolns arrived at the White House, there was no system in place to smooth the transition from one administration to the next. For much of the twentieth century, advice on running the building passed verbally between the outgoing First Lady and her successor, and nowadays the chief usher prepares detailed guidebooks for the new presidential family. In Mary Lincoln's time, the transition was left up to the individuals involved. The outgoing First Lady, Democrat Harriet Lane, James Buchanan's niece, did not hide her disdain for her successor. In early 1861, Lane supposedly planned to meet with Mary Lincoln about the house, but for unknown reasons the meeting never took place. After the First Inaugural, the new First Lady walked through the building with a cousin from Springfield, and she was shocked by what she saw. She had no friendly predecessor to consult and nothing in print to guide her on managing the White House.[17]

Mary Lincoln also had to learn how to manage a large staff, a total of about twenty men and women who can be identified by name during her tenure, including native-born workers and immigrants, men and women, whites and blacks, longtimers and newcomers. Typically she had about ten people working for her at any point in time—cooks, maids, seamstresses, butlers, messengers, ushers, stable hands, coachmen, watchmen, and guards—more than she employed at the Springfield house but fewer than other presidential administrations had used. William Crook, who served as a guard, implied that there were too few servants in Lincoln's White House, and that the staff was smaller than the number of house servants (about twenty-four) who worked for most of the nineteenth-century administrations; some one hundred full-time staff work at the White House today. The house workers in Lincoln's times sometimes quarreled with each other, and as was the case for previous administrations, some had ill-defined job descriptions. Thomas Pendel, who worked as a watchman, also lit candles in windows and took care of the visitors' hats and coats. The top jobs paid well for the mid-nineteenth century: the steward earned $1,200, and a messenger, $900.[18]

The First Lady was supposed to be in charge of the staff, but Mary Lincoln struggled to maintain her authority. The mansion had no equivalent to the powerful job of chief usher, created a generation later, or the social secretary, who serves today as the conduit between the first family and the staff. Every morning Mary Lincoln met with the steward, who was ostensibly in charge of the staff, but there was no strict hierarchy among the servants as in a country house in Victorian England. The staff has a history of quietly ignoring the First Lady's wishes, and Mary Lincoln had to engage in a "good deal of domestic supervision" over the servants, one guard observed. When a new family moved to the White House, there was usually some staff turnover, and she went through four stewards during her tenure. In comparison, James Buchanan and Harriet Lane went through three stewards, one of whom lasted a month. Many first families resented having to pay the steward's salary, and Mary Lincoln would periodically fire the stewards to save money and try to do the job herself.[19]

Furthermore, some of the staff members treated the house's material objects as if they were available to take at will. Theft had always been a problem at the White House because the building was open to the public, but the staff also pilfered all kinds of household goods, a common resort among employees who wanted to express hostility toward an employer. Abigail Adams, who occupied the White House in 1800, had to replace china that was broken or stolen by the employees during her brief residence. Their identities remain unknown, but some of the servants "appropriated" the newspapers delivered to the White House for President Lincoln before he had a chance to read them. Other servants damaged or stole the expensive china Mary Lincoln purchased in 1861. The stealing seems to have worsened at times when the building did not have a steward, when the servants were known to carry away pieces of furniture.[20]

Among the individuals who labored at the White House, the white male employees left more accounts of Mary Lincoln than anyone else. The female cooks, black and white, to whom she gave her orders before every meal, have left no records, and neither did any of the black men. Those white men on the staff caused her a good deal of trouble. The doorkeepers at the main entrance sometimes disappeared without notice, so that such dignitaries as Prince Napoleon and Robert Dale Owen came in unannounced on separate occasions and wandered unattended through the building. The doorkeeper Edward McManus occasionally lost the keys to the front door. Colonel Charles Halpine complained that the doormen routinely disappeared at night, which allowed anyone to enter the building.[21]

Mary Lincoln nevertheless had her defenders among the white male employees, including her secretary William O. Stoddard, watchman Thomas Pendel, and guard William Crook. Stoddard said she could be moody and sometimes unreasonable, but she gave instructions to the servants in a "kindly" manner. Pendel described her as generous and willing to help people when she could, and Crook offered that she quietly assisted people in need and was "very generally liked" among the staff. But when things went wrong, her decisions could become public scandals. A case in point is that of the irresponsible doorkeeper Edward McManus, hired in the Jackson administration and rumored to be a Confederate sympathizer. When Mary fired him at the end of 1864, the press attacked her for it, even though the president approved of the decision. An anonymous source defended the First Lady in the *New York Times*, insisting that McManus was fired for "insolence," carelessness, and drunkenness, but she was still blamed.[22]

In general, Mary Lincoln did not benefit from the contrast to her husband, who was mostly oblivious to his material surroundings. For all of his extraordinary gifts as a politician, Abraham Lincoln did not pay much attention to the White House as a dwelling place. He showed much less interest in the house than did his predecessors, such as the eager James Monroe; or John Quincy Adams, who requested an inventory of all of the furniture; or Martin Van Buren, who ordered the chandeliers restrung in the state rooms. Lincoln did not care about the condition of his living quarters, and his office furnishings were sparse. He dismissed the expensive furniture his wife purchased as "flub-dubs," ridiculous purchases in wartime.

The president asked a great deal of his political staff, expecting his secretaries John Hay and John Nicolay to work as hard as he did, which was very hard, but he was an undemanding employer when it came to the household. He sometimes forgot to eat, and when he did sit down for a meal, he ate whatever was put in front of him. He felt unperturbed when Robert Dale Owen entered the building without glimpsing a single staff person. Mary Lincoln, who was acutely aware of her material environment, asked much more of the household staff than he did.[23]

The First Lady's closest friend in the White House, and probably her best friend in Washington, was her seamstress, Elizabeth Keckley (sometimes spelled Keckly). Keckley had already established herself as a first-rate maker of fashionable attire prior to her employment at the White House. Born enslaved in Virginia in 1818, the same year Mary Todd was born in Kentucky, Keckley eventually purchased her freedom and made her way to Washington, where for a time she worked for Varina Davis, wife of the Mississippi senator and future president of the Confederacy, Jefferson Davis. Mary Lincoln hired Keckley in 1861, and the two women formed a genuine bond. They both supported the Union, and the Lincolns contributed to an organization founded by Keckley to assist fugitive slaves. The bond was also personal, for Keckley comforted Mary Lincoln after the deaths of her son William in 1862 and her husband in 1865. Keckley's special status did not blind her, however, to the First Lady's mistakes as a housekeeper. For example, Keckley thought it foolish to fire the stewards to save money.[24]

Mary Lincoln knew that each new administration received $20,000 to refurbish the house. After she had the mansion thoroughly cleaned, she began redecorating, which she believed would simultaneously prove her loyalty to the Union cause, her respect for the White House as the national house, and her value as a wife and mother. Her budget of $20,000 was four times higher than her husband's salary at its antebellum peak, so she could buy the top-of-the-line items, such as Wilton carpets. The men who served as commissioners of public buildings, first William Wood and then Benjamin French, did not put brakes on her spending. John Watt, the gardener, introduced her to some irregular financial methods, shifting money from one account to another. Other presidents and their families have received unreported gifts, other staff members have gotten kickbacks for government contracts, and other administrations have siphoned money from other agencies to cover expenses. In similar fashion, Mary Lincoln moved money around so she could have enough to spend on the building.[25]

Despite these maneuvers, the First Lady could not stay within a budget. In 1861, a journalist overheard her say she would try to be "economical" as she shopped, yet she quickly spent all $20,000 plus almost $7,000 more. Mary Lincoln spent unwisely, taking the consumption ethos of the antebellum period too far. In her zeal, she bought chairs, sofas, wallpaper, drapes, new editions of Sir Walter Scott and Shakespeare, a dinner service of Haviland china, and a rosewood bed carved with fretwork. She followed no particular style in her purchases but chose gleaming surfaces, bright colors, and plush materials. The results were visible at a grand reception in the East Room in February 1862. Several hundred people crowded into the room, which had a new velvet carpet of shimmering green and a table with a vase five feet tall, ringed by smaller vases, all of them brimming with fresh flowers. The guests consumed food and drink at a dazzling buffet with crystal plates, candelabra, and a candy statue of the Goddess of Liberty. The First Lady had remade her material environment to her satisfaction, and a few commentators praised her good taste. From Rhode Island, the *Newport Mercury* called the newly decorated salons nothing short of magnificent.[26]

Despite these reviews, most people were not favorably impressed. In fact, the First Lady's spending brought down a storm of criticism on her head. Timing is everything in politics, and her expenditures seemed crass, even offensive, because the country was at war. Washington society, which included many Confederate sympathizers, turned a cold shoulder to Mary Lincoln, although in the spring of 1861, when no one was sure if the war would last, the press often gave her the benefit of the doubt. A Philadelphia newspaper called her a "lady of taste and judgment," and the *New York Times* deemed her a "good" housekeeper. The press became more critical in the fall of 1861, when Yankee journalists began to object to her spending. After the East Room reception in February 1862, journalists focused on Mary Lincoln's choice of punch bowl, an ornate blue-and-white porcelain dish that the emperor of Japan had sent to the White House in January 1862. They described it as an enormous basin filled with strong drink, which a servant distributed to the guests. The First Lady should put aside the "oriental punch bowl," declared a newspaper in Sandusky, Ohio, and serve nonalcoholic drinks to soldiers protecting the U.S. capital. Even though she did not buy it herself, this luxury object from a foreign monarch came to symbolize what many people saw as her self-indulgence.[27]

The public and the press have accepted spending sprees by other First Ladies, such as Dolley Madison and Jacqueline Kennedy, in more ordinary circumstances, but Mary Lincoln did not live in ordinary times. In the twentieth century, Edith Wilson and Eleanor Roosevelt cut back on expenditures during World Wars I and II to show their support for the war effort, yet Mary Lincoln somehow could not grasp that important concept. Her shortcomings are understandable at the human level, since she had considerable talent for this task and she wanted to prove herself, but she made a political blunder. Her husband's disapproval somehow did not restrain her; perhaps she saw the house as her province alone; perhaps she was in the grip of a compulsion. In any case, she spent yet more money in 1864, buying even more beautiful objects for the residence. In New York, she "ransacked" stores on Broadway, one newspaper reported. Somehow she hid the cost of these new purchases from her husband.[28]

Journalists sometimes linked the First Lady's regional background to her poor management of the White House. One newspaper labeled her luxurious purchases absurd for someone from a "rural home in Illinois," but her contemporaries could not agree on her regional identity. One Yankee newspaper called her "quite Western in appearance," no details provided, while another newspaper implied that she was from the North like the vice president's wife, Ellen Emery Hamlin, a native of Maine. To ratchet up the confusion, other papers compared her to Queen Victoria, which was meant as a compliment. Historians do not agree on Mary Lincoln's regional identity, portraying her as a Southerner, a Westerner, or both Southern and Western. Stephen Berry calls the Todds, her family of origin, utterly American in their acquisitiveness and their individualism, and Stacy Pratt McDermott argues that her life straddles all three regions, South, North, and West. Jennifer Fleischner observes that Mary Todd Lincoln occupied a "geographical and political no-woman's-land."[29]

Mary did not make it any easier for historians, her peers, or herself when she made contradictory statements about her regional identity. At different times in her life, she called herself a Kentuckian, including while she was First Lady; a Westerner, because she once said, the Lincolns were poor; and a Northerner, because her sympathies were "entirely Republican." In fact, she did not have strong regional loyalties, as her varying self-descriptions reveal. She was loyal above all else to her husband, which is what the nineteenth century expected of women. She never fit the stereotypes that crystallized during the war, for example, that all whites from slaveholding states were ardent secessionists, and she hailed from a state that voted for the Unionist candidate John Bell in 1860. Her support for the federal cause seems clear. In a letter in July 1861, she portrayed herself as a Kentuckian who was loyal to the Union, declaring that allegiance to the country at large should be more important than state loyalties.[30] No matter what anyone said about her regional identity, she could not figure out how to manage the White House. She could not seem to relinquish what she had learned about material culture and the household before 1861.

In the war's last year, Mary Lincoln came to prefer Soldier's Home, a cottage outside Washington where she retreated to escape her troubles. Then came the calamity of her husband's murder in 1865. As Mary grieved in her living quarters for weeks afterwards, strangers made off with the silver, various ornaments, the lamps, the vases, and other pieces of furniture. Her contemporaries blamed that on her, too, rather than on the guards, who seemed unable to protect the household objects at any time and may have taken some things themselves. When Mary Lincoln left the White House, she gave away many of her husband's personal belongings to political figures, such as abolitionist Frederick Douglass. She took with her a dressing table as a souvenir, after which Elizabeth Keckley loyally pointed out that Commissioner French gave his permission, and then bought a replacement right away. Mary Lincoln denied the allegation that she took many other household objects with her. Sometime in 1865, she sold the Japanese punch bowl, just as some of her predecessors had sold White House furniture in the past. The bowl, which has changed hands many times, now resides at Wheatland, James Buchanan's estate in Pennsylvania.[31]

After Mary Lincoln departed the White House in 1865, she never again ran her own household. She did not return to the Springfield home because she said it harbored too many memories of her husband; instead, she bought a house in Chicago, decided to rent it out, and finally sold it. With her son Tad, she lived in a series of hotels in the United States and Europe, and after he died, she resided for a time with her son Robert in Chicago. As most Americans know, she spent part of 1875 in an insane asylum in Illinois after a dispute with Robert. When she was released, she lived in yet more hotels overseas, a household of one, where she had no material responsibilities and did not have to furnish the rooms in which she lived. Her failing health forced her to return to Springfield to live with her sister Elizabeth. She died there in 1882. The Lincoln home in Springfield is now a museum where, ironically, many of her carefully chosen objects are displayed for public view. There she had been able to express her gifts at homemaking, but the war disrupted antebellum premises about gender and material culture. Mary Todd Lincoln, a product of that era, could not adapt to new imperatives about how the First Household should be managed when the nation was at war.[32]

NOTES

1. Robert P. Watson, ed., *Life in the White House: A Social History of the First Lady and the President's House* (Albany: State University of New York, 2004), 227; Gilson

Willets, *Inside History of the White House: The Complete History of the Domestic and Official Life in Washington of the Nation's Presidents and Their Families* (New York: Christian Herald, 1908), 25–26; William Seale, *The President's House: A History*, 2 vols. (Washington, D.C.: White House Historical Association, with the cooperation of the National Geographic Society and Harry N. Abrams, 1986), 1:xv. I thank Patrick Clarke and Louise Stephenson for their conversations about the White House and its objects.

2. Watson, ed., *Life in the White House*, 226; J. B. West with Mary Lynn Kotz, *Upstairs at the White House: My Life with the First Ladies* (New York: Coward, McCann & Geoghegan, 1973), 368; Carl Sferrazza Anthony, *First Ladies: The Saga of the Presidents' Wives and Their Power, 1789–1961* (New York: Quill William Morrow, 1990), 108, 116, 152; Seale, *President's House*, 1:40–41.

3. David Herbert Donald, *Lincoln at Home: Two Glimpses of Abraham Lincoln's Family Life* (New York: Simon & Schuster, 1999), 22; Seale, *President's House*, 1:152–56, 80–81, 139, 146–48, xviii; Willets, *Inside History of the White House*, 31–32; Peter Mandler, *The Rise and Fall of the Stately Home* (New Haven: Yale University Press, 1997), 3–4, 76–78.

4. Jennifer Fleischner, *Mrs. Lincoln and Mrs. Keckly: The Remarkable Story of the Friendship between a First Lady and a Former Slave* (New York: Broadway Books, 2004), 209; Ruth Painter Randall, *Mary Lincoln: Biography of a Marriage* (Boston: Little, Brown, 1953); Justin G. Turner and Linda Levitt Turner, *Mary Todd Lincoln: Her Life and Letters*, with an introduction by Fawn M. Brodie (New York: Alfred A. Knopf, 1972); Jean H. Baker, *Mary Todd Lincoln: A Biography* (New York: W. W. Norton, 1987); Stephen Berry, *House of Abraham: Lincoln and the Todds, a Family Divided by War* (Boston: Houghton Mifflin, 2007); Catherine Clinton, *Mrs. Lincoln: A Life* (New York: Harper, 2009); Frank J. Williams and Michael Burkhimer, eds., *The Mary Lincoln Enigma: Historians on America's Most Controversial First Lady*, with an epilogue by Catherine Clinton (Carbondale: Southern Illinois University Press, 2012); Stacy Pratt McDermott, *Mary Lincoln: Southern Girl, Northern Woman* (New York: Routledge, 2015). Scholars need to explore further how Anglo-American women experienced the material world, including the houses in which they lived. See Amanda Vickery, *Behind Closed Doors: At Home in Georgian England* (New Haven: Yale University Press, 2009), 3.

5. Jack Larkin, *The Reshaping of Everyday Life, 1790–1840* (New York: Harper & Row, 1988), 110–11; Baker, *Mary Todd Lincoln*, 4, 17, 20, 28–32; Fleischner, *Lincoln and Keckly*, 9, 17; McDermott, *Mary Lincoln*, 20.

6. *Mary Todd Lincoln House*, http://www.mtlhouse.org/about.html, accessed August 31, 2015; Baker, *Mary Todd Lincoln*, 45, 32, 46, 28–29; Fleischner, *Lincoln and Keckly*, 63.

7. Fleischner, *Lincoln and Keckly*, 63, 149, 152; Katherine B. Menz, *The Lincoln Home: Lincoln Home National Historic Site, Springfield, Illinois* (Harper's Ferry Center, W.Va.: National Park Service, U.S. Department of the Interior, 1983), 5, 6, 38; Michael Burlingame, ed., *A Reporter's Lincoln: Walter B. Stevens* (Lincoln:

University of Nebraska Press, 1998), 161; *Abraham Lincoln Online.org*, http://abrahamlincolnonline.org, accessed July 1, 2015; Larkin, *Reshaping of Everyday Life*, 118, 120.

8. Douglas L. Wilson and Rodney O. Davis, eds., *Herndon's Informants: Letters, Interviews, and Statements about Abraham Lincoln*, with the assistance of Terry Wilson (Urbana: University of Illinois Press, 1997), 359; Menz, *Lincoln Home*, 6; Baker, *Mary Todd Lincoln*, 157; Salman Akhtar, *Objects of Our Desire: Exploring Our Intimate Connections to the Things around Us* (New York: Harmony Books, 2005); Fleischner, *Lincoln and Keckly*, 49; Marilyn Ferris Motz, "Introduction," 4, in *Making the American Home: Middle-Class Women and Domestic Material Culture, 1840–1940*, ed. Marilyn Ferris Motz and Pat Browne (Bowling Green, Ky.: Bowling Green State University Popular Press, 1988); Katherine C. Grier, *Culture and Comfort: Parlor Making and Middle-Class Identity, 1850–1930* (Washington D.C.: Smithsonian Institution Press, 1988), vii, 6–7.

9. Menz, *Lincoln Home*, 53; Eliza Leslie, *Miss Leslie's House Book: A Manual of Domestic Economy for Town and Country*, 8th ed. (Philadelphia: Carey & Hart, 1845), 4, 8, 172, 192, 190; Eliza Leslie, *Miss Leslie's Behavior Book: A Guide and Manual for Ladies* (Philadelphia: T. B. Peterson, 1839); Catherine E. Beecher, *A Treatise on Domestic Economy, for the Use of Young Ladies at Home and at School*, rev. ed. (Boston: Thomas H. Webb, 1843); Motz, "Introduction," 1–2.

10. Menz, *Lincoln Home*, 338–341, 346, 349, 161, 98, 35, 13, 42; Motz, "Introduction," 4; Leslie, *House Book*, 311.

11. Menz, *Lincoln Home*, 161, 44, 53, 55, 161, 166, 18, 37, 36; David Herbert Donald, *Lincoln* (New York: Simon & Schuster, 1995), 198; Katherine Helm, *True Story of Mary, Wife of Lincoln* (New York: Harper, 1928), 98.

12. Fleischner, *Lincoln and Keckly*, 177–78, 175; Beecher, *Treatise on Domestic Economy*, rev. ed., 1843, 205–7; Randall, *Mary Lincoln*, 92–93; David M. Katzman, *Seven Days a Week: Women and Domestic Service in Industrializing America* (New York: Oxford University Press, 1981), 146–83.

13. Fleischner, *Lincoln and Keckly*, 153, 159–60; Michael Burlingame, *The Inner World of Abraham Lincoln* (Urbana: University of Illinois Press, 1994), 268–356; Kenneth J. Winkle, *Abraham and Mary Lincoln* (n.p.: Concise Lincoln Library, 2011) 2, 53; Baker, *Mary Todd Lincoln*, 227–28; Carl Sandburg, *Mary Lincoln: Wife and Widow* (Bedford, Mass.: Applewood Books, 1995), 71–73.

14. Fleischner, *Lincoln and Keckly*, 208; Donald, *Lincoln*, 251–52, 270–71; Menz, *Lincoln Home*, 34, 45–46, 98, 135.

15. Donald, *Lincoln at Home*, 22–23; Seale, *President's House*, 1:317–19; Donald, *Lincoln*, 312; William O. Stoddard, *Inside the White House in War Times* (New York: Charles L. Webster, 1890), 13, 49.

16. Stoddard, *Inside the White House*, 9, 5, 14; Watson, *Life in the White House*, 226–27; Seale, *President's House*, 1:187, 185–86, 342; Randall, *Mary Lincoln*, 212; Donald, *Lincoln*, 313.

17. Henrietta Nesbitt, *White House Diary by Henrietta Nesbitt, F.D.R's Housekeeper* (Garden City, N.Y.: Doubleday, 1948), 26; Lady Bird Johnson, *A White House*

Diary (Austin: University of Texas Press, 2007), 10; Kate Andersen Brower, *The Residence: Inside the Private World of the White House* (New York: HarperCollins, 2015), 34; Seale, *President's House*, 1:363; "Preparation for the Inaugural Ball at Washington," *New London* [Conn.] *Weekly Chronicle*, February 21, 1861, 3; Turner and Turner, *Mary Todd Lincoln*, 84.

18. Fleischner, *Lincoln and Keckly*, 204–5, 208; William H. Crook, *Through Five Administrations: Reminiscences of Colonel William H. Crook, Body-Guard to President Lincoln*, ed. Margarita Spalding Gerry (New York: Harper, 1910), 17; Seale, *President's House*, 1:181, 194; Brower, *The Residence*, 11; Thomas F. Pendel, *Thirty-Six Years in the White House: Lincoln–Roosevelt* (Washington, D.C.: Neale, 1902), 33, 35; Shirley Anne Warshaw, *Guide to the White House Staff* (Los Angeles: CQ Press, an imprint of Sage, 2013), 3.

19. Stoddard, *Inside the White House*, 62; Seale, *President's House*, 1:257, 299, 336–37, 395, 409, 2:611; West and Kotz, *Upstairs at the White House*, 9, 133; Brower, *The Residence*, 13; Crook, *Through Five Administrations*, 17; Elizabeth Keckley, *Behind the Scenes, or Thirty Years a Slave, and Four Years in the White House* (New York: G. W. Carleton, 1868), 206–7; Asa Briggs, *Victorian Things* (Chicago: University of Chicago Press, 1989), 256–57.

20. Seale, *President's House*, 1:195; Alison Light, *Mrs. Woolf and the Servants: An Intimate History of Domestic Life in Bloomsbury* (New York: Bloomsbury Press, 2008), 141; Phyllis Lee Levin, *Abigail Adams: A Biography* (New York: St. Martin's Press, 1987), 388; F. B. Carpenter, *Six Months at the White House with Abraham Lincoln: The Story of a Picture* (New York: Hurd and Houghton, 1866), 153; Baker, *Mary Todd Lincoln*, 259; Keckley, *Behind the Scenes*, 206–7.

21. Turner and Turner, *Mary Todd Lincoln*, 96; Randall, *Mary Lincoln*, 339; Carpenter, *Six Months at the White House*, 65–66, 98–99; Stoddard, *Inside the White House*, 10.

22. Stoddard, *Inside the White House*, 62, 86; Pendel, *Thirty-Six Years in the White House*, 30–31; Crook, *Through Five Administrations*, 18; Seale, *President's House*, 1:393; "Kitchen Cabinet Meddling," *New York Times*, January 11, 1865, n.p.; "Years in the White House," *New York Times*, October 10, 1886, 6.

23. Noah Brooks, *Washington in Lincoln's Time* (New York: Century, 1895), 276–77; Seale, *President's House*, 1:170, 214; Stoddard, *Inside the White House*, 24; Donald, *Lincoln*, 310, 313; Carpenter, *Six Months at the White House*, 99.

24. Fleischner, *Lincoln and Keckly*, 28–30, 147–48, 231–32, 248, 251–52, 286–87; Joan E. Cashin, *First Lady of the Confederacy: Varina Davis's Civil War* (Cambridge: Harvard University Press, 2006), 94–95; Keckley, *Behind the Scenes*, 206. On similar relationships in England, see Lucy Lethbridge, *Servants: A Downstairs History of Britain from the Nineteenth Century to Modern Times* (New York: W. W. Norton, 2013), 121–24.

25. Donald, *Lincoln*, 312; McDermott, *Mary Lincoln*, 98; Seale, *President's House*, 1:385–94; West and Kotz, *Upstairs at the White House*, 265–66; Nesbitt, *White House Diary*, 38. Both Wood and Watt had left their posts by early 1862.

26. "Mrs. Lincoln's Shopping in New York," [Columbus, Ohio] *Crisis*, May 30,

1861, 8; Seale, *President's House*, 1:390, 385–86, 382; Turner and Turner, *Mary Todd Lincoln*, 88, 130; Mary Clemmer Ames, *Ten Years in Washington* (Hartford, Conn.: A. D. Worthington, 1873), 171; "High Jinks in Washington," *Boston Post*, February 10, 1862, 4; "Life in Washington," *Newport* [R.I.] *Mercury*, February 8, 1862, 3.

27. Fleischner, *Lincoln and Keckly*, 210–11; "City Items," [Philadelphia] *Press*, May 4, 1861, 3; "Local Military Movements: Visit of Mrs. Lincoln to the Park Barracks," *New York Times*, May 18, 1861, n.p.; "Mrs. Lincoln," [Cleveland] *Plain Dealer*, September 11, 1861, 2; "The New Japanese Presents," [Washington, D.C.] *National Republican*, January 28, 1862, 2; "Mrs. Lincoln's Party," *Providence* [R.I.] *Evening Press*, February 14, 1862, 2; "A Good Suggestion," *Sandusky* [Ohio] *Register*, February 12, 1862, 3; "White House Junketing," [Belfast, Maine] *Republican Journal*, February 14, 1862, 2.

28. Betty Boyd Caroli, "The First Lady's Changing Role," in *The White House: The First Two Hundred Years*, ed. Frank Freidel and William Pencak (Boston: Northeastern University Press, 1994), 180; Seale, *President's House*, 2:823–25, 977, 994; Fleischner, *Lincoln and Keckly*, 271–72; "Mrs. Lincoln," [Washington, D.C.] *Daily Constitutional Union*, May 6, 1864, 2.

29. "Mrs. Lincoln's Shopping in New York," [Columbus, Ohio] *Crisis*, May 30, 1861, 8; "Burleigh, the New York Correspondent," [Middletown, Conn.] *Constitution*, February 20, 1861, 3; "It Is a Curious Circumstance," Hartford [Conn.] *Daily Courant*, April 29, 1861, 2; "American Women at Home and Abroad," *New York Herald*, April 29, 1863, 6; Randall, *Mary Lincoln*, 30; Fleischner, *Lincoln and Keckly*, 5; Winkle, *Abraham and Mary Lincoln*, 25; Clinton, *Mrs. Lincoln*, 129; Jerrold M. Packard, *The Lincolns in the White House: Four Years That Shattered a Family* (New York: St. Martin's Press, 2005), 15; Turner and Turner, *Mary Todd Lincoln*, 77; Daniel Mark Epstein, *The Lincolns: Portrait of a Marriage* (New York: Ballantine Books, 2009), 9, 453; Frank J. Williams, introduction to *Mary Lincoln Enigma*, ed. Williams and Burkhimer, 8; Berry, *House of Abraham*, 22–23; McDermott, *Mary Lincoln*, 2; Fleischner, *Lincoln and Keckly*, 210–11.

30. Turner and Turner, *Mary Todd Lincoln*, 107, 112, 447; Joshua Zeitz, *Lincoln's Boys: John Hay, John Nicolay, and the War for Lincoln's Image* (New York: Viking, 2014), 287; "A Letter from Mrs. Lincoln," *New York Times*, July 14, 1861, n.p.

31. Seale, *President's House*, 1:411, 424; Ames, *Ten Years in Washington*, 240; Fleischner, *Lincoln and Keckly*, 291–92; Keckley, *Behind the Scenes*, 202, 205–6; Randall, *Mary Lincoln*, 388–89; "The Emperor's Bowl, 100-Year Symbol of Japanese-American Relations," *Georgetowner*, February 25, 1960, 1, Accession File, Wheatland Collection, LancasterHistory.org.

32. Fleischner, *Lincoln and Keckly*, 290; McDermott, *Mary Lincoln*, 134–37, 141–51; Menz, *Lincoln Home*.

Householder and General

Lee's War as a Household War

JOSEPH M. BEILEIN JR.

In the antebellum South, every man belonged to a household. Over the past few decades, scholars of gender, race, and class have worked to return men to their households with deep running historical consequences. However, for all of this work, some Southern men have not yet been restored to their appropriate social location. Many of the so-called great men still seem to exist outside the basic social, economic, and political unit of the antebellum South, the household, somehow unmoored to the foundation of their society. Robert E. Lee is perhaps the best example of these detached men, floating at the very surface of Southern history without any real human attachments grounding him to the terra firma of his historical world. Although he is best known as the commanding general of the Army of Northern Virginia, Lee was also the head of a large slaveholding household when the war broke out, a fact that too often escapes the scrutiny of historians. In the rare instances when Lee's role within his household is studied, it is often isolated from his role as a military commander. Thus in Southern and Civil War histories Lee is either the general or the man; he is rarely, if ever, both.[1]

Indeed, Lee was the connection between the household and the war, a fact that he would struggle to fully comprehend over the course of the Civil War. In part, his status made this recognition difficult, if not impossible. As the head of a household and the head of an army, his perspective gave him a great view of others but no real view of himself. Looking down at his family, home, and property or gazing out upon his army, Lee—and men like him—imagined his army and his household as objects to manipulate, entities that could even be segregated from one another so that they might exist in distinct worlds. Yet Lee's very identity as a soldier and a husband, an officer and a father, a general and a planter bound these spheres together, one inside the other. Lee's war was in fact a household war.[2]

Lee was raised in the household of a warrior, which left a permanent imprint on him and influenced his actions throughout his life. He was born in one of the great plantation houses in Virginia, Stratford Hall. Like other boys of his generation, he grew up in the shadow of the American Revolution. For Lee that shadow loomed larger than it did for most others because his father, Henry Lee, had been a hero of the war. Fighting in the Southern theater where the Americans relied heavily upon militia and partisans and where entire districts were swept up in internecine warfare, Henry Lee saw and participated in some of the bloodiest irregular combat of the revolution in which his dashing character and unconventional command earned him the moniker "Light-Horse Harry." More than that, he helped to orchestrate and lead both guerrillas and the formal forces of the Continental army in the decisive campaign of the war. As such, Light-Horse Harry was one of the most important men in bringing the mighty British army to its knees in Virginia in 1781. After the war, Henry Lee would hold distinguished posts, first as the governor of Virginia and later as a member of Congress. Perhaps his greatest postwar contribution to American history was in delivering the eulogy for George Washington. It was Light-Horse Harry who spoke those famous words describing his fellow Virginian and father of the young republic: "First in war, first in peace, and first in the hearts of his countrymen."[3]

Despite his fame, Henry Lee's actions would destabilize and ultimately destroy his once great and wealthy household. Even before the war had ended, he began damaging his reputation, although no one knew then how self-destructive he would become. During a period of time in which the fighting phase of the Revolution had come to a close but no treaty had been signed, Henry Lee grew frustrated with his place in the army. Disgruntled by the lack of promotion, he resigned his commission and returned to his family lands to become a gentleman planter. Ambitious but directionless, it was not long before he began taking out loans that he could not repay. Piece by piece, he sold off portions of the Lee family lands to pay his balance, but he was never able to break the destructive pattern of debt. Ultimately, the Lee family had to move off their estate and into the town of Alexandria, and Henry spent time in debtor's prison. The Lee name took yet another hit when Henry was nearly beaten to death for coming to the aid of a Federalist friend whose newspaper was attacked by a Democratic-Republican mob. In an attempt to recover from his wounds, he left his family for the Caribbean, but he never healed. When he died on March 25, 1818, Henry left his wife without a husband, his children without a father, his family without a home, his name without honor, and his household without a head.[4]

Growing up in a fractured, vulnerable home must have caused anxiety for young Robert. It certainly created a vacuum in his mind where the voice of his father should have resonated. He only knew the specter of his father, but he would be haunted by the ghost of Light-Horse Harry for the remainder of his life. Born in 1807, Robert was eleven when his father died, and his father had been away for most of those years. It is unclear how many, if any, of his stories of the American Revolution Henry shared with Robert. Permanently absent and obscured by rumor, Henry Lee probably came to his son in the form of fireside tales told by kith and kin who were brave enough to speak of him. Whispered words like "partisan," "cavalryman," "guerrilla," "debtor," "scoundrel," "blackguard," and "Light-Horse Harry" must have danced around in the boy's imagination like smoke swirling up the chimney. Left with only the fleeting images of a ghost, a greater responsibility was placed on Robert to decide which parts of his father's identity to follow, should he choose to pursue any part of his father at all.[5]

Lee's mother did what she could to hold the pieces of their domestic life together and provide a suitable home for her children. Although they had suffered the loss of family lands, enslaved workers, income, and reputation, Ann Hill Carter Lee was able to tap into the support of an extensive kinship network. By this point in the history of Virginia, a great many of the oldest and wealthiest families were intermarried, and the Lee and Carter families were as enmeshed in this web of bloodlines as any. Ann Lee's kin made sure that her family had a home and that the children received what they needed. William Henry Fitzhugh provided the family with a home in Alexandria and often invited them out to Ravensworth, his plantation in the country. Ann's father, Charles Carter, established a trust fund from which Ann received more than $1,000 annually. Henry Lee's brother Charles also put the family up from time to time at his plantation. It was not the life that Ann had expected for herself or her children, but it was a dignified existence.[6]

Even as a boy, Robert worked to fill the role in the household vacated by his father. The best example of his efforts to be the man of the house, so to speak, can be seen in his relationship with his mother. Whether it was their somewhat unstable, mobile life or perhaps the physical closeness that would preclude letter writing, there is little direct evidence of the way in which mother and son related to each other. That said, it seems likely that Robert was something of a caretaker for his mother. Ann Lee became ill in her thirties with what historians have speculated was tuberculosis. With his older brother off at school and his stepsiblings removed from the plight of Ann and her children, Robert was the oldest male in the household and felt the responsibility to take charge of it. It would seem that the greatest exertion of his energy was providing his mother with a pillar on which she could lean. He nursed her, he took her for daily carriage rides, and he managed what household business she was incapable of doing. Mother and son were dependent upon one another.[7]

There were several men who stepped in to help Robert in his quest to attain manhood and mold him into a very different kind of man than his father had been. The first to step into the breach and directly work to shape Lee was a relative on his mother's side, William Fitzhugh, who would serve as something of a mentor for the young Lee. After seeing the boy through school, it was Fitzhugh's connections that allowed Lee to attain an appointment to the U.S. Military Academy at West Point, New York. In an iconic moment, Lee was given a letter of recommendation by Fitzhugh to the secretary of war that he asked the boy to hand deliver to John C. Calhoun. Of course, the young Lee did exactly that. If there was any question of whether or not Lee was a worthy candidate for acceptance, it was seemingly answered by his willingness to deliver the letter himself. Indeed, it appeared that Lee was learning what it was to be a man—the right kind of man.[8]

After receiving his appointment, Lee entered the exclusively male barracks of the U.S. Army. As his time at West Point demonstrated, he thrived in this world. The stories about his time at West Point have become fixtures of the Lee biography: he maintained an unblemished record as a cadet; he finished at the top of his class—technically second, although he was first among the young men who stayed in the army; he was in one of the last classes to matriculate under the guidance of headmaster Sylvanus Thayer and among the first students to study under Professor Dennis Hart Mahan, two legends of West Point; and he was appointed to the esteemed corps of engineers. Quite a few scholars have pointed to his education on the Hudson as the primary influence on his strategic and tactical thinking during the Civil War. The military training Lee received at West Point was of the conventional nature. He was being taught to lead the young formal army of the United States by looking to Europe and the large European armies that had waged the Napoleonic Wars for guidance and inspiration.[9]

In the military, the ghosts of Lee's childhood seemed to disperse and were replaced by the ethos of the regular army, which insisted upon occupying the whole of a young man. In addition to the content of his coursework, the culture of the army played a significant role in Lee's vision of the conduct of war. Both the Military Academy and later the institution of the U.S. Army provided a welcome alternative to the household of his youth. The military provided a structure—a seemingly unchanging, unbreakable structure—in which rules were enforced, standards were kept, and merit was rewarded, all of which must have provided Lee with a deep sense of security. Although family names and reputations carried across state lines and followed men into places as exclusive and as isolated as West Point, institutions like the army also offered a sense of anonymity that would have relieved a young man trying to shake the negative connotations of his name. West Point would also provide an endless list of male role models for Lee to look up to and brothers in arms with whom he could commiserate. For a boy without a father, who rarely spent time with his brothers and whose home life was unstable and demanding, Lee was just the type of young man who was able to grow into a man and make a name for himself in this setting.[10]

Almost immediately after his graduation from West Point, Lee set out to create a household of his own. His mother, to whom he had been so attached, died soon after he returned home in the summer of 1829, which cut him free from the household of his youth. However, his father's reputation still haunted Virginia. He would have to prove to others in his community that he was not Light-Horse Harry. Lee courted a young woman from a wealthy Virginia family, a family with bloodlines that went back as far as his own. Mary Ann Randolph Custis was the daughter of George Washington Parke Custis, the stepgrandson of George Washington. (His father was adopted by Washington when he married Martha, the widow of Daniel Parke Custis.) George Custis must have seen the same thing in Lee that Fitzhugh, Calhoun, and Thayer had seen in him. In 1831, just a couple of years after Robert's graduation from West Point, the couple married.[11]

From that time through the Civil War, Lee would be responsible to dependents in two institutions: his household and his army. As the head of a household, Lee indeed proved to be very different than his father. He and Mary had seven children, all of whom were living in 1861 when the Civil War began. By all accounts, it was a happy and loving marriage in which Robert and Mary built up and maintained a stable household, one that was much more stable than the household in which he was raised. More than anything else, Lee was present. That is, he was as present as any army officer could be during the antebellum period. He served in places like St. Louis and Michigan and often tried to keep his family with him. However, Mary eventually returned to her father's home at Arlington where she had support and assistance in child rearing. When Robert was not at home, he was living with and leading soldiers. These men depended on him for guidance and order, which he provided, and in exchange they gave him their obedience and respect. It could have felt to Lee that he traveled between two worlds that were sometimes separated by great physical distances as well as emotional and intellectual space. However, moving from one world to another did not necessarily mean leaving the other behind, only that bonds could change by being pulled, stretched, and compressed and that the man who moved between the family and the army was altered in ways minor and major.[12]

The greatest geographic distance that Lee traveled from his household was during the Mexican-American War. In an army of men, far from home, he came to embody the ideal American officer. He served as a staff officer for General Winfield Scott, the preeminent hero of the antebellum period. Scott had been an effective officer in the War of 1812, and he continued to actively command forces in the various Indian wars of the antebellum period, including the Black Hawk War and the Second Seminole War. As the most experienced officer in the army, he was given command of the forces set to invade Mexico, only to be relieved by General Zachary Taylor. Scott would get into the war by persuading President James K. Polk to allow him to lead a seaborne invasion of Mexico at Vera Cruz and then march inland to take Mexico City. Here Lee witnessed and helped to execute a campaign that was considered at the time to be one of the most daring and genius in the history of warfare.[13]

Returning home to Arlington on June 29, 1848, Lee was confronted with the more direct management of his household, which was far from perfect. Although some of his responsibilities with the army lessened during peacetime, so too did the excitement and sense of purpose that came with warfare departures. The energy of combat gave way to the tedious but necessary work of heading a household that seemed more and more in need of leadership. Over the course of their marriage Mary Lee proved to be a poor housekeeper who was seemingly incapable of performing anything beyond the most basic tasks of a wife and mother. Eventually, her health issues precluded any kind of domestic work or management. She began to suffer from an array of health problems that would ultimately get so bad that she needed a wheelchair. Just as he did with his mother, Lee served as a nursemaid to his wife when he was present, and he made sure her needs were met when he was away.[14]

Just a couple of years before shots were fired at Fort Sumter, the Lee household grew tremendously. In 1857, his father-in-law passed away and

left all of his enslaved workers and the estate at Arlington under Lee's control. As the executor of George Custis's will, Lee also oversaw the distribution of other estates. For instance, Robert and Mary's son William Henry
Fitzhugh "Rooney" Lee inherited the Ravensworth plantation. Also, it was
Lee's task to manage his various new holdings in such a way that he could
fulfill one of his father-in-law's requests, which was to free the more than
one hundred enslaved African Americans within five years of his death,
a task that would prove all the more difficult with the outbreak of war.
Regardless of this caveat, it must be acknowledged that in 1861 Lee was
the head of a very large slaveholding plantation and one of the elite house-
holders in the South. Furthermore, the arc of Lee's story had moved in the
opposite direction from his father's biography. Henry was born with everything and over time lost it all. Considering the deficits of capital and honor
his father had left him with, Robert was born with less than nothing, and
after decades he became a wealthy planter. None of this was coincidence.
Lee actively worked in the opposite direction of his father. It is possible to
look at Robert E. Lee at this moment, just on the cusp of the war, and see
a man who had redeemed his family name.[15]

When the Civil War began and Virginia seceded from the Union, Lee
famously acted to protect his home. Whether he meant his state—the state
in which his household was located—or his family—those who resided in
his household as well as the families of his sons and daughters—the protection of his household was implied as a motivation for resigning his commission from the U.S. army. Lee said that he could not draw his sword
against Virginia, or as he told his sister, "I have not been able to make up
my mind to raise my hand against my relatives, my children, my home."
With the express desire to protect his family and his homeland, he joined
the Confederate forces in Virginia. Serving as an adviser to President Jefferson Davis and eventually becoming the head of the Army of Northern Virginia, Lee pursued a strategy of conventional warfare that he hoped would
keep his soldiers under discipline, provide order to the war, and allow him
to choose when and where battles took place. In his mind, a conventional
war waged by a formal or "regular" army offered the best chance to win the
war. Given his motivations for leaving the Union and joining the Confederacy, Lee must have also considered conventional warfare and the victories
it would generate as the best way to defend his household.[16]

The war, however, quickly swept into Lee's household. One of Lee's
greatest concerns in its first days was getting his wife away from Arlington House, which sat on the Potomac River in the direct path of the Union
army. Although this concern was representative of a common desire by

men in the conventional armies to move their mothers, wives, sisters, and sweethearts away from the battlefront, the nature of Lee's relationship with his wife gave him an even greater sense of urgency. Also, considering his father's abandonment of Lee's own sickly mother, he felt a great degree of guilt for the circumstances in which he left his wife. In May 1861, Robert wrote Mary, "I want you in a place of safety." He tried to be as empathetic as possible, saying in another letter, "I grieve at the necessity that drives you from your home. I can appreciate your feelings on the occasion, and pray that you may receive comfort and strength in the difficulties that surround you." Mary Lee would move to Ravensworth. However, when that plantation was overrun, the U.S. army forced her to withdraw to Richmond.[17]

Even as the war ran roughshod over his household, so too did the household seep into Lee's war. Either due to Mary's physical limitations or Lee's preferences, Mary did not join her husband at the front. Lee would leave the lines of battle from time to time to visit his wife when he traveled to Richmond on official business. Unlike Lee, some officers brought their households with them when they went on campaign. On both sides, the wives of officers, especially general officers, joined their husbands at the battlefront. Throughout the war Union generals John C. Frémont, George B. McClellan, Ulysses S. Grant, and William T. Sherman all received visits from their wives and sometimes children. There were a few Confederate officers whose wives were also present at times with the army. The wife of George Pickett, one of Lee's generals, lived with her husband, as did the wife of Richard Ewell. In addition to demonstrating the unrelenting power of the household even in war, the presence of these women in command tents revealed the direct influence of wives and mothers on the war, even in the highest reaches of the formal armies.[18]

For his part, Lee constructed an alternative, all-male household under his command tent. The officers and soldiers of his command took on imagined kinship roles; they were his brothers, nephews, and sons. It was not uncommon for Lee to refer to the soldiers in the Army of Northern Virginia as his "boys." Occasionally these relations were real—Lee had sons and a nephew in the Confederate army—but mostly these familial roles were imagined. To these men, Lee was a father figure of sorts, earning him nicknames like Uncle Robert and the Old Man. Lee's tent may have been the largest of these homosocial, moveable, and metaphorical households, but it was not the only one. From the corps commanders on down through the divisions, brigades, and regiments, and finally down to the messes of the enlisted men, these were social units in which men would slide into familial roles and develop relationships with other men that drew on the organic bonds more commonly associated with peacetime households.[19]

U.S. and Confederate armies segregated themselves from other members of domestic households, but there was little they could do to move all of the households from the theater of war. The Union embraced this reality sooner than did the Confederacy. In Virginia, Union general John Pope directed his men to subsist off the land and target the homes of Confederates during the summer of 1862. Pope's General Orders 5, 6, and 7 permitted his soldiers to take food from local farms, force enemy inhabitants to contribute to the required two days' worth of rations each of his soldiers was to carry, and hold the local citizenry responsible for guerrilla violence and sabotage. From that point onward, Union forces began to live off the Virginia countryside, entering homes, taking what they needed, and sometimes even destroying property. Eventually, in 1863, the Union would articulate a universal policy for engaging the Southern citizenry as enemies in General Order 100, also known as the Lieber Code for its main author, Francis Lieber. Immediately in the wake of Pope's orders and continuing throughout the war, the men in the Army of Northern Virginia were angered and frustrated by their enemy's actions. Generally they viewed these new Union policies as a shameful step away from civilized warfare and an assault on civilization itself. On a personal level, any soldiers or officers whose homes were destroyed or whose women were humiliated—or worse—became enraged.[20]

Lee may have been critical of Union policies that brought the war into households and saddened by the enemy's occupation of his home at Arlington, but he nevertheless directed his own army to live off the households of the enemy during the Gettysburg campaign in the summer of 1863. On June 21, with his entire army across the Potomac, Lee issued General Order 72 in which he stated, "No private property shall be injured or destroyed by any person belonging to or connected with the army, or taken, excepting by the officers hereinafter designated." Lee stipulated that these officers pay the market price for whatever they procured from the local populace with Confederate money. Given the worthlessness of the Confederate dollar in Pennsylvania, most Northerners saw this appropriation as stealing. Moreover, Lee said that if "authorities or inhabitants neglect or refuse to comply with such requisitions, the supplies required will be taken from the nearest inhabitants so refusing," and "If any person shall remove or conceal property necessary for the use of the army, or attempt to do so, the officers herein before mentioned will cause such property, and all other property belonging to such person that may be required by the army, to be seized." In short, Lee instructed his men to enter enemy households and take what they needed one way or the other.[21]

When viewed through a glass darkly, Lee's Order 72 looked a lot like the Union army's General Order 100 and the orders that had preceded it. This murky reflection of the Union strategy can be seen in the racial implications of Lee's policy. Just as the Union army was working directly and indirectly to emancipate enslaved people, the Confederate army, with Lee at its head, was working to stop and even reverse the flow of freedom and to return these black men and women to the mudsill of the Southern household. One of Lee's cavalry brigades under the command of General Albert Jenkins rode about southeastern Pennsylvania kidnapping free African Americans and driving them south where they would be enslaved. Jenkins's Raid may appear to be shocking, but this component of the Gettysburg campaign was perfectly congruent with the proslavery politics of the Confederacy.[22]

Although the racial element of Order 72 fit with the worldview of a man who had headed a slaveholding household before the war, actions taken by some of his soldiers against white women in Pennsylvania caused Lee to realize that he had violated the gendered boundaries of civilized warfare. In response to these violations, Lee issued General Order 73 one week after Order 72, in which he reminded his soldiers "that the duties expected of us by civilization and Christianity are not less obligatory in the country of the enemy than in our own." Furthermore, Lee considered "that no greater disgrace could befall the army, and through it our whole people, than the perpetration of the barbarous outrages upon the unarmed, and defenceless and the wanton destruction of private property that have marked the course of the enemy in our own country." As he wrote these words, it must have occurred to Lee that even the most civilized and Christian invading armies had to live off the land and that even disciplined regular army soldiers were capable of abuse.[23]

More than simply scolding the few soldiers who misbehaved, Order 73 offered declarative statements regarding Lee's definitions of war and its practitioners. The order itself implies that Lee believed that his men had clearly forgotten the rules of conventional and therefore civilized warfare. He reminded these soldiers that "we make war only upon armed men, and that we cannot take vengeance for the wrongs our people have suffered without lowering ourselves in the eyes of all whose abhorrence has been excited by the atrocities of our enemies." War, then, was an exercise performed by men against men. In Lee's mind, true war could not include the "unarmed" or the "defenseless," meaning women, and any soldier who violated this basic dynamic of warfare immediately forfeited his claims to true manhood. As soon as a man assaulted another man's dependents, he made his own household fair game and delivered up his women and children to the whims of the invader. Up until this point, Lee's "boys" had been true men: protectors of the household rather than its violators.

And yet without Order 72, the Confederate army would never have reached Gettysburg. It was quite possible that the real source of defeat during the summer of 1863 came from Lee's unwillingness to engage in an offensive against the Union household. Military failures—Pickett's Charge or another moment in and around Gettysburg from July 1 through July 3 (Ewell's decision to hold his ground rather than take Culp's Hill on the battle's first day, Longstreet's delay in executing his echelon attack on July 2, etc.)—have served as the all too obvious sources of Confederate defeat for historians since the end of the war. For Lee and Davis and millions of other Southerners, it was easier, even honorable, to recall the moment when fifteen thousand men battered themselves against walls of stone, lead, and enemy soldiers as the pivot point of the war. From this perspective, war was safely contained to armies and to men and preserved for posterity within the limits of a neatly demarcated field where it could be visited at leisure with its memory protected and its meaning contained. Pickett's Charge may have been the moment of defeat, but it was just as likely that the Confederate army was so close to breaking through the blue wall atop Cemetery Ridge because they had invaded, pulled resources from, and otherwise destroyed the households of their enemies. Despite Lee's narrow focus on the field of battle, the Gettysburg campaign failed.

In the aftermath of the failures in Pennsylvania, the household and the war would come to share a thought in Lee's mind. In late July, Lee wrote to President Jefferson Davis articulating his concern that the people of the Confederacy had turned on him and the army because of their defeat on the third day of the battle. Lee promised that his tactics and the strategy that he and Davis were employing would be vindicated once the official reports were finished. Then, on August 8, 1863, Lee sent a missive to Davis in which he accepted blame for the failures of his army, made reference to his failing health as a growing source of frustration and limitation, and requested some lesser command for which he would be a better fit. Of course, Davis told his general that he could not accept his resignation. On August 22, 1863, in Lee's final rebuttal to his faithful president, he reiterated to Davis, "I am as willing to serve now as in the beginning in any capacity and at any post where I can do good. The lower the position, the more suitable to my ability, and the more agreeable to my feelings." Now, however, he concluded his letter by stating, "Beyond such assistance as I can give to an invalid wife and three houseless daughters, I have no object in life but to devote myself to the defense of our violated country's rights." Right next to one another were his household and his war. Yet in Lee's mind there was still a disconnect: they were associated, correlated, and somehow coexistent, but they were not directly related.[24]

Lee's household, past and present, explained much of his behavior during and after the Gettysburg campaign. Given his frame of reference, it made perfect sense that Lee thought of his dependents in the wake of the Gettysburg campaign. There he had undertaken a policy that came to harm vulnerable women and exposed unprotected households to the horrors of war. Moreover, his part in turning out Union women and leaving them without a home must have caused Lee to reflect that his own wife and daughters were made "houseless" by the enemy. In hearing about households left vulnerable, women forced to fend for themselves, children neglected, and men misbehaving, visceral feelings and recollections born of his youth must have been awakened inside him. Order 73 as well as his final plea to Davis that he would be better served tending to his family seemingly point to such anxiety.[25]

Upon returning to Virginia, Lee, his officers, and other Confederate officials began to articulate more clearly the relationship between the war and the household as one of victimization. In particular, they saw Southern guerrillas, bushwhackers, partisans, and any other irregulars as violators of the household—enemy households, Confederate households, and even their own households. As early as 1863, there were reports from members of the Confederate leadership that many partisans were indiscriminate in their violence and that incorporating these men into the regular army would protect the Southern household. In his annual report to President Davis on November 26, 1863, Secretary of War James Seddon asserted that the partisans "have, indeed, when under inefficient officers and operating within our own limits, come to be more formidable and destructive to our own people than to the enemy." Exactly where Seddon procured the information on which he wrote his report was unclear. However, this report was the beginning of a movement against partisan warfare, earlier sanctioned in April 1862 with the passage of the Partisan Ranger Act, by the Confederate government because of the claim that irregulars were actively attacking the Southern community.[26]

Over the coming months, Lee's officers became more and more frustrated by irregular soldiers and what they saw as the detrimental effect guerrillas had on both the Southern household and the Confederate army. During the second half of 1863 and into 1864, the officers of the Army of Northern Virginia asserted that households served as a major draw, pulling men out of the regular army and into the partisan or guerrilla ranks.

In a January 11, 1864, letter to Lee, Brigadier General Thomas Rosser suggested that the partisan ranger corps was the primary source of desertion among his soldiers and that it should be disbanded. His first criticism of guerrilla warfare was that fighting as a guerrilla kept a potential soldier out of the formal army; the second was that "they cause great dissatisfaction in the ranks from the fact that these irregular troops are allowed so much latitude, so many privileges. They sleep in houses and turn out in the cold only when it is announced by their chief that they are to go upon a plundering expedition." And, third, the presence of the partisan rangers "renders other troops dissatisfied; hence encourages desertion." Rosser said that his soldiers "see these men living at their ease and enjoying the comforts of home, allowed to possess all that they capture, and their duties mere pastime pleasures compared with their own arduous ones; and it is a natural consequence in the nature of man that he should become dissatisfied under these circumstances."[27]

Lee seemed to agree that partisans were a threat to both the army and the household. Regarding the army, an increase in desertions from 1863 to 1864 among soldiers of the Army of Northern Virginia led Lee to endorse Rosser's request, and by mid-February the Partisan Ranger Act was repealed. It remains unclear whether or not the repeal led these fighters to join the formal army forces, but it seems unlikely. Lee continued to be critical of irregular fighters, suggesting that the guerrilla war was an attractive option for Southern men in and around Virginia. Again, his greatest criticism of the guerrillas was his claim that the irregular war allowed for violence against the Southern citizenry. Lee stated that it may not have been partisans per se but that the lack of formal army discipline or uniforms among partisan units allowed for the existence of brigands. In an April 1, 1864, letter to the inspector general of the Confederacy, Lee articulated that his greatest concern with the partisan system was that it "gives license to many deserters and marauders, who assume to belong to these authorized companies and commit depredations on friend and foe alike."[28]

However, the Confederate fear of the irregular was misguided. At the very least it was based on a misunderstanding of the triadic relationship of the guerrillas, the households, and the war. Perhaps stemming from the crisis facing the Confederate war effort, they seemed to project the failings of the formal military on the partisans. This shifting of blame was no more evident than in Lee's admission that it was "deserters and marauders" late of the Army of Northern Virginia—his own "boys"—who were terrorizing Southern households; he immediately followed this admission by attributing these depredations to the partisans. In keeping with the pattern of this misattribution, Lee and his fellow Confederate officers spoke of the siren song of the household, with its warm beds and the "comforts of home," which must be taken to mean the company of women who lured otherwise committed soldiers out of the army and into the warm embrace of guerrilla service. But, in seemingly the next thought, they reported these same men fled the army to join the partisan ranks so that they might rape the women and pillage the homes of their fellow Southerners. It seems rather unlikely that the same men were responsible for both the nurturing interactions with their women and also the victimizing of the weak.[29]

The view of the guerrillas from Lee's household was distorted because he looked out at them through the eyes of Henry's son. Lee seemed to admire the irregular fighters that he met firsthand. He certainly spoke well of John S. Mosby, for example. But when he imagined the other guerrillas, those he did not know, the image that came to mind did not resemble Mosby, John H. McNeill, or any other partisan; instead, he saw someone who failed to meet the standard of conventional manhood, who made vulnerable the very households he should be protecting, who lacked honesty and honor. It is perhaps a reach to claim that when Lee pictured the guerrilla of his war, he saw his father. However, it would be shortsighted to contend that nothing of his father—or at least the way Lee imagined his father—came to color or shape his ideas about the Southern partisan in the Civil War.[30]

Had Lee known his father better or at least known more of his father's service in the Revolution, he might have thought better of disregarding the contribution of the guerrillas outright. Well born, educated, patriotic, skilled in warfare, and fearless, his father was the embodiment of the dashing cavalier. At twenty years old in 1776, Henry Lee was in the prime of his life when the American Revolution exploded in Britain's American colonies. Coming from a prominent and wealthy Virginia family, Lee was made a captain at the outset of hostilities. He quickly rose to lieutenant colonel and became the commander of a group of partisans from Virginia known as Lee's Partisan Legion. Even though he attained such a relatively high rank, he was nevertheless quite young and able to ride and shoot with the best of his men while also being comfortable living in the brush. Even his sobriquet, Light-Horse Harry, an eloquent splicing of his chosen tactics and informality, gives the impression of a young, dashing, masculine figure rather than a plodding old man.[31]

Light-Horse Harry's brand of warfare was both courageous and successful in the face of long odds. He led from the front, executing the kind of attacks that slowly chipped away at the British and their colonial allies. On

February 25, 1781, Light-Horse Harry executed a brutally successful ambush on a few hundred Tory dragoons led by a loyalist named Colonel John Pyle. Using disguise to his advantage, Lee approached the Tories very casually. Because Lee's Legion and Tarleton's Dragoons both wore green uniforms, Lee let the Tories believe that he was his British counterpart, Lieutenant Colonel Banastre Tarleton, and that his men were British dragoons. Pyle's battalion halted along the right side of the road and let Lee's Legion ride up alongside them on the left side of the road, making it as easy for the patriots to use their pistols and muskets as it was difficult for the loyalists to access and fire their weapons. Light-Horse Harry remembered that he "passed along the line at the head of the column with a smiling countenance, dropping, occasionally, expressions complimentary to the good looks and commendable conduct of his loyal friends." Finally, Lee reached the head of Pyle's column where he greeted Pyle. Then, while he was "Grasping Pyle by the hand," the ambush was executed. According to Lee, "The conflict was quickly decided, and bloody on one side only. Ninety of the royalists were killed, and most of the survivors wounded." As for Lee's part in the bloodshed, he did not directly say. He did recall, however, "Pyle, falling under many wounds, was left on the field as dying, and yet he survived."[32]

The guerrillas of the Revolution also executed a strategy that conserved manpower. In his memoirs of the Revolution, Light-Horse Harry described himself and his fellow guerrilla Francis Marion as "singularly tender of the lives of their soldiers; and preferred moderate success, with little loss, to the most brilliant enterprise, with the destruction of many troops." For a variety of reasons, including the highly democratic nature of guerrilla warfare and the war aims and strategies shared by guerrilla movements generally, the lives of individual fighters were valued much more than they were in conventional warfare. If guerrillas thought their captains were negligent with their lives, they could leave or refuse to follow orders and elect a new captain. From a military perspective, most guerrilla wars took a particular form where the survival of the resistance force was a victory. It was fine to retreat from a skirmish or to lose a battle in guerrilla warfare because as long as the guerrillas continued to fight, the guerrillas were winning the war. And win the Revolutionary War they did.[33]

Regardless of the historical model the American Revolution provided for the Confederacy, Lee saw guerrilla warfare as an existential threat, which in the end was a greater threat to him than the Yankees. Consequently, he attempted to bolster his ranks and protect Southern households from wayward stragglers with little effect. Lee was only able to sustain the war for another year. When the Army of the Potomac broke through Confederate lines around Petersburg on April 2, 1865, the Army of Northern Virginia, with perhaps more than forty thousand soldiers, made its breakout. As the Confederates marched westward in an attempt to regroup, men deserted by the thousands, making their way to their own nearby homes. Whether or not they plundered friendly homes along the way is unclear but also unlikely. As these soldiers deserted, the Union cavalry attacked the Army of Northern Virginia day after day for nearly a week, killing, wounding, and capturing thousands of Confederate soldiers and destroying supply trains.[34]

Despite all of its losses, on the morning of April 9, the Army of Northern Virginia still had nearly twenty-eight thousand men in its ranks—enough to fight on, or at least Lee's chief of artillery, General Porter Alexander, thought so. As Alexander presented it, the Army of Northern Virginia "must either surrender; or, the army may be ordered to scatter in the woods & bushes," presumably to continue the fight as guerrillas. Even after Lee patiently listened to the enthusiastic pleas of his subordinate, he could not bring himself to endorse guerrilla warfare. Rather, he reminded Alexander that their soldiers' "homes have been overrun by the enemy & their families need them badly." Lee worried that if he were to send his soldiers into the brush, "The men would have no rations & they would be under no discipline. . . . They would have to plunder & rob to procure subsistence. The country would be full of lawless bands in every part, & a state of society would ensue from which it would take the country years to recover." Additionally, Lee himself was feeling the fatigue of old age. He told Alexander, "You young fellows might go out bushwhacking, but the only dignified course for me would be to go to Gen. Grant and surrender myself." Lee concluded, "I expect to meet Gen. Grant at ten this morning . . . to surrender this army to him."[35]

When given this final choice to fight on in the form of a guerrilla, Lee made the same decision as the soldiers who left the army in its final days. When he was approached by Alexander, Lee had already made up his mind to go home, and he did not plan to bring the war with him. Of course, the war had already been to his home, Alexander's home, and the homes of his men. In articulating his reasons for rejecting guerrilla warfare and raising the white flag, Lee foresaw his "boys" making war on the Confederacy's mothers and daughters. His frightful vision, as compelling as it was, revealed the limits of his own knowledge of the nature of man. Although he imagined that the discipline of the army provided order for his troops, he forgot that his so-called boys were in fact someone else's very real sons. Or that these sons had very real mothers and fathers, and they were as likely to turn on their own households, their own people, as Lee was to turn on his.[36]

Indeed, Southern men were of the household. In April, May, and June 1865, tens of thousands of men returned to their loved ones, their homes, and their lands. Before, during, and after the war, the household was a constant force, regardless of one's mental, emotional, or physical distance from it. Even though he could not see it, Lee, the men of the Confederate army, and the guerrillas were members of their respective households, even while they set out to explore the universe of battle. They carried inside them their households and the war, with their minds, bodies, and souls holding these two cosmic entities together with such strength that only death might rip the two spheres asunder. If there was any difference among these men, it was that the fighters of the guerrilla war could see more clearly the influence of the household on the war while Lee and many of his fellow Confederate leaders lived in denial of this relationship. And yet, when it was all said and done, each returned home.[37]

In an unlikely epilogue, Lee made peace with his father's ghost. In 1869, he published a second edition of his father's recollections of the American Revolution, *Memoirs of the War in the Southern Department of the United States*, which Henry had written and published in 1812. On the title page of the work, Lee proudly maintained his father's official rank and designation as the commandant of the Partisan Legion. He must have come to grips with Light-Horse Harry's identity as a guerrilla and recognized how important that partisan status had been to his father. Perhaps, in a quiet moment, while writing the introduction to his father's story, he pondered what might have been if he had been a bit more like Light-Horse Harry and a bit less like the image people have sculpted of him as a Marble Man. Perhaps not. Although both men were of the same household, at different points in their lives, each man lost sight of that ever-present bond, a blind spot that led to their worst defeats.[38]

NOTES

1. Douglas Southall Freeman, *R. E. Lee: A Biography* (New York: Charles Scribner's Sons, 1934); Thomas Lawrence Connelly, *The Marble Man: Robert E. Lee and His Image in American Society* (Baton Rouge: Louisiana State University Press, 1977); Gary Gallagher, *Lee and His Generals in War and Memory* (Baton Rouge: Louisiana State University Press, 1998); Emory Thomas, *Robert E. Lee: A Biography* (New York: W. W. Norton, 1997); Alan T. Nolan, *"Rally, Once Again!" Selected Civil War Writings of Alan T. Nolan* (Lanham, Md.: Rowman and Littlefield, 2000). The book that best demonstrates social and cultural issues on Lee's generalship is Michael Fellman, *The Making of Robert E. Lee* (New York: Random House, 2000).

2. LeeAnn Whites, *The Civil War as a Crisis in Gender: Augusta, Georgia, 1860–1890* (Athens: University of Georgia Press, 1995), 4–14; Susan Bordo, "Feminism,

Postmodernism, and Gender-Skepticism," in *Feminism/Postmodernism*, ed. Linda Nicholson (New York: Routledge, 1990), 133–56; Thomas Nagel, *The View from Nowhere* (New York: Oxford University Press, 1986).

3. Henry Lee, *Memoirs of the War in the Southern Department of the United States* (New York: University Publishing, 1869).

4. Thomas, *Robert E. Lee*, 23–37.

5. Thomas, *Robert E. Lee*, 36–37.

6. Thomas, *Robert E. Lee*, 34–40.

7. Thomas, *Robert E. Lee*, 39.

8. Thomas, *Robert E. Lee*, 42. A number of significant studies of nineteenth-century manhood have been produced in the past few decades. They include Nina Silber, *The Romance of Reunion: Northerners and the South, 1865–1900* (Chapel Hill: University of North Carolina Press, 1993); Stephen W. Berry II, *All That Makes a Man: Love and Ambition in the Civil War South* (New York: Oxford University Press, 2003); Amy Greenberg, *Manifest Manhood and the Antebellum American Empire* (New York: Cambridge University Press, 2005); Lorien Foote, *The Gentlemen and the Roughs: Violence, Honor, and Manhood in the Union Army* (New York: New York University Press, 2010); Brian Craig Miller, *John Bell Hood and the Fight for Civil War Memory* (Knoxville: University of Tennessee Press, 2010).

9. Thomas, *Robert E. Lee*, 47–54; Fellman, *Making of Robert E. Lee*, 11–12.

10. Thomas, *Robert E. Lee*, 47–54.

11. Thomas, *Robert E. Lee*, 56–66.

12. Fellman, *Making of Robert E. Lee*, 34–53.

13. Thomas, *Robert E. Lee*, 111–36.

14. Thomas, *Robert E. Lee*, 70–84.

15. Fellman, *Making of Robert E. Lee*, 12. Evidence suggests that Lee did not feel as if he had been able to restore his name. He wrote to his son that he hoped his progeny might "resuscitate" the name of the Lee house. Letter from Lee to William Henry Fitzhugh Lee, April 2, 1860, in *Life and Letters of Robert Edward Lee, Soldier and Man*, ed. J. William Jones (Washington, D.C.: Neale, 1906), 112.

16. E. Porter Alexander, *Fighting for the Confederacy: The Personal Recollections of General Edward Porter Alexander*, ed. Gary Gallagher (Chapel Hill: University of North Carolina Press, 1989), 532; Gary Gallagher, "The Idol of His Soldier and the Hope of His Country: Lee and the Confederate People," in *Lee and His Generals*, 3–20.

17. Robert E. Lee Jr., *Recollections and Letters of General Robert E. Lee* (Old Saybrook, Conn.: Konecky & Konecky, n.d.), 30; Thomas, *Robert E. Lee*, 195–96.

18. Candice Shy Hooper, *Lincoln's Generals' Wives: Four Women Who Influenced the Civil War for Better and for Worse* (Kent, Ohio: Kent State University Press, 2016).

19. Aaron Sheehan-Dean, *Why Confederates Fought: Family and Nation in Civil War Virginia* (Chapel Hill: University of North Carolina Press, 2007), 58–59; Lee, *Recollections*, 69–90.

20. U.S. War Department, *The War of the Rebellion: A Compilation of the Official Records of the Union and Confederate Armies* (Washington, D.C.: Government Printing Office, 1880–1901) [hereafter cited as *OR*], vol. 12, pt. 2:50, 51; Mark Grimsley, *The Hard Hand of War: Union Military Policy toward Southern Civilians, 1861–1865* (New York: Cambridge University Press, 1997), 38–39, 86–92, 148–51; Sheehan-Dean, *Why Confederates Fought*, 100. The topic of soldier-enemy household interaction has yielded a number of important works that analyze this interface from the perspective of invading soldiers, women, slaves, and even men far removed from their violated homes. Much of this work has focused on Sherman's March, but it would seem that similar conclusions regarding the ways that these violations affected women and their men can be assumed about feelings of Virginians. For examples of this literature, see Lisa Tendrich Frank, *The Civilian War: Confederate Women and Union Soldiers during Sherman's March* (Baton Rouge: Louisiana State University Press, 2015), and Lisa Tendrich Frank, "War Comes Home: Confederate Women and Union Soldiers," in *Virginia's Civil War*, ed. Peter Wallenstein and Bertram Wyatt-Brown (Charlottesville: University of Virginia Press, 2005), 123–36.

21. General Order 72, Headquarters Army of Northern Virginia, June 21, 1863.

22. Margaret S. Creighton, *The Colors of Courage: Gettysburg's Forgotten History: Immigrants, Women, and African Americans in the Civil War's Defining Battle* (New York: Basic Books, 2005).

23. General Order 73, Headquarters of the Army of Northern Virginia, Chambersburg, Pennsylvania, June 27, 1863; Creighton, *Colors of Courage*, 103–4.

24. Stanley F. Horn, ed., *The Robert E. Lee Reader* (Indianapolis: Bobbs-Merrill, 1961), 337–38; *OR*, series 1, vol. 29, pt. 2: 639; vol. 51, pt. 2: 1076.

25. Horn, *Reader*, 337–38.

26. *OR*, series 4, vol. 2: 1003, 990–1018; series 1, vol. 33: 1252; series 1, vol. 33: 1082–83.

27. *OR*, series 1, vol. 33: 1082–83; Sheehan-Dean, *Why Confederates Fought*, 92–94, 227n17.

28. *OR*, series 4, vol. 2: 1003, 990–1018; series 1, vol. 33: 1252; series 1, vol. 33: 1082–83.

29. In guerrilla studies there is a school of thought that would agree with Confederate leadership that the guerrillas turned on their own people. For prominent works in this school, see Michael Fellman, *Inside War: The Guerrilla Conflict in Missouri during the American Civil War* (New York: Oxford University Press, 1990); Daniel Sutherland, *A Savage Conflict: The Decisive Role of Guerrillas in the American Civil War* (Chapel Hill: University of North Carolina Press, 2009).

30. Lee said of Mosby, "Attention is invited to the activity and skill of Colonel Mosby, and the intelligence and courage of the officers and men of his command as displayed in this report. . . . The services rendered by Colonel Mosby and his command in watching and reporting the enemy's movements have also been of great value. His operations have been highly creditable to himself and his command." *OR*, series 1, vol. 43, part 1: 635.

31. Lee, *Memoirs of the War*, 11–79.

32. Lee, *Memoirs of the War*, 256–58.

33. Lee, *Memoirs of the War*, 225.

34. Sheehan-Dean, *Why Confederates Fought*, 189–90, 252n4; Elizabeth R. Varon, *Appomattox: Victory, Defeat, and Freedom at the End of the Civil War* (New York: Oxford University Press, 2014), 70–78; William Marvel, *Lee's Last Retreat: The Flight to Appomattox* (Chapel Hill: University of North Carolina Press, 2002), 205–6.

35. Alexander, *Fighting for the Confederacy*, 531–33.

36. Alexander, *Fighting for the Confederacy*, 532.

37. See Joseph M. Beilein Jr., *Bushwhackers: Guerrilla Warfare, Manhood, and the Household in Civil War Missouri* (Kent, Ohio: Kent State University Press, 2016).

38. Lee, *Memoirs of the War*.

The Divided Houses of Ulysses S. Grant

BROOKS D. SIMPSON

Sometimes solving major problems in one's public life resolves tensions in one's private existence. Such was the case for Ulysses S. Grant during the American Civil War. At the beginning of the conflict, Grant was still trying to secure his future amid a series of struggles to make ends meet. At the same time, he wrestled with the consequences of having been born into an antislavery household presided over by a demanding and hypercritical father who all too often kept his eye on the main chance and of having married into a proslavery household where his wife delighted in the comforts of slavery and his father-in-law preached a Southern proslavery gospel. By war's end, Grant's military success gained him economic security as well as national fame, freeing him from dependence on his father and father-in-law, and the end of slavery freed him from trying to reconcile his personal beliefs with those of his wife by removing the reason for the uneasiness. However, family matters continued to dog Grant for the remaining two decades of his life, as an indulgent father found his life complicated by the choices of his children, while other family members sought to turn their relationship to prominence into personal profit and advantage. Finally, as death closed in on him, he managed to complete the most enduring memoir penned by an ex-president, thus providing for his wife and family long after he had passed from the scene.[1]

Born in a small frame house in Point Pleasant, Ohio, just north of the Ohio River outside Cincinnati, the boy originally christened Hiram Ulysses Grant was the eldest child of Jesse Root Grant, an aspiring businessman trying to make his mark in the tanning business. In pursuit of that goal Jesse

as a young man had worked in several tanneries, including one in Deer-
field, Ohio, run by Owen Brown: perhaps he crossed paths with Owen's son
John, who would later make a name for himself in the fight to end slavery.[2]
Some of that attitude may have rubbed off on Jesse, although other family members in Virginia just across the Ohio remained in slavery's land.
His marriage to Hannah Simpson in 1821 brought him into more contact
with antislavery advocates such as Thomas Morris, who had befriended the
Simpson family when they arrived in Ohio.[3] The next year Hannah gave
birth to their first son, who was delivered by Dr. John Rogers, an abolitionist; years later the Grant family relocated to Georgetown, a few miles away,
moving into a house built for Morris with land Jesse bought from him.[4]

Thus young Ulysses grew up surrounded by antislavery influences, although it remains unclear as to the degree to which they left an impression
upon him. His boyhood friend Daniel Ammen was the son of an antislavery
newspaper editor. Closer to home, Jesse and his half-brother Peter helped a
woman named Leah and her son Archibald secure their freedom. The family knew the Reverend John Rankin, and it was to Rankin's private school
that Jesse dispatched Ulysses. Rankin had another claim to fame: he was
an influential player in helping enslaved African Americans escape north-
ward through what would become known as the Underground Railroad.[5]

Ulysses found a more immediate obstacle to making his way in the world
in his father. He had to wrestle continually with both the opportunity and
burdens associated with being Jesse Grant's son, for Grant was not a modest man. He was proud and outspoken, prone to quarreling when challenged, and he wanted to be counted among the town's elite while he failed
to conceal his true sentiments about his fellow townspeople. He loved the
give-and-take of local and national politics, although he was far better at
the former than the latter. He liked to brag about the boy he took to calling
"my Ulysses," so much so that others would mock the phrase. Sometimes
people took aim at the son when they wanted to target the father, hurting
the sensitive boy far more than the irrepressible father.

Political rivalries helped chart young Grant's path to a college education. Jesse wanted his son to attend the United States Military Academy
at West Point, New York. To do that he had to secure a nomination from a
member of Congress. Thomas Hamer, a Democrat, represented Jesse's district. The two men had been friends and allies until some undisclosed incident in 1832 drove them apart, with Jesse finding a warm home in Whig
ranks, where he proved to have a sharp way with words in print in David
Ammen's newspaper. During the 1830s Jesse pursued a career in politics,
becoming mayor of Georgetown in 1837. Realizing that he need not expect

any favors from partisan foe and personal enemy Hamer, Grant first turned to Morris, then senator from Ohio, only to learn that the antislavery Whig (and future vice presidential candidate on the Liberty Party ticket in 1844) had no appointment to give. Jesse thus reluctantly approached Hamer, who had no trouble setting aside old rivalries in favor of helping Ulysses, although he had more trouble recalling the teenager's name. It being the last day of the session (as well as the last day of Hamer's congressional service), the congressman had no time to check facts, and so off went a recommendation for the nomination of Ulysses S. Grant—Hamer having never heard the young man called by his given name of Hiram and assuming that his middle initial must reflect his mother's maiden name. The bureaucratic snafu was never undone.[6]

In traveling to West Point in 1839, Ulysses knew that he would soon mix with young men drawn from across the nation in as geographically diverse an environment as he was likely to encounter in Jacksonian America. That meant that he would now meet sons of slaveholders, some who were perhaps slaveholders themselves, at a time when debates over slavery were escalating. He soon befriended several Southerners, notably James Longstreet of Georgia and Frederick Dent of Missouri, who became his roommate during his last year at the academy. Years later a story would circulate that the roommates had nearly come to blows while debating slavery until Ulysses burst out laughing. If this story was indeed true, the young man from Ohio either did not have strongly held views on the issue of slavery or did not see them as a barrier to befriending Southerners who might believe differently.[7]

Graduating from the academy in the middle of his class in 1843, the new brevet second lieutenant was given orders to report to Jefferson Barracks, Missouri, just outside St. Louis. Fred Dent's family lived not far away, on a large plantation christened White Haven by its owner, "Colonel" Frederick Dent, the title apparently an honorific one. Before long the young officer was paying frequent visits to White Haven, sometimes staying for dinner (anything was better than the fare at the officers' mess) while the Colonel, a lifelong Democrat, debated politics with the young fellow from Ohio with Whig proclivities. There was plenty to talk about, for the debate over whether to annex Texas was sure to play a role in the 1844 presidential contest.[8]

Soon there was another reason for the young lieutenant to make his way to White Haven. Seventeen-year-old Julia Dent was her father's oldest daughter and clearly his favorite among the three girls, and perhaps among the three older brothers. She had been away at St. Louis when Grant first visited, but once she appeared at White Haven, something changed. Like Ulysses Grant, Julia liked to ride horses, and soon the two of them were going off on long excursions. The lieutenant even braved accompanying the young lady to dances, although he never liked either music or dancing. Sometimes he was away for so long that he returned late for dinner at the officers' mess and paid the fine of a bottle of wine. Apparently it was worth it: when Grant learned that his regiment was headed to western Louisiana, he suddenly realized that the reason the news made him sad was that those orders would take him away from Julia. Returning from leave in Ohio, Grant rode out to White Haven. Drenched from fording an overflowing creek—nothing was going to stop him from seeing Julia—Grant pulled up at the house of Julia's brother John, changed into some oversized civilian clothes, and continued on to White Haven, where he planned to stay a few days while he mustered up the courage to make his intentions known. One day Grant commandeered a buggy to take Julia to a wedding in St. Louis. Once more he encountered an overflowing stream, with water reaching up to the bridge. Although Julia volunteered to go back, the lieutenant declared that they were going on; as they approached the bridge, Julia turned to Ulysses and declared, "Now, if anything happens, remember that I shall cling to you, no matter what you say to the contrary." Making his way safely across the bridge, Ulysses turned to Julia. Did she mean what she had said? Would she cling to him always?[9]

In proposing to Julia, the young lieutenant deliberately overlooked the fact that she was a slaveholder's daughter, surrounded by enslaved people who appeared and disappeared to serve her every need. Whenever she went off into the woods, "a dusky train" of slaves followed her and catered to her whims. That romanticized and self-centered view of the peculiar institution persisted throughout her life. "I think our people were very happy," she recalled in her memoirs. "At least they were in mamma's time, though the young ones became somewhat demoralized about the beginning of the Rebellion, when all the comforts of slavery passed away forever." She remembered her father as being "most kind and indulgent to his people, too much so perhaps," which is just how one might expect an adoring daughter to remember her father. For Grant, who was aware of the debate over slavery and of the efforts blacks made to escape their enslavement, these opinions might seem strange. When Julia told of how enslaved workers implored her to give them some money to help one of the Dent slaves buy something for which they rewarded her with fruits and animals from the surrounding grounds, Grant may have seen the purity of her heart and remained silent about how the enslaved people used her to get what they wanted. After all, one could be a kind and caring slaveholder, but one was still a slaveholder.[10]

Colonel Dent was not altogether happy with the news when he learned of the engagement the following year—anticipating his objection, the couple had kept it secret for many months. Grant gained the old man's permission to let the couple court through correspondence, although the colonel withheld his final approval for the match. That would have to suffice for the moment, because Grant's regiment soon received its marching orders, first for New Orleans, then for the northern bank of the Rio Grande. With the annexation of Texas an accomplished fact, the challenge of defining its disputed border with Mexico promised the possibility of military hostilities.[11]

In later life, Grant would deplore the waging of the Mexican-American War as immoral, suggesting that the Civil War was divine punishment for American arrogance. However, he did not share those opinions in his correspondence at the time. Given his Whig background, one can suppose that he was not enthusiastic about the conflict, but perhaps the best reason he deplored war was that it took him away from Julia. He had little to say about the war as a vehicle to expand slavery: his commentary instead focused on what he judged to be the harmful effect of the Catholic Church upon the Mexican people, whom he found likeable enough. After several years of credible service, at war's end Grant returned to St. Louis, secured Colonel Dent's blessing (an endeavor aided in part by Grant's having rescued Fred Dent during the battles outside Mexico City), and married Julia on August 22, 1848. Having once pondered resigning his commission to seek a career as a mathematics professor, Grant remained in the peacetime army, moving periodically from post to post. Julia gave birth to the couple's first son, Fred, in 1850; she was pregnant with her second child when Ulysses received orders to journey to the West Coast. Believing that such a trip was dangerous for Julia, especially in her condition, Grant left his family behind and made his way to the Pacific coast, surviving what proved to be a harrowing passage across the Panamanian isthmus.[12]

Separated from his wife and two sons (Ulysses Jr., nicknamed Buck, was born on July 22), Grant struggled to make money to reunite the family, but nothing worked. Growing ever more lonely and isolated, struggling to maintain his health, and increasingly bored by the humdrum of routine military life, Grant took to drinking. In his case it did not take long for the effects of alcohol to tell on him: Americans were far more concerned about the inability of a man to hold his liquor than they were concerned about alcohol abuse itself. Another assignment placed him under the command of an officer with whom he did not get along—the same officer who had fined him a bottle of wine each time he appeared late at the officers' mess back in Missouri. By 1854 Grant had taken enough. On the very day he received his commission as captain, he tendered his resignation. He needed to return to Julia.[13]

Grant's departure from the army overshadowed his credible military service in the eyes of his father, who bemoaned that the military had ruined his son for business. In fact, Jesse tried to get the War Department to decline his son's resignation, only to be rebuffed. Then Jesse offered to put his son in the family business, now located in the northwest corner of Illinois in Galena, while Julia and the two boys stayed in Kentucky. The former captain rejected the offer: he had come home to be with his family, not separated once more from them. Instead of following in his father's footsteps, he planned to become a Missouri farmer, a pledge that was easier made than fulfilled. His father-in-law set aside some land to plow, and the family could stay in the house once occupied by Julia's brother Lewis before he made his way west to California.[14]

During the next six years Grant struggled to make ends meet. A combination of bad luck, poor health, and the impact of the depression following the Panic of 1857 proved too much to overcome. Although family members disputed notions that these years were ones of failure, Grant himself would not have termed them a success. The federal government bothered him about funds due from his service as a commissary officer and quartermaster (the army held officers responsible for losses incurred under their supervision). His father-in-law seemed loath to let go of his little girl. As a local physician later noted, Grant "chafed under this condition of things." With his family expanding by the addition of a daughter, Nellie, in 1855, Grant needed to find a way to provide for his family.[15]

As he toiled as a farmer, cut logs and brought them to St. Louis for sale, and even erected his own log cabin which he labeled "Hardscrabble" as a jab at the pretentious names of surrounding houses, Grant worked alongside enslaved laborers. Some of these people were enslaved by Colonel Dent, and others Grant hired out as laborers from other slaveholders. At one point Grant gained ownership of a slave, William Jones, from one of the Dents, although the precise circumstances remain unclear. Neighbors later said that Grant failed as a slaveholder, because he could not compel or coerce them to work. As one of Julia's cousins put it, "He was no hand to manage negroes. He couldn't force them to do anything. He wouldn't whip them." As if that were not enough, he overpaid his hired laborers, much to the chagrin of surrounding farmers, leading one worker to declare that the former army captain "was the kindest man he ever worked for." In letters to his father Grant called the slaves "servants," as if to hide their true condition, even if he knew Jesse knew better. One of the Dent slaves later recalled that Grant went so far as to declare that should he ever secure title to the rest of the Dent family slaves, he would free them . . . as, indeed, he eventually freed William Jones. However, even as Julia's sister Emma noted that Grant disliked slavery, she added, "I do not think that Grant was such a rank abolitionist that Julia's slaves had to be forced upon him"—even if it appears that the Colonel never passed on formal title to those enslaved people to Julia. However the fact that Grant had anything to do with slavery infuriated Jesse Grant, who had no good words for what he called that "tribe of Dents" and their slaveholding ways.[16]

Grant also found himself brushing shoulders with the politics of the time, including the debate over slavery. He hauled wood to Henry T. Blow's house and often chatted with Blow, who was engaged in trying to secure the freedom of a former family slave and his wife—namely Dred and Harriet Scott. Blow was a member of the newly established antislavery Republican Party serving in the Missouri state senate at the time, and his abolitionist preferences were well known. Yet when it came time for Grant to cast his first presidential ballot in 1856, he passed over the former Whig Millard Fillmore, now heading the nativist Know-Nothing ticket, as well as Republican standard-bearer John C. Frémont in favor of Democratic candidate James Buchanan. Doubtless it pleased Dent to see that his son-in-law was in political agreement with him for once, although Grant later explained he voted as he did because he knew about Frémont from his time in the military. Nevertheless, being identified with the Democratic Party would have consequences.

Even as he continued to farm and cut wood, Grant looked to his father for financial assistance. In December 1856, after detailing his struggles with farming, he hinted that a loan for $500 for a year at 10 percent interest would be very useful. The following February he became more explicit. Reminding his father of a previous offer to give him $1,000, Grant now asked for the loan outright. "It is always usual for parents to give their children assistance in beginning life," he wrote, although he acknowledged that he was now thirty-five. He detailed his situation, including his tight family budget—he had spent a total of $50 over two years to clothe his family of five—and his difficulties with making a living as a farmer.[17] Although he later reported some success with that year's crop, with the onset of the depression he was in trouble again, enough so that he pawned a watch at Christmastime.[18]

The Grants welcomed a fourth child in February 1858, a boy. They decided to name him Jesse, perhaps as a way to curry favor with his namesake. Later that year the elder Jesse Grant paid a visit. He came armed with an offer to have his eldest son join him in business at Covington. Suffering from malaria and chills, Ulysses prepared to accept the offer, much to Julia's displeasure. Fortunately, at least to Julia, Grant's meddling sisters somehow thwarted the offer, leaving Grant to pursue his destiny elsewhere.[19] After selling portions of the White Haven property (including Hardscrabble) to help his father-in-law get along, he moved the family to St. Louis, where he hoped to make money in real estate. Never very good when it came to handling money in a business, Grant soon sought work elsewhere. Once more family connections bedeviled him. Applying for the office of county engineer, he found that Republicans rejected him because of his ties to the Dents, while some Democrats remained suspicious of his Northern birth. The post went to a German American favored by the Republicans, which may well have sparked Grant's dalliance with a local Know-Nothing lodge.[20] Meanwhile he searched for other opportunities, managing to find work at the customs house for a month. As winter came to a close in 1860, he decided to travel to Kentucky and seek support once more from his father.

Jesse's solution was an easy one. He would put his eldest son to work in a general store he owned that was managed by his other two sons, Simpson and Orvil, in Galena, Illinois, tucked away in the northwest corner of the state near the Mississippi River. Simpson's health problems had created the opportunity to put his brother to work on free soil, away from the Dents and slavery. This time Grant accepted the offer. It meant leaving Julia's slaves behind: Grant sought to hire them out to St. Louis Republicans to guarantee that they were well treated, a rather interesting if curious solution.

Although Ulysses did not exactly enjoy working in the general store, where he was under the supervision of his younger brothers, it looked as if his fortunes were turning upward at last. People overlooked his shortcomings as a businessman to listen to his stories about the Mexican-American War or to hear his views on politics. Having arrived too late in Illinois to establish citizenship, Grant watched the election of 1860 from the sidelines. Although he professed to be a supporter of Democrat Stephen A. Douglas, he did not find Illinois's native son, Abraham Lincoln, objectionable, and he actually helped drill the members of the local Republican "Wide Awake" club for its fall rallies. In the weeks after the election Grant expressed his opposition to secession and speculated on whether there would be a war. When news of Fort Sumter came, he attended rallies in support of the

Union and found himself elected to drill the town's volunteers. His road back into military service lay before him.

Grant outlined his political position to both his father-in-law and father within weeks of Fort Sumter. He reminded both men that he differed from them in key particulars in a way that demonstrated a newfound assertiveness. He told Colonel Dent that "now is the time, particularly in the border Slave states, for men to prove their love of country." Whatever one's previous political allegiances, "now all party distinctions should be lost sight of and every true patriot be for maintaining the integrity of the glorious old *Stars & Stripes*, the Constitution and the Union." He blamed the South for the commencement of hostilities; he also believed that the coming of war meant "the doom of Slavery," for the cotton market would seek other suppliers, resulting in a decline in the value of slaves.[21] From his father Grant sought approval for reentering the service, since he would have to leave the family business, while reaffirming his support for the Union cause, whatever his previous partisan inclinations may have been.[22] Before long he predicted that the war would be of short duration: he was more concerned that there might be "a negro insurrection" that would have to be put down by Union troops. He also predicted that the Yankees "would go on such a mission . . . with the purest motives."[23]

Although Grant's choice was an easy one, no one else in either the extended Grant or Dent families followed suit. Over in Virginia, one of his aunts proved a loyal secessionist, snapping to Grant's sister Clara: "If you can justify your Bro. Ulysses in drawing his sword against those connected by the ties of blood, and even boast of it, you are at liberty to do so, but [I] can not."[24] In May Grant traveled to Missouri and stopped to visit his father-in-law, who said that while he was for the Union he was opposed to the effort to sustain it by force. Grant concluded that Dent was a secessionist in wish, but he no longer felt dependent upon his goodwill.[25]

After spending more than a month helping to enlist and drill soldiers in Springfield, Grant looked for a colonelcy, and his quest for a commission resulted in success when he was named colonel of the Twenty-First Illinois in June. Several months later, his prewar profile in Galena paid off, when the town's congressman, Elihu B. Washburne, forwarded his name to Lincoln to be commissioned as a brigadier general. Jesse Grant was proud of his son, but that did not stop him from imposing on him. Before long the new brigadier had to tell his father that he would have nothing to do with securing government contracts for anyone and that he declined to share his plans with his father.[26] Nor did Jesse always express confidence in his son's abilities. After capturing a Confederate force at Fort Donelson, Tennessee, in February 1862, a triumph that made his name a house-hold word—especially when it was rendered "Unconditional Surrender Grant"—Grant received word that he had been promoted major general of volunteers. Recalling that his father had wondered whether he could handle the responsibilities of being a brigadier general, Grant now asked his wife, who was visiting the elder Grant in Kentucky: "Is father afraid yet that I will not be able to sustain myself?"[27] He almost spoke too soon. A few weeks later, Jesse visited his son in Tennessee; as he was leaving, Ulysses received orders detaining him at his headquarters while his men made their way south along the Tennessee River under the command of one of his sub-ordinates. What Jesse made of this we do not know, but Grant found him-self "in a very poor humor."[28]

Somewhat more troubling was Jesse Grant's willingness to wage war with the local Cincinnati press, which on the whole had not treated his son well.[29] Sometimes he penned his own letters; after Shiloh he shared with the press several letters from headquarters, including one from Grant him-self. The appearance of such correspondence simply reinvigorated news-paper criticism.[30] At first Ulysses quietly hinted that he would not defend himself in print and would not "permit it from any one around me"; how-ever, in September 1862 he was far more blunt. He declined once more to share details of military operations, because Jesse was "so imprudent" with such information. What followed next was even more direct. The news-paper articles had exasperated him. "I have not an enemy in the world who has done me so much injury as you in your efforts in my defence. I require no defenders and for my sake let me alone." Jesse was free with his criti-cism of other generals, and listeners inferred that he was relaying his son's sentiments.[31]

Nor did Julia's visits to the Grants always turn out well. Directing his wife to lend his father some money in the wake of a family visit, Grant growled: "I feel myself worse used by my own family than by strangers," adding that it always seemed his father tended to look askance at his eldest son.[32] In November 1862 he snapped back at a letter from his father appar-ently critical of Julia, regretting that "all that comes from you speaks so con-descendingly of every thing Julia says, writes, or thinks. You without prob-ably being aware of it are so prejudiced against her that she could not please you. This is not pleasing to me."[33] By the beginning of 1863 things had got-ten even worse between Julia and Ulysses's sisters, to the point that Ulysses endorsed Julia writing to Virginia Grant to explain how difficult it was for Julia and the children to stay with the Grants in Kentucky.[34]

Perhaps one of the reasons the Grants clashed with Julia was her continuing interest in using enslaved labor to help her take care of the children. Of particular interest was an enslaved woman she fondly called "Black Julia." When Julia brought the children and Black Julia to the front to visit her husband, tongues wagged. Back in 1861 one of the general's critics, who charged that Grant was a drunk, declared that "until we can secure pure men in habits and men without secesh wives with their own little slaves to wait upon them, which is a fact here in this camp with Mrs. Grant, our country is lost."[35] When Colonel Dent began divesting himself of his slaves in 1862 by formally giving them to his daughters through a bill of sale, Grant instructed that he should do that with all the enslaved people to avoid their being sold, presumably to satisfy debts. However, he made it clear that he did not want Julia to have any of them: "It is not probable we will ever live in a slave state again but [I] would not like to see them sold under the hammer."[36]

If Julia's continuing involvement with slavery embarrassed Grant, so too did his father's avarice. Like many other people, Jesse Grant saw in the war an opportunity to make a dollar, and he soon settled upon trying to secure a permit from his son to trade cotton. In the process he struck up a partnership with two Cincinnati businessmen who hoped to use the general's father to secure a trading permit.

It so happened that the two businessmen were Jewish. They hoped to capitalize on reestablishing prewar business relations with other Jewish businessmen, especially in the Memphis area, to take advantage of trading in captured cotton. They reckoned without Grant's personal hostility to the cotton trade in general and to his belief that Jewish traders in particular were seeking to profit off the conflict. Although in later years some people would claim that Grant was no anti-Semite, some of his comments at the time betrayed sentiments commonly associated with anti-Semitism, and when Jesse approached him to secure a trading permit, the general snapped. Instead of lashing out at his father, who was surely a conniving businessman who happened to be a Methodist, Grant issued General Order 11, banishing Jews "as a class" from his department—an order with such sweeping implications that it was quickly revoked by the authorities in Washington, but not before it left a stain on Grant's reputation. For the rest of his life he sought to atone for his mistake in issuing what Julia once called "that obnoxious order." Grant's anger at his father does not excuse what he did, and it alone does not explain it, although it may illuminate the order's timing and intemperate language. However, it does suggest that just as Jesse had no problem blaming his son when he failed, he also had no qualms about cashing in on his success.

Thus, as 1863 opened, Ulysses S. Grant found himself in trouble. His military record to that point had been uneven, with spectacular victories offset by more controversial performances that subjected him to scrutiny and criticism. He was not yet Mr. Lincoln's general. Indeed, the president's willingness to embrace a proposal by John A. McClernand to take Vicksburg suggested that his faith in Grant was less than complete. Matters did not improve over the next several months as Grant struggled to devise a plan to take Vicksburg rather than to await the advent of spring, when the roads would dry and rapid movement would be possible. Erstwhile supporters now shared second thoughts about whether Grant was the coming man. Impatience mounted as rumors circulated that perhaps the general was once more seeking solace in the bottle. Washington authorities sent out envoys to see what was going on.

Then came one of the most brilliant and daring campaigns ever to unfold on American soil. As spring came, Grant prepared to move, and when he did so, he moved quickly. The result was the capture of Vicksburg on July 4 and the surrender of its garrison of some thirty thousand men who found themselves surrounded after a whirlwind campaign in which Grant won five battles in less than three weeks before settling down to siege operations in May. Doubters and critics now sang his praises, as did the envoys sent to spy on him; rivals found themselves displaced or silenced. Lincoln celebrated Grant's achievement, going so far as to admit that he was mistaken about the course he thought Grant should have pursued. One sign of his confidence was the decision to promote Grant to major general in the regular army. Unlike his previous commissions in the volunteer service, this promotion meant that Grant would have a position in the army at the end of the conflict. At last he had found a job that he could do and that he could keep. He would sustain himself.

As Grant emerged into the spotlight, family members took a backseat. Jesse might still try to meddle, but he was reduced to letters retelling tales about young Ulysses for the biographers who sprang up to chronicle the life of the hero of Vicksburg. Colonel Dent was struggling even more. The people he had enslaved had been liberating themselves throughout the conflict, long before Missouri formally abolished slavery early in 1865. White Haven was in serious trouble, as creditors hovered about while Dent leased out land from the estate. Even Black Julia liberated herself, escaping in February 1864 when Julia Grant planned to return to St. Louis, where Black Julia feared she would be reenslaved for good, much as Dred Scott himself had been. The general refused to lift a finger to secure her return.[37]

Ever the family man, Grant worked whenever possible to have his wife and at least some of his children with him for stretches throughout the war. Most prominent among the boys was Fred, who accompanied his father during the entire Vicksburg campaign: at Big Black River on May 17, he got so close to the action that he was slightly wounded. He was still with his father when Vicksburg surrendered on July 4, 1863, although he spent much of the siege recovering from the aftereffects of his wounding. In 1864 Nellie posed as the little woman who lived in a shoe for a charity; later, while the older children went to school, little Jesse romped around headquarters when Julia visited her husband at City Point, Virginia, in 1865. By that time Grant had secured a new house through the benevolence of others in Burlington, New Jersey, across the river from Philadelphia, away from the Grants and the Dents, but within commuting distance of Washington, D.C.

Grant needed to live near Washington because by 1864 he had a new position, that of general in chief of the armies of the United States with the rank of lieutenant general in the regular army. His record of military success in 1863 at Vicksburg had continued with the triumph at Chattanooga, propelling him to the top spot that winter. Yet he still sought to spend as much time with his family as possible, and Fred accompanied him to Washington when he accepted his new commission from President Lincoln. Although Grant found himself in the spring and summer of 1864 busy battling Robert E. Lee's Army of Northern Virginia while coordinating the overall Union war effort, once he had settled down outside Petersburg and Richmond, Virginia, he could send for Julia. Staff officer Horace Porter once entered the general's headquarters to find him holding hands with his wife, causing the usually imperturbable general to blush; another time Porter found him playing with his children. Other family responsibilities remained, as Grant remembered when he had to secure the release of his imprisoned brother-in-law John, who had been captured by Confederate authorities despite the fact that he had leaned toward the Confederacy early in the war.

Julia liked to think that she knew something about politics, and in February 1865 she nearly had a chance to practice some statecraft of her own. Meeting Confederate general James Longstreet to discuss various military matters, Union general Edward O. C. Ord recalled that Longstreet's wife, Louise, was a distant cousin of Julia Grant. Perhaps the cousins could convene for a social visit in Petersburg, opening the door to negotiations to bring the war to an end. Confederate authorities actually approved of his outlandish scheme and prepared to bring Louise to Petersburg, but Grant quashed the idea. When Julia, who thought the scheme was "enchanting" and "thrilling," persisted, Grant ended the conversation by calling the idea "absurd," adding: "The men have fought this war and the men will finish it."[38]

The men indeed soon finished it. Julia remained behind in City Point with the Lincolns, who had been visiting with the Grants, as her husband set out on what became the final campaign of the war in Virginia at the end of March 1865. Alongside her was Mary Todd Lincoln, who treated Julia as an aspirant for the position of First Lady. The two women did not get along well, and Mary Lincoln was prone to make her displeasure rather public. The Lincolns returned from City Point to Washington just before news arrived that Lee had surrendered his army to Grant; Julia awaited her husband's return, and the couple made their way back to Washington. There concern about Mary's behavior led the Grants to excuse themselves from a visit to Ford's Theatre on the night of April 14, 1865 (which happened to be Good Friday), on the grounds that the Grants needed to hurry back to Burlington to see their children. That night, Grant learned that the president had been shot and was not expected to live. Mary Lincoln would no longer be First Lady. It remained an open question as to whether Julia Grant ever would take possession of that title.

Appomattox secured Ulysses S. Grant's place in history. The Union victory also fortified his future. Over the next several years he would receive several houses in Galena and Washington, money courtesy of a fund-raising effort in New York, and various gifts, including a library donated by Boston-based patrons. In 1866 he would add a fourth star to his shoulder straps, reinforcing the fact that he now held a lifetime position as commanding general. As if that were not enough, in 1868 he was elected president, the youngest man to assume that office at the time. It seemed he had come out on top at last.

Yet the man who had once struggled to provide for his family now discovered that he had to provide, one way or another, for other family members as well, and it was a growing family, including in-laws. From the time he left Wilmer McLean's parlor in Appomattox Court House until the day he left the White House in 1877, Grant was besieged by family and friends who sought to take advantage of him or who claimed to others that they could influence him. Jesse Grant found himself appointed postmaster of Covington, Kentucky, by Andrew Johnson, who also had no problem in sending Frederick Grant to West Point in order to curry favor with the general. Before long Virginia Grant, who had struggled to marry, found true love in Abel Corbin, whom she wed in May 1869: Corbin used his new access to the president to entangle Grant and his family in the efforts of Jay

Gould and Jim Fisk to corner the gold market that September. Mary Grant had already married Michael J. Cramer, a Methodist minister and diplomat who suddenly found himself minister to Denmark in 1870, courtesy of Mary's brother. Sneakiest of all was Orvil Grant, who sought to capitalize on his blood ties to the chief executive to line his own pockets through manipulating Indian post traderships, reminding everyone of his powerful brother.

Julia's family was not any better. Grant stepped in when his father-in-law faced economic disaster and began buying up parcels of land that had once formed White Haven and the surrounding plantation. Along the way he discovered that he had to cut through a thicket of mortgages and title disputes due to the colonel's ineptitude. Although Grant occasionally imagined retiring to the farm to raise horses, one senses that he made these purchases to please his wife by preserving her childhood home. With White Haven having passed into the hands of the son-in-law he once questioned, Colonel Dent traveled to Washington to remind people of the superiority of the Southern way of life, much to the general's amusement. Julia's sister Emma had married James Casey, who became a prominent Republican in Louisiana, deriving most of his influence from his marital ties. Brother Lewis Dent tried to take advantage of those ties when he ran for governor of Mississippi in 1869, but the president would have nothing to do with supporting a Democrat, dooming that quest. Meanwhile, Julia's brother Frederick Dent capitalized upon his place as a member of his brother-in-law's staff to ascend to a job as one of Grant's private secretaries in the White House.

In providing for such relatives, Grant came under political fire, as enemies claimed that nepotism ruled the day. The charge had enough merit to sting. True, some of these relatives had been active in public life before Grant became president, but it could not be denied that many of them had taken advantage of their proximity to power to advance their fortunes. The practice was not as uncommon as it seemed—chief executives have always been surrounded by family members clamoring for something—but never did it seem so visible, so mundane, and in some cases so sordid or blatant. Although Grant did not appear to profit by these associations and upon occasion distanced himself from them, the impression remained that the administration was a little too much in the family way. He had become the Great Provider.

Eight years in the White House proved to be the longest time Ulysses and Julia Grant lived together in the same place, although the family often made its way in the summer to Long Branch, New Jersey, where the ocean breeze proved far more inviting than Washington's relentless humidity.

Fred squeezed his way through West Point—it paid to be the president's son; Ulysses made his way through Exeter and Harvard before going into business; and little Jesse provided much entertainment. However, the highlight of family life during those eight years was Nellie's White House wedding to Englishman Algernon Sartoris. Grant was not wild about the match, and he warned Sartoris's father that being president did not make him a wealthy man. With the ceremony over, someone noticed that the president was missing. A determined search found him, face down, sobbing in Nellie's bedroom.

During the White House years both Jesse Root Grant and Colonel Frederick Dent passed away, leaving Ulysses as the head of the family. Had it been up to Julia, her husband would have stood for a third term: indeed, the president had to smuggle out of the White House a message that he had no such desire before informing his indignant wife that it was time to look forward to life beyond the presidency.[39]

Upon leaving the White House in 1877, Ulysses and Julia Grant embarked on a tour of Europe that eventually turned into a trip around the world. The endeavor ate deeply into family funds: only shrewd investment decisions by Buck enabled the former first couple to be away for so long. Upon returning to the United States in 1879, Grant attempted to settle in Galena, and it was from there that he made an unsuccessful bid for the presidency in 1880. The Grants then decided to move to New York City, a relocation made possible by the generosity of admiring donors who established a trust fund and purchased a house just east of Central Park. With all four children seemingly making their way in the world, Grant could now look forward to retirement, but he remained restless. Some people still thought of him as a possible presidential candidate in 1884, and he played the role of party statesman to the hilt, if not always successfully. Then there was the lure of business opportunities, headed by the presidency of the Mexican Southern Railroad. Having resigned his general's commission in 1869 to accept the office of president of the United States, he had forfeited military retirement pay. Former presidents were not awarded pensions, so he had to work if he wanted to live a lifestyle that could stand scrutiny besides those of his well-heeled admirers. Finally, there was Buck's offer of a place in the investment firm run by Ferdinand Ward and himself, with offices on Wall Street opposite Trinity Church. Perhaps somewhere in the back of the general's mind was the notion that he could at last show his father that one could make an honest dollar and do so while working alongside one's son. To outsiders it was not obvious that the Grant in Grant and Ward was the former president's son and not the retired general himself.

Grant thought he was making himself financially secure. However, Ferdinand Ward was a swindler, pure and simple, and a master of Ponzi schemes. Having duped the son, he now duped the father as well, along with a sufficient number of other investors who never looked carefully at where their money was going—namely, into Ward's own pocket. Grant thought he was providing for the future: instead, he was placing the family's financial security in peril. It appeared that Buck was as naïve and vulnerable as his father, and the former general's trust in his son, perhaps shaped in part by memories of his own father's lack of trust in him, backfired. Finally, in 1884 the bubble burst, ruining Grant, his sons, and a goodly number of investors. The general and his family retreated to Long Branch for the summer, where he embarked on writing a series of articles about various campaigns in an effort to bring in some money. Once more he was fighting to make ends meet.

Soon he was fighting something else. A sharp pain in his throat turned out to be the first sign of cancer, although it was not diagnosed for several months. Needing money, Grant contemplated writing his memoirs. Once more his business sense nearly did him in, for he was on the verge of agreeing to a deal that promised merely a fair return when Mark Twain swooped in and begged Grant to allow him to publish the book on terms that promised to make Julia rich should it sell well. As cancer ate away at his body in a never-ending battle of attrition, Grant fought back, struggling to complete the memoirs in order to provide for his family long after he was gone. At last he was determined to tell his story, to share with readers how he had seen the war that made him as he had fought to save the Union.

Less than a week after he had finished his memoirs, Ulysses S. Grant died on July 23, 1885, in a cottage in Mount McGregor in upstate New York, surrounded by members of his family. The fruits of his endeavors soon manifested themselves that December when Mark Twain presented Julia Grant with a check for $200,000, the first installment of royalty payments that reached some $450,000 in all. Perhaps he had done it the hard way, but Grant had provided for his family by writing a book that remains a masterpiece of American literature.

We remember Ulysses S. Grant primarily as a general and a president. Lesser known is how those triumphs and what they meant helped a son, a husband, and a father resolve the simple questions of how to make a living so as to secure his independence from both his family and that of his wife. The events of the Civil War gave him job security and rid him of the burdens associated with his wife's entanglement with slavery. The years after the war saw him rise, fall, and struggle to rise again, each time thinking about his family. Perhaps it is no accident that when one enters Grant's Tomb, one encounters Ulysses and Julia lying side by side, together in death as they had been in life, united forever.

NOTES

1. Previous scholarly treatments of Ulysses and Julia Grant can be found in John Y. Simon, "A Marriage Tested by War," in *Intimate Strategies of the Civil War*, ed. Carol K. Bleser and Leslie J. Gordon (New York: Oxford University Press, 2001), 123–37, and Candice Shy Hooper, *Lincoln's Generals' Wives: Four Women Who Influenced the Civil War—for Better and for Worse* (Kent, Ohio: Kent State University Press, 2016).

2. G. L. Corum, *Ulysses Underground: The Unexplored Roots of Ulysses S. Grant and the Underground Railroad* (West Union, Ohio: Riveting History, 2016), 15–16.

3. Corum, *Ulysses Underground*, 16.

4. Corum, *Ulysses Underground*, 20.

5. Corum, *Ulysses Underground*, 39–45; Brooks D. Simpson, *Ulysses S. Grant: Triumph over Adversity, 1822–1865* (Boston: Houghton Mifflin, 2000), 6–9.

6. Simpson, *Grant*, 9–11.

7. Simpson, *Grant*, 14–17.

8. Simpson, *Grant*, 18–20.

9. John Y. Simon, ed., *The Personal Memoirs of Julia Dent Grant* (New York: G. P. Putnam's Sons, 1975), 49–50; Lloyd Lewis, *Captain Sam Grant* (Boston: Little, Brown, 1950), 106–13.

10. Simon, *Personal Memoirs*, 34–36.

11. Simpson, *Grant*, 25–29.

12. Simpson, *Grant*, 30–54, *passim*.

13. Simpson, *Grant*, 54–62.

14. Simpson, *Grant*, 63–65; Simon, *Personal Memoirs*, 76.

15. Simpson, *Grant*, 63–69.

16. Simpson, *Grant*, 67.

17. USG to Jesse Grant, December 28, 1856, in *The Papers of Ulysses S. Grant*, 32 vols., ed. John Y. Simon et al. (Carbondale: University of Southern Illinois Press, 1967–2012), 1:334 (hereafter *PUSG*); USG to Jesse Grant, February 7, 1857, *PUSG* 1:336–37.

18. USG to Mary Grant, August 22, 1857, *PUSG* 1:338; Pawn Ticket, December 23, 1857, *PUSG* 1:339.

19. Simon, *Personal Memoirs*, 80.

20. USG to Jesse Grant, August 20, 1859, *PUSG*, 1:350; USG to Jesse Grant, September 23, 1859, *PUSG* 1:311–52.

21. USG to Frederick Dent, April 19, 1861, *PUSG* 2:3–4.

22. USG to Jesse Grant, April 21, 1861, *PUSG* 2:6–7.

23. USG to Jesse Grant, May 6, 1861, *PUSG* 2:20–22.

24. *PUSG* 2:15.

25. USG to JDG, May 10, 1861, *PUSG* 2:26–28; USG to JDG, May 15, 1861, *PUSG* 2:30–32.

26. USG to Jesse Grant, November 27, 1861, *PUSG* 3–226–28.

27. USG to JDG, February 22, 1862, *PUSG* 4:271.

28. USG to JDG, March 5, 1862, *PUSG* 4:326–27.

29. USG to JDG, February 26, 1862, *PUSG* 4:292–93.

30. *PUSG* 5:79–83.

31. USG to Jesse Grant, August 3, 1862, *PUSG* 5:263–64; USG to Jesse Grant, September 17, 1862, *PUSG* 6:61–62.

32. USG to JDG, March 5, 1862, *PUSG* 4:326–27.

33. USG to Jesse Grant, November 23, 1862, *PUSG* 6:344–45. There are hints of another family rift in USG to JDG, March 6, 1863, *PUSG* 7:396–97.

34. USG to JDG, February 13, 1863, *PUSG* 7:321–22.

35. *PUSG* 4:119.

36. USG to JDG, May 16, 1862, *PUSG* 5:123–24.

37. Simon, "A Marriage Tried by War," 128–29.

38. Simon, *Personal Memoirs*, 140–41.

39. Simon, *Personal Memoirs*, 185–86.

PART 2

The Wartime View of the Household

The Soldier's Dream of Home

Jonathan W. White

Whether awake or asleep, soldiers thought of home. Indeed, more than anything else, Union and Confederate officers and enlisted men dreamed about their loved ones. "Last night I dreamed of being at home as I often do and sweet were the kisses what I took all around," wrote a New Yorker to his wife. A thirty-six-year-old Virginian similarly told his sixteen-year-old sweetheart that he had "som mighty good dreams about you." Such dreams of home were often sweet and romantic, but sometimes they focused on mundane things that soldiers missed. A Wisconsin soldier wrote to his mother from the Pine Woods of Georgia in 1864, "I dreamed last night about the cheese which you wrote about in the letter I got three days ago" and how much "I would like a taste of it."[1]

Americans North and South were absorbed with their unconscious lives during the Civil War. In their dreams they relived distant memories, envisioned a return to peace, kissed loved ones they had not seen for months or even years, traveled to faraway places, enjoyed luxurious meals with members of their households, and communed with the dead. Distant spouses relished hearing each other's voices in their dreams, and parents and children loved seeing one another. Many soldiers became dependent upon their dreams for release from the stress of the battlefield. The conversations created by their sleeping brains felt to them like real communication with those at home. Indeed, the dream lives of soldiers and civilians became tangible sources of sustenance between the homefront and the battlefield. Whether nighttime visions were uplifting or distressing, ordinary or bizarre, soldiers and civilians reported their dreams to one another, freely expressing their deepest and most intimate feelings, vulnerabilities, aspirations, and anxieties. In the process, they overcame—albeit only temporarily—the barriers of time and space that seemed so insurmountable during the war and that were often compounded by infrequent correspondence.

Sharing dreams had been an important part of antebellum life. Every morning in households around the country, husbands, wives, children, and friends shared their dreams of the previous night. Young and old alike sought to discern their meaning.[2] Many Americans continued this tradition during the war, but now these dream reports took place in letters rather than over the breakfast table. As historian J. Matthew Gallman argues, "Citizens at home turned to familiar means, aided by detailed letters, to cope with the harshest wartime losses."[3] Dream reporting, in a very real sense, helped soldiers and civilians develop intimacy with one another despite the great physical distances that separated them.

Dreaming of home enabled soldiers to find emotional comfort and psychological healing during a time of great turmoil. As one scholar explains, home represented "so much more than any particular place." It "is a conglomeration of memories and senses, it is the knowledge and familiarity of locale." Thoughts of home evoked a sense of belonging. Indeed, soldiers who dreamt of home envisioned their mothers, sisters, wives, and sweethearts—women who were important "sources of nurture, kindness and sympathy" and who were "crucial to maintaining the stability of the home environment and [the] local communities many soldiers believed they were fighting to protect."[4]

The concept of home, for soldiers, was also a static one—"a stable source of identity," writes historian Susan J. Matt, and a place that did not change despite the tremendous social upheaval of civil war.[5] Soldiers knew that those at home were anxiously awaiting their return—and from the field they also often imagined themselves back home. At night they believed that they were going to bed around the same time as their families, and this knowledge gave them a special connection to their homes. Many found comfort in thinking that they and their wives were looking at the same moon and stars before turning in. Such quiet moments helped soldiers cope with long separations. Although they could not be at home to protect their families, many soldiers believed that they were fighting so that their households could be safe and their children could sleep in peace.

Many soldiers came to view their dreams as visitations. "I question whether any other class of men have better dreams than true hearted soldiers," wrote James H. Burke of the Thirty-Seventh Indiana Volunteers. "Of course it is because their dreams are apt to be associated with the loved ones at home." As soon as a soldier's head hits the ground, Burke contin-

ued, "he returns to them in his slumber, and—as some have related to me—
sometimes has a merry romp again around his own cheerful hearth stone."
In some dreams, soldiers' families came to the front "and seem to mingle
their sweet spirits with his." Thinking about the "soldier's dream of his
love" caused Burke to remember a poem by George D. Prentice, which he
then wrote out by heart. "Come, in beautiful dreams, love, / O, come to me
oft," it began.[6] Dreams, for men like Burke, became a welcome new reality
where soldiers could enjoy the comforts of home, even if only for a fleeting
moment. Of equal importance, such dreams admonished soldiers, as leaders
of their households, to serve with honor and faithfulness as they were fighting for their firesides as much as for their nation.

The concept of "the soldier's dream of home" was ubiquitous in American popular culture during the Civil War, although the idea did not orig-
inate in the United States. Scottish poet Thomas Campbell's poem "The
Soldier's Dream" (circa 1800) began appearing in American anthologies as
early as the 1820s, and by the 1830s it was being read by children in primary schools.[7] By the 1850s, others were imitating Campbell in both written words and artistic renderings. In March 1852, *Godey's Lady's Book* produced a story by the English novelist Henry William Herbert as well as a
print of a Scottish soldier dreaming of home in faraway Egypt. Upon seeing
the print, two American women composed their own verses, both entitled
"The Soldier's Dream of Home," which appeared in the magazine seven
months later.[8] About this same time an unknown printmaker produced a
full-color print of a Scottish soldier sleeping in the foreground with the
pyramids behind him and his family above him in a dream. Beneath the
serene image were Campbell's lyrics. Currier and Ives would borrow heavily from this template a decade later, replacing the soldier's green kilt with a
blue woolen uniform, while the pyramids in the background were replaced
by canvas tents.

The Civil War took place in the era of Victorian romanticism when
even the most experienced soldiers could be moved to tears by a poem
about dreams and family. In 1862, Confederate general J. E. B. Stuart copied Campbell's poem in its entirety and then added a few lines of his own
in an album for a young woman in Virginia. Other soldiers similarly tran-
scribed the whole poem—or several stanzas from it—in their letters home.
They may have done so from memory, for in the 1850s Campbell's words
had been set to music, and many young men knew them by heart. Some
soldiers sang the song in their tents at night. For others, meditating on this
poem was the best way to capture their emotions after a battle. Soldiers
sought out stationery with Campbell's poem and brought the verses to the

attention of their wives and sweethearts. "Is not this beautiful?" wrote one Ohio soldier to his fiancée in April 1862.[9]

Missouri infantryman John C. Hughes was so moved by a piece of letterhead featuring Campbell's poem that he penned an affectionate letter on the subject to his wife. "O the sweete visions that I hav saw when all was still when the trobeles and hardships and bustels of war was forgoten in sweet repose," he wrote on February 27, 1863. But these dreams "onley serve to increac my sorrow when I awoke to a true sence of my condition." He described seeing his wife and four sons in his dream, but "when i would awake and find that it was all a dream i hav often bathed my pillow in tears and almost wished that I could quit this world of sorrows and disappointment and meat my friends on shoars of sweet deliverance." Hughes wished that "wars would ceac" and he could return to his home and family in times of peace. Only then "could we realise those sweete visions of the night."

Hughes closed his letter with two stanzas from "Fare Thee Well," by Lord Byron, which he must have copied from a poetry book because the spelling was accurate, unlike that in the rest of his letter. Following those eight lines of poetry, he added a few from the song "I'd Offer Thee This Heart":

> but now my dreams ar sadly o'er
> fate bids them all depart
> and i must leav my nativ shore
> in brokenness of heart
>
> and O dear one when far from thee
> i'll never know joy again
> I would not that one thought of me
> should giv thy bosom pain
> i'd ofer thee this hand of mine
> if i could lov thee less but heart
> so pure as thine should
> never know distress

The romanticism of these lines—which Hughes clearly knew by heart— reflects the anguish of a lonely soldier who knew he was nearing death. Suffering alone in a military hospital so far from home, his dreams of his family—and his longing to be with them—had become his most cherished possessions. But soon they, too, would be taken from him. Sadly, Hughes died of disease less than two months after writing this letter on a hospital boat near Helena, Arkansas.[10]

Women writers on both homefronts also expounded on these themes during the war, building on the ideas first popularized by Campbell's poem. South Carolinian Caroline H. Gervais wrote an oft reprinted poem called "In His Blanket on the Ground," about a weary Confederate soldier who dreams of "home, and friends, and loved ones."[11] In Massachusetts, the Unitarian poet Caroline A. Mason's "The Soldier's Dream of Home" touched soldiers as deeply as Thomas Campbell's verses had. Union soldier H. B. Howe was so moved by Mason's poem that he told her that his own family was "almost [an] exact copy of the picture you have painted." "Such lines," he continued, "carry with them many a blessing as they are read by the exiled soldier—self exiled as many of us are, away from home, kindred and friends, especially from the dear ones of his heart."[12] It is little wonder that so many soldiers penned their own clumsy and often melodramatic lines about dreams of home, seeking to capture the emotions of the more popular verses. Such poems are preserved on scraps of paper, in letters and diaries, account books, newspapers, and even regimental histories.[13]

Music also incorporated dream-related themes, and songs about dreams could be heard along the front lines. Songs unrelated to the war continued to focus on dreams, just as many had in the antebellum era. Some of the most touching songs related to the experiences of soldiers and their families. A beautifully illustrated piece entitled "The Soldier's Vision" featured an enlisted man dreaming of "my home and friends so dear"—the place where he could relive "boyhood scenes" and never again see "blood stained fields" or hear "the cannon's thunder roar." "I Dreamed My Boy Was Home Again" related the story of a "lonely, weary, broken-hearted" mother who had a bright, joyous dream of her son returning home. One of the most popular Northern war songs, "All Quiet along the Potomac Tonight," described Union soldiers "peacefully dreaming" of home. In the Southern counterpart, "All Quiet along the Savannah To-Night," a Confederate picket sees "visions of loved ones . . . back home in his dreams." Among the Confederate ranks, "See Her Still in My Dreams" was also popular.[14]

"Mother Kissed Me in My Dream" was a widely reprinted Union song based on the account of a dying soldier at Antietam. One song sheet included a brief account of the story behind the song as well as a touching image of a faithful mother praying for her son and then visiting him as an angel the night before he died. The lyrics beckoned soldiers to do their duty on the battlefield while assuring them that their pain and suffering would be alleviated by visitation dreams from their mothers, and the song quickly gained an audience among Northern soldiers. During the Battle of Gettysburg, a wounded private in the Eighty-Sixth New York sang it "to cheer his comrades" while they were resting near the Wheatfield on July 3, 1863.[15]

Sometimes the sentimentality of music even influenced soldiers' dreams. Writing two weeks after the Battle of Fredericksburg, surgeon William Child of the Fifth New Hampshire Volunteers told his wife, "The soldiers have gone to rest and to dream of home. Such is the scene from my tent door. I walk among the tents and hear the sweet notes of 'Sweet Home'—and think of my own home so far away—when shall I return—what changes may transpire—shall I ever return—are they all well there—do they think of me—will my children remember me—Oh a thousand thoughts come rushing in producing one of those thrills of emotion that I love so well." That night Dr. Child "dreamed of home every hour."[16]

Of course, pleasant dreams of home could lead to disappointment after sunrise. Frequently soldiers wrote about hugging and kissing their wives but then waking up feeling angry that they were away from home sleeping on the hard, cold earth.[17] Lieutenant Richard Goldwaite's unconscious nighttime wanderings revealed his longing for his wife—and perhaps also his fears that he might never see her again. He dreamed that "you came here to see me and we were a going to have a good time in my tent when night came and when I woke up in the morning and did not find you, I was mad enough to go over to Baltimore and get drunk."[18] Such dreams could have emotional effects on the soldiers who dreamed them, even when they weren't about actual women at home. After dreaming of an imaginary "fair lady last night," one Maine soldier "felt home sick all day as a consequence."[19]

Ironically, visitations with loved ones in soldiers' dreams were not always pleasant, and soldiers' sleeping brains sometimes created scenarios that revealed unease about family life that might have been rumbling just beneath the surface of the soldiers' subconscious. Feelings of guilt also often materialized in dreams, and remorse for secret sins sometimes manifested itself in soldiers' sleep. The most striking and common iniquity to appear in dreams was marital infidelity. Young men away from home feared that their wives and sweethearts might lose hope, or believe that their lovers had died, and fall into the arms of a sneaking coward at home. Such worries that another man—or men—might disrupt their households caused some soldiers to write home about their concerns.

Soldiers were remarkably candid in bringing up their fears of abandonment and adultery. To soften the difficulty of the issue, however, they often situated it within a discussion of their dreams. Doing so enabled them to maintain a certain level of intimacy while broaching a difficult subject. In September 1862, Surgeon William Child told his wife, Carrie, that in his dream she did not say she loved him when they first saw each other, but soon thereafter "you kissed me—and told me you loved me." A year and a half later, his insecurities still revealed themselves in his letters and dreams. "I can not tell you how I desire to see you," he wrote in April 1864. "You seem more dear to me than ever. I love—love you. I dream of you almost nightly. . . . And nothing would cause me more misery than to feel that my wife should have no love for me—for then she certainly could not be happy." Despite his entreaties Carrie wrote to him infrequently, and her letters were rather short and perfunctory. By November 1864, he was feeling great trepidation about his marriage. He reflected on the fact that she had never appeared very passionate when they were together before the war. And as he thought about these things, an "awful idea" crept into his head— that perhaps she might be in love with another man.[20]

It is little wonder that a vague word of a dream in one of Carrie's letters put Dr. Child on edge. "You say you had a dream about me," he wrote to her in January 1864. "Why did you not tell me all about or not say anything about it? You make me feel as though there was something very bad about me—or that you at least thought so." He then reiterated that he dreamed about her "often" and that they were "always good and pleasant dreams too." Carrie apparently never revealed her dream. Two months later he again implored her to tell him. Again, she refused. A year later, in January 1865, he was still tortured by her dream. "Last night I dreamed of you a long and pleasant dream," he wrote. "You mentioned that you once dreamed of me— an unpleasant dream—awful dream, but you would not tell it to me. Why not? You always tell me just enough to excite my curiosity, then leave me to wonder."[21]

Other soldiers had dreams that explicitly exposed their fears of spousal infidelity, abandonment, or other marital difficulties. Captain Thomas Jefferson Hyatt of the 126th Ohio had several "very queer" dreams one night. "First I dreamed that we had been married some years, and the time had run out and we were about arranging another term," he told his wife. But then "I dreamed you had abandoned me and had or was about to form an alliance with Lt. [Joseph C.] Watson of this Regt." At first Hyatt was content with this new arrangement, "as I supposed I was free to go where I chose." But soon he "began to feel very badly, and could not think of the separation." In his dream his wife seemed "offish," and he grew jealous of how she looked at Watson. But eventually she began "to regret the steps you had taken and began to think I was a *little* better than your second choice. I just then awoke, and behold it was all a dream, and I was very glad of it."[22]

These kinds of dreams were ubiquitous. Minnesota infantryman Duren F. Kelley dreamed that he saw his wife on a street back home but that she "seemed to take no notice of me and kept right on." South Carolinian Jesse W. Reid's wife "would hardly speak to me" in his dream. In like manner, New Yorker John Hartwell dreamed he came home, but his wife "took about as much notice of me as you would if I had been out to get an armful of wood." But things only went downhill from there, likely revealing some of Hartwell's deepest anxieties. As the dream progressed, Hartwell saw his wife "take the hand of a finely dressed gentleman & jump into a carriage & ride away."[23]

Bad dreams of home often resulted from lack of correspondence with loved ones.[24] After not receiving a letter from his wife for almost two months, Wisconsin soldier Miles Butterfield had a "very strange Dream" that he could not get out of his mind, which he described in a twelve-page letter to his wife. Butterfield dreamed that he had gotten out of the service and gone home to see his wife and baby, but she refused to "take any notice of me." Eventually he learned that she "did not intend to live with me anymore," and she wanted him to get his furniture out of the house. He pleaded with her, but to no avail. He then walked into town and saw several friends, including one who claimed that he had been living with Butterfield's wife for three weeks "and that he was not the only one that had been with you, but he was the one that you was going off with." Now Butterfield felt even worse. In his dream he returned home and told his wife he could "forgive all and live with you as before," but again she rejected him and left town on a train.

Suicidal thoughts now flooded Butterfield's sleeping brain. "I was going to wait until the next train come along and I would put an end to my Miserable life by lying down on the track and letting the cars run over me," he told her, "for now I had nothing to live for as you and the Baby was gone, but I began to think how you had been acting, and concluded that I would go back and let you go, and thought that it was a good thing that you had gone as I did with one once before as you know." After several pages of this vivid description, Butterfield again asked his wife to send him more letters. Clearly lack of communication from home was having a destructive effect on this soldier's psyche. In this case dreams were a bitter communion; only real and affirmative contact from home could rid him of his nightmares. Perhaps only by describing such a dream could he induce enough guilt in her to get her to send more letters.[25]

Other soldiers had similarly violent dreams about adultery—some of which, like Butterfield's, involved their wives cheating with multiple men. On September 4, 1861, William Hardy dreamt that he had returned home to Mississippi and that his wife, Sallie, "received me cooly." He watched her get into "a buggy with a young man and left in a gay and fastidious manner." He followed them to a party, where he now saw her "in a fine glee, entertained by two nice-looking gentlemen." Sallie still ignored William, so that his "heart sunk, and the tears gushed forth from my eyes." She chastised him and rejoined her two boyfriends. At this point Hardy "became enraged and determined to settle the matter. I got my double barrel shotgun heavily loaded, and after killing both the young men, I drew a dagger and determined to terminate your life and my own with the same knife at the same time." But before he could execute "this horrible deed, I awoke." He wrote, "My mind was contorted, my whole physical frame convulsed, and I almost crazy." Only after he had become convinced that it was a dream did he finally relax. Hardy attributed such a "terrible dream" to having heard of a comrade's wife being unfaithful, as well as being "tired and worn down, completely exhausted from a long and tedious drill."[26]

Lack of correspondence also had psychological effects on women, and wives longed for a word from the army to assure them of their husband's love. "What can be the matter that you don't write?" Kate Peddy of Georgia asked her husband in the Confederate army. "It has been nearly three weeks since you wrote a single line. I fear my dream is coming true that you have learned to love me less." Such doubts plagued many women for the duration of the war. "I dreamed you came home the other night, and I was nearly crazy with joy, but you seemed indifferent," wrote Peddy in December 1862 in an echo of the common soldier's dream. "I wanted to know if you did not love me. You said, yes, but did not love me as much as you did before you had learned to stay away. I awoke in great distress, and all the next day it would come into my thoughts oftener than I wished."[27]

The reporting of such dreams reveals a remarkable level of intimacy that persisted between husbands and wives. Despite the great distances between them, even bad dreams became a mechanism for emotional connection. To be sure, these dream reports by men may reveal a way that some soldiers tried to maintain a measure of control over their households—unsophisticated attempts to compel their spouses to remain faithful. But something more than manipulation seems to have been going on in these dream reports between spouses. Ironically, as soldiers and their wives were experiencing severe doubts about their partner's faithfulness, they still felt close enough to share their insecurities. And, unlike Dr. Child's case, most spouses responded with words of kindness and affirmation.

Not all soldiers had monogamous dreams, and many likely dreamed of multiple women back home. One Confederate officer dreamed of visiting a Miss Sallie. "She was standing on [the] porch," he wrote. "I cried out to

Miss S., 'Here comes your sweetheart.['] She ran in the house. Met me at door. Went in and was having a nice time when awoke & 'twas all a dream." Two nights later he dreamed of a different girl. "Suddenly Miss Kate opened the door and came in looking beautiful as an angel. I spoke to her. Told me, she congratulated me on being married. Told the miss she was mistaken, but if she was willing I'd soon be. Don't remember her answer." Four days later, he dreamt that he was about to "pop the question" to a Miss Frances.[28]

Most soldiers were modest—even shy—when describing romantic dreams to their wives and sweethearts. Confederate surgeon George W. Peddy of the Fifty-Sixth Georgia Volunteers told his wife, Kate, "Honey, I wish I could tell you what a dream I had of you last night. I will tell you about it when I get to see you. Oh that I could realize such facts as the dream perpetrated!"[29] Giving slightly more detail, Dr. William Child assured his wife on a cold night in November 1864 that he missed "home with its thousand comforts among which a comfortable bed—with a comfortable bed-fellow and warm—is not the least." He then told her that he "dreamed of home more than once in my restless sleep. It might cause you to laugh should I tell you what I dreamed—perhaps blush. I have concluded to tell you at another time if I should ever see you." Instead of sleeping with her, he lay on the frozen ground in a blanket next to a hospital steward. "You would laugh to see us in bed curled up like two pigs with our heads covered," he wrote.[30]

Other soldiers, by contrast, described explicit dreams that probably made their women blush and avert their eyes. Union general Godfrey Weitzel wrote a colorfully descriptive and romantic letter to his future wife, Louisa Bogen, on March 4, 1864:

> I have pinched your picture and it does not holler. I have bitten it and it does not holler. I have kissed it and it does not return my kisses. I have hugged it and it does not return my hug. So just consider yourself pinched, bitten, hugged and kissed. I have been dreaming about you all last night. I was back at home and had only 12 hours to stay. You and I sneaked away from the rest of the folks and went upstairs to that little front room in your house and we had such a pleasant time. But alas! It was only a dream.[31]

For some soldiers, dreams of girls led to wet dreams. In one graphic letter, a Pennsylvania soldier encouraged his wife to masturbate by their fireplace after describing a dream he had had about her in which he "was having the sensation, as my shirt fully attested."[32] Not all soldiers saw seminal emissions as a positive effect of dreams, however—or something to write home about. A chaplain in the 145th Pennsylvania Volunteers noted a peculiar reason that two men in his regiment claimed for a discharge: "Both of them have been married for some years; and yet such are the pernicious effects of the early indulgences, that now they frequently have nocturnal emissions, foul dreams, etc.—besides rheumatism and general debility— such as renders them unfit for service."[33] Although these soldiers may have believed that they had a legitimate disability, other soldiers realized that they could feign wet dreams by masturbating in order to get out of the service. One team of army surgeons, for example, found that three out of the four patients under their care who claimed to suffer from "spermatorrhoea" had actually produced "manufactured" evidence of the disorder.[34]

Nevertheless, most soldiers saw romantic dreams as a welcome comfort. Some even concluded they could offer protection on the battlefield. One Georgia volunteer believed that if he dreamed of his sweetheart before a fight it was "a good omen" and he could go into battle "with the full relief that I will come out safe." He reckoned, "Maybe it is the spirit of my wee little sweetheart that hovers over me in battle and protects me from death or injury."[35]

This last dreamer captures the essence of most soldiers' and civilians' dreams during the Civil War. Dreams functioned as pleasant visitations between loved ones at home and in the field. Indeed, civilians in both North and South frequently experienced the inverse of "the soldier's dream of home." While soldiers regularly dreamed of *going* home, women and children often dreamed of their menfolk *coming* home. Lonely women desperately longed to have these dreams, and some would do whatever they could to induce them. One night in 1863, Dollie Vermilion of Iowa put one of her husband's letters under her pillow hoping she would dream of him. Unfortunately, the technique didn't work. Instead of dreaming of her husband coming home, she "dreamed of a battle somewhere, all night" with the sounds of "drums beating, and cannon booming, and the shout of the distant soldiers." When Dollie awoke the following morning and wrote a letter to her husband, she told him, "It troubles me." Clearly Dollie's attempt to influence her dreams in a positive way had exactly the opposite effect. Instead of having pleasant dreams of her husband coming home, her unconscious mind traveled to the danger he was experiencing—something that undoubtedly preoccupied her waking thoughts.[36]

Dreams often catapulted civilians into the battlefield—another inverse of "the soldier's dream of home." Some, like Lizzie Hardin of Kentucky, daydreamed about charging up a hill while "under a heavy fire from the summit."[37] Other Northern women had dreams of combat after reading about it in the newspapers. One Wisconsin woman told her mother that she was "disturbed by dreadful dreams of battles" after reading "war news," while a Philadelphia woman similarly experienced "bad dreams ... about the War" after hearing "alarming war news, rumours of an impending battle, [and] that Washington is not safe."[38]

Women's dreams of battle could be quite intense, even for those who had never come close to combat. In June 1862, a Louisiana girl dreamt that she went to a battlefield with an "American flag flying over it. I looked, and saw we were standing in blood up to our knees, while here and there ghastly white bones shone above the red surface."[39] In September 1864, after reading in the papers about William Tecumseh Sherman's capture of Atlanta, a Pennsylvanian dreamed that she was fighting against several armed Confederates in a hotel. "I was lying on the floor to prevent their bullets striking me," she wrote. "I know I expected to be killed and I wondered if I would be much missed. I was just as cool as you please and wondered if everyone was as cool when in action," she told her husband proudly.[40] A number of women experienced this sensation of fearlessness in their dreams, and some dreams led women to wish they could actually join the ranks. One Illinois schoolteacher dreamed that she was at General Ulysses S. Grant's headquarters helping him capture the Confederate stronghold at Vicksburg. The next day she wrote, "I more than ever wish I was a man that I might fill one place left vacant by some brave soldier. At times when I first hear of the fearful loss of life in some engagements I can scarcely proceed with my duties in womans province."[41]

Not all women were euphoric about their warlike dreams—most were likely terrified. After dreaming that the Confederates had captured one of the federal forts around Washington, D.C., Elizabeth Blair Lee dreamed herself onto Pennsylvania Avenue "in a scene of great anguish and trouble." She then wrote to her husband about it. "I tell you this to let you see how these terrible times haunt me."[42]

Most civilians, like Elizabeth Blair Lee, likely longed for peaceful dreams that foreshadowed an end to the conflict and a reunion with loved ones.[43] Just like their menfolk, women longed to be reunited with their husbands, fathers, brothers, and uncles. Dreams became a way for them to diminish the distance between homefront and battlefield, just as they were for soldiers. "It is well that thoughts can travel over the space, and imagination picture you all, for otherwise it would be very lonely," wrote General Benjamin F. Butler's daughter to her parents about her thoughts as she fell asleep at night.[44] One woman explained to her husband that dreams were evidence that "there is some magnetic chain between us and I can almost always tell ... when you are in danger."[45] In like manner, Varina Howell

Davis told her husband during his long imprisonment after the war for serving as president of the Confederacy, "No bars or bolts can keep me from you in dreams."[46]

Within this context, we can make sense of the commercial demand for depictions of soldiers dreaming peacefully of home. Northern printmakers created and sold images of idealized soldiers' dreams to reassure families of their menfolk's fidelity to home and country. Soldiers portrayed in deep, restful sleep could be found on envelopes, stationery, song sheets, and *cartes de visite*, in pictorial newspapers, and on prints by firms like Currier and Ives. These images—with titles such as *The Soldier's Dream, The Soldier's Dream of Home, The Union Soldier's Dream of Home,* and *The Soldier's Dream of Peace*—depicted volunteers in slumber on the night before battle, faithfully serving their country but dreaming of home. Some prints contained other related themes of the era, such as *The American Patriot's Dream*, in which a dreaming soldier envisions his return home not only as victorious but also as triumphant because of his promotion to an officer. In this case he longed not only to be reunited with his family but also to be successful in the glories of war.[47]

Many of these images carried "a double message," according to one scholar. Not only did they emphasize the importance of victory and reunion but also they underscored what soldiers longed for in their family lives. Their wives were "to be virtuous and chaste, a source of encouragement to their absent husbands, and the mainstay of the home and farm during his time of military service."[48] Families likely hung prints of dreaming soldiers in their homes to convince themselves that their soldiers' thoughts were on them. Mothers, fathers, wives, and children eagerly opened letters that arrived from the front in envelopes featuring depictions of *The Soldier's Dream*. One soldier in the Ninth Vermont Infantry inscribed a copy of the Currier and Ives print *The Soldier's Dream of Home* to his wife.[49] A Pennsylvania soldier created a pose to capture these themes in two *cartes de visite* he took in uniform. In one he pretends to sleep with a letter in his hand, ostensibly dreaming of his wife who sent it; in the other, the photographer superimposed a woman hovering over him as he has his head down on a table—presumably his wife, about whom he dreams.[50] The theme even emerged in parlor activities. Mothers taught the words of "The Soldier's Dream" to their children.[51] And in 1865 a Quaker family in Virginia—with both men and women participating—performed a tableau of *The Soldier's Dream* in their home.[52] The concept of "the soldier's dream of home," in short, became part of the American vernacular—even part of the daily routine of some households.

One modern scholar views these popular depictions as part of "the myth of America" and "a cultural cover-up" because they offer "tidy depictions of men and women in their correct roles, spaces, and places" rather than portraying "the controversial activities of female reformers prior to the Civil War, which had fostered fears and anxieties about 'monstrous women.'" This scholar implies that these images functioned to keep women bound in subservience, concluding, "Perhaps the soldier's dream was, in part, a dream of postwar normalcy: average men living normal lives with normal wives."[53]

Such an anachronistic critique wholly misunderstands the Victorian culture of Civil War America—not to mention the perfectly natural desires of families separated by war. Although patriarchy still reflected the nature of marriage as a public institution, it did not capture the private realities of many households. By the antebellum period, American families had become less patriarchal and more democratic than they had been earlier. As one scholar explains, marriage was increasingly "characterized by a companionate relationship between husband and wife" and "attitudes toward children within the family became gentler." In other words, husbands and wives experienced marriage as a partnership based in romantic love, and they no longer tended to view their children primarily as sources of supplemental income, as had been typical in earlier times. As historian J. Matthew Gallman explains, "As the century progressed it appears that increasing numbers of married couples—especially in the northern states—embraced the notion that the ideal marriage should be a partnership grounded in love and respect, even when the legal system recognized no such equality."[54]

Within this context it is little wonder that soldiers and their wives longed for normalcy. In its most primal sense, normalcy meant survival. Most soldiers naturally longed for that, as did their loved ones. But even more, normalcy represented relief from the hardships and anxieties of wartime. With so many men off in faraway, dangerous places for years at a time with very little communication to and from home, it should not be at all surprising that images like *The Soldier's Dream* appealed to soldiers and their wives. In most cases, married soldiers wanted to be home with their families. These images resonated with them, therefore, precisely because the scenes on paper captured the daily experiences and expectations of Union and Confederate soldiers. In a practical sense, the concept of *The Soldier's Dream* became a comfort to lonely spouses who were separated by war—a representation of the communication they longed to have, and often did have, in their dreams.[55]

Of equal importance, these images publicly emphasized the companionate nature of the marriage relationship that existed in many households.

Indeed, rather than subjugate women by relegating them to the domestic sphere, such images were intended to support those who remained at home by boosting their morale. "Such scenes were meant to reassure families that their men in arms remained inspired, perhaps even protected and blessed, by thoughts of home and hearth," write historians Mark E. Neely Jr. and Harold Holzer. Historian Alice Fahs adds, "The image reassured the viewer that soldiers had not become killers, but instead remained connected to their homes. . . . The image at once reassures the viewer that soldiers have not fundamentally changed, and provides a narrative 'happy ending' to the war within the dream itself."[56] Indeed, images like these reinforced sentimental notions and understandings of how families ought to experience the war.

At the same time, these commercial depictions of "the soldier's dream" struck nineteenth-century Americans as authentic. Soldiers could relate to these mass-market appeals in large measure because the images captured the very dreams they were having in their tents and bivouacs at the front. "Did you ever see a picture called the soldiers dream?" a Confederate soldier asked his wife in October 1862. "I have seen it somewhere, possibly in an old magazine. The artist had certainly seen life in camps and had a wife and baby."[57] Indeed, soldiers truly believed that the commercial images captured the reality of their experiences. In August 1864, while encamped near Atlanta, Lieutenant Russell M. Tuttle of New York awoke from a nap and, although his sleep had been "filled with dreams," he could not remember what they had been. This realization caused him to ruminate on the many "Golden Dreams" that all of his comrades had in camp, around the campfire, while out on picket, in battle, or on the march. "Dreaming ever, and of what?" he wrote. "Almost always of home, of the glad return to old friends, and scenes which [are] to follow all this peril and hardship, which is to compensate for all we are now deprived of, which is to make substantial the honors gained in the field." Tuttle remembered seeing old European prints of soldiers' dreams of affectionate familial reunions after war. "And I have read poetry picturing similar scenes," he wrote. "I can realize the sentiment of all this now, and I can tell you there is a deal of romance in these same visions of happier scenes that come to gladden the soldier with bright hopes."[58]

Soldiers like Tuttle longed to have the idealized soldier's dream of home. Like many people, they wished they could control their sleeping thoughts so that they could make a visit to their loved ones. And when they were fortunate enough to travel those dreamy miles, they felt a kinship to other soldiers from generations gone by. "I dream the soldiers dream sometimes," wrote one Confederate soldier from Arkansas. "I wish I could dream it in reality."[59]

In a remarkable way, popular images of "the soldier's dream" helped humanize the enemy, causing some Yankee soldiers to see Southern households as not so different from their own. An Indiana soldier described being in the "dilapidated old village" of Decatur, Georgia. Among the old wooden houses, he wrote, "Only a few of the citizens remain, and they are 'poor white trash.'" One caught his eye, however. A "pretty little girl, with bright black eyes and glossy curls" who "gazed upon us, from a window— a beautiful picture in a decayed frame." As he looked at this little girl, he recalled the children he and his comrades had left behind in the North. The thought caused a "tear to steal, unbidden, down the bronzed cheek." "These little episodes," he continued, "seemingly unimportant in themselves, often call our minds afar from the scenes of war. We dream, but we are awake. I often see a picture, 'The Soldier's Dream'; it is of home. We are not always asleep, when these visions come. Happy the remnant of us, who shall enter the promised land of a restored Union."[60]

The concept of "the soldier's dream of home" resonated so thoroughly with both Union and Confederate soldiers precisely because most soldiers often dreamed pleasant dreams of the people and things they had left behind. "Home" was not simply a symbol in the popular lithography of the day—a sphere on the periphery of the war effort. On the contrary, "home" was the focal point of soldiers' deepest longings and a source of real support when soldiers lay upon the ground in utter weariness. It is little wonder that "home" occupied the most intimate thoughts of soldiers' unconscious minds. Whether waking or sleeping, soldiers desperately wished to be home.

To be sure, many soldiers suffered from nightmares and night terrors, but more bad dreams appear to have been caused by lack of correspondence or fear of infidelity than by the experience of combat. So great were these domestic travails that some soldiers even dreamed about not receiving letters from their families.[61] Letters from home could ameliorate the effects of bad dreams. As one Minnesota soldier told his wife in November 1863, "Another letter from you at last, which somewhat relieves me from the gloom of that horrible dream."[62] An Illinois soldier "had a sweet dream over [his sweetheart's letter] last night."[63] Similarly, a Pennsylvanian wrote his wife that it was a "pleasure" to read a letter he had just received from her. "I read it twice, then re-read it, then closed my eyes to dream of my 'dear good wife,'" he told her. "The letter so lifted my heart."[64] For these soldiers—

as for so many civilians—an occasional letter and a dream would have to suffice for conversation during times spent apart.

Of even greater significance, however, is that most soldiers reported happy, peaceful, and romantic dreams of home. Far more common than nightmares of battle were those dreams of soldiers like John Jones of the Forty-Fifth Illinois, who told his wife of a dream in which she "gave me a most enrapturing kiss." William Wallace of Wisconsin slept with pictures of his wife and children under his pillow so that he might dream of home. One Mississippian wrote happily to his future wife after waking from a dream, "My soul thanks the great Giver of all good that He has endowed us with the faculty of dreaming, that the overwrought, wearied soul may wander a season, through the mystic regions of the Dreamland . . . of another and happier world." Henry Graves of New York saw dreams of home as "angels of mercy" sent to the "soldier mortal." Sam Farnum of Rhode Island told a friend in November 1862, "I have dreamed often enough of sisters but of picket duty & fights I have never had the luck to dream."[65] Even during the heat of battle, soldiers' minds could not help but return to their homes. During the fighting at Spotsylvania Courthouse in 1864, two exhausted New Hampshire soldiers fell asleep next to each other—only to wake up a few minutes later when one of their comrades was shot and cried out in pain. The two awakened men looked at each other and recounted their dreams. Both had dreamed of going home to see their families, and one remarked, "I wish it were all real."[66]

The candor of soldiers' letters to their spouses and friends is remarkable. When they had a bad dream, they shared it. However, the dream lives of soldiers—on the whole—do not appear to have been dark or terrifying. Some soldiers even awoke from their dreams in laughter.[67] Those who awoke in sadness often did so because they missed in reality the closeness they had felt to their families while they were asleep. Their dreams had been happy; waking up led to a bitter parting. Perhaps even more important, thoughts and dreams of home helped sustain soldiers in their cause, giving them a visual reminder of what—and who—they were fighting for.[68]

In short, most soldiers delighted in their dreams of home.[69] The dreams of Civil War soldiers—both Union and Confederate—thus reveal an intense intimacy between soldiers and their families. Sharing their dreams with one another helped sustain them through long periods of separation, anxiety, and sadness. Rather than growing distant and uncommunicative, soldiers strove to maintain strong lines of communication in their letters, even when doing so meant divulging embarrassing secrets or insecurities. "Do you like to have me tell you my dreams?" one Union sailor playfully asked his wife. "If I cant see you during the day it is at least pleasant to see you in my dreams."[70]

NOTES

Portions of this essay appeared in Jonathan W. White, *Midnight in America: Darkness, Sleep, and Dreams during the Civil War* (Chapel Hill: University of North Carolina Press, 2017).

1. George Tillotson to wife, January 9, 1862, in *The Soldier's Pen: Firsthand Impressions of the Civil War*, ed. Robert E. Bonner (New York: Hill and Wang, 2006), 52; M. B. Thurman to Jane Rosser, November 30, 1861, in *Love and War: A Southern Soldier's Struggle between Love and Duty*, ed. Robert H. Crewdson (Buena Vista, Va.: Mariner, 2009), 26–27; Bob Blaisdell, ed., *Civil War Letters: From Home, Camp, and Battlefield* (Mineola, N.Y.: Dover, 2012), 178. See also William Ward Orme to Nannie, June 22, 1863, in Harry E. Pratt, ed., "Civil War Letters of Brigadier General William Ward Orme, 1862–1866," *Journal of the Illinois State Historical Society* 23, no. 2 (July 1930): 282; Robert G. Evans, ed., *The 16th Mississippi Infantry: Civil War Letters and Reminiscences* (Jackson: University of Mississippi Press, 2002), 5, 14, 25, 40, 55; Samuel Gilbert Webber to Nannie, December 21, 1862, Webber Letters, The Mariners' Museum Library, Newport News, Va. (hereafter TMM); H. E. Coleman to wife, March 10, 1862, TMM.

2. See, for example, Emily Foster, ed., *American Grit: A Woman's Letters from the Ohio Frontier* (Lexington: University Press of Kentucky, 2009), 124; Andrew Burstein, *Lincoln Dreamt He Died: The Midnight Visions of Remarkable Americans from Colonial Times to Freud* (New York: Palgrave Macmillan, 2013), 179, 182.

3. J. Matthew Gallman, *Mastering Wartime: A Social History of Philadelphia during the Civil War* (New York: Cambridge University Press, 1990), 79.

4. David Anderson, "Dying of Nostalgia: Homesickness in the Union Army during the Civil War," *Civil War History* 56 (September 2010): 250, 262.

5. Susan J. Matt, *Homesickness: An American History* (New York: Oxford University Press, 2011), 99–100.

6. Cincinnati *Western Christian Advocate*, January 1, 1862.

7. *The Wreath: A Collection of Poems from Celebrated English Authors* (Hartford, Conn.: Silas Andrus, 1821), 147–48; S. G. Goodrich, *The Fourth Reader for the Use of Schools* (Boston: Otis, Broaders, 1839), 203–4; Epes Sargent, *The Standard Speaker; Containing Exercises in Prose and Poetry for Declamation in Schools, Academies, Lyceums, Colleges* (Philadelphia: Thomas, Cowperthwait, 1852), 147.

8. Henry William Herbert, "The Soldier's Dream: An Incident of Egypt," *Godey's Lady's Book*, March 1852, 178–80; poems by J. L. Swan and Fanny Fales, "The Soldier's Dream of Home," *Godey's Lady's Book*, October 1852, 380.

9. Charles V. Mauro, *A Southern Spy in Northern Virginia: The Civil War Album of Laura Ratcliffe* (Charleston, S.C.: History Press, 2009), 56–57; Robert Bruce Don-

ald, ed., *Manhood and Patriotic Awakening in the American Civil War: The John E. Mattoon Letters, 1859–1866* (Lanham, Md.: Hamilton Books, 2008), 92–93; Richard M. McMurray, ed., *An Uncompromising Secessionist: The Civil War of George Knox Miller, Eighth (Wade's) Confederate Cavalry* (Tuscaloosa: University of Alabama Press, 2007), 65; Elias Winans Price to Henrietta McDowell Price, September 8, 1863, Price Papers, Southern Historical Collection, Louis Round Wilson Special Collections Library, University of North Carolina at Chapel Hill (hereafter SHC); Lysander Wheeler to parents, March 15, 1863 (GLC 07460.022), Gilder Lehrman Institute of American History, New York (hereafter cited with Gilder Lehrman number only); Burstein, *Lincoln Dreamt He Died*, 213.

10. Grata J. Clark and Jeffrey S. Clark, eds., *A Soldier's Dream of Home: The Civil War Letters of John C. Hughes to His Wife, Harriet* (Fort Worth, Tex.: Arcadia-Clark, 1996), 78–83, 87. For another soldier who used similar stationery, see Raymond G. Barber and Gary E. Swinson, eds., *The Civil War Letters of Charles Barber, Private, 104th New York Volunteer Infantry* (Torrance, Calif.: Gary E. Swinson, 1991), 86.

11. H. M. Wharton, *War Songs and Poems of the Southern Confederacy, 1861–1865* (Philadelphia: American Book and Bible House, 1904), 308–11.

12. Quoted in Alice Fahs, *The Imagined Civil War: Popular Literature of the North and South, 1861–1865* (Chapel Hill: University of North Carolina Press, 2001), 106–7. The full text of the poem is available in Frank Moore, ed., *Lyrics of Loyalty* (New York: George P. Putnam, 1864), 139–41, as well as a number of other books and periodicals from the period.

13. John Worrell Northrop, *Chronicles from the Diary of a War Prisoner in Andersonville and Other Military Prisons in the South in 1864* (Wichita, Kans., 1904), 124; James F. Clarke Account Books, College of William and Mary, Williamsburg, Va.; J. Waldo Denny, *Wearing the Blue in the Twenty-Fifth Mass. Volunteer Infantry, with Burnside's Coast Division, 18th Army Corps, and Army of the James* (Worcester, Mass.: Putnam and Davis, 1879), 102–3; "To My Wife" in the Columbus, Ohio, *Crisis*, September 3, 1862.

14. Christian McWhirter, *Battle Hymns: Music and the American Civil War* (Chapel Hill: University of North Carolina Press, 2012), 22; C. Everest, "The Soldier's Vision" (Philadelphia: Lee and Walker, 1862); Charles Carroll Sawyer, "I Dreamed My Boy Was Home Again" (Brooklyn: Sawyer and Carroll, 1863); Fahs, *Imagined Civil War*, 118; Edmund L. Drago, *Confederate Phoenix: Rebel Children and Their Families in South Carolina* (New York: Fordham University Press, 2008), 30.

15. Dudley H. Miles, ed., *Photographic History of the Civil War*, 10 vols. (New York: Review of Reviews, 1911), 9:350. Several editions of this song are available at the Library of Congress and other repositories.

16. Merrill C. Sawyer, Betty Sawyer, and Timothy C. Sawyer, eds., *Letters from a Civil War Surgeon: The Letters of Dr. William Child of the Fifth New Hampshire Volunteers* (Solon, Maine: Polar Bear, 2001), 75.

17. Steven J. Ramold, *Across the Divide: Union Soldiers View the Northern Home Front* (New York: New York University Press, 2013), 45; Benjamin Hirst to wife,

March 6, 1863, in *The Boys from Rockville: Civil War Narratives of Sgt. Benjamin Hirst, Company D, 14th Connecticut Volunteers*, ed. Robert L. Bee (Knoxville: University of Tennessee Press, 1998), 88; Grant Taylor to wife and children, May 25, 1862, and November 15, 1863, both in *This Cruel War: The Civil War Letters of Grant and Malinda Taylor, 1862–1865*, ed. Ann K. Blomquist and Robert A. Taylor (Macon, Ga.: Mercer University Press, 2000), 25, 196. For similar examples, see Peter S. Carmichael, "One Man's Turning Point," *Civil War Times* 42 (August 2003): 68; Melvin J. Hyde to Alice L. Holcomb, March 4, 1864, in *In the Field: Doctor Melvin John Hyde, Surgeon, 2nd Vermont Volunteers*, ed. Geraldine Frances Chittick (Newport: Vermont Civil War Enterprises, 1999), 72; Randall Allen and Keith S. Bohannon, eds., *Campaigning with "Old Stonewall": Confederate Captain Ujanirtus Allen's Letters to His Wife* (Baton Rouge: Louisiana State University Press, 1998), 33–34; George C. Rable, *Fredericksburg! Fredericksburg!* (Chapel Hill: University of North Carolina Press, 2002), 112; William H. Haigh to wife, June 1, 1865, William H. Haigh Papers, SHC.

18. Marti Skipper and Jane Taylor, eds., *A Handful of Providence: The Civil War Letters of Lt. Richard Goldwaite, New York Volunteers, and Ellen Goldwaite* (Jefferson, N.C.: McFarland, 2004), 70.

19. Hiram Smith Williams, April 19, 1864, in *This War So Horrible: The Civil War Diary of Hiram Smith Williams*, ed. Lewis N. Wynne and Robert A. Taylor (Tuscaloosa: University of Alabama Press, 1993), 49–52; William B. Jordan Jr., ed., *The Civil War Journals of John Mead Gould, 1861–1866* (Baltimore: Butternut and Blue, 1997), 76, 95.

20. William Child to wife, September 22, 1862, April 1, November 20, 1864, in *Civil War Surgeon*, 34, 211, 310–11.

21. William Child to wife, January 29, February 4, March 17, 20, 1864, January 8, 1865, in *Civil War Surgeon*, 201–9, 314. The Childs' marriage survived until Carrie died in 1867, at which point William married her sister. See also Gustave Cook to wife, December 10, 1862 (GLC02570.36).

22. Hudson Hyatt, ed., "Captain Hyatt: Being the Letters Written during the Years 1863–1864, to His Wife, Mary, by Captain T. J. Hyatt, 126th Ohio Volunteer Infantry," *Ohio Archeological and Historical Quarterly* 53 (April–June 1944): 171. For other examples like these, including dreams in which Confederate soldiers feared that their wives were sick or had died, see Drago, *Confederate Phoenix*, 30–32; Stephen W. Berry II, *All That Makes a Man: Love and Ambition in the Civil War South* (New York: Oxford University Press, 2003), 225.

23. Duren F. Kelley to Emma, December 24, 1863, in *The War Letters of Duren F. Kelley, 1862–1865*, ed. Richard F. Offenberg and Robert Rue Parsonage (New York: Pageant Press, 1967), 83–84; J. W. Reid, *History of the Fourth Regiment of S.C. Volunteers, from the Commencement of the War until Lee's Surrender* (Greenville, S.C.: Shannon, 1892), 46–47; Ann Hartwell Britton and Thomas J. Reed, eds., *To My Beloved Wife and Boy at Home: The Letters and Diaries of Orderly Sergeant John F. L. Hartwell* (Madison, Wisc.: Fairleigh Dickinson University Press, 1997), 36–37.

24. Carol Reardon argues that lack of correspondence had a negative effect on soldiers' "sense of personal confidence and well-being." See Reardon, *With a Sword in One Hand and Jomini in the Other: The Problem of Military Thought in the Civil War North* (Chapel Hill: University of North Carolina Press, 2012), 112.

25. Miles Butterfield to Libbie Butterfield, September 15, 1864, Butterfield Papers, University of Wisconsin–Milwaukee. For another bad dream connected to lack of correspondence from home, see Leander Harris to Emily S. Harris, September 6, 1863, Leander Harris Collection, University of New Hampshire. Other soldiers also mentioned lack of correspondence immediately before or after a description of a dream of home. See, for example, Nina Silber and Mary Beth Sievers, eds., *Yankee Correspondence: Civil War Letters between New England Soldiers and the Home Front* (Charlottesville: University Press of Virginia, 1996), 145; Allen and Bohannon, *Campaigning with "Old Stonewall,"* 14.

26. William Harris Hardy to Sallie Johnson Hardy, September 4, 1861, in *16th Mississippi Infantry*, ed. Evans, 22.

27. George P. Cuttino, ed., *Saddle Bag and Spinning Wheel: Being the Civil War Letters of George W. Peddy, MD, Surgeon, 56th Georgia Volunteer Regiment, CSA* (Macon, Ga.: Mercer University Press, 1981), 30, 136, 208, 282, 296–97. See also Marilyn Mayer Culpepper, ed., *Women of the Civil War South: Personal Accounts from Diaries, Letters, and Postwar Reminiscences* (Jefferson, N.C.: McFarland, 2003), 146. For other examples of women who connected their dreams to correspondence from their husbands, see Isabel Shaw Brown to John A. Brown, June 13, 1864, in *Dear Isa, Dear John: The Civil War Correspondence of One of Ohio's Hundred Days' Men, First Sergeant John A. Brown, 148th Ohio National Guard*, ed. Natalie H. Lee (Dexter, Mich.: Thomson-Shore, 1998), 63; Mary Eliza Rose to Charles Rose, n.d. [ca. summer 1863], Rose Family Papers, Virginia Historical Society, Richmond.

28. Jonathan W. White, ed., "Dream Reports: Excerpts from the Dream Journal of Alexander S. Paxton, 4th Virginia Infantry," *Military Images* 35 (Summer 2017): 8–10.

29. George W. Peddy to wife, March 18, 1863, in *Saddle Bag and Spinning Wheel*, ed. Cuttino, 158.

30. William Child to Carrie, November 13, 1864, in *Civil War Surgeon*, ed. Sawyer, 299.

31. Quoted in Thomas P. Lowry, *The Story the Soldiers Wouldn't Tell: Sex in the Civil War* (Mechanicsburg, Pa.: Stackpole Books, 1994), 170.

32. J. A. H. Foster to wife, January 21 and March 1, 1864, in *Letters from the Storm: The Intimate Civil War Letters of Lt. J. A. H. Foster, 155th Pennsylvania Volunteers*, ed. Walter L. Powell (Chicora, Pa.: Firefly, 2010), 182, 193.

33. John H. W. Stuckenberg, diary entry for October 12, 1862, in *I'm Surrounded by Methodists: Diary of John H. W. Stuckenberg, Chaplain of the 145th Pennsylvania Volunteer Infantry*, ed. David T. Hedrick and Gordon Barry Davis Jr. (Gettysburg, Pa.: Thomas, 1995), 17. See also Berry, *All That Makes a Man*, 144–48.

34. William W. Keen, S. Weir Mitchell, and George R. Morehouse, "On Ma-

lingering, Especially in Regard to Simulation of Diseases of the Nervous System," *American Journal of the Medical Sciences* 48 (October 1864): 374–76. Not all medical experts at the time believed wet dreams were a legitimate excuse for discharge from the service unless their effects were "sufficiently decided and pronounced." See, for example, John Ordronaux, *Hints on the Preservation of Health in the Armies* (New York: Appleton, 1861), 185; Roberts Bartholow, *A Manual of Instructions for Enlisting and Discharging Soldiers* (Philadelphia: J. B. Lippincott, 1864), 21–22. For a contemporary medical explanation of the physical and medical causes of wet dreams from the era, see Bartholow, *Spermatorrhoea: Its Causes, Symptoms, Results, and Treatment* (New York: William Wood, 1870), 5–27.

35. Richard M. Mcmurry, ed., *Footprints of a Regiment: A Recollection of the 1st Georgia Regulars, 1861–1865* (Marietta, Ga.: Longstreet Press, 1992), 109.

36. Dollie Vermilion to William Vermilion, March 18, 1863, in *Love amid the Turmoil: The Civil War Letters of William and Mary Vermilion*, ed. Donald C. Elder III (Iowa City: University of Iowa Press, 2003), 71.

37. Adrian Schultze Buser Willet, "Our House Was Divided: Kentucky Women and the Civil War" (PhD diss., Indiana University, 2008), 112. On Confederate women wishing they could fight, see George C. Rable, *Civil Wars: Women and the Crisis of Southern Nationalism* (Urbana: University of Illinois Press, 1989), 151–53, 178.

38. Hannah Aldrich to mother, August 21, 1861, in "Hannah's Letters: The Story of a Wisconsin Family, 1856–1864, Part II," ed. Elizabeth Krynski and Kimberly Little, *Wisconsin Magazine of History* 74 (Summer 1991): 296; Hannah to Emily, October 28, 1861, in "Hannah's Letters: The Story of a Wisconsin Family, 1856–1864, Part III," ed. Elizabeth Krynski and Kimberly Little, *Wisconsin Magazine of History* 74 (Autumn 1991): 42; Elizabeth Ingersoll Fisher, diary entries for September 16–17, 1861, Sidney George Fisher Collection, Historical Society of Pennsylvania, Philadelphia.

39. Charles East, ed., *Sarah Morgan: The Civil War Diary of a Southern Woman* (New York: Touchstone, 1992), 128, 442, 525–26.

40. Sophia Stockett Sellman to John Henry Sellman, September 6, 1864, in Sophia Stockett Sellman Letters, Library of Virginia, Richmond.

41. Harriet M. Buss to parents, March 31, 1863 (this part of the letter is actually dated April 1), Kislak Center for Special Collections, Rare Books and Manuscripts, Van Pelt Library, University of Pennsylvania; Charles Royster, *The Destructive War: William Tecumseh Sherman, Stonewall Jackson, and the Americans* (New York: Random House, 1991), 245.

42. Elizabeth Blair Lee to Phil, September 10, 1861, in *Wartime Washington: The Civil War Letters of Elizabeth Blair Lee*, ed. Virginia Jeans Laas (Urbana: University of Illinois Press, 1991), 77.

43. Some women dreamed of returning to the "peaceful everyday duties" of prewar domestic life. See, for example, Carl H. Moneyhon, ed., "Life in Confederate Arkansas: The Diary of Virginia Davis Gray, 1863–1865, Part I," *Arkansas Historical*

Quarterly 42 (Spring 1983): 53. Others overcame bad dreams by becoming more involved in civic and economic matters at home. See, for example, Thomas R. Taber, ed., *Hard Breathing Days: The Civil War Letters of Cora Beach Benton, Albion, New York, 1862–1865* (Albion, N.Y.: Almeron Press, 2003), 18–19, 81, 101, 224–25, 314, 316, 327, 331–32, 416.

44. Blanche Butler to mother, December 14, 1862, in *Chronicles from the Nineteenth Century: Family Letters of Blanche Butler and Adelbert Ames*, 2 vols., ed. Blanche Butler Ames (Clinton, Mass.: Colonial Press, 1957), 1:87.

45. Mary Watkins to Richard Watkins, September 24, 1862, in *Send Me a Pair of Old Boots and Kiss My Little Girls: The Civil War Letters of Richard and Mary Watkins, 1861–1865*, ed. Jeff Toalson (New York: iUniverse, 2009), 136.

46. Lynda L. Crist et al., eds., *The Papers of Jefferson Davis*, 15 vols. (Baton Rouge: Louisiana State University Press, 1971–), 12:79.

47. I have located a dozen visual images of soldiers' dreams from the Civil War years. Most are available in the catalog of the Library of Congress's Prints and Photographs Division. For a selection of patriotic covers, see William R. Weiss Jr., *The Catalog of Union Civil War Patriotic Covers* (n.p., 1995), 213. In 1862, Currier and Ives produced a beautiful image entitled "The Soldier's Home, the Vision," which depicts a woman sleeping peacefully on a couch as she dreams of her husband leading a charge beneath an American flag. This image makes a clear connection between dreams and correspondence as the woman holds a letter from her husband in her hand.

48. Steven R. Boyd, *Patriotic Envelopes of the Civil War: The Iconography of Union and Confederate Covers* (Baton Rouge: Louisiana State University Press, 2010), 82.

49. Currier & Ives Lithograph, "The Soldier's Dream of Home," collection of the author.

50. Ronald S. Coddington, "Comforting Spirit," *Military Images* 34 (Autumn 2016): 72.

51. Lucy Pier Stevens, diary entry for December 20, 1864, provided via email by Vicki Adams Tongate (the original diary is held at Southern Methodist University).

52. John E. Divine, Bronwen C. Souders, and John M. Souders, eds., *"To Talk Is Treason": Quakers of Waterford, Virginia, on Life, Love, Death, and War in the Southern Confederacy* (Waterford, Va.: Waterford Foundation, 1996), 94.

53. Amy E. Hughes, *Spectacles of Reform: Theater and Activism in Nineteenth-Century America* (Ann Arbor: University of Michigan Press, 2012), 133–37.

54. Dennis E. Suttles, "'For the Well-Being of the Child': The Law and Childhood," in *In Tender Consideration: Women, Families, and the Law in Abraham Lincoln's Illinois*, ed. Daniel W. Stowell (Urbana: University of Illinois Press, 2002), 46–47; J. Matthew Gallman, *Defining Duty in the Civil War: Personal Choice, Popular Culture, and the Home Front* (Chapel Hill: University of North Carolina Press, 2015), 189–90; Steven Mintz and Susan Kellogg, *Domestic Revolutions: A Social History of American Family Life* (New York: Free Press, 1988), 43–65.

55. On the power of sentimental literature in the Civil War era, see Fahs, *Imagined Civil War*, chap. 3; Frances M. Clarke, *War Stories: Suffering and Sacrifice in the Civil War North* (Chicago: University of Chicago Press, 2011).

56. Mark E. Neely Jr. and Harold Holzer, *The Union Image: Popular Prints of the Civil War North* (Chapel Hill: University of North Carolina Press, 2000), 91–97; Alice Fahs, "Picturing the Civil War 2: Sentimental Soldiers," http://picturinghistory.gc.cuny.edu/?p=916 (accessed December 29, 2014).

57. Allen and Bohannon, *Campaigning with "Old Stonewall,"* 173.

58. George H. Tappan, ed., *The Civil War Journal of Lt. Russell M. Tuttle* (Jefferson, N.C.: McFarland, 2006), 147–48.

59. James M. Harrison to mother, January 14, 1863, James M. Harrison Letters, Special Collections, University of Arkansas, Fayetteville. For other soldiers who wrote home about having the soldier's dream, see Nat Turner, ed., *A Southern Soldier's Letters Home: The Civil War Letters of Samuel Burney, Cobb's Georgia Legion, Army of Northern Virginia* (Macon, Ga.: Mercer University Press, 2002), 100; William A. Blair, ed., *A Politician Goes to War: The Civil War Letters of John White Geary* (University Park: Pennsylvania State University Press, 1995), 195; Barber and Swinson, *Civil War Letters of Charles Barber*, 63, 161.

60. John J. Hight, *History of the Fifty-Eighth Regiment of Indiana Volunteer Infantry* (Princeton, Ind.: Press of the Clarion, 1895), 414.

61. See, for example, Joseph Jones to wife, September 7–9, 1862 (GLC02739.010), and George W. Clark to sister, June 4, 1863 (GLC06167.05).

62. James Madison Bowler to Elizabeth Caleff Bowler, November 14, 1863, in *Go If You Think It Your Duty: A Minnesota Couple's Civil War Letters*, ed. Andrea R. Foroughi (St. Paul: Minnesota Historical Society Press, 2008), 211.

63. Gene Barr, ed., *A Civil War Chaplain and His Lady: Love, Courtship, and Combat from Fort Donaldson through the Vicksburg Campaign* (El Dorado Hills, Calif.: Savas Beatie, 2016), 287.

64. Jonathan E. Helmreich, ed., *To Petersburg with the Army of the Potomac: The Civil War Letters of Levi Bird Duff, 105th Pennsylvania Volunteers* (Jefferson, N.C.: McFarland, 2009), 106.

65. John Jones to wife, March 12, 1863 (GLC05981.20); William Wallace to Sarah, December 7, 1862, in John O. Holzhueter, ed., "William Wallace's Civil War Letters: The Virginia Campaign," *Wisconsin Magazine of History* 57 (Autumn 1957): 59; Burstein, *Lincoln Dreamt He Died*, 215; Henry Graves to wife, August 7, 1862, quoted in Wanda Burch, "The Home Voices Speak Louder Than Drums," New York History blog (April 30, 2012), available at www.newyorkhistoryblog.com/ (accessed May 29, 2015); Sam Farnum to Frank, November 14, 1862, War Letters, New-York Historical Society.

66. Lyman Jackman, *History of the Sixth New Hampshire Regiment in the War for the Union* (Concord, N.H.: Republican Press Association, 1891), 252–53.

67. George Hulslander to John Reeser, March 2, 1865 (GLC03523.43.24).

68. Earl J. Hess, *The Union Soldier in Battle: Enduring the Ordeal of Combat* (Lawrence: University Press of Kansas, 1997), 124.

69. Only a few soldiers saw their dreams of home as unwelcome or as a sign of weakness because they took their focus off the battlefield. See, for example, Ted Ownby, "Patriarchy in the World Where There Is No Parting: Power Relations in the Confederate Heaven," in *Southern Families at War: Loyalty and Conflict in the Civil War South*, ed. Catherine Clinton (New York: Oxford University Press, 2000), 230; William C. Davis and Meredith L. Swentor, eds., *Blue Grass Confederate: The Headquarters Diary of Edward O. Guerrant* (Baton Rouge: Louisiana State University Press, 1999), 526, 596; Jordan, *John Mead Gould*, 175; Burstein, *Lincoln Dreamt He Died*, 300n45. For an analysis of why so many soldiers thought of their loved ones during battle, see Reid Mitchell, *Civil War Soldiers: Their Expectations and Their Experiences* (New York: Simon and Schuster, 1988), 77.

70. Samuel Gilbert Webber to Nannie, December 22, 1862, Webber Letters, TMM. Soldiers and sailors had similar dreams of home during peacetime. For an antebellum sailor's dreams of home, see William McBlair to wife, May 12 and 20, 1857, September 25, 1857, January 21, 1858, and February 3, 1858, all in McBlair Papers, TMM.

"Now I Can Bear My Ills Patiently"

The Expanding Realm of Wisconsin Households during the Civil War

JULIE A. MUJIC

Mrs. C. L. Morgan of Sylvester, Wisconsin, wrote to her state's governor, Edward Salomon, on March 31, 1863. She implored him to consider the condition of wounded soldiers who were "unable to bear the fatigue, and hardships of camp life." Morgan insisted that military officers and army surgeons agreed that "home is the only spot where they can be restored to health" but that bureaucratic red tape prevented the soldiers' return into the households that would restore their vitality. She requested that Governor Salomon figure out a way around the obstructive policies that caused some soldiers to languish in hospitals, where commanding generals care "no more for them than . . . about the inhabitants of some other planet." It was in the homes of their mothers, Morgan vowed, that injured soldiers could regain the dignity of human life, and she held Salomon, "as legal Guardian of the rights of the people of Wisconsin," accountable for each soldier who died while yearning for home. Morgan insisted that she spoke for all "broken hearted mother[s]" who believed that their deceased sons might have recovered from their illnesses or injuries if they "could have come home"—back to the households on the Wisconsin homefront that yearned for their presence.[1]

The Civil War disrupted the household in Wisconsin, and state residents responded by shifting the place of the household, by flexing it and expanding it outward to encompass the battlefield. Soldiers welcomed the accompaniment of the household onto the battlefield and in many respects felt comforted and protected by it. This essay utilizes a sample of nearly 350 letters to the four Civil War governors of Wisconsin to examine the relationship between Wisconsin households, the state, and the battlefield. As part of a collection labeled "Wisconsin, Governor Relief Work" at the Wisconsin Historical Society, these letters include pleas for financial help, applications for jobs, demands for information, and political entreaties. This essay will focus on the letters in this collection that specifically demonstrate the way that women expressed their belief that the state acted as an intermediary in the movement of the household to the field of battle.[2]

In 1860, Wisconsin was a rapidly changing state. It had only attained statehood in 1848, yet the population grew 154 percent to more than 776,000 people between the 1850 and 1860 censuses. Most people lived in the southern half of the state, and New England transplants and immigrants from Germany and Ireland dominated the landscape. The population was divided into 147,473 households, according to the census, which is as close as we can come to an estimate for this period. The state was heavily agricultural—second in the nation in wheat production—and retained many qualities of a frontier society, including high personal debt, unreliable currency, and inadequate public schools. Politically, the rise of the Republican Party in the 1850s had attracted many voters, and the state's growing population shifted it firmly into that political camp. Lincoln carried Wisconsin by more than twenty thousand votes.[3]

The outbreak of war in 1861 took an immediate toll on many of these newly established Wisconsin households. Response to Lincoln's call for troops after Fort Sumter was enthusiastic; the federal government requested only one regiment of ten companies, but thirty-six companies volunteered within one week. Ultimately Wisconsin furnished more than ninety-one thousand soldiers to the war effort, which equated to one per every nine people living in the state and one soldier for every two voters (the highest percentage of eligible voters of any state in the North). This means that perhaps 60 percent or more of Wisconsin households underwent significant transformation when one of their members answered Lincoln's call for troops. Additionally, by the fall of 1861, Wisconsin faced economic depression due to the economic shifts caused by secession, and the governor's pleas for more financial support for soldiers' families went unheeded by the state legislature for many months. It was within this context that women on the Wisconsin homefront tried to figure out their role in the war.[4]

Women, as individuals and as members of Ladies' Aid Societies, sent contents of the household to the battlefield and, when that was not enough, went themselves, as representatives of the household and its responsibilities toward the soldiers. They labored in this manner in order to keep the household intact. Through these actions, they represented the household sphere in ways that contributed to the success of armies. They turned to what they knew best—providing for their family members within the paradigm of the household—but they did it in a new way. Wisconsin women appealed directly to the state, through the office of the governor, and expressed their expectation that state officials were duty-bound to serve their needs as constituents. The state had taken away their men; therefore, the state had to answer to the women. They inundated the governor with requests. The arriving letters demanded a separate filing system because they had not been received in such large numbers before. The collection is dated 1861–91, but twenty-two of the twenty-six folders are from the period 1861–65. Women viewed the governor as an intermediary in their determination to prevent the war from fracturing the household. Women in Wisconsin undertook steps to make sure that the value of their household remained recognized, and they hastened to inform the governor that he should in fact assist them in that goal. Wisconsin women—mothers, wives, and sisters—maintained that they had every right to see to the needs of their soldiers in the field. They argued that they should be able to participate in the war by applying the dynamics of the household to the battlefield wherever possible, both with supplies and with their personal attention.[5]

Ten days after the outbreak of war, Governor Alexander Randall issued a proclamation to the "Patriotic Women of Wisconsin." Recognizing immediately the crucial role women could play in the upcoming conflict, Randall highlighted his expectations for female participation. He asked them for "lint and bandages" for the army but then moved quickly to the plea for their support, something much more intangible. "Your husbands and brothers and sons are called upon to aid in subduing rebellion," he began, and then assured women, "It is your country and your government as well as theirs." He hoped that they would find it in their hearts to "give strength and courage and warm sympathies and cheering words to those who go to do battle." Essentially he expected women to support the soldiers and the war effort with both material and emotional support, much as they did within their households already.[6]

Wisconsin mothers, sisters, and wives took this call for support seriously and spent the next four years in conversation with the state regarding their contributions to both the homefront and the battlefront. Addie Ballow captured this spirit when she wrote to the governor that she did not want to "sit idly by while Fathers husbands sons and brothers fall." In her mind, women who "battle to sustain" a government "that *protects* them" should be "given a voice or hand to aid" it. Ballow believed that women's "influence *directs* in smaller ways the shafts that tell upon the mens hearts who hurl those well aimed shattering elements into the enemy battlements." She believed that the governor should allow her to fulfill this call through a nursing position among Wisconsin soldiers so that she could "toil again in their behalf." The word *again* illustrates the negotiations that opened between the governor and the women in response to the governor's request for loyalty. Women had toiled for men before the war in the households and therefore during the war should be sent where they could continue that work.[7]

Just as the government organized and paid men to serve in the war, women anticipated similar mobilization and financial support for their efforts at accumulating and shipping supplies to the soldiers. By the end of 1861, the state boasted forty-nine local organizations aimed at supplementing governmental supplies for the soldiers. One report to the governor in late 1861 listed sixty-nine packages sent to Wisconsin soldiers in St. Louis hospitals containing such things as bedding, socks, hospital supplies, books, and newspapers, as well as food items including dried fruits and berries. Officers there asked for additional donations from home, such as towels, underwear, and mending materials. This typical refrain resonated throughout the collection of letters—the soldiers needing more, the soldiers wanting more, and households scrambling to provide it.[8]

The request for funds to subsidize the shipments was the most frequent purpose of these letters related to supplies for the soldiers. Moreover, the letters revealed the expectation on the part of Wisconsin households that the effort to sustain the soldiers in the camps would be a joint one between "the Ladies" and the governor. "In behalf of the Ladies of Manitowoc," Mrs. C. C. Barnes wrote to the governor in May 1861 to find out whether "the soldiers of this state are sufficiently supplied with flannel shirts." The women in her community volunteered to make "two or three hundred for them" but only if the "Government [will] furnish the material."[9] A few months later, the Ladies' Patriotic Society of Reedsburg wrote that they had "prepared a box of lint, bandages, havelocks, pillows, &c" for the soldiers but wondered whether the state would pay for the transportation costs.[10]

Letters to the governor indicated that women who ran into problems funding shipments or figuring out where to send them expected the governor to provide solutions. They did not hesitate to instruct him on how to mobilize the homefront with more focus on care for the soldiers. In their minds, women should be his partners in these efforts. One mother asked the governor to "give hundreds of Mothers and Sisters in our State an opportunity of sending, to our brave boys who are nobly risking their lives in an unhealthy climate, some of the abundance, that we have at home." She wanted Governor Lewis to instruct the women of Wisconsin to gather supplies to relieve the men of their suffering from scurvy and other ailments. Earlier in the war, Martha Cook told Governor Salomon that after spending time over the past year at her husband's side in the army, particularly at Vicksburg, she saw that the "scarcity of sanitary supplies are great." Unsure of what to do, she had "sent off a box at my own expense," and she wrote to the governor in the fall of 1863 to request a position that would organize and transport materials from the households of Wisconsin to the soldiers in the field.[11]

Even as Wisconsin residents adjusted to the financial challenges that the war wrought on their households, they continued to send to their soldiers the kinds of materials that would be utilized in times of need at home. By 1863 the variety and quantity of supplies coming from the household had increased. Women recognized that soldiers at the front suffered for want of basic materials and stretched their already thin means to provide what they could. One "barrel of Hospital stores" that went from Madison, Wisconsin, to Memphis included rags, shirts, towels, pillows, slippers, dressing gowns, linen coats, lint, bandages, woolen socks, combs, and buttons. The women of this particular aid society also sent slippery elm, an herb used to treat sore throat, cough, diarrhea, skin wounds, and acid reflux. This kind of herbal remedy was used regularly in Wisconsin households and would have offered the soldiers a reminder of the comforts of home. The shipment also contained "reading matter," which was highly valued among soldiers to keep them abreast of news at home and to entertain them during the long days and nights in camp.[12]

Beyond medical supplies and clothing, Wisconsin residents sent available luxuries from home, with the belief that they would comfort "the sick and wounded" or help soldiers in camps avoid conditions such as scurvy. Even in these cases, they perceived the governor as the liaison between their efforts and the success of the soldiers. The Ladies of Prairie du Chien "prepared a box containing brandies, wines, preserves, and other delicacies" in May 1862 that they hoped would reach hospitalized Wisconsin soldiers. One aid society sent porter beer to the wounded of Gettysburg "to strengthen them and build them up."[13] The Platteville Ladies' Aid Society explained that their shipment of articles to soldiers was designed to "alleviate your sufferings." They hoped that the materials gathered and sent would relieve "monotony" and remind the boys in the field that they "are our pride: and when rebels are in the dust we will welcome you home with pride and joy and thankful hearts."[14] The aforementioned prevalence of scurvy in the camps in particular prompted soldiers to request household goods from Wisconsin. One general asked the Milwaukee Soldiers' Aid Society to send antiscorbutic goods, which provide vitamin C to combat scurvy. The society intended to ship pickles, dried fruit, and vegetables to the regiment but asked the governor to cover the shipping costs.[15] The same society secretary wrote again in February 1865 for funds to cover another shipment of goods to help fight scurvy in a regiment with thirty-five soldiers suffering from the condition.[16]

The women who worked tirelessly to provide these kinds of supplies to army camps and hospitals were rewarded by reports of the positive impact of their efforts. They shared that news with the governor regularly. One mother from Racine sent a letter to Governor James T. Lewis in September 1864 in which she included an excerpt from a letter she had received from an officer in the Twenty-Second Wisconsin Infantry, then entrenched outside Atlanta. He mentioned a lack of variety in their rations and a dearth of sanitary supplies, including bedding, hospital necessities, and food. The officer argued that the state should organize a way to obtain needed items from the homefront as "these good things" furnished from Wisconsin's households would *"prevent* very much sickness, strengthen our army, and, I believe, save many valuable lives." As an example, he shared the reaction of two Indiana regiments who received pickles, pickled onions, and dried fruit from their state: "You can hardly imagine how they improve the health and spirits of the boys."[17]

Many female residents were not satisfied with sending household goods to the front or campaigning to transport sick loved ones home; they wanted to go themselves. The two most numerous types of letters in this category were applications for nursing positions and requests for passes to visit a sick or wounded relative. This physical extension of the household was intended to protect and provide for loved ones in ways that only the household could provide satisfactorily. The majority of letters to the governor requesting positions outside the state were seeking opportunities as regimental nurses. One-third of these letters date from the first year of the war. Those who rushed to the front did so for a variety of reasons, mirroring the diverse motivations of soldiers themselves. Some women offered their services generally wherever they were needed in the South, while other applicants specified regiments that they wished to accompany.

Women who applied to serve as nurses believed that they could reunite or even re-create a household near the battlefield. Applications for nursing positions came from all corners of the state, from all ages, from all marital statuses, and from all stages of emotional strain due to the war. The letters to the governor in this category spoke of duty, gender, honor, and courage, but their constant refrain was that of family. Mrs. J. A. Torrey already had two years' experience by 1864 when she petitioned for another nursing position. She had "been in battles and taken care of wounded men, [had] nursed the sick in hospital, had charge of and distributed sanitary supplies, spent days upon hospital boats and in camp." She lost her husband and son in the war and did not want to "live through the long dreary days perhaps years which may be allotted me with nothing but tears.... I must have something to do, some care which will give me no time to dwell upon these things. A life of idleness will kill me or make me a burden to myself and those around me."[18] A second letter spelled it out clearly for the governor: "I have given my husband, my only and noble son for my country. It was all I had to give. The sacrifice has been complete. I only ask for employment, for care, to make my lonely saddened life endurable."[19] Even though the war took her two closest family members, she felt that continuing her work of nursing wounded soldiers was a healthy responsibility for her. The war allowed her the opportunity to create a new household for herself, and in so doing, perhaps she could save lives to help her heal her own wounds.

Many letters revealed a simple desire to be with those they loved. Nursing seemed to provide a way to justify to the governor women's presence at the front. Women sought and gained entrance to the realm of the battlefield because the emptiness left by the soldiers' absence was more than some families could bear. One group of women from Baraboo wanted to accompany the Sauk County Riflemen in May 1861, while the father of an orderly in the Fourth Wisconsin Regiment offered to care for the sick and wounded for free if only to satisfy his "natural desire to be with [his son] if possible."[20] One woman from Hartford, Frances Helmer, asked to go with her brother's company because she believed "they would fight better if their sisters were their to take care of them."[21] The pastor of a Congregational church in Union Grove addressed Governor Salomon in February 1863 on behalf of two women who wished to be nurses at the hospital in Nashville because one had a husband and the other had a brother "stationed at that place." Pastor Dickinson closed his letter by stating his hope that the governor "will find it consistent to grant the commissions they desire."[22]

Women who applied to be nurses did not hesitate to advise the governor on military policy. Often women combined comments about how nursing was one of the only options available to them with an argument that employing women in this capacity would allow more men to be relieved for service at the front. This line of reasoning demonstrated their willingness to use political rationale for their own wartime purposes and their belief that the governor acted as the person who could effect change. "Is there not places now occupied by men," Susan Chapman wondered in August 1862, "that might be by ladies, and let those that are now there go forth to duty?"[23] J. Lurvey insisted that women in her community "wish to take the place of those waiting upon our sick & wounded & allow them to return to their Regts." "Why why," she demanded, "*cannot* their places be filled by our Noble & Patriotic Ladies?"[24] Addie Ballow added that "woman . . . does her work of love infinitely better than men in and about hospitals," and men should be sent back to their regiments to prevent "broken ranks." After chastising the governor about taxing the families of volunteer soldiers, Ballow returned to the importance of women near the fields of battle, asking, "Is there no way for women to be recognized as *help* to put down this rebellion?"[25]

The governors' responses to these applications regarding nursing opportunities varied. It is not difficult to see why women were confused about their powers in this matter and continued to apply directly to that highest state office. In some cases, the governors advised women on where and when to proceed to begin a nursing position in an army hospital. Those responses were rare, however, and the majority of responses fell into a few categories: the state's budget for nurses was used up; the governor did not have the power to appoint nurses at that time; the colonels had the right to appoint a certain number of nurses to their regiments, but the governor himself had no control over it; the applicant should apply directly to the Sanitary Commission (the governors usually recommended the North West Sanitary Commission in Chicago); and the governor might be able to send some additional nurses soon, so please write back again.

The governors were careful to express appreciation for the women's support in their responses and direct them as to how to accomplish their goals if the state could not address their demands. This type of response was especially necessary because the governors also read in these letters quite direct opinions regarding contemporary political issues facing the state. Wisconsin women recognized the concerns imperative to their communities and communicated them, often laced with political messages. In using this language, the letter writers expanded the household to influence the military situation, expecting the governors to realize that their treatment of the citizens during this time of crisis would result in their future electoral success or failure. Women expressed views that governors had to take seriously because they understood that they depended on the women of the homefront to support the soldiers. As supplies and direct care from the households became ever more crucial during the war, governors could not afford to overlook the political opinions coming from within Wisconsin's homes.

Wisconsin women whose husbands were already at war as volunteers demanded that the governor lessen the burden on their families while increasing it on those who shirked their duty. In particular, the challenging political climate of the midwar period only added to Wisconsin women's belief that the governor should listen to their ideas, often regarding how to manage dissent on the homefront. The zenith of Copperhead popularity in Wisconsin, as in much of the North, occurred during the first six months of 1863 as a response to the Emancipation Proclamation. Desertion increased across regiments, and after this point enlistment relied heavily on men of Republican leanings. In Wisconsin, Democrats came down strongly against the war and emancipation and spoke harshly against the threat of conscription. Fear of economic competition from freed slaves who might migrate north drove much of this opposition. White men who had recently moved to Wisconsin themselves did not want an abolitionist war to hinder their economic potential, and they avoided the war as a way to express their distaste for its changing goals.[26]

Questions of loyalty and devotion to the cause raised the ire of many letter writers, even though those discussions were not usually the main purpose of their missives. In sending their loved ones to war, many Wisconsin women anticipated that political leaders would consider their opinions when shaping the outcome and meaning of that sacrifice. For example, in 1862 Susan Chapman asked Governor Salomon whether a draft would occur soon because she was worried that "it will fall on our farming community." Ultimately, though, she felt so strongly that "our country must be saved" that she conceded to the governor that she supported the conscription of that already "diminished" class.[27] E. M. Hecock concurred but asked the governor specifically to "draft and take some of these confederates out from among us." She was dismayed by the lack of financial support for the families of soldiers and told the governor that men in her county did not help struggling families and boasted that they would only serve if drafted. Hecock stated that she was unsure whether it was because they had "so much secession in their hearts" or because families of men who already enlisted "have been so neglected by the state."[28] Hecock did not seem to care which was the cause. She wanted the unhelpful, and therefore in her mind unpatriotic, men gone either way. Marietta Hawes chimed in with her expectation that men who enlisted voluntarily, and the women who thus gave up "our dear Husbands and our all for the sake of our beloved country," should receive more praise and recognition than "one that has hung back until the last minute."[29] Emma Kelty challenged the governor in March 1864 on whether war widows should be taxed to raise "bountys for volunteers, for the sake of keeping copperheads & slinks at home." She connected taxing the households and the issue of disloyalty in her letter and ended her remonstration regarding the failures of the state to provide for widows with this: "I tell you the soldiers in the Army don't like to have there familys served so while they are fighting in the defence of there country."[30]

As the war progressed through these challenges, appeals for passes through the lines to visit or nurse a specific soldier arrived in increasing numbers. The women who wrote these pleas did not bother to justify their demands in terms of patriotism or duty to the country. Their only goal was to save the life of a loved one deemed to be on the verge of death. Arriving mostly in the last three years of the war, these letters demonstrate how the war began to take its toll on the households of Wisconsin and how women on the homefront believed that their presence on the military front, the expansion of their household that their presence represented, was the only hope for the recovery of their family member. In their eyes, this responsibility could no longer be left to the military; only the household could serve the needs of the soldiers. Furthermore, the women insisted, the governor was responsible for granting these passes, and they expected them in a timely fashion.

Women informed the governor that their methods for care and tending were required at the front to supplement those provided by the military bureaucracy. The requests for passes to minister to sick and wounded sons, brothers, and husbands began to trickle in during the second half of 1862, as military campaigns in all theaters of war saw increased action. Susan Jordan begged the governor to let her go to her husband in a hospital in Norfolk, Virginia. She had just buried their only child and wanted a chance to save her child's father.[31] In another letter J. Fowler gave the governor explicit instructions about how to pave her way safely into the South to nurse her wounded husband back to health, including a reminder that she expected to obtain the pass because her husband was "a faithful man & devoted soldier."[32] Desperate to get to her brother who was "sick, nigh unto death" in Nashville, Melissa Pope relied on emotional and religious pressure to sway the governor's hand. "Oh if you have a heart do for the love of God grant it [to] me," she wrote in December 1862.[33]

The bulk of this genre of letters appeared in 1863 and 1864, and as the Union army moved deeper into the South, women's requests for passes followed that lead. They demanded to travel further east in Tennessee and into Georgia, Texas, and Virginia, for example, undeterred by the increasing distances of these locations from their homes in Wisconsin.[34] In their eyes, the household could stretch even across these long miles. Husbands themselves began to push for household presence, as Sarah Van Allen informed the governor in October 1863 that her husband "is sick and requests me to come to him."[35] Albert Winchell of the Eighth Wisconsin Battery wrote directly to the governor himself, appealing for a pass for his wife to join him in Murfreesboro, Tennessee, because he was "desirous of having her come through as I have been sick for some time."[36] In November 1864, when Winchell sent this request, the Union army still faced a threat from Confederate forces moving through this part of the South, and it could not have been clear yet when those forces would be quelled.

Women also felt no qualms about asking to go to places wrought with destruction and danger. Amanda Brown requested a pass as she made plans to rush to her husband's side in Vicksburg, just four days after the Confederates surrendered there.[37] She was determined to go, as was Mrs. Lynch of Sheboygan, but the latter expected to head to Vicksburg in March 1863, right in the middle of the siege. Lynch explained to the governor that she would "leave [her] little ones for a while to go and see their dying father," who was with the Seventeenth Wisconsin Regiment in Vicksburg. She told the governor that if he granted her request, she would teach her "little ones" to pray for him.[38] Margaret Herron went one step further, asking for a pass to go to her husband, who was wounded and "in the hands of the enemy." She did not know whether he had yet been exchanged, but she wanted the governor to determine his situation and then send her personally to see to his well-being. "Believe me," she assured the governor, "he is worthy a true womans love for he is all that is noble brave and true."[39]

Women who asked for passes to tend sons, brothers, and husbands deep in the South are all dated late 1864, after the Union army had made progress into that region through Sherman's March. As the Union gained control of more territory, women from Wisconsin believed it to be their right to enter those spaces as rightful representatives of the households who claimed and supported the soldiers. Rebecca Hinchly requested a pass to go to her sick son in Rome, Georgia, and asked that the governor write whatever was necessary to make her loyalty clear to commanding officers in the region. She wanted to start for Georgia within a few days' time, and she asked the governor to rush his response to her request, "for I fear he will be dead before I get there."[40] Mary Sickler asked the governor if she could go to the Union hospital in Alexandria, Virginia, in November 1864, where she could nurse her sick husband, who was "unfit for field service," and assist with the other patients there who "were suffering for want of proper care"— "proper" in her eyes meaning someone from home, someone from within Wisconsin households.[41] Letters of this nature kept arriving—Mrs. J. A. Rapp wanted to go to Chattanooga; Maranda Lewis hoped to tend to her husband in Nashville; Jane Cassin intended to find her son in Missouri.[42]

Governors had somewhat more power to grant these requests for passes

than they did to hire nurses, so these letters met with success more frequently than did the nursing applications. In these cases the variety of
responses included the governor had no power to grant a pass to that location and he suggested applying to the military officials in charge of that
area; the governor had no passes at his disposal at that time; the governor
could not issue a pass but would try to find out more information from state
agents near the soldier in question; the legislature had not given the governor funds to issue passes/pay for travel for residents; or he answered affir-
matively with instructions as to how and when to proceed to the desired
location. Again, the diverse range of responses was what likely continued
the stream of requests into the governor's office.

By the time war prosperity arrived in Wisconsin in the fall of 1863,
women had firmly established a line of communication with the governor that reflected their belief in his ability to see to their needs. However,
letters from soldiers' families also illustrated that the growing Wisconsin
economy was slow to trickle down to their homes. The majority of letters
related to pleas for financial assistance arrived in 1863 with only a slight
downturn in 1864. Still, the highest number of letters received directly from
soldiers asking for a woman from their household to come to the battlefield
occurred in 1862 and 1864; the former was when the financial crisis worsened, and the latter was when those affected by it the most were still suffering. War prosperity translated into success at the polls for Republican
candidates in the fall of 1863, effectively beating back the short-lived Copperhead appeal in the state, and by the end of the war Wisconsin held a
place of prestige among the victorious states of the North.[43]

Wisconsin households proved that the Northern war effort required the
mobilization of the whole society, not just its citizen soldiers. People who
made a life in a place like Wisconsin in the 1860s, where almost everything
was new and somewhat tenuous, moved beyond the challenges created on
the frontier to shape households that actively supplied and supported the
soldiers in the field.[44] Even in the farthest reaches of the Midwest, those
who remained behind on the homefront negotiated the changes in their
households caused by war by flexing their household realms to encompass the battlefield. Women in particular attempted to provide continuity
to their sons, brothers, and husbands by sending aspects of the household
to the military camps. When they did not feel that the government was
providing adequate care, whether medical or otherwise, these women petitioned the government to fill those voids themselves. Thus the household
remained central during the war as a counterweight to the demands and
influence of the military establishment.

Furthermore, women contributed to the maturation of the state of Wisconsin during the war. They helped push the state past its prewar frontier mentality into an institution that had clear ties, obligations, and a history with the people who called it home. When war began, many Wisconsin residents had only just arrived and had little in the way of loyalty or affiliation with the state government. Granted, Wisconsin may have been far away from the location of most of the conflict that shook the nation, but women saw no reason why they should not assert their value across those distances and demand assistance from the government in their midst. Wisconsin women believed that the household rightly belonged merged with the field of battle during the Civil War, and they demonstrated this conviction through a tremendous dedication to the movement of goods and their own bodies. As the war went on and their letters to the governor became increasingly politicized in nature, governors could not afford to overlook the opinions coming from Wisconsin's households. Governors did their best to address the demands radiating from the homefront, and each letter received an individual response. The contributions of women and their perceptions of war impacted enlistment, homefront stability, and the flow of supplies and nurses going from the state.

The presence of the household on America's Civil War battlefields was pivotal to the success of armies, and both the families and the soldiers knew it. The four wartime governors of Wisconsin surely could not disagree when, in July 1863, George Smith, a state agent in Memphis hospitals, sent Governor Salomon an update regarding how local women who had accompanied him to the South as nurses were contributing to the well-being of the soldiers. "They are doing much good in their wards," he noted, "and also visiting our Wisconsin soldiers in other wards and Hospitals." The women from Wisconsin had received a warm welcome in Memphis, and Smith quoted a soldier who was astonished that the people of the state "think so much of us at home as to volunteer to come way down here to take care of us." "Now I can bear my ills patiently," said one Wisconsin soldier. In the end, Wisconsin's soldiers benefited from the women in their state who recognized that the governor could help them make whole again what the war had threatened to tear asunder.[45]

NOTES

The title is taken from George C. Smith, July 13, 1863, box 2, folder 5, Wisconsin, Governor Relief Work, 1861–91, Wisconsin Historical Society Archives (hereafter listed just with box and folder information).

1. Mrs. C. L. Morgan, March 31, 1863, box 2, folder 4.

2. Alexander W. Randall served in the office until January 1862, when he was replaced by Louis P. Harvey. Harvey died in an accident four months into his term while visiting Wisconsin soldiers in the South and was succeeded by Edward Salomon. In January 1864 James T. Lewis took office. All four were Republicans.

3. Census of 1860, Miscellaneous Statistics, 350; Frank L. Klement, *Wisconsin and the Civil War* (Madison: State Historical Society of Wisconsin, 1963), 4–10.

4. Klement, *Wisconsin and the Civil* War, 15–16. For more information on the economic hardships facing the Wisconsin homefront early in the war, see Frank Klement, "Copperheads and Copperheadism in Wisconsin: Democratic Opposition to the Lincoln Administration," *Wisconsin Magazine of History* 42, no. 3 (Spring 1959): 182, 184. The letter collection to the governor of Wisconsin that serves as the main source for this essay also contains evidence that residents, especially families of soldiers, faced financial difficulties. In fact, letters from soldiers' families requesting help from the state to aid in relieving destitution formed 22 percent of the collection. They alone would make a fascinating future case study.

5. Recent scholarship confirms this notion of the strength and flexibility of households in the Midwest during the Civil War era. Ginette Aley and Joseph Anderson explain that "mid-nineteenth-century farm husbands and wives tended to view themselves as partners, both of whose contributions to the farm were absolutely necessary." Aley and Anderson, eds., *Union Heartland: The Midwestern Home Front during the Civil War* (Carbondale: Southern Illinois University Press, 2013), 85. Considering that the Midwest was 88 percent rural in 1860, it is likely that most of the women writing to the governor during the war lived in a rural area. Aley and Anderson, *Union Heartland*, 3. Additionally, there were few cities in Wisconsin at the time, and review of the letters in the file reveals that the majority derived from outside of Madison, the capital, and Milwaukee. Also, Aley notes in her essay in that volume that "a woman's life [was defined] almost entirely by her relationships and in terms of her family," according to gender norms of the era. Looking at the relationship between the household and the battlefield is a natural line of inquiry when taking into account how invested both men and women in Wisconsin households would have been in the stability of that familial system. Aley argues that midwestern women focused on "preserving their world [as] their primary mission." Aley, "Inescapable Realities: Rural Midwestern Women and Families during the Civil War," in Aley and Anderson, *Union Heartland*, 126, 133.

6. Alexander W. Randall, April 22, 1861, Proclamations by the Governor, box 1, folder 1.

7. Addie L. Ballow, August 27, 1864, box 3, folder 5.

8. H. A. Reid, box 1, folder 1.

9. Mrs. C. C. Barnes, May 25, 1861, box 1, folder 1.

10. Mrs. E. Danforth, August 19, 1861, box 1, folder 1. See also letters in box 1, folder 7 dated October 23 and November 20, 1862, from the Ladies' Aid Societies of Lancaster and Jefferson, respectively.

11. Mother to James T. Lewis, September 5, 1864, box 3, folder 5. See also Mrs.

Hopkins to George Smith, August 3, 1863, box 2, folder 6; Martha Cook, October 13, 1863, box 2, folder 7.

12. Mrs. B. Hopkins to George Smith, August 3, 1861, box 2, folder 6.

13. W. Y. Selleck, August 23, 1863, box 2, folder 6.

14. Letter from Platteville Ladies' Aid Society, n.d., box 3, folder 2.

15. August 19, 1864, box 3, folder 5.

16. February 21, 1865, box 3, folder 3. With regard to the first request from the Milwaukee Soldiers' Aid Society, the governor answered that a state agent would come pick up the materials and deliver them south to the proper recipients. In February 1865 he responded that the Society could forward the materials directly and then submit receipts to him for reimbursement.

17. Mother to James T. Lewis, September 5, 1864, box 3, folder 5.

18. Mrs. J. A. Torrey, August 29, 1864, box 3, folder 6.

19. Ibid. There are two letters from the same date—one addressed to the governor and one addressed to a Mr. Allen at the governor's office. Both letters ended up in the same file.

20. May 14, 1861; George W Durgin, July 25, 1861, box 1, folder 1.

21. Frances Helmer, May 10, 1861, box 1, folder 1.

22. D. Dickinson, February 28, 1863, box 2, folder 2.

23. Susan Chapman, August 18, 1862, box 1, folder 4.

24. J. Lurvey, August 16, 1862, box 1, folder 6.

25. Addie L. Ballow, August 27, 1864, box 3, folder 5.

26. Klement, *Wisconsin and the Civil War*, 47–52.

27. Susan Chapman, August 18, 1862, box 1, folder 4.

28. E. M. Hecock, July 31, 1862, box 1, folder 4.

29. Marietta Hawes, August 2, 1862, box 1, folder 4.

30. Emma Kelty, March 31, 1864, box 3, folder 7.

31. Susan Jordan, August 27, 1862, box 1, folder 4.

32. J. E. Fowler, September 28, 1862, box 1, folder 6.

33. Melissa Pope, December 29, 1862, box 2, folder 1.

34. See letters dated May 30, 1864, November 9, 1864, November 11, 1864, and November 26, 1864, box 3, folder 4.

35. Sarah E. Van Allen, October 2, 1863, box 2, folder 7.

36. Albert Winchell, November 20, 1864, box 3, folder 4.

37. Amanda Brown, July 8, 1862, box 2, folder 5.

38. Mrs. Michael Lynch, March 31, 1863, box 2, folder 4.

39. Margaret Herron, May 24, 1864, box 3, folder 6.

40. Rebecca Hinchly, November 2, 1864, box 3, folder 4.

41. Mary J. Sickler, November 9, 1864, box 3, folder 4.

42. Mrs. J. A. Rapp, November 26, 1864; Maranda Lewis, November 7, 1864, box 3, folder 4; Jane Cassin, July 20, 1864, box 3, folder 5.

43. Klement, *Wisconsin and the Civil War*, 72–78, 95–105.

44. State historian Ruth DeYoung Kohler noted that at the time of the outbreak of war, "Wisconsin was a young state with a relatively small population. Its organization was new and struggling, and its financial condition was poor in comparison with eastern states." Ruth DeYoung Kohler, *The Story of Wisconsin Women* (Committee on Wisconsin Women for the 1948 Wisconsin Centennial, 1948), 38.

45. George C. Smith, July 13, 1863, box 2, folder 5.

Written on the Heart

Soldiers' Letters, the Household Supply Line, and the Relational War

LeeAnn Whites

In May 1863 John Smith, a local postmaster and dry goods merchant in Plains, Ohio, decided to do his friends and neighbors a favor by hand delivering their mail to them instead of waiting for them to pick it up in his store as was customary. Smith knew that many of these families were waiting with concern to hear from their brothers, sons, and husbands who were far off fighting for the Union cause in the Civil War. He perhaps considered it part of his patriotic duty to walk the extra mile for the members of his community who were sacrificing so much for the war, and perhaps the joy and the relief he witnessed delivering that mail prompted him to suggest to Montgomery Blair, U.S. postmaster general, that the practice should be made universal. Taken with the idea, Blair passed it to the president, and in July 1863 Abraham Lincoln initiated the practice of home delivery of the mail by the U.S. Postal Service.

Today's Americans are still the beneficiaries of the force of that bond between the soldiers who fought on the military front and their kin at home. Archives all over the country hold thousands of these letters, eagerly read at the time and carefully saved for posterity. Historians still work their way through this truly vast array, publishing an ongoing stream of individual soldiers' letters as well as exploring the collections as a whole. It was perhaps Bell Wiley, in his two now classic works, *The Life of Billy Yank* and *The Life of Johnny Reb*, who first realized the possibilities that the soldiers' letters offer the historian to answer questions about the experience and the motivation of the common soldier in the field. Few historians, however, have considered the correspondence of Civil War soldiers as what remains, the physical detritus of what was at the time a domestic supply line, the tip of the iceberg of a critical wartime household exchange. The hundreds of thousands of letters written during the war remain as a testimony to the way household relations persisted, even as those relationships warred against distance, distress, and, sadly, the death of household members that the war brought.[1] The war itself was in fact born out of struggle over household relations, that is, whether some households would be built on the backs of enslaved people, and whether those enslaved people had the right to their own households. It should then come as no surprise that the household played a critical role in the war itself if only because the demands of fighting the war posed an immediate, practical threat to so many households, regardless of their position on slavery and the rights of enslaved people and slaveholders. The tens of thousands of Civil War letters that remain to this day reflect the extent of the contribution that individual households made to the supply of their men in the field. For although members of soldiers' households may or may not have cared about the causes of the war, whether Union or Confederate, they cared about the fate of their soldier kin and the viability of their households.[2]

From the outset of the war, households on both sides confronted the question of how the emotional and material exchange systems upon which households were built would reconfigure in the face of the departure of so many men to the front. In *All That Makes the Man*, historian Stephen Berry suggests that on an emotional level, letters from home, especially letters from wives to their husbands, could literally make the difference between men who were able to maintain sufficient morale to soldier on and survive the conflict and those who could not. A soldier's letters can then be read as a critical supply line in providing that soldier with the emotional sustenance he needed for his very survival. He depended on those letters every bit as much as he needed formal military provisions.[3]

The correspondence between George Lowe and his wife, Lizzie, demonstrates the vital nature of household correspondence. George Lowe served in the Fifth Regiment of the Iowa Volunteers out of Burlington. His correspondence with his wife began on July 12, 1861, shortly after his enlistment. In his first letter home he wrote that the "fare is first rate" and that the soldiers were all in "good spirits and anxious to make a blow at the rebels." In his next letter, George began a refrain that would only grow louder until the day he died. He wrote to complain that Lizzie had failed to answer him. "What makes me feel so bad about not getting a letter from you," he wrote, "is that nearly every man that went from Monroe and Newton have got letters and have begun to throw it up already that your Wife don't think anything of you or she would have wrote to you before this time." Sadly, for George this pattern of what he saw as neglect by his wife would persist. In subsequent letters he wrote of the joy the occasional letter from her brought to him as well as of the long drawn-out misery he experienced when he received no reply to his own frequent letters home.[4]

It is perhaps because of the way in which soldiers experienced their emotional loss so acutely as well as the intense significance that they attached to the receipt of letters from loved ones that we have failed in large part to see the need for material supply that these letters also document. In the case of the correspondence between George Lowe and his wife, there is a record not only of the emotional supply that letters provided soldiers but also of the material supply associated with the nurturing work of wives and mothers. By the time of his second letter home, George was bemoaning his miserable lack of mail and the neglect he was suffering as a result of it, and he was also reporting to his wife on the condition of his health, which had been "alright," although "a majority of our company has been complaining, mostly of Diarrhea." His letters continued to detail complaints about life in camp. He wrote that he did not like the "fare we get here at all. . . . nothing for dinner but salty side meat, bread and water and for breakfast we had the same with the exception we had some coffee." By August 3 he described to her how the men were "hungry as dogs and glad to get a piece of dry bread to knaw at. . . . This kind of living made me have the sick headache very bad and I have it now so that I can hardly write."[5]

Indeed, not only did the food and bad water give men the sick headache and diarrhea but also it often killed them. As a result, their families at home, especially their wives and mothers whose responsibility it was to care for their health, had good reason to be concerned. As is well documented, more Civil War soldiers died of disease than died of battlefield wounds. In fact, the number one killer of soldiers was dysentery. The military ration of beef or pork and some sort of starch that the soldiers regularly described in their letters home, even if unspoiled and in sufficient quantity, was not enough to keep them healthy. In some cases, soldiers could supplement the standard issue diet. Sometimes delegations of the local ladies would provide nearby soldiers with food, but other times the acquisition of supplies from civilians was more irregular and had to be taken on by the soldiers themselves. Soldiers' letters reflected this unpredictability. For example, one soldier wrote home that "Major Cleveland and myself went out and took a hog prisoner and had some fresh meat for breakfast," and another wrote of "liberating a rebel pig." In addition, soldiers could purchase almost anything from sutlers, although often for a highly inflated price. Nelson Huson

wrote to his parents in Illinois in March 1863 to note his naïveté in enlisting some six months earlier. "I thought then," he commented, "that there
was nothing like being a soldier & getting 13 dollars a month. . . . But if a
fellow buys anything here he has got to pay for it." He noted the high price
of potatoes, "ten cents a pound for some and everything in proportion."[6]

Soldiers also described the ways in which standard issue military clothing was insufficient, as it generally did not include boots, socks, gloves,
hats, or overcoats—the sorts of things soldiers desperately needed on long
exposed marches, or nightly picket duty in the rain, or even just in camp in
the dead of winter. Soldiers received a $2 a month clothing allotment, but
they found that the cost of being properly outfitted regularly outstripped
that amount. Furthermore, no matter how careful a soldier was with money,
how rarely he bought a pound of potatoes or a piece of fruit, how long he
tried to go into the winter without a proper coat, how often he "liberated"
a pig or caught a fish rather than spend his wages with the sutlers, little
could make up for the fact that both armies routinely failed to pay their
men for months at a time. As one Union soldier wrote to his family after
six months of not being paid and upon hearing a rumor that the paymas-
ter was finally coming, it still would not amount to the total due as it was
"general practice" to hold back the last two months' pay.[7]

To combat these shortages and acquire the necessary provisions, these
soldiers wrote home and asked for help. The people that soldiers most often
turned to in their letters to ask for the desired shirt, gloves, hat, tea, cakes,
meats, and butter (especially butter as soldiers struggled to keep weight on
to better withstand the bouts of dysentery) that they needed to meet their
basic needs were their female kin. Soldiers turned to women because it was
their place in the household order to provide not only their love and affection for their kin but also their food and clothing. If the soldier were an
unmarried man, as most soldiers were, he would likely make these requests
of his mother and sisters, and if he were married, he would request them of
his wife. Soldiers' letters frequently began with an account of the state of
their health, the items that they needed, and their appreciation for what
they had already received through the domestic supply line from home.

George Henry Mellish of Woodstock, Vermont, who enlisted in Company C, Sixth Vermont Regiment in February 1862 at age eighteen and
served until discharged three years later at the end of the war, left behind
a treasure trove of letters. He began writing to his mother during his first
month of service, and his existing 160 letters document in great detail the
supply of food and clothing she sent to him. On October 23, 1862, some six
months after his initial enlistment, Mellish wrote of supplies he expected

and wanted from home: "Oh I want that box. I want a pair of boots, shirts, gloves and stockings." He was not looking for supplies only for himself. "I want two pairs of gloves, one a size larger than mine, for another fellow. I want good ones. I want a fancy woolen knit cap for winter evenings in camp." Furthermore, Mellish hoped the anticipated box would contain "some good navy tobacco." He left any other supplies to his mother's discretion. "If there is anything else you think of that you think I need you may send it but my wants grow fewer, as I grow older in the service. And in time I think I should want nothing."[8]

Although Mellish was undoubtedly correct in perceiving himself as toughening up under the rigors of military life, his letters over the next few months recorded the receipt of butter, cakes, pickles, stamps, paper, tobacco, and even money to buy more things from the sutlers when he was not paid on time. Mellish was, in fact, fortunate to have a hardworking and devoted mother and a large household that was willing and able to part with all the provisions he wanted that they unquestioningly sent to him. His father was a shoemaker, and there was only one other child in the household, George's younger sister, Martha, so the family could focus on George's needs. Even so, it was no small thing for the Mellish family to part with all these supplies. In order to better keep track of what she sent him, George's mother, Mary, regularly numbered each of her letters. Indeed, much of the correspondence between them consisted not only of George's requests but also of his mother's queries concerning what had arrived and in what condition it had arrived. George reported on the contents of his packages, remarking about one package that "the box came through as nice as possible, everything was just as good as it was when it started. I got everything you spoke of but the dried apple."[9]

The Mellish family offers an example of a household, although stressed emotionally and materially by the loss of their son to the Union war effort, that was able to successfully reconfigure and carry on. When George did not receive his wages, they sent him money. When George needed clothing or food, they sent what he requested. When he lost his knapsack in a hasty retreat, his mother replaced his stamps and his paper so he could write home. Supplies from the Mellish home were also regularly accompanied by motherly advice regarding the dangers of drinking and gambling, endeavors that were widespread in military camps. In addition, when George, tired and depressed at the seemingly endless nature of the war, wrote to his mother, she encouraged him to remain with his regiment, counseling him to consider the long-term consequences of anything less than honorable behavior. Altogether then the Mellish household supply line enabled George to avoid the high costs of the camp sutlers and still have clothing and decent food. Furthermore, the entire household benefited from this domestic supply line, as George was able to save his pay and ultimately send some of his money home. As he proudly wrote to his mother on January 24, 1864, "I don't worry a cents worth about the money I have sent home, I know it is in good safe hands and I want father to use it just as he has a mind to . . . to get a cistern. Won't it be handy."[10]

Although the correspondence in the Mellish household was maintained by the mother and much of it revolved around her continued provision of food and clothing for her son—a vital aspect of her normal household role—Mellish's father also sometimes sent messages in his wife's letters concerning financial matters. For example, Mary Mellish told George that his father wanted to know what George planned to do with his bounty. George also wrote to his father within his letters to his mother, specifically asking her to tell his father about certain things—occasionally about politics and more frequently about finances. In November 1863 he wrote directly to his father, "I have saved out of my clothing money since I have been out here $34 and some odd cents and shall get it with my next pay. . . . I shall send home more next payday than I have before." In addition, occasionally George asked that his father make him a nice pair of boots or he complimented the gifts his father sent. In a December 1862 letter to his sister he wrote, "Martha, tell Father the boots were just a fit." The following May, he again wrote to his father through his sister: "I wish you would ask father to get me a knife." As with his letters to his mother, George's messages to his father reflected the supply that his father as the male head of household would have given him were he still at home. These requests clearly highlighted the gendered division of labor in this household where the father, as head of household, was responsible for financial matters and as a shoemaker was of course responsible for the family shoes.

Although the Mellishes were able to shift the labor and relations of the household to successfully supply their soldier son, other households were less able to do so. Twenty-one-year-old John Robert Lowery joined Company E of Mallett's Battalion in July 1862 and served as a member of the North Carolina Camp Guards. His correspondence with his mother serves to illustrate how the basic resources of a household mattered in what a mother was able to provide. Lowery, known as Rob, was a teacher and the eldest of the family's eight children. As yeomen farmers who owned several slaves, the Lowerys appear to have had the resources to supply their son with at least what the Mellish household was able to provide for their son.[11]

Misfortune struck the Lowerys, however, even before the war began, when the father, Hugh, died in February 1861. By the time Rob wrote his first letter home to his mother in June 1862, two of his brothers, William and James, were also enlisted in the Confederate army. Left on the family farm were his sixteen-year-old brother, Hugh, his mother, and his four sisters, ranging in age from five to thirteen. The Lowerys also had three enslaved laborers. Much like George Mellish and so many other soldiers, Rob Lowery wrote about the conditions of camp life. In his first letter home he described his rations: "We get bacon which is black and very badly cut up with skippers, plenty of flour with a little rice and salt." In his next letter, two days later, he answered his mother's question as to what he needed; in this letter the difference in the resources between the Lowery household and the Mellish households appeared. Although George Mellish always included a long list of items he needed, Rob Lowery's reply was simple and unselfish—he told her that he had "his uniform, it is enough." However, "If you wish," he continued, "you may send me two or three colored shirts but do not put yourself to too much trouble." Later, upon receiving his bounty for enlisting, Rob wrote to his mother to ask her to send him a bedtick, which he paid for, and also a pair of gloves. Apparently his mother made him at least one shirt during the war because he requested that she put a pocket inside it. Even so, he noted that "there are a great many things that I want, but can make out very well without."[12]

Rob knew that his mother was in a difficult situation, especially because she only had her youngest son left on the farm to help her. He urged his mother to get a dispensation for the boy to remain at home, an effort that ultimately failed. By 1864 Hugh, too, was in the Confederate service. That spring, Rob was appalled to hear that his mother had to do outdoor work. It is possible that by that point in the war the household's enslaved members were able to escape, leaving the white family to do all the work required for their survival. This loss would have turned the household's early ability to use enslaved labor to compensate for the initial Confederate enlistment of so many Lowery sons into an almost unsustainable strategic error. It put the burden of the sustenance of the household upon those remaining at home—the mother and her four young daughters. Despite these challenges, Rob's mother continued to write to him frequently. She inquired about how he was sleeping, what he was eating, and how he was washing his clothes. When she asked if he had shoes, he responded that the ones he brought from home were in fact nearly worn out, "but you need not mind that, I am working for the government and I think it will find me shoes." His most common topic of discussion, the food, was not positive, but he did not often complain. He described his food as consisting of "plenty of poor beef" or "plenty of meat and bread and a little rice, the pork is very good but the beef is pretty black." He never mentioned sending his pay home. He probably could not do that, just as she could not send him much in the way of supplies. He did, however, mention the occasional splurge he made when the soldiers actually got paid. For example, he let her know on March 30 that he had bought four eggs at Easter to make up for not being home to have dyed eggs; he spent twenty-five cents for the four.[13]

Perhaps not surprisingly, within a year of his enlistment Rob Lowery fell seriously ill. By June 6, 1863, he reported that the camp was not well. On July 9 he wrote to say that he was sick in bed for the fourth day, and on July 12 he wrote to say that he was in the hospital with a pretty severe case of diarrhea and asked his mother if she might be able to come nurse him to health. On July 18 his mess mates wrote to Rob's mother to tell her that he was "very bad" in the hospital, out of his head, and thinking she was already with him. Perhaps because she had so many children at home, his mother was unable to visit Rob, but his uncle did. For her part, his mother sent Rob the clothing that he needed, and on August 4 he wrote to say that he was improving, and he thanked her for the clothes. "I reckon that I was as proud as I was the first time I put on breeches," he wrote. "Consequently I can walk about but I am very careful and do not go out of doors in the sunshine but sit in the house."[14]

His uncle's visit and the clothing and food that his mother sent with him helped Rob Lowery survive this bout of illness, but he would not survive the next one. He wintered through another year and reported on the measles and mumps in camp and how men were dying. On January 11, 1864, when food was surely scarce, he finally wrote to his mother and said not only that men were dying but also that he had heard from his brother, who "thinks that a 1/4 lb of bacon and a pound of flour is not enough for a man of his appetite." At this point his mother sent Rob another box of supplies. On January 24, he responded that he was "much obliged to you for the victuals, which you sent me, I assure that they were very thankfully received for our rations are very scanty at present." His reports home make clear that the soldiers were going hungry for months at a time. Not until April 11 was he finally able to report that "as for rations we get flour bacon and a little rice, which is very good living. Oh it is so good and plentiful." At this point, for Rob Lowery the fact that the soldiers had food to eat that was not spoiled and that there was enough of it was all that he wanted. Sadly, his body needed more and he died in the hospital some months later.[15]

Like Mary Mellish and other mothers, Elizabeth Ann Lowery cared about the health and well-being of her son. She wrote to him regularly, and like Mary Mellish she always inquired about his conditions and sent what she could. The difference in this case was that Lowery undoubtedly had less to send. In addition, perhaps her son, unlike George Mellish, was not inclined to ask for more than he thought he absolutely needed or that his family could spare for him. It is also possible that Rob Lowery went into the war less well nourished than did George Mellish. The large family may not have been able to nourish anyone fully. Consequently, Rob's youngest brother, Hugh, survived only a year in the Confederate military. He returned home in January 1865 on extended furlough and died of dysentery and anemia one month later.[16]

As important as the labor of a soldier's female kin was in supplying the food and clothing the soldier needed to survive, her ability to nurse sons and husbands back to health was equally vital. In Rob Lowery's case, his uncle stood in for his mother and came to see him and perhaps to contribute to his nursing. Distance from the domestic supply line and the uncertainty of place put many soldiers into especially dangerous situations. Soldiers in the worst circumstances were those who were required with no warning to move suddenly and to march long and hard; some literally dropped of exhaustion along the way and could not go further. Although soldiers were fortunate if their kin could be spared to make the trip to nurse them, households never even had the option to provide this type of aid if they did not know where their soldier kin were or what their condition was.

The domestic supply line was only as successful and strong as its ability to deliver necessary items. The practice of numbering letters as Mary Mellish did as well as soldiers' careful accounting of what arrived and what did not arrive reflects the understandable concern that the mail itself could not necessarily be trusted. The most secure domestic supply lines tended to be those closest to home. The safest and most secure way to get needed items to soldiers was by having family or neighbors hand deliver them. That personal route was the only way to ensure that the soldiers received the supplies that they needed so desperately. However, few soldiers were privileged enough to be close to home. Historians have discussed the desirability of serving in the Home Guard because it allowed men to remain close to home and thus able to protect their households. However, they have given less attention to the fact that staying close to home also meant that soldiers' households were better able to supply them. The Civil War was largely a matter of Union invasion and occupation of Southern territory, and certainly it was understood at the time that the long supply lines through enemy territory threatened the ability of the Union army to maintain the regular military supply. It is likely then that along with the home advantage, the Confederacy held in formal military terms, and the same was true for the household supply line. Confederate soldiers were closer to home than Union soldiers. Of course, if the household simply had little it could provide, like the Lowerys, it mattered little how close your fighting sons were. On the other hand, a household could have all the resources needed and the willingness to send them, like the Mellish household, but it mattered little if they did not arrive.[17]

Proximity to home certainly aided those soldiers lucky enough to have that advantage. George Whitaker Wills, who enlisted into the First Regiment of the North Carolina Volunteers on May 12, 1861, in Raleigh, North Carolina, was able to spend much of the war in the surrounding region, although his regiment would eventually move as far north as Gettysburg. He enlisted with other men of his community in the infantry as a corporal, and he would serve with these men as their regiment was reorganized into the Forty-Third North Carolina Infantry. Being drawn from the same community meant that these men were not only brothers in arms but also often brothers or at least extended kin. This familial connection would prove critical to the ability of their individual households to supply these men in the field; they would rely upon each other to move those items to the front. Wills's father and uncle made regular trips to the Confederate camp with supplies. Those deliveries, combined with packages brought back to camp by the men who came home on furlough regularly, meant that there was a secure line of mail and supplies from home for the regiment. As Wills noted in a letter home, "Every time one man from home gets a notion to come here, someone else will come too, we are now living finely, the day after Uncle L came, Mrs. Jones and J. Kimbrell came in with another large supply."[18]

George Wills was also fortunate that he came from one of the better-educated and wealthier households of his county, valued at $5,220 in real estate and $29,725 in personal estate in the 1860 census. His father, William H. Wills, was a Methodist minister, as was his older brother, Richard. At the war's outbreak, nineteen-year-old George was attending school as were three of his siblings; only three children, ages eight, five, and two, were too young to attend. The Wills household was a highly literate household, able to maintain regular correspondence with their son, George. After all, soldiers had long periods in camp with time to write and were motivated to do so. However, often their families, busy at home, found keeping up regular correspondence to be more difficult. Schoolteachers, like Rob Lowery, and a family of ministers, like the Wills, had literary resources that many of their fellow soldiers must have envied. Indeed, while George did sometimes write to both his mother and father, he wrote most often to his younger sister, Lucy, who at age sixteen was sufficiently literate to be responsible for maintaining the correspondence with her brother and conveying to their mother the news of the items he most needed from home.

As with George Mellish and Rob Lowery, food and clothing were the first items George Wills requested of his household. In July 1861, after two months in service, George wrote to Lucy that as "it seems that neither the government or state either is going to give us any clothes so I must have a pair of pants made. If I hadn't received those from home I would have been without nearly." From the outset of his service, George Wills also wrote to his sister about the widespread "camp colic" and the inedible nature of the food. "Mother always told me I was too particular about eating and I find it so. I haven't eaten anything from the table in over a week." Fortunately, he had received two boxes from a Mr. Willard Dosage, and together with the one from home these provided him with sufficient fare to avoid the military standard issue altogether. The ability of Wills's household and community to supply the men would continue and intensify throughout the war, particularly as prices for purchased goods skyrocketed and the Confederacy failed to pay the soldiers even the minimal $11 wage.[19]

Although George Wills's basic needs for food and clothing from home were not different from those needed by other soldiers, what differed was the one resource his household could provide to him that others could not. The Wills household decided to part with one of their more than twenty slaves, a man named Wash, and send him to the front to assist George. Wash was himself a married man with a wife named Leah and several small children. George first noted Wash's arrival from home with a Mr. Page in a letter home on July 3, 1861. He let his sister know that "Wash brings news from home. That the horses are doing well, the corn crop was good, the cotton was not. He says to tell their father that he should have planted the big field in corn, not cotton."[20]

Even more than a mother willing to sew and cook for her son, a sister willing to write letters, or a father willing to make his son shoes, an enslaved man like Wash could offer these and other types of aid but at the front lines. Wash also made regular trips back and forth between camp and home, bringing supplies as well as news of the Wills household. When George was far from home, Wash scoured the local markets in what George referred to as "speculative tours." In addition to improving George's own basic supply of needed goods, Wash's skills and his use of them also improved life in camp in general. It was, therefore, as George wrote to his sister in April

1862, "an agreeable surprise" to have Wash return so quickly from his trip home for supplies. "We were living pretty badly before he came as our bread was made altogether as meal and half cooked, so of course we partook very lightly but since he came we had as good cooking as anyone could do."[21]

It was doubly fortuitous that Wash returned when he did, because George soon was writing home about the regiment being on the march. As much as George benefited from Wash's ability to acquire supplies and news from home and be of help around the camp, Wash's greatest single contribution may have been the help he gave on the long marches that the regiment made during that spring and summer as well as in 1863. In a June 9, 1862, letter home from Camp Davis near Wilmington, North Carolina, George noted, "Wash as usual had fine tales to tell you I reckon. . . . Did he tell you how much he carried to Wilmington? If not make him tell you for Pat says (I reckon he has told you who Pat is) he had at least three tons, a right big load isn't it?" Although George was joking about the amount Wash claimed to be carrying for him on these long marches, he knew on some level that Wash made those marches possible for him. "The regiment is moving again . . . so after expecting to leave every day until Tuesday, I took up my knacksack (No I didn't either but Wash did) and walked."[22]

The following spring found George's regiment even further from home. On May 25, 1863, George wrote from a few miles away from Fredericksburg, Virginia, and mentioned that they were marching about twenty-six miles each day. "The regiment was very indignant at it, and while a great many of the men fell out, I stood up but was very tired when I got here." Of course, George's advantage was that he had Wash to carry his pack. By June 28 the regiment was marching into Pennsylvania; George had no idea where they were going, but knew that they were in Union territory. On the outside envelope of this letter George conveyed a message from Wash to his wife, Leah. Wash wanted her to know that he was getting on well and that an "old woman tried to persuade Him to desert on me the other day, asked him if he was treated well [and] didn't he think he could better himself by stopping there. He says this is beautiful country but it doesn't come up to home in his eye."[23]

In all the letters George wrote home, there were only a few notes that George passed on for Wash. In this case, the note may well have been more for the benefit of George and the rest of the Wills family than it was for Leah and Wash's own kin. After all, Wash, still enslaved to the Wills family, was now in free territory. Although his service to George had given him the autonomy to go on "speculative tours" and travel back and forth from home to camp, he perhaps rightly saw the story of his conversation with the Union woman as a good way to reassure the Wills family that he had no intention of attempting to escape. This potential reassurance did not mean that Wash did not have a sharp eye for the extent to which the war opened opportunities for himself and presumably the other enslaved members of the Wills household. In fact, Wash was a sharp trader. The remainder of his notes home consisted in large part of comments to his wife concerning business matters. For example, on April 12 he wrote to his "dear Wife" on the back of "Master George's letter" that he thought that she was undoubtedly rather peeved at him for not writing. His excuse was that he had "so much moving about to do, it is hard to write." He continued to give her some directions. "John can have the timber for $100 and Master Dick can have the book for $200." He concluded with a comment on one of his money-making schemes to sell soap in camp to what were undoubtedly very grateful and very dirty Confederate soldiers: "Tell Mister Ed to buy all the soap he can get at that price. I will sell it for him and go shares into it."[24]

Although the Wills family sent Wash off with George in an effort to make life easier for their soldier son and brother, Wash turned this breach in household relations to his own empowerment and to that of his own kin. The war created many opportunities for enslaved members of households, depending on their individual circumstances. Military-aged men, especially those in the border areas, were able to enlist in the Union army and gain their freedom. As Union troops approached their area, entire enslaved families were able to escape to freedom beyond the military lines. For Wash and his kin, his loyal service to George Wills at the front was a strategy that also worked to the increased integrity of his own household. Every penny Wash made for himself through his "speculative tours" out marketing for George at the front, every clever idea he came up with to take advantage of the needs of soldiers such as selling soap at the front, every item he sold or traded back home, expanded the space and integrity of his kin relations even during their enslavement. There is no record of what happened to Wash, only that he survived the war, but presumably his family was strongly situated to take up a more autonomous place in freedom as a result of his wartime efforts.

When men left their households for the military front, the work attached to them followed them to a much greater extent than we have previously understood. The focus on the rendering of the work of the household as public—as in publicly organized charitable work like the Ladies' Aid Societies, fund-raising fairs, or the formation of the sanitary commissions—and the emergence of women as wage workers during the war, only represents the tip of the iceberg of a larger household relational breach created by the massive departure of so many men. That breach, that turning of the household economy inside out, was addressed by government large and small and by the militaries that struggled to keep these men even partially fed and clothed. What has been overlooked, however, is the role that the household itself continued to play in the supply of the men at the front. In particular, composite figures of the material advantages of the Union and the Confederacy fail to capture the relational war of households because of the way that the war was not structured by region so much as by the resources of individual households and the labor of those household members.

Not only has the extent to which soldiers were supplied directly by their families and thus what contributions the households made to the war effort been neglected, the connection to how the household itself was transformed in the process of fighting the Civil War has also been overlooked. In terms of the larger systemic change that the war was pivotal in creating, what mattered in the long run was not so much which side had more or less in the way of resources, who won or who lost, or even who lived or who died, so much as the way in which the very process of fighting the war served to move the household relations in the direction of a modern social order of free homes, shorn of unfree labor and grounded in an increased respect for the importance of women's emotional and material work. When George Lowe finally received a letter from his wife, when George Mellish received his box and his mother's wise counsel, when Rob Lowery was able to get up and walk around in the clothes that his mother sent him, when soldiers sent all those thousands of letters home, they were written on the heart and sent through the household supply line, and they underwrote the victory of a relational war.

NOTES

1. Bell I. Wiley, *The Life of Johnny Reb: The Common Soldier of the Confederacy* (Baton Rouge: Louisiana State University Press, 1943) and *The Life of Billy Yank: The Common Soldier of the Union* (Baton Rouge: Louisiana State University Press, 1952). For more recent lines of discussion, see James McPherson, *For Cause and Comrades: Why Men Fought in the Civil War* (New York: Oxford University Press, 1997); Chandra Manning, *What This Cruel War Was Over: Slavery and the Civil War* (New York: Vintage, 2008); and Reid Mitchel, *The Vacant Chair: The Northern Soldier Leaves Home* (New York: Oxford University Press, 1993).

2. Some of the most central works to date on the Civil War as a household war are Joseph M. Beilein Jr., *Bushwhackers: Guerrilla Warfare, Manhood, and the*

Household in Civil War Missouri (Kent, Ohio: Kent State University Press, 2016); Victoria E. Bynum, *The Free State of Jones: Mississippi's Longest Civil War* (Chapel Hill: University of North Carolina Press, 2001); Lisa Tendrich Frank, *The Civilian War: Confederate Women and Union Soldiers during Sherman's March* (Baton Rouge: Louisiana State University Press, 2015); LeeAnn Whites and Alecia P. Long, eds., *Occupied Women: Gender, Military Occupation, and the American Civil War* (Baton Rouge: Louisiana State University Press, 2009); and LeeAnn Whites, *Gender Matters: Civil War, Reconstruction, and the Making of the New South* (New York: Palgrave Macmillan, 2005).

3. Stephen W. Berry II, *All That Makes a Man: Love and Ambition in the Civil War South* (New York: Oxford University Press, 2004).

4. George W. Lowe to Lizzie Lowe, July 12 and 26, 1861, George W. Lowe Papers, Huntington Library, San Marino, Calif. This essay is drawn from a larger study of close to fifty letter collections held at the library, the Gilder Lehrman Collection at the New York Library, and the holdings of the Southern Historical Collection (SHC) at the University of North Carolina, Chapel Hill.

5. George W. Lowe to Lizzie Lowe, July 26 and August 3, 1861.

6. John Robert Lowery to Ann Elizabeth Lowery, February 21, 1863; January 24, 1864; January 31, 1864, John Robert Lowery Papers, SHC.

7. Nelson C. Huson to Maria Huson, March 8, 1863, Nelson Huson Papers, Huntington Library.

8. George H. Mellish to Mary Mellish, October 23, 1862, George Mellish Papers, Huntington Library.

9. In the 1860 census, Stephen Mellish, the father, is listed as having a shoe store, $1,500 in real estate and $500 in personal estate. George is listed as being a painter, his mother as being a "wife," and both Martha, age four, and George, sixteen, are listed as attending school. I assume that along with owning a shoe store, Stephen Mellish was in fact a shoemaker.

10. George Mellish to Mary Mellish, January 24, 1863, George Mellish Papers, Huntington Library.

11. John Robert Lowery to Hannah Vance Lowery, July 20, 1862, July 22, 1862, February 21, 1863, August 7, 1862, John Robert Lowery Papers, SHC. In the 1860 census, Hugh Lowery, the father, aged fifty-seven, is listed has having $2,000 in real estate and $4,500 in personal estate, so the Lowery household was worth more than the Mellish household, but if the $4,500 was largely in slave property and without the father and the four sons to work the land, there is only the mother, Anna Lowery, forty-one in 1860, and four daughters, ten, eight, five, and two, to somehow make a living. While no 1860 slave schedule has been found to date, the 1850 slave schedule lists Hugh Lowery as owning three slaves, one seventeen-year-old female and two males, fifty and thirty. Rob Lowery mentions the slaves in his correspondence home in 1862. It isn't clear how long they remained or if the youngest brother was able to keep them working.

12. Rob Lowery to Hannah Lowery, June 6, 1862, September 14, 1862, September 18, 1862, October 10, 1862, Lowery Papers.

13. Rob Lowery to Hannah Lowery, March 30, 1863.

14. Rob Lowery to Hannah Lowery, June 6, July 9, July 12, July 18, and August 4, 1863.

15. Rob Lowery to Hannah Lowery, January 11, January 24, and April 11, 1864.

16. Hugh White Lowery, Find A Grave Memorial #77073193.

17. Beilein, *Bushwhackers*, 90–95.

18. George Wills to Lucy Wills, July 21, 1861, George Whitaker Wills Papers, SHC.

19. George Wills to Lucy Wills, July 21, 1861, May 11, 1861, March 1864.

20. George Wills to Lucy Wills, July 3, 1861.

21. George Wills to Lucy Wills, April 1862.

22. George Wills to Lucy Wills, June 9, 1862.

23. George Wills to Lucy Wills, May 25 and June 28, 1863.

24. Wash to Leah, April 12, 1863, Wills Papers.

PART 3

The Household as the Site of War

A "Fearful Family Quarrel"

The Union Assault on Southern Households
as Battle Strategy

Lisa Tendrich Frank

When Union troops bombarded the "rebellious city" of Atlanta in the summer of 1864, they did so knowing that it was filled with civilians, what one soldier called "a Great good many inoffensive ones."[1] The presence of civilians, with their homes and property, shaped how Yankees understood how "our shell had torn the city to pieces considerable." U.S. soldiers blamed Confederates for the presence of the civilians because "Hood never gave orders for the noncombattants to remove."[2] The civilian population did little to dampen the troops' wholehearted joy at taking the city, as U.S. soldiers rejoiced that "the Rebs have received a sound & wholesome lesson." Union soldiers lionized their commander: "*Vive la Sherman!* May his praise be on the lips of thousands and a grateful nation fail not to do him honor."[3] His troops considered General William Tecumseh Sherman "a *big man*" for his successes in the Atlanta campaign, which "struck the rebellion a great blow."[4] When Sherman ordered the removal of the Confederate civilians from the city, U.S. soldiers continued to support him. After all, the women and children "should not have 'waited for us to come south' if they did not expect to suffer the consequences."[5] Confederate women did not share this praise of the Union general or his soldiers, especially once Sherman issued orders to expel the women from the captured city. In Upson County, Georgia, Loula Kendall Rogers lamented that "Atlanta, 'that great city' with all its might 'bulwarks and towers' has fallen!"[6] Closer to Atlanta, Minerva McClatchey refused to leave her Marietta home, despite the fact that Sherman ordered "that we must go one way or the other." Instead, she proclaimed that "unless Genl Sherman 'ordered me personally and preemptorily'" to leave, she would not budge because "this is my home. I have a right to stay at it."[7]

The 1864 forced removal of Southern women and children from Atlanta evokes provocative images that shape scholarly and public understandings of Civil War households. The flight of women and children has been memorialized in countless manifestations of American popular culture, including Margaret Mitchell's *Gone with the Wind*. Depictions of the event similar to the one portrayed in the novel and then movie have been recounted by Ladies' Memorial Societies and have been preserved in monuments, paintings, and sketches, as well as in works by modern historians. The public memorials offer two contrasting images of Atlanta's evacuation. In some depictions, desperate women and children flee from the rampant destruction that accompanied the occupation of an enemy town. In others, these civilians are graciously encouraged to leave their homes so they will be spared from harsh military tactics seen as antithetical to civilian life. These competing versions of Atlanta's evacuation reveal a shared misunderstanding of the connection between the Union's military tactics and Confederate households. In both descriptions, civilians must leave Atlanta because war, as Sherman asserted, was no place for families. However, a different explanation emerges through a reexamination of Sherman's writings about war and a close analysis of how his policy played out in Atlanta.

The evacuation of Atlanta's civilians resulted from Union commanders' explicit ambition to treat households as legitimate military targets and to blur distinctions that typically separated civilians from enemy combatants. This policy predated its implementation in 1864 Atlanta and can be seen in the actions, experiences, and writings of Sherman and others. Although this essay focuses on Sherman's eviction of households from Atlanta in 1864, the tactic of attacking and destabilizing households was not unique to this particular campaign. Throughout the war, Sherman and other Union commanders realized that if they could undermine enemy households, the Confederacy could not sustain the war. This recognition led directly to the decision to evict civilians from their homes.[8]

On several occasions prior to the Atlanta campaign, the U.S. military forcibly emptied entire towns of their civilians and otherwise removed families from their homes. Sherman's actions in Atlanta may be the most memorable, but similar large-scale evictions took place in Roswell, Georgia, Memphis, Tennessee, and, perhaps most dramatically, in four counties in Missouri.[9] Although all of these instances resulted in the forced removal of civilians from their homes, they have often been described as "evacuations." Treating them as evacuations, however, has created the understanding that the tactic was something done on behalf of the civilians rather than something done to them—as an attempt to shield families from the war rather than as a policy that brought war's "hard hand" down on households.[10] This use of the term "evacuation" draws attention away from the benefits that eviction provided the U.S. army and instead attributes responsibility for their actions to the unintended or unfortunate consequences of war. In fact, the removal of families was not a benevolent act to keep women out of the line of fire. The Union army intentionally and coercively expelled women and children from their homes because doing so allowed the Union to make a quick military strike at enemy households without waging a sustained war against them.[11] Sherman understood the importance of such a strike in making Confederate families "know the consequences of their actions."[12]

The premeditated eviction of female-headed households in Atlanta and elsewhere both resolved and revealed an aspect of the Civil War's "crisis in gender."[13] On one hand, Sherman and other U.S. officials recognized that the rules of war and of nineteenth-century propriety required them to adhere to various restraints when it came to the treatment of women and children.[14] On the other hand, Sherman and other Union officers understood that "all the South is in arms and deep in enmity."[15] They knew that these women and the wartime households they headed served as the backbone of Confederate morale and nationalism and provided much-needed resources and labor for the Confederate war effort. In addition, Confederate women were known to undermine occupying Union forces by waging feminine forms of guerrilla warfare or by engaging in other less aggressive but still menacing gendered practices. Eviction allowed Union officers to apparently follow their mandate to protect and provide for households in their midst as long as they were known to be loyal, while absolving them of responsibility for those households that were not under their control. In Atlanta that required wholesale eviction since most households were not. Eviction could even be justified by the Lieber Code, which proclaimed that "the more vigorously wars are pursued, the better it is for humanity" and which recommended that a commander "throw the burden of the war, as much as lies within his power, on the disloyal citizens."[16] Sherman insisted that disloyal Confederate households could not be shielded from the harm that would unavoidably occur through eviction or occupation. It would be impossible to protect them entirely from these adversities. As he acknowledged, "You might as well appeal against the thunder-storm as against these terrible hardships of war. They are inevitable."[17]

Sherman contemplated the problem created by enemy civilians and households long before he set off to capture Atlanta in 1864. As a nineteenth-century student of war, Sherman learned firsthand the centrality of civilians to modern warfare. From his earlier experiences and observations during Florida's Seminole Wars as well as from those he gained during the Civil War, he learned that civilians were just as much the enemy as were soldiers. He discovered that defeating an army required that he defeat the soldiers' household support systems. When Sherman fought in the Second Seminole War (1835–42), for example, the U.S. army attempted to starve Seminole civilians into submission. Under Winfield Scott and other generals, the United States burned cornfields and villages, slaughtered cattle, and cut off Seminoles from cornfields, gardens, and wild coontie fields. In many cases, these homefront actions received a higher priority than did the pursuit of enemy warriors or capture of military leaders. The United States and the colonial powers that preceded it waged what some scholars have called "feed fights" against Indians from the colonial era to the late nineteenth century.[18] U.S. officers realized that a strike at Native American families often achieved the same ends as a military battle against Native American warriors.

Sherman's experiences fighting irregular Confederate units early in the Civil War further prepared him for his 1864 campaign against civilians in Atlanta. In 1861 and 1862, Sherman faced enemy combatants in Tennessee, Mississippi, and elsewhere who intermingled with and, when they were not fighting, appeared indistinguishable from civilians. Because guerrilla warfare made it nearly impossible to distinguish combatant from noncombatant, Sherman struggled to enact military policies that affected one but not the other. It also confirmed for Sherman that civilians were an integral part of the Confederate war effort. Contemporary military tacticians have confronted this reality more dramatically when they wage what is euphemistically called "urban warfare," but Sherman confronted analogous situations. Like many tacticians who followed, Sherman concluded that he could either act in ways that some might "style . . . cruel and barbarous" and extend warfare to some civilians or else suffer from the depredations that irregular fighting could inflict.[19]

In October 1862, for example, Sherman concluded that he could not effectively fight the enemy and ignore the families of Confederate guerrillas. The difficulties presented by an enemy who used guerrilla tactics led him to assert that he was "unwilling longer to protect the families and property of men who fire from ambush upon our soldiers." His solution was to expel civilians from their homes and "compel such families to go forth and seek their husbands and brothers." Although he acknowledged the ethical implications of this decision, Sherman "[knew] his heart" and followed it as he rid Memphis of its enemy civilians.[20] Guerrilla attacks upon two Union steamboats on the Mississippi River in 1862 further convinced Sherman that "the families of men engaged in such hellish deeds shall not live in peace where the flag of the United States floats."[21] Sherman ordered the U.S. military to confront and subdue all Confederate civilians. Women may not have attacked the steamboats themselves, but their moral and material support of their soldiers certainly aided and abetted it.

Civilians, Sherman explained, did more than allow soldiers to hide in their midst. Southern women and households provided essential support for a Confederate military that ultimately relied on them for both material and ideological support. This reality led him, as well as other Union commanders, to pursue campaigns that placed these households at the forefront of their actions. This desire to undermine households led to tactics that included the emancipation of enslaved African Americans, the destruction of railroads and agricultural fields, and the invasion of and burning of civilian homes. All of these measures struck at the Confederate economy, but they also created instability and disrupted households, the basis of the South's political structure and economy. In addition, Union commanders articulated their belief that a war on households could undermine the political legitimacy of the Confederacy, foster political dissent, weaken morale, and force enemy leaders to allocate military resources to the homefront.[22]

As early as 1862 then, Sherman recognized the power civilians had to affect the soldiers and the course of the war, and he held them responsible for their roles. "Instead of inflaming the minds of their husbands & brothers to lift their hands against the Government of their Birth and stain them in blood," Sherman stated that "ladies" should have encouraged Southern men "to exhaust all the remedies afforded them by our glorious Constitution and thereby avoid 'horrid war.'"[23] As he would later do in Atlanta, Sherman justified his removal of families in Memphis with descriptions of his behavior that made it analogous to actions taken by a caring father who meted out corrective punishments. On one hand, he asserted that "no measures would be too severe" for these Rebels and that "the absolute destruction of Memphis New Orleans & every city town and hamlet of the South would not be too severe a punishment" for Confederate offenses. On the other hand, he excused his actions and claimed to be helping the families whom he was "requiring . . . to leave." Sherman claimed "there Can be no hardship for the wife and Children going to their own husbands and families." Furthermore, these Confederates "ought to be glad of the opportunity & the measure instead of being severe is very mild."[24] In other words, evicted Southerners should thank him for his "kindness."

In 1863, Sherman employed and justified similar tactics in his treatment of Mississippi civilians after the Union capture and occupation of Vicksburg. In response to protests against his attitude toward civilians and assumed noncombatants, he asserted, "We are justified in treating all the inhabitants as combatants." He refused to be swayed by requests for leniency or help. "Of necessity in War the Commander . . . may take your house, your fields, your everything, and turn you all out, helpless to starve. It may be wrong, but that don't alter the case. In War you can't help yourselves, and the only possible remedy is to stop war."[25] His goal, as always, was to bring the war to a close and bring the South back into the Union. This necessity, he explained, required that he treat white women as the enemy. He defended his belief to his daughter, Minnie, by writing that "whenever a result can be accomplished without Battle I prefer it," and attacking households was one way he could avoid the larger "fight."[26] Even so, he believed that "In war we have a perfect right to produce results in our own way." He was not concerned with the "scruple" involved as long as the "means . . . are effectual."[27] This tactical approach continued into 1864. As he approached Atlanta, Sherman once again looked for ways to avoid the deadly battles on the military field while understanding that another kind of battle needed to be waged on the homefront. After all, he acknowledged, "We have to combat not only with the organized resistance of the Confederate forces, but the entire people of the South."[28]

In early 1864, Sherman's thoughts about waging war on female-centered households revealed his approach in the future Atlanta campaign. In a letter specifically devoted to discussing "the treatment of inhabitants known or suspected to be hostile or 'Secesh,'" Sherman outlined a prescient rationale for war and an attack on the homefront that military historians have largely overlooked. He asked: "Should we treat as absolute enemies all in the South who differ from us in opinion or prejudice, Kill or banish them, or should we give them time to think and gradually change their conduct?" The answer for "men [who] take up Arms" was clear to Sherman—kill them—as was the case for seizing personal property "because otherwise they might be used against us." He also justified the military confiscation of Confederate homes because during war "all houses left vacant by an inimical people are clearly our Right, and such as are needed as Storehouses, Hospitals & Quarters." Sherman acknowledged that not all homes were vacated, and therefore he carefully delineated the rules that governed the behavior of his army when they found "dwellings used by women, children & non-combatants." Here, in his discussion of civilians, Sherman specifically distinguished public from private and masculine from feminine. "So long as non-combatants remain in their houses & Keep to their accus-

tomed peaceful business, their opinions and prejudices can in no wise influence the War & therefore should not be noticed; but if any one comes out
into the public streets & creates disorder he or she should be punished,
restrained or banished."[29]

In this explanation, Sherman opened the door for the hard war homefront campaigns in Atlanta and during the subsequent March to the Sea
and through the Carolinas. Using a broad definition of disorder and defiance, he contended that his army had an obligation and a right to silence
women who engaged the public discourse on the war through their vocal
or material support. His definition of disloyalty was similarly broad and
included households that provided aid of any kind to the Confederate army.
"If the people or any of them Keep up a correspondence with parties in
hostility they are spies & can be punished according to Law with death
or minor punishment. These are well established principles of War." Sherman's justification for a war on households went beyond limiting the ability of soldiers to fight. After all, he asserted, "a People who will persevere
in a War beyond a certain limit ought to Know the consequences."[30] As
Sherman understood it, occupied women were the key to the Confederacy's
supply and communication lines, recruitment of men, and moral support
and needed to be treated accordingly.[31]

By the time Sherman approached Atlanta, he was prepared to treat its
inhabitants as enemies who were deserving of hard war tactics. Sherman
did not march into Atlanta and then discover that he was unprepared to
deal with a city filled with unarmed civilians. He knew the types of people
he would encounter in the railroad city and therefore emptied the city in
order to prevent civilians from continuing to fight the war. Forcibly evicting these families, he had learned, was a savvy military strategy designed to
deal with an overwhelmingly female enemy. Two years earlier, for example,
Sherman acknowledged that the demography of Southern towns and cities
had changed because "all the young & middle aged [men] have gone to the
war."[32] Similarly, in June 1863, he "found as is the case of all farms here a
bevy of women waiting patiently the fate of husbands & sons." Throughout the homefront, Sherman noticed that "not a man is seen—nothing but
women."[33] The Civil War had changed the Southern homefront and Sherman designed homefront tactics accordingly. After capturing and entering a
city that he knew to be primarily occupied by enemy women and children,
Sherman selected a military tactic he had used in the past. Long before
he approached the city, he vowed to "take Atlanta & Disturb the peace of
the Inhabitants of Central Georgia."[34] As he explained, "We have to combat not only with the organized resistance of the Confederate forces, but

the entire people of the South."[35] As a result, once he captured it, he emptied Atlanta in order to prevent Confederate civilians from continuing to fight. Displaced Confederates, he understood, would be unable to feed, clothe, or otherwise sustain the army, and these exiles would further disrupt surrounding areas. The resulting refugee crisis was a consequence of this attempt by the U.S. military to break the social and material support that households provided to the Confederate war effort.

Sherman's forces captured Atlanta on September 2, 1864, after a long campaign for the city that often left civilians fearing for their lives. When Confederate troops finally fled the railroad city, more than one thousand civilians—Southern women, children, and mostly elderly men—remained in their homes. They were not soldiers, but Sherman and others already had a clear policy on how to deal with them.[36] As a result, on September 8, 1864, Sherman issued Special Field Orders 67, which turned the citizens of Atlanta into displaced people. Instead of presenting the forced removal of Confederate families as an unfortunate by-product of war, Sherman pursued eviction to "utterly . . . negat[e] Davis' boasted threat and promises of protection."[37] In short, evicting women limited their ability to support the war as it simultaneously emasculated Confederate men. Sherman waged war on women in order to bring their men to their knees.

In one of his most famous and repeated statements, Sherman justified his attack on Confederate households as both inevitable and deserved. In response to the protests of white Confederates about the immorality of his eviction of Atlanta's civilians, Sherman countered that "war is cruelty, and you cannot refine it." He further justified his actions asserting that "those who brought war on the country deserve all the curses and maledictions a people can pour out."[38] Although scholars and others have segregated the debate over the eviction of Atlanta's civilians into the domestic realm as opposed to showing it as a deliberate military tactic, Sherman saw it as strategy. Defenders of Sherman's policies declare that women needed to be removed or evacuated because they were distractions from the war or faced physical danger if they stayed; others repeat the concerns of Atlanta's leaders by describing it as unnecessarily cruel. When placed in the larger context in which these words were written and Sherman's actions against civilians occurred, however, it becomes clear that Sherman's policy was a deliberate tactic designed to subdue the enemy in a war that he characterized as a "fearful family quarrel."[39] Sherman developed these ideas before the Civil War and employed them in various campaigns, but the military's war on households had its most emphatic rendering after the capture of Atlanta.

Despite Sherman's repeated comments on treating civilians as enemy combatants, most historical interpretations of the events in Atlanta have emphasized Sherman's assertion that eviction shielded women and families from the horrors of war. It has become commonplace to understand—often without further explanation—that Atlanta needed to be evacuated because, as Sherman put it, "The use of Atlanta for warlike purposes is inconsistent with its character as a home for families." After all, he cautioned, families would be unable to survive: "There will be no manufactures, commerce, or agriculture here, for the maintenance of families, and sooner or later want will compel the inhabitants to go."[40] This explanation was only half of the equation, as Sherman was well aware. He frequently stated his intention to treat Atlanta and its civilian population as a military target. "I feel perfectly justified in taking whatever & whereever I can find."[41] Sherman, in short, felt warranted in taking what he needed from women and other civilians and in ridding himself of the burdens of caring for those whose lives he left in shambles. Although he claimed he wanted to protect women and children from the gendered dangers of occupation, Sherman actually emptied Atlanta because the presence of hostile civilians endangered his wartime policies. By definition, bringing war home to civilians made Atlanta "inconsistent with its character as a home for families."[42]

Privately and sometimes publicly, Sherman and other U.S. leaders acknowledged that the eviction of Confederate noncombatants served Union war aims. In particular, it prevented "secesh" women from harassing soldiers and interfering in military operations. Sherman did not want female Confederates waging gendered war on his troops as women in occupied New Orleans had done to Benjamin Butler's. Evictions would deny any possibility of chamber pots being dumped on Union soldiers or of women otherwise resisting the occupation.[43] As Sherman told Halleck, "I want it a pure Gibraltar and will have it so by the first of October."[44] In comparing Atlanta to an isolated military post and key base of the British Royal Navy during the Crimean War, Sherman demonstrated his true aim: he wanted a base that had no interference from Confederate civilians, who had a "vindictive nature."[45]

In his letters to his wife, Sherman repeatedly stressed his desire to maintain the distinction between the work of war, an endeavor that required able-bodied men, and the household, a feminized space and set of ideals that would have required his attention to the concerns of female civilians. He alerted Ellen to both the military and personal reasons for evicting enemy civilians from the city. Sherman did more than "take the ground that Atlanta is a conquered place" that he "propose[d] to use ... purely for our own military purposes which are inconsistent with its habitation by the families." He also bragged that after his orders were fulfilled "the town will be a real military town with no women boring me at every order I give."[46] In his mind, a "real military town" would have no interference from women, especially not enemy women who would endlessly question and protest every move he made as well as every order he gave, while simultaneously demanding aid and protection from Union soldiers. In addition to eliminating this feminine nuisance, eviction resolved the uncertainty of how Confederate civilians might behave if they remained in Union-occupied Atlanta. "I will have been a silly fool to take a town at such cost, and left it in the occupation of a helpless and hostile people."[47] He again stressed the dangers of what "hostile people" might do, especially because "the entire South, man, woman, and child are against us, armed and determined."[48] As a result, their forced removal was of military importance. "I know the vindictive nature of our enemy, and that we may have many years of military operations from this quarter." Therefore, he claimed "it wise and prudent to prepare in time" by evacuating the "vindictive" enemy, regardless of her sex.[49]

Perhaps recognizing that it would be unwise to counter Sherman's argument that women were inconsequential to the war effort and unable to defend themselves, Confederate men and women played along and responded to Sherman's argument with their own paternalistic language and judgments. For example, Atlanta's mayor and two councilmen "petition[ed]" Sherman "to reconsider the order requiring [civilians] to leave Atlanta." As they urged him to rethink his actions toward civilians, they specifically cast Sherman's treatment of women and children as unmanly. They subsequently appealed to his masculine obligations and urged him to acknowledge the civilians' need for aid: "You know the woe, the horrors and the suffering cannot be described by words." In their response to Sherman, Atlanta's public officials also purposely ignored white women's active participation in the Confederate war effort as they instead stressed the purported blamelessness of female Confederates: "What has this helpless people done, that they should be driven from their homes to wander strangers and outcasts and exiles?"[50] This image, which has been dutifully repeated by white Southerners and scholars since its publication, confirms the mythology that "helpless" women needed to be spared from the horrors of an occupying force.[51] White women across the South similarly used the language of paternalism to express their outrage against Sherman's orders. For these women the language and logic of paternalism made the banishment from Atlanta into evictions and violations rather than evacuations and acts of charity that Union officials portrayed them as. In Confederate women's eyes, Sherman "promulgated an Order so infamous that a Russian example must be sought if we would find a parallel amongst civilized nations."[52] Another woman stressed that in the "darkened annals of history," there were no others who, like the Union, "wage[d] war upon helpless women and children."[53] Like many others, she used the paternalistic language of "helpless women" to emphasize the inhumanity of the tactic.

In the face of repeated public criticisms, Sherman never wavered in his confidence in his actions. Although he publicly insisted that he acted with charity in his homefront campaigns, during and after the Atlanta campaign Sherman echoed the belligerent justifications he had expressed earlier in the war. In a letter to Halleck days before he issued Special Field Orders 67, Sherman contemplated its reception. "If the people raise a howl against my barbarity & cruelty, I will answer that War is War & not popularity seeking. If they want Peace, they & their relations must stop War."[54] For Sherman, women's roles in sustaining the Confederate war effort justified their eviction: "Now that war comes to you ... you deprecate its horrors, but did not feel them when you sent car-loads of soldiers and ammunition, and moulded shells and shot, to carry war into" other places.[55] Sherman's response to complaints about the ethics of waging war on women clearly highlighted his beliefs. Feminized households were fair game because they initiated and sustained Confederate disloyalty and otherwise brought the war on themselves.[56]

Sherman's eviction of Atlanta's civilians reflected a larger desire by Union soldiers and civilians to eschew paternalism and instead treat Confederate women as the enemy. Like their commander, many Union soldiers believed that Confederate women deserved to feel the hard hand of war. For example, one commissary officer reported to his wife in a very matter-of-fact way that "this may look hard to some at first thought," but the eviction of civilians was necessary and "the Exodus commences tomorrow."[57] Similarly, although J. Dexter Cotton acknowledged that "it seems very hard," he justified the necessity of uprooting households. He proclaimed that it "serves them right for most of the women of the south are generally stronger secess than the men."[58] One soldier urged his family to "read ... Sherman's letters to Hood in reference to the removal of the women & children of Atlanta" because "they are so good, just the sentiments of his whole army."[59] Another reported with pride that Sherman ordered that "a Southern Lady on the street ... is to be considered no better than she ought to be and sent right away." He also described the trains leaving the city filled with Southern civilians because "Gen Sherman does not intend to have them inside of our lines . . . he intends to make a military Gibraltar of Atlanta."[60] These and other Union soldiers relished the fact that Confederate women were finally being treated as enemies in their own right and that enemy households were being turned upside down.[61] From the safety of the Union homefront Sherman's wife expressed her delight in her husband's actions. "I am charmed with your order expelling the inhabitants of Atlanta as it has always seemed to me preposterous to have our Government feeding so many of their people." She, like her husband, recognized that to feed enemy civilians would be counterproductive to U.S. war aims and a misappropriation of resources. Furthermore, she too believed that the Union should punish civilians for their disobedience. She decried, in particular, the Confederacy's "insolent women particularly for they are responsible for the war and should be made to feel that it exists in sternest reality."[62] Many Union women shared Ellen Sherman's perspective and applauded the harsh treatment of their Confederate counterparts as a valid wartime tactic and a necessary step in ending the "fearful family quarrel."[63]

In Atlanta, Sherman put into action the lessons he had learned during his military career and pursued a campaign designed to undermine the Confederacy by turning households upside down.[64] He crafted Special Field Orders 67 as a military tactic designed to dismantle enemy households rather than as a paternalistic evacuation of helpless civilians.[65] Recognizing that war could not be confined to armies and acknowledging the importance of households to the Confederate war effort, the policy provided him an effective way to bring war to "all the South," regardless of age or sex.[66] In making war directly on the household, Sherman and his soldiers aimed to destroy Confederate support and to bring about a rapid end to the war. Emphasizing this event as an eviction highlights its original intent as well as its role in the hard hand of war. As Sherman clearly recognized, war did not confine itself to armies; irregular fighting and armies brought untold difficulties; gender conventions created burdensome obligations on occupying armies; and households sustained armies. The eviction of civilians from Atlanta allowed Sherman to address all of these issues and provided him with an effective way to fight what was a household war.

NOTES

1. Robert Stuart Finley to Mary A. Cabeen, July 26, 1864, Robert Stuart Finley Papers #3685-z, Southern Historical Collection (SHC), Wilson Library, University of North Carolina at Chapel Hill; George Washington Baker to Mother, September 3, 1864, George Washington Baker Papers #4909, SHC.

2. Baker to Mother, September 3, 1864, Baker Papers #4909, SHC.

3. Finley to Cabeen, September 8, 1864, Finley Papers #3685-z, SHC.

4. John J. Metzgar to Carrie Metzgar, September 15, 1864, John J. Metzgar Papers #4939, SHC.

5. J. Dexter Cotton to Ann Cotton, September 22, 1864, J. Dexter Cotton Papers, Library of Congress (LC), Manuscript Division, Washington, D.C.

6. Loula Kendall Rogers, September 13, 1864, Loula Kendall Rogers Papers, Special Collections Department, Robert W. Woodruff Library, Emory University, Atlanta.

7. Minerva Lea Rowles McClatchey, September 19, 1864, McClatchey Family Papers, 71-601, Georgia Department of Archives and History (GDAH), Atlanta.

8. Similar tactics were used during Philip Sheridan's campaign in the Shenandoah Valley. See Lisa Tendrich Frank, "War Comes Home: Confederate Women and Union Soldiers," in *Virginia's Civil War*, ed. Peter Wallenstein and Bertram Wyatt-Brown (Charlottesville: University of Virginia Press, 2005), 123–36. Also see Lisa Tendrich Frank, "The Union War on Women," in *The Guerrilla Hunters*, ed. Barton A. Myers and Brian D. McKnight (Baton Rouge: Louisiana State University Press, 2017), 171–91.

9. In retaliation for William Clarke Quantrill's raid on Lawrence, Kansas, on August 25, 1863, Sherman's foster brother and brother-in-law, Thomas Ewing Jr., issued General Order Number 11. This order forced the evacuation of more than twenty thousand civilians from four counties in Missouri. For a look at these events through the lens of gender, see LeeAnn Whites, "Forty Shirts and a Wagonload of Wheat: Women, the Domestic Supply Line, and the Civil War on the Western Border," *Journal of the Civil War Era* 1, no. 1 (March 2011): 56–78. After his troops captured the manufacturing town of Roswell, Georgia, Sherman's orders were to cause "utter destruction" and "arrest all people male & female connected with the factorys no matter what the clamor and let them foot it under guard to Marietta, whence I will send them by cars to the North." Sherman to Kenner Garrard, July 7, 1864, U.S. War Department, *The War of the Rebellion: A Compilation of the Official Records of the Union and Confederate Armies* (Washington, D.C.: Government Printing Office, 1880–1901) [Hereafter cited as *OR*], series 1, vol. 38, pt. 5:76. Sherman further noted that the female factory workers "being exempt from conscription they are as much governed by the rules of War as if in the Ranks." Sherman to Henry W. Halleck, July 7, 1864, *Sherman's Civil War: Selected Correspondence of William T. Sherman, 1860–1865*, ed. Brooks D. Simpson and Jean V. Berlin (Chapel Hill: University of North Carolina Press, 1999), 662.

10. In contrast, Ulysses S. Grant "expelled" Jews from the areas under his control in Tennessee, Kentucky, and Mississippi. See Jonathan D. Sarna, *When General Grant Expelled the Jews* (New York: Schocken Books, 2012).

11. The difference in terminology becomes clearer in the contrasts between Sherman's decision to evict Confederate civilians from Atlanta and the decisions of Confederate officials to evacuate Southern civilians from places in the line of battle. Despite the implications of the term *evacuation* Sherman gave his orders to suit his

wartime objectives, he did not make them on behalf of Confederate civilians. Although the validity of the order to evacuate in the latter case is ripe for discussion in another context, the term *evacuation* has obscured the experiences of Confederate women and children and misstated the military intent of the tactic.

12. Sherman to R. M. Sawyer, January 31, 1864, *Sherman's Civil War*, 598–601.

13. See LeeAnn Whites, *The Civil War as a Crisis in Gender: Augusta, Georgia, 1860–1890* (Athens: University of Georgia Press, 1995).

14. On wartime ideas about masculinity, see Lorien Foote, *The Gentlemen and the Roughs: Manhood, Honor, and Violence in the Union Army* (New York: New York University Press, 2010); Stephen W. Berry II, *All That Makes a Man: Love and Ambition in the Civil War South* (New York: Oxford University Press, 2003). On the need to recognize the homefront as an important aspect of Civil War decisions and battles, see LeeAnn Whites and Alecia P. Long, eds., *Occupied Women: Gender, Military Occupation, and the American Civil War* (Baton Rouge: Louisiana State University Press, 2009).

15. Sherman to Ulysses S. Grant, October 4, 1862, *OR*, series 1, vol. 17, pt. 2:261.

16. General Orders No. 100, April 24, 1863, *OR*, series 3, vol. 3, 148–64. On the Lieber Code, see John Fabian Witt, *Lincoln's Code: The Laws of War in American History* (New York: Free Press, 2012), esp. 231–49; Mark Grimsley, *The Hard Hand of War: Union Military Policy toward Southern Civilians, 1861–1865* (New York: Cambridge University Press, 1995), esp. 149–51. Grimsley notes that the ambiguity of the Lieber Code both "enjoined Union forces to behave with humanity" and "declined to set specific limits on what those forces might do to achieve victory." *Hard Hand of War*, 151.

17. Sherman to James M. Calhoun, mayor, E. E. Rawson, and S. C. Wells, representing the City Council of Atlanta, September 12, 1864, *Sherman's Civil War*, 708.

18. John K. Mahon, *History of the Second Seminole War, 1835–1842* (Gainesville: University Press of Florida, 1967); Andrew K. Frank, *Before the Pioneers: Indians, Settlers, Slaves, and the Founding of Miami* (Gainesville: University Press of Florida, 2017), chap. 3.

19. Sherman to Thomas C. Hindman, October 17, 1862, *Sherman's Civil War*, 317.

20. Sherman to Hindman, October 17, 1862, *Sherman's Civil War*, 317.

21. Sherman to Miss P. A. Fraser, October 22, 1862, *Sherman's Civil War*, 318.

22. This need for the Confederacy to allocate resources to the homefront would be a reversal of the traditional connection between civilians who supplied the soldiers and otherwise supported the war effort.

23. Sherman to Fraser, October 22, 1862, *Sherman's Civil War*, 318–19.

24. Sherman to Valeria Hurlbut, November 6, 1862, *Sherman's Civil War*, 321.

25. Sherman to H. W. Hill, September 7, 1863, *Sherman's Civil War*, 536, 537.

26. Sherman to Maria Boyle Ewing Sherman, January 19, 1864, *Sherman's Civil War*, 587.

27. [Sherman] Report, Vicksburg, March 7, 1864, as quoted in Michael Fellman, *Citizen Sherman: A Life of William Tecumseh Sherman* (New York: Random House, 1995), 174.

28. Sherman to Lorenzo Thomas, April 12, 1864, *Sherman's Civil War*, 621.

29. Sherman to R. M. Sawyer, January 31, 1864, in *Sherman's Civil War*, 599.

30. Sherman to R. M. Sawyer, January 31, 1864, *Sherman's Civil War*, 598–601. Other officials similarly viewed all Confederates, regardless of age or sex, as enemies. Thaddeus Stevens noted, "The necessities of State require that all the inhabitants of a hostile country should be treated as enemies, whether in arms or not. Even women and children are enemies, and are to be treated as such in every respect. . . . There can be no neutrals in a hostile country." April 4, 1863, in *The Selected Papers of Thaddeus Stevens, Volume 1: January 1814–March 1865*, ed. Beverly Wilson Palmer and Holly Byers Ochoa (Pittsburgh: University of Pittsburgh Press, 1971), 391.

31. For more on Sherman's warfare against Southern households as a result of their integral role in supporting the Confederacy, see Lisa Tendrich Frank, *The Civilian War: Confederate Women and Union Soldiers during Sherman's March* (Baton Rouge: Louisiana State University Press, 2015); Lisa Tendrich Frank, "Bedrooms as Battlefields: The Role of Gender Politics in Sherman's March," in *Occupied Women*, 33–48.
Sherman also repeatedly included women in his discussions of the enemy. For example, he argued that "to the petulant and persistant secessionist, why death or banishment is a mercy, and the quicker he or she is disposed of the better." Sherman to R. M. Sawyer, January 31, 1864, *Sherman's Civil War*, 602. Other generals similarly included women and households as valid targets of military might. See Philip H. Sheridan, as quoted in *History of the Sixth New York Cavalry (Second Ira Harris Guard), Second Brigade—First Division—Cavalry Corps, Army of the Potomac, 1861–1865*, compiled by Hillman Allyn Hall and William B. Besley, Veteran Association of the Sixth New York Cavalry, Committee on Regimental History (Worcester, Mass.: Blanchard Press, 1908), 537–38.

32. Sherman to John Sherman, January 6, 1862 [1863], *Sherman's Civil War*, 352.

33. Sherman to Ellen Ewing Sherman, June 27, 1863, *Sherman's Civil War*, 492.

34. Sherman to Ellen Ewing Sherman, May 22, 1864, *Sherman's Civil War*, 639.

35. Sherman to Lorenzo Thomas, April 12, 1864, *Sherman's Civil War*, 621.

36. Sherman considered all white Southerners, civilian or military, as working for the Confederacy and had used this justification for eviction earlier in his career. In Memphis, families of guerrillas were sent away because of their support for their men, and prior to his arrival in Atlanta, Sherman had evicted the female factory workers in Roswell because "they had been for years engaged exclusively at work for the confederate Govt." Sherman to Henry W. Halleck, July 7, 1864, *Sherman's Civil War*, 662.

37. Sherman to Ulysses S. Grant, November 6, 1864, *Sherman's Civil War*, 751. On Sherman's goals for the entire campaign, see Frank, *Civilian War*. Although later scholars would debate the importance of the homefront, Sherman had no doubts about its power. In all of his tactics and many of his writings, Sherman acknowledged women's power to affect the course of war.

38. Sherman to James M. Calhoun, mayor, E. E. Rawson, and S. C. Wells, rep-

resenting the City Council of Atlanta, September 12, 1864, *Sherman's Civil War*, 708. Uttered in response to the protests by Atlanta's mayor and councilmen that Sherman had acted immorally by evicting Confederate civilians, these words have led scholars and others to segregate the debate over the eviction of Atlanta's civilians into the domestic realm rather than to see it as a military tactic.

39. Sherman to Ellen Ewing Sherman, January 1864, as quoted in Lee Kennett, *Marching through Georgia: The Story of Soldiers and Civilians during Sherman's Campaign* (New York: HarperPerennial, 1995), 12.

40. Sherman to Calhoun, Rawson, and Wells, September 12, 1864, *Sherman's Civil War*, 708. For interpretations that negate the larger tactical reasons for expelling women from Atlanta, see Grimsley, *Hard Hand of War*, 186–90; Thomas G. Dyer, *Secret Yankees: The Union Circle in Confederate Atlanta* (Baltimore: Johns Hopkins University Press, 1999), 202–8; Kennett, *Marching through Georgia*, 207–11; Anne J. Bailey, *The Chessboard of War: Sherman and Hood in the Autumn Campaigns of 1864* (Lincoln: University of Nebraska Press, 2000), 15–16.

41. Sherman to Grant, April 10, 1864, *Sherman's Civil War*, 618.

42. Sherman to Calhoun, Rawson, and Wells, September 12, 1864, *Sherman's Civil War*, 708.

43. On Butler's conflict with women in occupied New Orleans, see Alecia P. Long "(Mis)Remembering General Order No. 28: Benjamin Butler, the Woman Order, and Historical Memory," in *Occupied Women*, 17–32; Jacqueline Glass Campbell, "'The Unmeaning Twaddle about Order 28': Benjamin Butler and Confederate Women in Occupied New Orleans, 1862," *Journal of the Civil War Era* 2 (March 2012): 11–30.

44. Sherman to Halleck, September 9, 1864, *Supplemental Report of the Joint Committee on the Conduct of the War*, vol. 1 (Washington, D.C.: Government Printing Office, 1866), 193.

45. Sherman to Calhoun, Rawson, and Wells, September 12, 1864, *Sherman's Civil War*, 707.

46. Sherman to Ellen Sherman, September 17, 1864, *Sherman's Civil War*, 717.

47. Sherman to Ellen Sherman, October 1, 1864, *Sherman's Civil War*, 728.

48. Sherman to John Sherman, September 22, 1862, in *The Sherman Letters: Correspondence Between the General and Senator Sherman from 1837 to 1891*, ed. Rachel Sherman Thorndike (New York: Charles Scribner's Sons, 1894), 162.

49. Sherman to Calhoun, Rawson, and Wells, September 12, 1864, *Sherman's Civil War*, 707. In this portrayal, Sherman compared female Confederate civilians to cornered animals—unpredictable, desperate, and thereby dangerous.

50. Calhoun, Rawson, and Wells to Sherman, September 11, 1864, in William Tecumseh Sherman, *Memoirs* (New York: Penguin, 2000), 493.

51. For a recent examination of the mythology and memory surrounding Sherman, see Anne Sarah Rubin, *Through the Heart of Dixie: Sherman's March and American Memory* (Chapel Hill: University of North Carolina Press, 2014).

52. Catherine Ann Devereaux Edmondston, September 16, 1864, in *Journal of a Secesh Lady": The Diary of Catherine Ann Devereaux Edmondston, 1860–1866,* ed. Beth Gilbert Crabtree and James W. Patton (Raleigh: Division of Archives and History, 1979), 615.

53. Sarah Elizabeth Wilson to J. H. Wilkes, November 19, 1864, Edward Marvin Steel Papers, Collection of Heiskell, McCampbell, Wilkes, and Steel Family Materials, Wilkes Family Correspondence, SHC.

54. Sherman to Henry Halleck, September 4, 1864, *Sherman's Civil War,* 697. Sherman frequently used the word *howl* when referring to reactions to his military decision. As James Reston Jr. recognized, "Neither states nor soldiers howl; civilians do, particularly women." Reston, *Sherman's March and Vietnam* (New York: Macmillan, 1984), 93. Other commanders similarly agreed that disrupting households would be an effective and justified way to wage war. For examples, see Philip Sheridan to A. A. Humphreys, May 13, 1866, *OR,* ser. 1, vol. 36, pt. 1:801; Philip Sheridan to William Tecumseh Sherman, March 18, 1870, *Executive Documents Printed by the Order of the House of Representatives during the Second Session of the Forty-First Congress, 1869–70* (Washington, D.C.: Government Printing Office, 1870), 70. Executive document number 269.

55. Sherman to Calhoun, Rawson, and Wells, September 12, 1864, in *Sherman's Civil War,* 709.

56. Sherman to Calhoun, Rawson, and Wells, September 12, 1864, *Sherman's Civil War,* 708.

57. George Williamson Balloch to Jennie Balloch, September 11, 1864, George Williamson Balloch Papers, 1852–1907, David M. Rubenstein Rare Book and Manuscript Library, Duke University, Durham, N.C.

58. J. Dexter Cotton, September 17, 1864, Cotton Papers, Library of Congress. Henry Hitchcock, a commander on Sherman's March, berated a woman because "you have done all you could to help the war, and have not done what you could to prevent it." Henry Hitchcock, November 25, 1864, *Marching with Sherman,* ed. M. A. DeWolfe Howe (Lincoln: University of Nebraska Press, 1995), 92.

59. Edward Allen, September 25, 1864, Allen Papers, SHC. See also Horatio Dana Chapman, September 20, 1864, *Civil War Diary: Diary of a Forty-Niner* (Hartford: Allis, 1929), 95. The idea that Confederate women were getting what they deserved continued throughout the campaign. One described it as "a horrible state of affairs [that] they had brought upon themselves." James Leath, December 23, 1864, Journal, Henry E. Huntington Library, San Marino, Calif.

60. John J. Metzgar to Carrie Metzgar, September 15, 1864, John J. Metzgar Papers #4939, SHC.

61. Even Union clergy rejected the idea that Confederate women deserved protection. Reverend George S. Bradley, who traveled with Sherman's troops, ridiculed the notion that soldiers should treat Confederate civilians with charity. He saw mercy as something that enemy Confederate women did not deserve. "So far as the women are concerned, we might as well spare our pity, for they are the worse

secessionists, and why should they not suffer." He further wanted these civilians to feel the consequences of their actions. Writing, "They have urged on the brutal treatment of Yankee prisoners. They have personally insulted these poor men," he agreed that they needed to be treated as military enemies. Bradley urged that women needed to "understand that secession means something more than a holiday parade." Bradley's attitudes showed not only a paternal outlook that dismissed white women as frivolous girls who reduced war to nothing "more than a holiday parade," but also a need to treat all secessionists as military enemies. George S. Bradley, December 28, 1864, *The Star Corps; or, Notes of an Army Chaplain, during Sherman's Famous "March to the Sea"* (Milwaukee: Jermain and Brightman, 1865), 225.

62. Ellen Sherman to William T. Sherman, September 17, 1864, as cited in Marszalek, *Sherman: A Soldier's Passion for Order* (Carbondale: Southern Illinois University Press, 2007), 286.

63. Sherman to Ellen Sherman, January 1864, as quoted in Kennett, *Marching through Georgia*, 12.

64. See Marszalek, *Sherman*, 188–201, esp. 195–96; Fellman, *Citizen Sherman*, 135–48. While in Memphis, Sherman evicted families of Confederate guerrillas and threatened to evict all civilians. "I will expel every secession family from Memphis if [guerrilla] war is to be continued." Sherman as quoted in Fellman, *Citizen Sherman*, 141.

65. See Sherman to Calhoun, Rawson, and Wells, September 12, 1864, *Sherman's Civil War*, 709; Sherman to Grant, November 6, 1864, *Sherman's Civil War*, 751. On Sherman's goals for the entire campaign, see Frank, *Civilian War*.

66. Sherman to Grant, October 4, 1862, *OR*, series 1, vol. 17, pt. 2:261; William T. Sherman to John Sherman, September 22, 1862, *Sherman Letters*, 162.

War's Domestic Corollary

Union Occupation Households in the Civil War South

MARGARET STOREY

It seams like home to see so many woman in camp.

—Orin England, 1862

In the early fall of 1863, General James B. McPherson hosted "*the event of the season*" at the Balfour House on the corner of Cherry and Crawford Streets in Vicksburg, Mississippi. An elegant brick home with a commanding view of the city and river below, it boasted "sun parlors, conservatories, fountains, and large spacious rooms." McPherson held the ball to honor the wives of Union officers who had traveled down the Mississippi River to winter in the recently conquered city. Among them were a number of young women, recently married to their fiancés after Vicksburg fell, who arrived at the party "decked in their bridal robes." Guests enjoyed a live orchestra and ate delicacies prepared by a New Orleans caterer, who had shipped the fare—and the waiters to serve it—up the river for the occasion. Sarah Jane Hill, married to a First Missouri Engineers brigade commander, remembered the event with pleasure. She danced "nearly every set and with a number of celebrities," including Generals McPherson and Mower. "It was the finest ball given that winter, and I am sure it was never forgotten by those who had the pleasure of attending it."[1]

There was perhaps no more ostentatiously domestic way to demonstrate the Union's newly regained control of the Mississippi River. In one of the most elegant homes in the South, fantastic food was served to Northerners only a few months after many of Vicksburg's residents (including its most elite) had had little but vermin to eat. In what was almost a fertility ritual, newlyweds were feted in their wedding finery, surrounded by the officers who had laid the mines, saps, and fortifications central to the most aggressive warfare against civilian and domestic institutions yet seen in the war. Here, Union officers and their wives enjoyed the height of domestic security in a home that had, just a few years earlier, stood as a monument to the Confederacy's slaveholding republic. If the objective of General Ulysses S. Grant's campaign in Mississippi was to destroy the material and psychological supports of the Confederacy, General McPherson's ball was war's domestic corollary.

Events on the scale of the Balfour House ball were rarities, but the presence of Union wives in occupied Southern cities and towns was far more common and significant than historians have acknowledged. If this reality is noticed at all by historians, it is usually passed over quickly, recorded as a feature of some other and more central matter being examined—the actions or ideas of a given general, the particular circumstance of a battle or other event, or as an aspect of a marriage itself.[2] The movement of wives into occupied territory was so commonplace, however, that to overlook it misses an essential feature of the Civil War itself. If we accept, as most historians do, that occupation was itself a form of warfare, then we must pursue the question of what women's role was within that form of warfare.[3] When we take cognizance of their often sustained presence in these military zones, we have to begin to take seriously that the Union's occupation of the South was not simply a male prerogative but also undertaken by Northern women as *wives*, acting in roles distinct from the women who traveled south to perform occupation service as nurses, teachers, or missionaries.[4]

Like other women's "war work," this spousal migration was a gendered form of war mobilization.[5] At its heart was the occupation household—the transient domestic arrangements through which Union officers and their wives reestablished the prerogatives and pleasures of their domestic relations within the military sphere of the garrisoned town. These sites of loyalist domesticity operated in a variety of ways. At the most fundamental level, Union officers and their wives desired a return to comfort—the warmth and love of family, the pleasure of sanctioned sexual relations—and hoped to restore the social and domestic stability that had been so disrupted by the war.[6] Officers and their wives took advantage of Union territorial control in the South to reassert those relations as quickly and as often as possible. It is also true that many wives simply wanted to be at the front—like their husbands, they found it exciting, not to mention patriotic, to experience firsthand the great conflict of their country. In the words of one soldier, "The Army seems to possess a strange fascination for some women." Indeed, some spent so much time with the armies that they later referred to themselves as "old campaigners" or "old soldiers."[7] As Mary Elizabeth Massey has argued, "Most wives were in camp because that was where they wanted to be, and no amount of dissuasion would keep them away."[8]

But these households also operated at an ideological level.[9] Wrapped up in a highly articulated system of manners and gender conventions, Union occupation households both endorsed and elided the coercion that underlay their existence. Without the conquest of Southern landscapes and homes, they would not exist, but once in place, they were rarely directly martial.[10] Their gentility did not make them less significant expressions of power. When Union officers' wives set up occupation households, however temporary, they used what John Kasson has called "the structures of everyday conduct" to assert their own and the Union's conquest of the South.[11] Like colonizers, Union households grafted themselves and their social practices onto local geographies, forming secure enclaves protected by the military might that had created them in the first place.

Union couples set up occupation households just as Southern households began to shatter under the pressure of invasion. The two phenomena were interconnected. "Hard war" tactics in occupied areas, particularly the confiscation of Southerners' property and the expulsion of Confederate sympathizers were designed to allow Union military control to stabilize into pacification. This meant undermining the power base of resistant secessionists, especially Southern wives and mothers who remained behind Union lines. A key power base of secessionist resistance in occupied places was the household—the home itself, the material means to maintain it, and the kinship and social networks within which it thrived.[12]

Scholars often describe this confrontation as a contest between U.S. soldiers and secessionist women, and so it was.[13] But that is not all it was. The same men who were the policy architects and enforcers of "hard war" tactics in the western theater—Ulysses S. Grant, William T. Sherman, Benjamin F. Butler, and their many subordinates and staff officers—also invited their wives and children into territory that they were attempting to subdue and frequently acted against civilians while their wives were present. When in the summer of 1862 Grant asked for permission to expel from Memphis the "great many families of rebel officers here who are very violent," he did so only days after his wife, Julia Dent Grant, and children had joined him in the city, where they had enjoyed "the salvos of artillery" on the Fourth of

July.[14] When Benjamin Butler ordered the owner of the opulent St. Charles Hotel to open it for his use as military and domestic headquarters the day after New Orleans fell, he did so with his wife, Sarah, at his side. And on the very day that her husband issued Order No. 28—known then and now as "the Woman Order" because it declared that any New Orleans female who insulted soldiers of the United States should be treated as a "woman of the street plying her avocation"—Sarah Butler sent a copy of it to her sister back in Massachusetts. "Never has anything been more deserved," she fumed. "Their insolence is beyond endurance, and must be checked. . . . We . . . seem like the conquered and they like conquerors."[15] The degree to which Sarah Butler—highly intelligent, ambitious, and keenly interested in political and military matters—played a role in the conception of the Woman Order is impossible to determine. But that she had influence in the decision seems clear from General Butler's own comment to her a few months later: "You said it was right at the time, and therefore I knew it was right."[16]

Similarly, when William Sherman threatened to banish secessionist sympathizers from Memphis in retaliation for a series of steamboat attacks on the Mississippi River, he did so against a backdrop of wifely migration.[17] Many of his officers' families were traveling on the river into Memphis during the height of these attacks in the summer and fall of 1862. His own wife, Ellen, managed to get safely to Memphis by steamboat after numerous attempts were foiled by the hazards of the river. Sherman was quite explicit about the fact that he was punishing rebels in kind when he defended his orders to a critical Memphis woman: "I will not permit the families and adherents of secessionists to live here in peace," he explained, "whilst their husbands and brothers are aiming the rifle and gun at *our families* on the free Mississippi."[18]

We well understand the significance of these tactics against Southern civilians within the evolution of the Union's military policy, but we often overlook the fact that "war on women and children" about which Southerners complained so bitterly was also something that Union officers believed was being waged by Confederates against *their* families—guerrilla warfare was not just a threat to the army or an abstraction of the national family but a menace against actual Northern women and children.[19] For the Union officers occupying the South with their families, the distance between the Northern household and the battlefront was considerably shorter than we may tend to imagine. It reminds us that the women who came to live in the occupied South did not simply wander into some neutral or pacified territory. They traveled through and into active military zones—zones whose character could change depending on which neighborhood or even home one found oneself in. Here the household itself was often the locus of conflict.

All modes of nineteenth-century transportation carried physical risks: steamboat accidents and explosions were commonplace, and railroads, too, were fraught with complication and danger. During the war, these normal risks multiplied significantly once passengers moved out of uncontested Union territory. Military, commercial, and passenger traffic frequently occurred on the same routes and in the same conveyances, and all were subject to attack by Confederate partisans. Throughout 1862 and 1863, Confederate guerrillas heavily targeted both railroads and steamboats, and the degree to which the roads or rivers could be declared "safe" at any time varied considerably. Colonel John Miller of the Twenty-Ninth Indiana advised Mary Chess Miller that, though he believed the railroad from Louisville to Nashville would be free of "Secesh cavalry" a mere month after Nashville had fallen, she would have to make the call herself as she traveled. He left it to her to determine, once at Louisville, "the safest route" to get to him.[20] In July, the wife and children of one Union general, along with one of his staff officers and his family, were injured and three soldiers were killed south of Nashville when their train derailed due to sabotage. The cars were "broken to pieces" and the railroad "badly torn up for some distance."[21] By early 1863, such attacks on railroads in southwest Tennessee had become an endemic feature of the war in the region. Sarah Jane Hill, traveling from Trenton to Memphis with her small child, had to duck between the seats when guerrillas fired into her train car, and threats of more such activity were reported at every station along the way.[22] A train carrying a large number of wives traveling to meet their husbands west of Memphis was similarly threatened by guerrillas who, having pulled up the tracks, next planned to ambush the cars. They were apparently dissuaded by the well-armed contingent of Union soldiers who set out to repair the damage.[23]

If railroads were risky, steamboats were equally attractive targets for guerrilla activity. Occasionally transport steamers were caught up in naval warfare carried on between Union steam rams and Confederate batteries in contested waterways. In late July, the uss *Sallie Wood*, carrying soldiers on leave as well as civilians, including multiple women, fell afoul of intense artillery fire from concealed batteries in the north Mississippi. Confederate partisans disabled, captured, and burnt the ship and took the passengers prisoner.[24] By the fall of 1862, Confederate guerrillas had begun to deliberately target transport steamers, both for plunder and to destabilize Union occupation of the Mississippi River valley. The activity was intense. As newspaperman Franc Wilkie caustically noted, "one of the amusements" before the fall of Vicksburg "was to take a run on a steamer up to Cairo," running a gauntlet of banks "haunted by guerrillas" ready to fire into the craft.[25] Even after Vicksburg fell, there was little distinction between "civilian" and "military" travelways. Matilda Gresham's husband encouraged her to come to Mississippi early in 1864 because the "navigation of the river is not so perilous now as it was some time back." She debated whether to go, especially after learning that two women had recently been killed by guerrillas who had fired on their boat. "Running the gantlet [*sic*] from Memphis to Natchez on a frail Mississippi River steamboat did not seem to me an ideal opportunity to visit my husband," Gresham remembered, but she "mustered up" her courage and her two children and struck out. The trip was harrowing—she learned only once aboard that the boat was loaded with ammunition and that the captain consequently expected to be attacked. Gresham sat up all night in terror while her children slept. Though the boats ahead and behind them both fell under rebel fire, her transport escaped unscathed.[26] Traveling to occupied areas exposed Union wives to the realities of warfare, but it also heightened their sense that, in transporting their domestic affairs into these areas, they had, in Gresham's words, run a gauntlet; their visits and their reunited households were hard won.

Actually living in occupied areas further blended domestic and military imperatives. Union wives had to rely for their shelter and sustenance, directly or indirectly, on the mechanisms of hard war, especially the confiscation of secessionist property and the expulsion of Southerners from their homes and cities.[27] In larger towns like New Orleans, Memphis, or Nashville, women could stay for brief periods in respectable hotels, but many occupied towns had no hotel, and even when there was one, families preferred the control and privacy of a house. In some instances, houses were vacant—abandoned by their Confederate owners either by volition or force. Upon reaching Memphis in late June 1862, Provost Marshal William S. Hillyer explained to his wife, Anna, that he and General Grant "intend taking a suburban residence for our families—of which there are some beautiful ones."[28] The Grants moved into the Hunt Mansion, abandoned by its secessionist owners just before the Union army took the city, and the Hillyers set themselves up in the "splendid house" of Fannie Galloway, just days after she was arrested and expelled from the city "for carrying on treasonable correspondence" with her own husband, a noted secessionist editor, and for employing her slave to transport contraband mail to and from rebel women all over the city.[29] Taking the house was both an act of punishment for Galloway's resistance and that of her husband and a way to obtain a comfortable home that could also serve as a beacon of Union patriotism in the midst of what was still a very resistant city.[30] "We have a beautiful flag hanging in the front of our house," Hillyer explained to her cousin in a letter. "[It is] very large and hangs over the front pavement."[31] The Hillyer and Grant families set up similar arrangements throughout the western theater over subsequent months—in LaGrange, they occupied a "large house with fine grounds" owned by a "runaway rebel." "We were in the enemy's country," Anna Hillyer admitted, "but feeling all the security which fifty thousand 'never defeated' soldiers afforded."[32] Though Julia Grant made a point of explaining in her memoirs that they "never occupied a house unless it was vacant," this neatly obscured the circumstances under which the houses were made vacant in the first place.[33] Whether the owners had fled of their own volition in anticipation of being occupied or had been forced out by the military authorities after occupation occurred, these relocations were functions of warfare and the Union army's advance into Southern territory.

Union appropriations frequently involved evaluations of homes for their beauty, comfort, or refinement. In Memphis, the Fifty-Fifth Illinois quartermaster and his wife occupied a "large fine house" near the main camp of the regiment, where they lived "in the highest style" and invited other officers to board.[34] Julia Hascell's husband, an officer in the Twenty-Ninth Indiana stationed in Knoxville, was "very nicely situated in an Elegant Brick House" with "every thing comfortable about him," before making arrangements to send for her.[35] In Nashville, when General John Miller confiscated a home for his wife, Mary, and their daughter, he described it as "a good one, though not the finest, but good enough," with a "large carpeted room for one bed room upstairs" and a "large fine library . . . left by the proprietor."[36] Later, after a hiatus away from the city, the family again needed a home, as Miller had been made military commander. In a letter to Mary, who had not yet returned, he explained, "I have taken the Evans House. Everybody says it is one of the finest houses in town and well furnished."[37]

The expansive houses of the Southern elite held many charms for itinerant wives seeking a comfortable dwelling, a fact painfully obvious to women who had been displaced; the fact of female presence made the displacement all the more devastating. Mrs. Barnett Graham of Memphis returned to her home after a brief social call to find that her house had been invaded not simply by soldiers but also by "two strange women" who were sitting "in her rocking chairs making themselves comfortable and ordering a different arrangement of her things," as well as "two other women at her bureau using her toilet articles"—one of whom was "cleaning her teeth at the wash basin"—all the while "laughing and making merry with one another."[38]

Upon learning that her family home in Baton Rouge had been occupied by "a Yankee Colonel and his wife," Sarah Morgan bemoaned the "debasement" of the luxuries and family heirlooms in it. "O my garden! do they respect you?" she asked her diary. The family dining table, the "old lamp," "father's little ebony stand," all were artifacts of the Morgans' harmonious household, now torn asunder by the war. But worst of all, Union people with "neither ancestry or family to be proud of" had colonized it, polluting and debasing the things with their grubby hands. "And mother's bed," she cried, "belongs now to a Yankee woman!"[39]

If the furniture and amenities of the confiscated home were insufficient, officers and their wives could appropriate accoutrements from other local households. Sarah Butler, living in a rough shanty on Ship Island for the three weeks prior to the Union assault on New Orleans, noted that, even if the home was merely a "room," it was "furnished with a wardrobe, secretary, which we use for dishes, a highposted bedstead hung round with a mosquito net, safe, chairs, washstand, china bowl and pitcher, dining table and stove," all of which were "captured the day before we arrived."[40] Auctions of the contents of abandoned Southern homes furnished considerable material for the comfort of Union wives at low cost. The household goods of "Mrs. Capt. Newell," including "Parlor, Bedroom, and Kitchen Furniture of the best and most Modern Styles" were auctioned off from her presumably abandoned residence in Memphis in the weeks following her husband's defeat in the river battle that preceded the city's fall.[41] In Nashville, the "auction stores are full of crockery & table ware and sell cheap," General Miller explained to his wife. "I am going to buy enough to do as well. We can sell it when we are through."[42] In New Orleans, Sarah Butler thought her husband "paid high" for "three oil paintings and a bronze clock"—she felt certain that three hundred dollars was too much "for this place where so much will soon be sold at auction."[43]

Union officers and their wives also regularly boarded in Southern homes that continued to be occupied by their owners. In some instances, the homeowners were Unionists, but far more commonly they were the wives and families of Confederate officers. Under the circumstances, occupiers could exploit the precarious financial and military position of elite Southerners to live in a socially elevated, even luxurious, manner. Most Union wives revealed few anxieties about adopting habits of "real Southern living"—a good number hailed from the Midwest, and though they might have found Southern slavery distasteful or even immoral, they had little argument with white supremacy and did not object to the conveniences of having black "servants" wait on them.[44] Julia Grant, of course, traveled for the first part of the war with her own slave, Jule.[45] Some had developed kinship or friendly connections to Southerners in the antebellum period and felt at home in a Southern setting, despite the obvious and violent conflict all around them. Southerners were often able to exploit this détente of manners thanks to such common social, class, or racial assumptions.[46] Confederates were well aware that their homes and property were in danger of confiscation, and women frequently stayed in homes rather than flee south of the lines as a way to anchor the family's property. In such tenuous circumstances, some made a conscious decision to wrap themselves in the additional protection and frequently the cash afforded by hospitality to Union officers and their families.

Sarah Jane Hill and her daughter, for instance, lived in the home of a Mrs. Wilson in Vicksburg, a "large white house with spacious upper and lower galleries," where they were provided with an elegant bedroom with a four-poster bed, lace curtains, satin bedclothes, and a slave to fold down the covers at night and bring in the tin bathtub every morning. "Our being there was a great protection to her," Hill later remembered.[47] Matilda Gresham's host was an "accomplished, refined woman" who provided "elegant dinners" to the boarders she kept for "the protection the presence of Federal officers afforded." Gresham approved of her strategy: "Many Confederates foolishly abandoned Memphis, and their houses were sacked."[48] Rachel Greene, her husband, and daughter boarded "in a secesh house" with other Union families, where all their meals were prepared by the slaves of their hosts, a widow and her sister. "O, but they are rebels, they would be glad to cut our throats or poison our food if they dared," she explained to her mother, "but their bread and butter depend on what they can get from Union soldiers."[49]

The power dynamics of these arrangements were sometimes exquisitely delicate. The authority of Southern women was limited almost entirely to the sphere of hospitality—providing it or withholding it—and the degree to which they deigned to extend courtesies commensurate with that hospitality. This ability was no small power, however. Behind the veneer of courtesy lay considerable possibilities for protest and active resistance. Sarah Hill's host, though lodging her Yankee guests in luxury in Vicksburg, did not remove the bed's "fluted silk upholstery" canopy, which had been ripped by the cannonball that also left a hole in the wall above the bed during the siege, a scar upon which Hill gazed every night and morning. Indeed, the ball itself stood in a place of honor on the mantelpiece, well in view of the occupiers whose presence had been facilitated by its fall.[50] And Matilda Gresham's host, Anne Fackler, was likely interested in any intelligence she might surreptitiously gather from her Yankee guests; she entertained noted mail runner Belle Edmondson alongside her Union boarders on multiple occasions.[51]

The power of Union women, on the other hand, derived almost entirely from the military might of the U.S. army, unless they and their hosts had ties of kinship or social connections predating the war. Stripped of middle-class and elite customs of courtesy, Union women were engaged in quite an aggressive or even extortionist act: that of moving into a strange woman's home and having her take care of them for money or other favors. Matilda Gresham, for instance, noted the importance of decorously avoiding the very thing that had brought her into Anne Fackler's home in the first place. "We discussed everything that women do," she noted, "but one subject we avoided—that was the *War*."[52] Though Gresham was respectful of these political boundaries in her interactions with Confederate women, other Union women, particularly those who subscribed to Republican Party or abolitionist ideas, were less interested in *bonhomie* and quicker to assert their role as conquerors. When Union wives arrived in the South, many were not just familiar but comfortable with the idea that Southern women, particularly those connected to guerrilla warfare, were legitimately part of the field of battle if they resisted Union authority. This recognition was in part due to the near obsession with the "she-rebel" in Northern news-papers, as well as the frank, often violent or sexually explicit, descriptions about Southern women that many Union soldiers included in their letters to their wives.[53] One provost marshal wrote with satisfaction to his wife that his men had knocked down the "thundering bitches" who had spat upon his men in the Memphis street.[54] Likewise, Illinois surgeon Hum-phrey Hood explained to his wife, Matilda, that it "would astonish you to see the insolence and impudence of these secesh women," describing their "clamoring," "begging and teasing and worrying" at the guards at Mem-phis's Irving Block Prison in an effort to get access to Confederate prison-ers. Unwilling to cast their efforts as understandable attempts to see their male kin, he ended by repeating a devastating rumor about the charac-ter of these otherwise "respectable" women. "It is said, in some instances, they have tried the power of personal charms—making promises that virtu-ous women cannot keep."[55] And Surgeon John Rice not only cast Southern women as little better than prostitutes but also introduced the complicating worry that he himself might have been subject to such secessionist charms when he told his newlywed wife that a Memphis woman had requested his picture. In a subsequent letter, she apparently reminded him of the dan-gers of such interactions. "Think you are entirely correct as to the object the lady had in wanting my picture," he assured her in his response. "She did not get it. The devil is in most of them. Many among them considered very respectable will grant almost any favor to promote their objects."[56] In these descriptions, Union officers held up a mirror to their, and their wives', own ideas about appropriate domestic and gendered behavior. In doing so, they engaged in a common practice throughout the Union during the war—that of tying disloyalty to a diminishment of female respectability—casting the fall from national loyalty as akin to a fall from virtue in ways that helped, ideologically, to justify harsh military treatment of Southern women.

Many Union women found their husband's stories about secessionist women confirmed by personal experience once they arrived in occupied areas. Wives of officers stationed in the South commented on the "very bitter" women who taught their children to avoid Union people and refused to walk underneath the U.S. flag.[57] Others observed, often with relish, harsh or humiliating physical altercations between Union soldiers and rebel women, as in the case of Sarah Hill, who watched with glee as a Union soldier, having been spat upon by a Confederate woman, grabbed the offender, wiped the spittle from his own face, and then vigorously rubbed the woman's nose in the soiled handkerchief.[58] Rachel Greene and other Union wives boarding in a Confederate house in Germantown, Tennessee, were gathered on the porch with their rebel hostesses when a train transporting U.S. troops came down the track within sight of the house. Greene and the other Union wives "snatched our handkerchiefs," and her little girl "caught hold of her little white apron," and all began "such a waving and bowing you never saw," to which the soldiers responded with cheers. All the while, the "secesh women stood and glowered" and hoped aloud that "the train would go to pieces and kill them all." Greene confessed to her mother that she "wanted to wring their necks," but satisfied herself with a cutting reply: "But it won't, though, if there is a just God in heaven."[59]

Encounters like these were not limited to front porch insults. For the smaller number of wives who lived outside garrisoned towns or traveled between them to reach their husbands, experiences more readily paralleled that of soldiers on the march. As such, they were more likely to participate in the kinds of punitive foraging and confiscation of Southern property that was endemic as the army moved through the Southern landscape and confronted active Confederates of both sexes. Sarah Hill, traveling in the dark on uncertain roads with fellow wives and a single officer on the way to meet her husband's engineering regiment in Tennessee, simply "took possession" of a poor farmer woman's home, despite the woman's protestations. "Very reluctantly" and "under compulsion," the woman of the house prepared their supper and made them space to spend the night. Hill was relieved when her husband, E. M., arrived early the next morning to pilot them to his camp, not least because she and the other women had figured out soon after taking the house that the sons of the household were keeping up communications with the guerrillas in the woods and thus refused to lie down to sleep after they had been given supper. E. M. promptly caught one of the boys and tied him up to the ambulance until the Union party was able to depart.[60] Martha Nicholson McKay, married to an officer of the Thirteenth U.S. Colored Troops, regularly went with her husband to get fresh food from the house nearby their camp in a small Middle Tennessee town where the men were building railroads. The owner of the house, it was rumored, longed to "shoot and poison" the soldiers. "They don't like us to have anything, even for a great price," she complained to her sisters at home. "They lie and say they have nothing. . . . Almost the only way to get a thing is to hunt for it, take it, & then pay for it if you're not too angry."[61] Sheer force never hurt, either. On a harrowing trek between camps, McKay and the officers' wives traveling with the regiment were installed for the night in a house situated in an area rife with guerrillas and very near where one of their officers had been shot only weeks before. The "lank woman" and the "Tennessee famer" who headed the household were "ordered to provide lodging for five ladies, supper & breakfast for eleven," doubtlessly impressed by the military force behind the order. As McKay remarked, "In the face of a Regt at night fall, who would not?"[62]

Most Union wives, however, did not find themselves in these situations for long, and in general they were rarely dependent on secessionists, overt or subdued, for their only company. Officers often coordinated when setting up arrangements for their families, and the entire affair was considerably more appealing to everyone if they could create a facsimile of the social life they were used to at home. Sarah Hill referred to the occupation households in Vicksburg as "a military social colony," an apt description in many respects.[63] Like colonizers, occupation households formed separate enclaves within the South, marked both by their loyalty to the Union and their domination of Confederate space, control that was manifested by the households' very existence. The sense of enclave was further intensified when the occupiers all hailed from the same town or county, as was often the case because of the manner in which regiments were recruited during the Civil War. The town of Gallatin, Tennessee, practically became an outpost of Pontiac, Illinois, and the citizens of Fremont, Ohio, would have found many old acquaintances in Memphis. When towns came under sustained occupations, friends and relatives could shuttle between the homefront and the occupied zone multiple times and keep up with the goings-on of others in the correspondence that was meant to be shared with all the neighbors and connections in both places.[64]

Central to the day-to-day social life of these occupation enclaves was the well-established custom of visiting and entertaining. Whether ensconced at hotels, boardinghouses, private homes, or camps in the field, Union families paid calls upon and hosted parties for one another regularly.[65] A Chicago visitor to Corinth, Mississippi, was delighted to be included in a "fine picnic" held by the post's "officers, with their ladies" in May 1863. "A fine band of music accompanied the party."[66] William and Ellen Sherman, along with their four children, made "frequent visits" to Vicksburg from Sherman's headquarters on the Big Black River, where they passed their days "very agreeably, visiting General McPherson at the Balfour House and the Grants at the Lum House."[67] The six women traveling with the Missouri engineers in Tennessee let no opportunity for convivial visiting go unanswered. In addition to organizing small quartet concerts featuring "old songs and the new patriotic ones" in the evenings, they "formed a whist club for amusement and a reading club. Our friends and relatives kept us well supplied with reading matter from home, and we would procure new books. Some one would read aloud, usually one of the young officers, and we women would busy ourselves with our fancy work and sewing."[68] Once established, these connections could be long lasting, sustained during wives' absences back at home, only to be refreshed upon their return or relocation to another spot. Ann Carter, for instance, wrote to Mary Chess Miller on one of her visits back to her home in South Bend from Nashville to give her updates about the social activities of the army families she knew. "The house has been verry gay for two weeks," she explained, thanks to "Gen Rosecrans and suit[e] being here his Wife also joined him here about ten days since I like her verry much says she had promised you a photograph which she would send."[69] General Miller reported to his wife about local activities on another occasion, noting, "Everybody enquires for you."[70] Mary Culver found life back home in Pontiac, Illinois, "dull and uninteresting," and her husband sympathized. "I can in a measure realize how dull it must be for you there. If I was there, it might be better, but I fear we will both find it dull after the excitement of Army life."[71] Carrie Goddard likewise remembered her time in camp with her husband and other wives at Murfreesboro with longing after she returned North; she thought often of "friends left behind" and "*whistled & hummed* all the old familiar band tunes—'*Bonny Eloise*' particularly—

with *my eyes shut*, trying to imagine myself once again in my pleasant quarters at Murfreesboro; where when free from anxiety, we passed our time so pleasantly."[72]

Leisure and entertainment are the activities of a secure people, and in locations where Southern Unionist populations were sizeable, the presence of occupation households created a longed-for social space for families who had suffered considerable social ostracism at the hands of secessionists. When General Hurlbut gave a "very large party" on Christmas Eve 1863, some twenty-five "ladies," nearly evenly divided between Southern Unionists and Northern visitors, attended along with about one hundred Union officers. "I think you wood [have] injoyed yourself," Orin England reported to his girlfriend back home, after describing the mutual acquaintances who had attended.[73] The Memphis social scene allowed numerous such activities. Union ladies there sponsored a fund-raiser to support the needs of wounded soldiers, and the Oddfellows Hall mounted a "Polyrama" depicting the war's history, to which Union officers and their families came.[74]

Within the context of occupation, such social activities were freighted with significance about loyalty, dominance, and conquest, and they were interpreted as such by many of the secessionist women in occupied towns. Sociability with Yankee families marked the divisions between conqueror and conquered, delineating clearly who belonged and who, even if allowed to stay in their homes under occupations, was exiled from power and influence. When General Ormsby M. Mitchel's three daughters passed through Athens on the way to their father's headquarters in Huntsville in June 1862, Mary Fielding noted that the family had "taken a house & is going to housekeeping there. I hope none of the ladies will call to see them."[75] Ellen Renshaw House of Knoxville, who bemoaned the idea of having "Yankee woman & children" in her house when her parents agreed to a boarding arrangement with Captain Charles McAlister and his family, despised the friendly relations between Union officers' families and the Unionist families in town. When the Captain and Mrs. McAlister called on the wife of Unionist William "Parson" Brownlow, she threatened in her diary that if "the tory women come here" to call on Mrs. McAlister, "I'll insult them certain and sure."[76] As it turns out, though she argued regularly and heatedly with Captain McAlister, Union authorities claimed it was her insult to his wife that ultimately prompted them to expel her from the city.[77] Similarly, the "Grand Military Ball," thrown by General Eleazar A. Paine in Gallatin, Tennessee, stuck in Alice Williams's craw. "The ball came off with great splendor," she noted in her diary, a day after "Old Dilsy (Mrs. Payne)" had arrived. "Old Dilsey" was a name given to "mammy" characters in minstrelsy, novels, and cartoons of the era, so Williamson's contempt for the wife of the commanding general is most evident. Two days later she commented sarcastically, "Old Dilse brought another daughter down. I wonder how many more there are."[78]

Whether insulted by or spied on by secessionist women or shot at by guerrillas while riding steamboats, most Union wives carried with them one certain piece of knowledge: they did not have to stay in the South. Their true households lay elsewhere, well out of the line of fire, and as long as their husbands lived through the war, most were confident that home would be waiting. This reality meant that the ways they behaved in the occupied South often had the quality of tourism—a sense that they were there to see the sights and to observe the mighty transformations wrought by the war. Sarah Butler was thrilled to be the only woman on a "quite delightful" trip down the Mississippi from New Orleans to see sugar being made on a plantation, "owned by an old bachelor," where she, her husband, and twenty gentlemen also had dinner.[79] In early 1863, Julia Grant, Minerva McClernand, the wife of General John McClernand, and Belle Reynolds, wife of Lieutenant Colonel William S. Reynolds, were among the guests for a similar excursion dinner aboard the steamer *Henry von Phul*, but this trip promised more than the typical entertainment. General Grant had ordered gunboats to run the blockade by Vicksburg, and the *Henry von Phul* followed them down the river, close enough to witness the "grand sight" of the Confederate batteries firing upon the blockade runners.[80] Sarah Hill remembered taking "long delightful rides through the beautiful woods" in Tennessee, touring past "rich and fertile farms or plantations which yet had not felt the devastating hand of war" and visiting both The Hermitage, Andrew Jackson's "quaint and primitive" home, as well as Adelicia Acklen's palatial Belair mansion, "a perfect fairyland" of a home.[81]

These excursions were fairly innocuous, but they could not have happened without substantial military control of the landscape. Other tours brought the wives of Union officers into far closer contact with the violent destructiveness of the war, experiences that were at once moving, awe inspiring, and troubling. The wives who arrived in Vicksburg in 1863, for instance, spent hours riding on horseback over the miles and miles of battlefield and siege defenses that ringed the city, developing new appreciation for the scope of the siege.[82] Sarah Hill and her husband were invited to dine with a well-to-do Vicksburg family whose home was "a partial ruin," including the dining room itself. "But the table service was perfect," she remembered, "the linen immaculate, the china and glass the best, and the silver service and salver, solid, heavy, and rich," and the family entertained their guests with "so many thrilling incidents" of the siege. Impressed by all she was hearing and seeing, Hill inquired about the "massive handsome coffee urn" that stood on the sideboard in the dining room, "battered and dented almost out of shape." That, she was told, was a "memento" of the family's "narrow escape," when the house had been struck by a shell, mere moments before the family was due to appear for breakfast, and where, presumably, they would have been killed alongside the coffee urn.

It seems clear that the Confederates who invited Union occupiers like the Hills to eat dinner with their perfect silver service, in a partially ruined dining room, wanted very much to preserve these traces as witnesses to the dignity and resilience of the vanquished. It also seems clear that Union occupiers relished these traces as proof of the legitimacy of the Union war and their own presence, even as those ruins elicited ambivalence and sorrow.[83] Rachel Greene captured the very mixed emotions that attended these visits in a letter to her mother from "the middle of secession" in western Tennessee, describing driving by "magnificent suburban homes" with "beautiful grounds and fountains" on her way to her husband's headquarters. One, a large, attractive brick house "with a world of verandas above and below," caught her eye for the forlorn aspect it presented. "Of course the owners had fled," she noted, and the home had been occupied by U.S. soldiers: "On the railings of the upper veranda hung long lines of blue army shirts, their sleeves hanging helplessly down; at the lower ones army coats were packed and the floors covered with debris of army life. To one statue a mule was hitched: on another an army shirt was hung to dry; the fountain was utilized as a reservoir for watering horses and mules; soldiers, horses, mules, and carts had taken possession in the name of Uncle Sam. Can we blame them?"[84]

The "helplessness" that Green ascribes to the soldiers' shirt sleeves is instructive, for she surely senses a greater helplessness in the face of the power of her husband's army. The gaze of an ambivalent tourist is at work here—triumph and regret mixed with a strange fascination and detachment. The experience of exploring the Vicksburg caves in which Southerners had sheltered during the siege was less forlorn than "uncanny," according to Sarah Hill. "You thought of the ancient cave-dwellers and the catacombs of Rome, and were glad you did not live in Vicksburg during the siege." She frequently referred to hearing the stories of suffering Vicksburg people as "thrilling," again evoking eeriness, as if she were traversing haunted territory. In similar fashion, Carrie Goddard and two other wives enthusiastically rode all over the battlefield of the Battle of Murfreesboro, "*fording* twice the *ever memorable Stone River.*" The experience was at first a lark—"We took up our long skirts—*held out* our feet as far as possible, and *heroically* made the *plunge*," but upon arriving at the battlefield itself, awe replaced levity. It was "still strewn with the marks of that terrible conflict," she wrote to her friend Mary back on the Indiana homefront with her husband, who had lost his eye in the battle. "Nearly all the trees are riddled with balls—some shivered in pieces—dead horses lying on the field in great numbers—& everywhere graves. Sometimes twenty in a row."[85]

In February 1863, Eliza Jane Anderson Veatch, married to General James C. Veatch, watched from the rooftop of a Memphis building as her husband carried out General Hurlbut's order to burn the entire town of Hopefield, on the Arkansas shore opposite the city, for having harbored guerrillas who fired on and destroyed a federal boat.[86] Her posture mirrored that of most of the Union wives who came to the occupied South during the Civil War—they were witnesses to, and beneficiaries of, the Union's conquest of Southern civilians. In this sense, the Union occupation of the South during the Civil War, like the war itself, was a project undertaken by women, and resisted by women, in relationship to their families, households, and communities. In establishing outposts of the idealized Northern household in territory that had, in the eyes of most Union people, been desecrated by disloyalty, U.S. officers and their wives accomplished more than simply making themselves whole again. By tying the Union military's invasion and destruction of households and communities to their ability to reconstitute their own family relations, Union people asserted the superiority of their forces, their society, and their culture.

NOTES

I am grateful for the comments, critique, and questions from a number of people as I wrote and revised this essay, especially LeeAnn Whites, Lisa Tendrich Frank, Matt Gallman, Jonathan Heller, and the discussants at the 2015 Southern Association for Women Historians triennial conference and the 2016 American Historical Association annual meeting.

1. Sarah Jane Full Hill, *Mrs. Hill's Journal: Civil War Reminiscences*, ed. Mark M. Krug (Chicago: Lakeside Press, R. R. Donnelley, 1980), 191–93. It is unclear whether McPherson was aware of the fact that the Balfour House had, less than a year earlier, been the site of an elaborate ball attended by Confederate officers and elites, an event cut short in its splendor by the appearance of Confederate soldiers alerting them to the arrival of Union troops in the area. This was the first day of the Battle of Chickasaw Bayou, itself a Union failure, but it marked the beginning of the long Vicksburg campaign. See Balfour House Application, National Register of Historic Places (1969), http://focus.nps.gov/pdfhost/docs/NRHP/Text/71000458.pdf.

2. Julia Dent Grant's near constant presence at the front, perhaps the most famous example, has been analyzed regularly for its relationship to Ulysses S. Grant's penchant for alcohol or as evidence of the depth of their romantic attachment. See, for example, John Y. Simon, "A Marriage Tested by War: Ulysses and Julia Grant," in *Intimate Strategies of the Civil War: Military Commanders and Their Wives*, ed. Carol K. Bleser and Lesley J. Gordon (New York: Oxford University Press, 2001), 127, 128–30. A notable early exception to this pattern was Mary Elizabeth Massey, whose chapter "Teeming with Women" outlines the degree to which the military camps of the Union armies were populated by women of all sorts and agendas, including wives. See Massey, *Women in the Civil War* (1966; rpt., Lincoln: University of Nebraska Press, 1994).

3. Historians of Civil War occupation have always taken, almost as a given, that occupation was itself an extension of warfare, but this did not mean that they have fully understood how occupation happened, nor have they understood women as warmakers within that context. Key modern treatments of the Union's occupation of the South include Stephen V. Ash, *When the Yankees Came: Conflict and Chaos in the Occupied South, 1861–1865* (Chapel Hill: University of North Carolina Press, 1995) and Mark Grimsley, *The Hard Hand of War: Union Military Policy toward Southern Civilians* (New York: Cambridge University Press, 1995), as well as important local studies, including Gerald M. Capers, *Occupied City: New Orleans under the Federals, 1862–1865* (Lexington: University of Kentucky Press, 1965); Walter Durham, *Nashville: The Occupied City* (Nashville: Tennessee Historical Society, 1985) and *Reluctant Partners: Nashville and the Union* (Nashville: Tennessee Historical Society, 1987); Louis S. Gerteis, *Civil War St. Louis* (Lawrence: University of Kansas Press, 2001); and Robert Tracy McKenzie, *Lincolnites and Rebels: A Divided Town in the American Civil War* (New York: Oxford University Press, 2006). All of these studies included women within the scope of their concerns, but only recently have scholars begun to argue that warfare had particular, gendered features in occupied regions, both under Union and Confederate rule. The essays in LeeAnn Whites and Alecia P. Long, eds., *Occupied Women: Gender, Military Occupation, and the American Civil War* (Baton Rouge: Louisiana State University Press, 2009), for instance, "offer evidence . . . that women were an integral part of the war of occupation," and cast the development of "hard war tactics" against "civilians" as driven not just by the active conflict between men but also by the gendered supply line, rooted in the household, that made guerrilla resistance in the South possible (7). See also Joseph M. Beilein Jr., "The Guerrilla Shirt: A Labor of Love and the Style of Rebellion in Civil War Missouri, *Civil War History* 58, no. 2 (June 2012): 151–79; and Margaret M. Storey, *Loyalty and Loss: Alabama's Unionists in the Civil War and Reconstruction* (Baton Rouge: Louisiana State University Press), 37–44.

4. The scholarship about Union women's war mobilizations is extensive and varied. I have relied particularly on Elizabeth D. Leonard, *Yankee Women: Gender Battles in the Civil War* (New York: W. W. Norton, 1994), xxii; Jeanie Attie, *Patriotic Toil: Northern Women and the American Civil War* (Ithaca, N.Y.: Cornell University

Press, 1998), 16, 22–25; Nina Silber, "A Compound of Wonderful Potency: Women Teachers of the North in the Civil War South," in *The War Was You and Me: Civilians in the American Civil War*, ed. Joan E. Cashin (Princeton: Princeton University Press, 2002), 37; Nina Silber, *Daughters of the Union: Northern Women Fight the Civil War* (Cambridge: Harvard University Press, 2005), 91–93; LeeAnn Whites, *Gender Matters: Civil War, Reconstruction, and the Making of the New South* (New York: Palgrave Macmillan, 2005), especially 9–24; and Judith Giesberg, *Army at Home: Women and the Civil War on the Northern Homefront* (Chapel Hill: University of North Carolina Press, 2009), 8–16, 68–91.

5. Margaret Storey, "A Conquest of Manners: Gender, Sociability, and Northern Wives' Occupation of Memphis, 1862–1865," *Ohio Valley History* 15, no. 1 (Spring 2015): 5.

6. The need to reestablish loving households also reflected the dominant gender conventions and identities of nineteenth-century Americans. Karen Lystra argues that "romantic love" was central to "women's power in the Victorian household" and that the "experience of love was rooted in the concept of an ideal self," a self "meant to be completely revealed to one person only." Separation during war could thus dramatically challenge, in this respect, a person's self-expression and identity. Such understandings of the marital relation were expanded into a particular reverence for the household that grew up around it. As Nina Silber argues, "In the North in the 1860s, few institutions were as hallowed and celebrated as the middle-class home," and the war had "dramatic effects on this sanctified domestic realm," not least because women relied on "the domestic sphere as a source of feminine authority." Similar dislocation doubtlessly occurred for men who, especially when in occupied areas where Southern women largely rejected their authority and their social niceties, found themselves unmoored from traditional gender roles that they associated very much with respectability, stability, and masculine restraint. See Karen Lystra, *Searching the Heart: Women, Men, and Romantic Love in Nineteenth-Century America* (New York: Oxford University Press, 1989), 7 (first quotation), 9 (second quotation); Silber, *Daughters of the Union*, 88.

7. Joseph F. Culver to Mary Murphy Culver, September 7, 1863, in *"Your Affectionate Husband, J. F. Culver": Letters Written during the Civil War*, ed. Leslie W. Dunlap (Iowa City: University of Iowa Libraries, 1978), 155 (first quotation); Hill, *Mrs. Hill's Journal*, 234 (second quotation); Carrie Goddard to Mary Chess Miller, January 19, 1864, John Franklin Miller Papers, M0059, Dept. of Special Collections, Stanford University Libraries, Stanford, Calif. (third quotation) [hereinafter SUL]. For general sentiments of women about toughing it out like soldiers, see Martha Nicholson McKay to Precious Mother & Sisters, October 3, 1864, Brandt and Helen McKay Steel Collection, 1805–1994, M1078, Manuscript and Visual Collections Department, William Henry Smith Memorial Library, Indiana Historical Society, Indianapolis [hereinafter IHS]; Memphis *Bulletin*, June 14, 1863.

8. Massey, *Women in the Civil War*, 66.

9. In *Loyalty and Loss*, especially 38–43, I argue that loyalty during the seces-

sion crisis and Civil War was understood in the South as a "family affair," but this concept easily extends to the entirety of the United States during this period. The notion that gender and kinship relations were reflections of idealized and ideological notions of political loyalty were commonplace. See LeeAnn Whites, *The Civil War as a Crisis in Gender: Augusta, Georgia, 1860–1890* (Athens: University of Georgia Press, 1995), 72–73; Whites, *Gender Matters*, 27–28; Amy Murrell Taylor, *The Divided Family in Civil War America* (Chapel Hill: University of North Carolina Press, 2005), 7–9; Stephanie McCurry, *Confederate Reckoning: Power and Politics in the Civil War South* (Cambridge: Harvard University Press, 2011), 29–37.

10. Historian Verity McInnis has argued in the case of British India and the American West that "military homes . . . functioned as operational sites of empire" and that in running those households, officers' wives "both designed and endorsed the principles of benevolent imperialism." There is something similar, but distinct, going on in the occupied South. Occupation households functioned more like outposts than as true colonial settlements, but they also shaped and supported the warfare and ideas that made them possible. Verity McInnis, "Indirect Agents of Empire: Army Officers' Wives in British India and the American West, 1830–1875," *Pacific Historical Review* 83, no. 3 (August 2014): 378.

11. John F. Kasson, *Rudeness and Civility: Manners in Nineteenth-Century Urban America* (New York: Hill and Wang, 1991), 5–7, quotation on 6.

12. Though scholars of hard war have tended to focus most closely on the expansion of Union military assaults into the homes of Southern civilians, it should be noted that Southern Unionists also relied on their kinship networks to resist the Confederacy, and the Confederacy, in turn, made war against Unionists, male and female, and the property they used to provided essential material support to the pro-Union resistance. See Storey, *Loyalty and Loss*, 78–86.

13. Many of the essays in Whites and Long, eds., *Occupied Women*, develop this historiography, but see, in particular, "Introduction," 6–7; Whites, "'Corresponding with the Enemy,'" 103–5; Lisa Tendrich Frank, "Bedrooms as Battlefields: The Role of Gender Politics in Sherman's March," 34–36; and Cita Cook, "The Practical Ladies of Occupied Natchez," 127–30. See also McCurry, *Confederate Reckoning*, 87–89, 113–14, and Joseph W. Danielson, *War's Desolating Scourge: The Union's Occupation of North Alabama* (Lawrence: University Press of Kansas, 2012), 41–57.

14. John Simon, ed., *The Personal Memoirs of Julia Dent Grant* (New York: G. P. Putnam's Sons, 1975), 101.

15. Sarah Butler to Harriet Heard, May 15, 1862, in *Private and Official Correspondence of Gen. Benjamin F. Butler*, 2 vols., ed. Jessie Ames Marshall (Norwood, Mass.: Plimpton Press, 1917), 1:486.

16. Benjamin Butler to Sarah Butler, July 15, 1862, in *Private and Official Correspondence*, 2:77. One Confederate Louisianan, likewise, located responsibility for the order squarely with Sarah Butler when he reported that the "infamous proclamation of Gen. Butler's was issued in consequence of the ladies of New Orleans hav[ing] sent back the cards sent to them by Mrs. Butler!" See entry dated May 16,

1863, in *Private Journal of Sarah L. Wadley*, Manuscript Volume No. 3, May 16, 1863–February 11, 1864, Sarah Lois Wadley Papers, Southern Historical Collection, Wilson Library, University of North Carolina at Chapel Hill [hereinafter SHC], http://docsouth.unc.edu/imls/wadley/wadley.html, last accessed January 10, 2016.

17. Between August and October eleven steamers were attacked, four of them between October 16 and 20. Earl J. Hess, *The Civil War in the West: Victory and Defeat from the Appalachians to the Mississippi* (Chapel Hill: University of North Carolina Press, 2012), 67–68; Hooper, *Memphis*, 20–21; Storey, "Conquest of Manners," 8.

18. Special Orders No. 254, U.S. War Department, *The War of the Rebellion: A Compilation of the Official Records of the Union and Confederate Armies* (Washington, D.C.: Government Printing Office, 1880–1901) [Hereafter cited as *OR*], ser. 1, vol. 17, pt. 2:240; *Memphis Appeal*, November 4, 1862; W. T. Sherman to Miss P. A. Fraser, October 22, 1862, *OR*, ser. 1, vol. 17, pt. 2:288 [emphasis mine]. Of the thirty families, twenty-six were households headed by women. Twenty of these were wives of Confederate soldiers; seven had sons in the Confederate army. See *Memphis Appeal*, November 4, 1862.

19. Again, Mary Elizabeth Massey drew this conclusion early on, though she assumed that most of the women targeted were actually expelled; in the end, only a few were forcibly removed. See Massey, *Women in the Civil War*, 67.

20. John Franklin Miller to Mary Chess Miller, March 20, 1862, John Franklin Miller Papers, SUL.

21. James S. Negley to Major General Buell, July 18, 1862, *OR*, ser. 1, vol. 16, pt. 2:178. Negley reports that this was the wife of Gen. Ormsby Mitchel, but she died in the summer of 1861, so there must have been some mistake about the woman's identity. His three daughters did join him in Huntsville in the summer of 1862, so perhaps there was confusion about an older woman who was accompanying them.

22. Hill, *Mrs. Hill's Journal*, 144–45; *OR*, ser. 1, vol. 24, pt. 3:154.

23. *Memphis Bulletin*, June 14, 1863.

24. *Chicago Tribune*, August 4, 1862.

25. Franc B. Wilkie, *Pen and Powder* (Boston: Ticknor, 1888), 283.

26. Matilda Gresham, *Life of Walter Quintin Gresham, 1832–1895, in Two Volumes, with Portraits* (Chicago: Rand McNally, 1919), 1:282–83.

27. In the First Confiscation Act of August 1861, Congress gave the government the right to seize the property of anyone who was actively participating in the rebellion. In July 1862, the Second Confiscation Act was signed into law; it gave the Union the right to seize the real and personal property of anyone who had aided the Confederacy directly or who had aided and abetted the rebellion. In many cases, these laws codified what had been increasingly common practice under martial law in some border states and a matter of pragmatic and tactical expediency in Confederate territory since the war began (and, of course, it was also used against foreigners, Northerners, and Unionists in the Confederacy from the moment the South seceded). LeeAnn Whites argues that such confiscations—used in Missouri as punitive assessments against rebel-sympathizing civilians and families—

embodied the "war of the households" waged in this politically divided state. Through it, displaced Unionist refugees arriving in St. Louis were supported materially by taxes in kind or in cash levied on known Southern sympathizing households, including those headed by women. Through this, Union households were planted, seeded, and watered in the city, while secessionist bases were undermined. See Whites, *Gender Matters*, 53–56. For Benjamin Butler's use of confiscation, see Capers, *Occupied City*, 86; for a discussion of the evolution of confiscation and communal punishment as military tactics in the West, and later, throughout the Union army, particularly the occupation of North Alabama and the military orders of General John Pope in mid-1862, see Grimsley, *Hard Hand*, 78–88; for a thorough analysis of the Union's confiscation laws, see Daniel W. Hamilton, *The Limits of Sovereignty: Property Confiscation in the Union and the Confederacy during the Civil War* (Chicago: University of Chicago Press, 2007). Hamilton explains that the Confederate government was also expansive in its confiscation of the property of Southerners who were living in the Union at the time the South seceded. "Those with family members living in the North suddenly found that a sibling or a parent or a child was an alien enemy whose property they had a legal duty to deliver to the courts." Hamilton, 112 and chaps. 5 and 6.

28. William Silliman Hillyer to Anna Rankin Hillyer, June 24, 1862, Papers of William Silliman Hillyer, Special Collections, University of Virginia, Charlottesville (hereinafter UVA).

29. DeeGee Lester, "Hunt-Phelan Home," in *The Encyclopedia of Tennessee*, http://tennesseeencyclopedia.net/entry.php?rec=673; Theopholis Lyle Dickey to Ann Dickey, June 25, 1862, Wallace-Dickey Family Papers, Abraham Lincoln Presidential Library, Springfield, Ill. (hereinafter AL); *Chicago Tribune*, July 9 and 11, 1862; see also Elizabeth Avery Meriwether, *Recollections of 92 Years, 1824–1916* (McLean, Va.: EPM, 1994), 68.

30. *Memphis Daily Union Appeal*, July 3, 1862. Matt Galloway was believed to have signed the house over to his wife before he left the city for Confederate territory.

31. Anna S. Hillyer to Cousin Mary, August 5, 1862, Papers of William Silliman Hillyer, UVA.

32. Anna Rankin Hillyer to My Dear Brother, December 13, 1862, Papers of William Silliman Hillyer, UVA.

33. Simon, ed., *Personal Memoirs of Julia Dent Grant*, 119.

34. William Kennedy to Jane Kennedy, William J. Kennedy Papers, 1861–63, AL.

35. Julia A. Hascall to Mary Chess Miller, February 4, 1864, John Franklin Miller Papers, SUL.

36. John Franklin Miller to Mary Chess Miller, March 19, 1862, John Franklin Miller Papers, SUL.

37. John Franklin Miller to Mary Chess Miller, June 8, June 15, and June 16, 1864, John Franklin Miller Papers, SUL.

38. Reminiscences of Elizabeth L. Topp, Robertson Topp Papers, 1805–1929, reel 1, Tennessee State Library and Archives, Nashville, 30 [hereinafter TSLA].

39. Charles East, ed., *The Civil War Diary of Sarah Morgan* (Athens: University of Georgia Press), 384.

40. Sarah Hildreth Butler to Paul and Bennie Butler, March 27, 1862, in *Private and Official Correspondence*, 1:384.

41. *Memphis Daily Union Appeal*, July 26, 1862. "Mrs. Capt. Newell" was likely Jane Newell, the wife of a local river captain, Thomas W. Newell, who had valorized himself at the outbreak of the war by hoisting a Confederate flag on his ship, the HRW *Hill*, in the face of Unionists in St. Louis, before running back down the river to an excited crowd at Memphis. Captain Newell and his ship went on to participate in the Battle of Belmont on November 7, 1861; the HRW *Hill* was captured by the Union navy in the Battle of Memphis on June 6, 1862. There is no other information about Jane Newell, but one presumes that she either fled the city after the fall or sold her home and its contents after her husband went to prison. See 1860 Census; J. M. Keating, *History of the City of Memphis and Shelby County, Tennessee, with Illustrations and Biographical Sketches of Some of Its Prominent Citizens* (New York: D. Mason, 1888), 1:482; and U.S. Naval Historical Center, *Confederate Ships Afloat* (Washington, D.C.: Department of the Navy, 2004; rpt., Booklife, 2011), 217.

42. John Franklin Miller to Mary Chess Miller, June 24, 1864, John Franklin Miller Papers, SUL.

43. Sarah Hildreth Butler to Harriet Hildreth Heard, November 2, 1862, in *Private and Official Correspondence*, 2:438. Under the auspices of the First and Second Confiscation Acts, General Butler made regular use of auctions to sell Confederate real estate and "personal effects" at "extremely low prices," amounting to something like $1 million worth of property. Capers, *Occupied City*, 86.

44. Hill, *Mrs. Hill's Journal*, 179; Storey, "Conquest of Manners," 13–14.

45. Simon, ed., *The Personal Memoirs of Julia Dent Grant*, 105.

46. Ash, *When the Yankees Came*, 219.

47. Hill, *Mrs. Hill's Journal*, 179.

48. Gresham, *Life of Walter Quintin Gresham*, 1:95.

49. J. Harvey Greene to Rachel Greene, January 30, 1863 (first quote), and Rachel Greene to Dear Mother, February 20, 1863 (second quote), in *Letters to My Wife: A Civil War Diary from the Western Front*, ed. Sharon L. D. Kraynek (Apollo, Pa.: Closson Press, 1995), 49, 53.

50. Hill, *Mrs. Hill's Journal*, 183.

51. Since Edmondson carried Fackler's mail to and from her husband through Confederate lines, she was a particularly welcome guest; in turn, Fackler aided Belle where she could, including helping her "fix my articles for smugling" on a trip into the city in 1864 by contriving a petticoat out of contraband gray cloth, pinning hats to the inside of hoops and secreting "brass buttons, Money &c in my bosom." Though it is unclear if most of Fackler's boarders were suspicious of Edmondson's activity, Edmondson clearly cultivated relationships with Union soldiers in Memphis, some of whom turned a blind eye to her doings and shared news with her that

allowed her to escape arrest. Loretta Galbraith and William Galbraith, eds., *A Lost Heroine of the Confederacy: The Diaries and Letters of Belle Edmondson* (Jackson: University Press of Mississippi, 1990), xxiv–xxvi, 97, 59–60, 96–99, 116–17, 197.

52. Gresham, *Life of Walter Quintin Gresham*, 195–96.

53. It is now a fairly commonly accepted notion that the attitudes of Union soldiers influenced the thinking of people on the homefront, particularly as regards antiwar dissent and hostility toward emancipation. And we have excellent explorations of the role of epistolary culture and kinship relations during the war from Taylor, *Divided Family in Civil War America*. For the partisanship of women on the Union homefront, see Silber, *Daughters of the Union*, 129–37.

54. James R. Slack to Ann P. Slack, June 29, 1862, James R. Slack Papers (L145), box 1, folder 2, Manuscripts and Rare Book Division, Indiana State Library, Indianapolis [hereinafter ISL].

55. Humphrey Hood to Matilda Hood, April 27, 1863, Humphrey Hood Papers, 1862–68, AL.

56. John B. Rice to Sarah Rice, July 28, 1864, John B. Rice Collection, RBH.

57. Anna S. Hillyer to Cousin Mary, August 5, 1862, Papers of William Silliman Hillyer, UVA.

58. Hill, *Mrs. Hill's Journal*, 141.

59. Rachel Greene to Dear Mother, February 20, 1863 (quote), in *Letters to My Wife*, 49, 53.

60. Hill, *Mrs. Hill's Journal*, 242–46 (first quotation, 243; second and third, 244).

61. Martha Nicholson McKay to Precious Mother and Sisters, August 16, 1864, Brandt and Helen McKay Steel Collection, 1805–1994, IHS.

62. Ibid.

63. Hill, *Mrs. Hill's Journal*, 184.

64. For Fremont and Memphis connections, see Ralph P. Buckland Papers, the John B. Rice Collection, the William Caldwell Family Papers, and the Orin O. England Collection, all at RBH. For the Pontiac and Gallatin Collection, see Dunlap, ed., *"Your Affectionate Husband,"* and the John Lewis Ketcham Collection (MO173), IHS.

65. Mrs. John A. Logan, *Reminiscences of a Soldier's Wife: An Autobiography* (New York: Charles Scribner's Sons, 1916), 130–31; Orin O. England to Cornelia Norton, January 11, 1864, Orin O. England Collection (LH-280), RBH.

66. *Chicago Tribune*, May 22, 1863.

67. William T. Sherman, *Memoirs of General W. T. Sherman*, Library of America ed. (New York: Literary Classics of the United States, 1990), 371. It was on the return from Big Black that the Sherman's oldest son, Willie, caught typhoid fever and died in Memphis at the Gayoso House (374).

68. Hill, *Mrs. Hill's Journal*, 255–56, 285–86.

69. Ann C. Carter to Mary Chess Miller, July 28, 1863, John Franklin Miller Papers, SUL.

70. John Franklin Miller to Mary Chess Miller, January 28, 1863, John Franklin Miller Papers, SUL.

71. J. F. Culver to Mary Murphy Culver, February 12, 1864, in Dunlap, ed., *"Your Affectionate Husband,"* 218.

72. Carrie Goddard to Mary Chess Miller, January 19, 1864, John Franklin Miller Papers, SUL.

73. Orin O. England to Cordelia Norton, December 12, 1863, Orin O. England Collection, RBH.

74. Storey, "Conquest of Manners," 11–12.

75. Entry dated June 15, 1862, in Mary Fielding's Diary, in *"To Lochaber Na Mair": Southerners View the Civil War*, ed. Faye Acton Axford (Athens, Ala.: Athens, 1986), 61.

76. Daniel E. Sutherland, ed., *A Very Violent Rebel: The Civil War Diary of Ellen Renshaw House* (Knoxville: University of Tennessee Press, 1996), 118.

77. Sutherland, *A Very Violent Rebel*, 127–28.

78. Entries dated March 29, 1864 (first quotation) and April 1, 1864 (second quotation), in Alice Williamson Diary, 1864, David M. Rubenstein Rare Book and Manuscript Library, Duke University, Durham, N.C. Digitized facsimile. http://library.duke.edu/rubenstein/scriptorium/williamson/. Paine was by all accounts one of the harshest Union commanders in the occupied South, though the case is hard to analyze because of the partisan nature of the accounts about him, both positive and negative. See Walter T. Durham, *Rebellion Revisited: A History of Sumner County, Tennessee, from 1861 to 1870* (Gallatin, Tenn.: Sumner County Museum Association, 1982), 158–95, and, for a less partisan account that treats Paine with greater historical rigor, see Berry Craig, *Kentucky Confederates: Secession, Civil War, and the Jackson Purchase* (Lexington: University Press of Kentucky, 2014), 261–76, 288–90.

79. Sarah Hildreth Butler to Harriet Hildreth Heard, November 18, 1862, *Private and Official Correspondence*, 2:489.

80. Simon, ed., *The Personal Memoirs of Julia Dent Grant*, 112.

81. Hill, *Mrs. Hill's Journal*, 255, 227–29.

82. Hill, *Mrs. Hill's Journal*, 187–88; Gresham, *Life of Walter Quintin Gresham*, 1: 239–40.

83. Historian Megan Kate Nelson has argued persuasively for Civil War Americans' fascination with the new ruins created by the war—at once moving, awe inspiring, and troubling. See Nelson, *Ruin Nation: Destruction and the American Civil War* (Athens: University of Georgia Press, 2012), chap. 2.

84. Rachel Greene to Dear Mother, February 20, 1863, in *Letters to My Wife*, 53.

85. Carrie Goddard to Mary Chess Miller, February 5, 1863, John Franklin Miller Papers, SUL.

86. Sylvester W. Fairfield to Mary Barker Fairfield, February 19, 1863, Sylvester Wellington Fairfield Civil War Letters, 1862–64, IHS.

Creek and Seminole Households on the Trail of Blood on Ice

ANDREW K. FRANK

In late 1861, hundreds of Creek and Seminole families left their homes in Indian Territory and formed a pan-Indian refugee community on the Deep Fork River at the eastern side of the Creek Nation. There, they united with families from several other Indian nations who found themselves with a similar need for safety. The Indians established temporary homes and campsites, performed ceremonies together, and gathered supplies that could help them survive the winter. Like many other Civil War refugees, these families fled their homes without a clear sense of direction or organization. They were not fleeing to join loved ones, and they were hardly organized as a group; they left their homes because the Civil War had torn their communities apart. This decision to leave their homes and the struggles that followed reveal the largely overlooked centrality of Indian households in the American Civil War. For the next few years, the importance of households—as social units and physical places—shaped the decisions that the displaced Creek Indians and Seminole Indians would make.[1]

The abandonment of homes and towns (*tawlas*) occurred as leaders from both the Confederacy and the United States pressured Native American communities to pledge their loyalty to one side or the other. The Creek Nation and Seminole Nation—two separate but historically related tribal nations with sizeable slave populations—officially and separately chose to sign treaties of allegiance with the Confederacy near the start of the war.[2] Nonetheless, many local Creek and Seminole towns and households warily rejected these alliances and instead proclaimed their neutrality.[3] They had good reason to be wary of the risks involved in wars with the United States.

In the first half of the nineteenth century, three Seminole wars and two Creek wars resulted in thousands of Indian casualties, the dispossession of most tribal lands in the East, and their forced removal from Georgia, Alabama, and Florida to Indian Territory. In these wars, the United States as well as individual Southern states repeatedly conflated and punished Native allies and Native enemies. In the Creek Civil War (1813–14), for example, the United States confiscated the lands of their Creek allies along with those of their enemies. As a result, many Creeks and Seminoles distanced themselves from the American Civil War even as their tribal leaders pledged their allegiances.[4]

As the population of the Deep Fork River swelled into the thousands, the refugees scrambled to withstand a brutal winter. Native American and Confederate officials saw it as an opportunity to obtain a quick military victory and "either compel submission to the authorities of the [Creek] nation or drive him [Creek leader Opothleyaholo] and his party from the country." Choctaw forces under Confederate Indian agent Douglas H. Cooper (formerly the U.S. Indian agent) attacked the temporary camps on November 19.[5] Rumors of the approaching soldiers reached the refugee camps before Cooper's 1,400 troops did. Threatened by the approach of Confederate soldiers, hundreds of Indian households rapidly abandoned the Deep Fork River community and began to march north.

Large groups of women, children, and the elderly led the path north while many of the adult men took up the rear in order to provide protection. Not content with letting the refugees leave unmolested, the Choctaw forces took up the chase. The rear guard did what it could to hamper the Confederates, offering enough resistance at the Round Mountains to allow most of their families to continue marching north. Cooper's forces remained in pursuit, and on December 9 they attacked the refugees at Chusto Talasah about forty miles away. Once again, most of the women and children fled before and during the fight, and a relatively small group of Native men prevented the Confederate forces from overrunning them. The refugee families regrouped a few miles away at nearby Chustenalah, where Cooper made his final attack on December 26. Rested and with reinforcements, Cooper's forces circled the camp, pushed the families out of their temporary homes, and otherwise stole whatever property was left behind. In the words of one historian, the Confederate forces "scattered Opothleyaholo's people over the heavily timbered hills of northern Indian Territory."[6]

As the refugees marched northeast that evening, a snowstorm increased the suffering of people who had left most of their personal belongings behind. For the next few weeks, the beleaguered families walked "in blood and snow" to southern Kansas. Hundreds died and hundreds more were captured, but the survivors made it to Kansas by late January. There, more than six thousand Creeks and Seminoles rebuilt their households in refugee camps along the Verdigris River.[7] George W. Collamore, the mayor of Lawrence, Kansas, who had previously served as the quartermaster general for Kansas's Union regiments, summarized their plight shortly after their arrival. "Large numbers of these [Indians who pledged neutrality were] driven from their comfortable homes, leaving their farms and their herds. . . . Their houses were fired by the enemy and their horses and cattle driven off."[8] These Native American families, in other words, had no choice but to seek safety in the unknown.

The story of "Opothleyaholo's migration" to Kansas has been told many times and from many perspectives. The contours of this story have not changed very much over the past generation, even as scholars have revolutionized the study of both Native Americans and the Civil War. Modern scholars still tend to focus on the Indian leaders—Creek chief Opothleyaholo and to a lesser extent Seminole chief Billy Bowlegs—as they negotiated their predicament with officials from the United States and the Confederacy. When the diplomatic overtures with the Union and Confederacy came to an end, scholars follow the charismatic leaders as they marched to Kansas, formed the First and Second Union Indian Brigades, and then returned as U.S. soldiers to fight in Indian Territory. In the process, scholars treat the mostly women and children refugees as colorful and dramatic appendages to the story. In these accounts, refugee families are worthy of description, but they exist in narratives largely to explain the moral outrages caused by the war or as a backdrop for military campaigns and diplomatic decisions. In short, the shattering of Native households and the flight to Kansas appear as the backdrop for the raising of Native regiments and the military's struggle in what became known as the Indians' Civil War. Rather than recalling it as "Opothleyaholo's migration," some Native Americans more aptly remember it as the "Trail of Blood on Ice."[9]

Contrary to their marginal place in the secondary literature, households and refugees belong at the center of the story. Creek and Seminole Indians engaged in the Civil War as female-centered, clan-based, matrilineal households, and they chose their diplomatic and military options accordingly. The centrality of households to this military campaign and to the Native American experience manifested itself throughout the war in at least four ways. First, before the fighting began, most Creeks and Seminoles declared through treaties and negotiations that their primary concern was to be able to protect their homes. Their subsequent behavior reflected this central concern, as they only abandoned the path of neutrality when Confederate forces attacked their households. Second, the targeting of or defending of households played a central role for Indian and non-Indian forces in the Confederacy and the Union. Opothleyaholo and other Native men—rather than fighting for the United States—marched behind their households out of a concern for their central role as men. The engagements in Indian Territory and on the road to Kansas were more about Native men defending women and children and protecting households than they were about fighting as a military force. Opothleyaholo and others marched as a rear guard for their households who led the way to Kansas. Native men were camp followers rather than camp leaders. Third, the concern for retaining and re-creating the household continued to shape the decisions of Native men and women once they became refugees. From Kansas, the men organized as "Home Guards" to return to Indian Territory to reclaim their homelands. They repeatedly demanded that the Union help them return home in order for them to "plant corn"—the staple of their diet and the symbolic center of households and female authority. Just as important, they repeatedly refused to support Unionist (or Confederate) ambitions if they failed to protect Native households. Finally, the concern for the household shaped the actions of Union forces in Kansas. In addition to providing regiments to support the reclaiming of Indian lands, the U.S. military allocated resources in order to sustain refugee families, aid their return to their homes, and otherwise convince potential Indian soldiers of the virtues of the Union cause. A good military policy, Union officers concluded, required the United States to supply Native women and children and otherwise allow Creek and Seminole men to protect and provide for their households rather than fight in distant battles.

Scholars of southeastern Native Americans have long recognized the centrality of households to daily life and the structure of traditional communities. Most of these studies emphasize the centrality of clans, extended matrilineal families that are named for a totemic animal, plant, or cultural force. A generation of scholarship on southeastern Indians has demonstrated how clan-based, matrilineal (and later patrilineal) households structured Native politics, economics, culture, diplomacy, and society. In southeastern Indian communities, men literally married into the physical households of their wives and their extended families. Husbands maintained their connection to their mothers and their households, even as they moved into new communities and sometimes into different nations. However, the households they joined were the ones that dominated their daily lives. Families connected by maternally related women clustered their homes together, danced at ceremonies together, and otherwise looked to each other to fulfill their daily needs. Women traditionally farmed—primarily corn but also beans, squash, cotton, and other staple crops—on lands controlled by their clans or extended families; men hunted or herded on the common lands that lay beyond towns. Removal to Indian Territory challenged many of these norms, as patrilineal descent became increasingly acknowledged and some families formed nuclear households that seemed more akin to those of their white neighbors. Centralized politics in the form of democratic councils played a similar role in marginalizing the importance of clans. However, the centrality of matrilineal clans and women planting corn in fields as well as in gardens continued long after their forced removal and the Civil War. Matrilineal descent continued to govern the spiritual world, and clan-based voting blocs and leadership shaped the new political structures. Even slaveholding fit within matrilineal clan norms, as men used enslaved laborers to plant and harvest cotton and thereby escape doing women's work in the field.[10]

The centrality of clans is often hidden in the diplomatic records of Indian Territory. Creek and Seminole towns tended to operate as independent entities before removal. Only limited power emanated from national councils. After removal and with the establishment of reservations in Indian Territory, the distribution of power looked and operated a bit differently than it did earlier. In limited form, centralization occurred in the West just as some centralization occurred before removal.[11] Councils and democratic elections placed new powers in the hands of tribal officials, and police forces enforced a range of national laws. Most of the powers of centralization resulted from the terms of treaties that were negotiated with the United States in the early nineteenth century. In each of the treaties, tribal governments were empowered to distribute resources—cash, trade goods, expertise, etc.—and secure the compliance of their constituents. For example, a treaty in 1856 between the United States and both the Creeks and the Seminoles empowered national leaders to settle land claims, distribute supplies, use federal money to "employ their own teachers, mechanics, and farmers," and negotiate and control their boundary with the Seminoles.[12] Neither the Creeks nor the Seminoles were as centralized as outsiders, especially the U.S. treaty negotiators, often imagined. On most issues, centralized power remained remarkably weak. Town leaders often attended national councils with explicit direction from their extended households, and implementation of tribal policies typically required the willing assistance of clan-based leaders. For example, Indian leaders typically needed permission from clan leaders to build roads, survey lands, and allow teachers or missionaries to enter a community. As much as national councils were the face of diplomacy and implemented a litany of national laws, local clans and household power prevailed in Indian country.[13]

When the Civil War began, both the United States and the Confederacy looked to secure alliances with the five largest southeastern Native American nations—Creek, Seminole, Choctaw, Chickasaw, and Cherokee. Each of these so-called Five Civilized Tribes had slaveholding and free black populations, centralized polities, and reputations for martial prowess. Obtaining their support required that Confederate and Union diplomats confront the Indians' ambiguous place in the United States. Although they were effectively reduced to "wards of the state," each of the southeastern Indian nations operated as semiautonomous "domestic dependent nations." They signed various treaties with the United States, were self-governed by tribal governments, and otherwise sought to preserve their sovereignty. These treaties—even as they often acknowledged allegiance and dependence on the United States—placed obligations on both the United States and each of the Indian governments. The treaties offered mechanisms to resolve disputes between the respective nations and their individuals, promised protection by the federal government, and frequently placed requirements on the United States to provide annual cash payments (annuities) and various vocational, social, and educational services. Despite these obligations, the federal government provided little oversight to Indian nations. When it served national purposes, the federal government underserved their Native allies. Annuities were frequently underfunded, obligations went unfulfilled, and Indian agents hired by the United States to mediate these issues complained incessantly about their lack of support from the federal government. Even agents inclined to assist Native communities rarely had adequate resources to do so.[14]

The reticence of many Creeks and Seminoles to forge wartime treaties with either the Confederacy or the Union stemmed partially from this recent history of unfulfilled promises. However, Native American leaders immediately recognized that diplomatic competition for Native allies offered them leverage that they did not have earlier. Native American leaders listened as Confederate and Union representatives made their respective pitches, as they all proclaimed that they could best protect the sovereignty of the Indian nations. Representatives used the wrongs committed in the past to justify their claims. Confederates proclaimed that they would fulfill the obligation of U.S. treaties in ways that the United States had not. Confederate Albert Pike, for example, warned a group of Creeks, Seminoles, and Cherokees "that we must fight for our Country. If we did not fight that, the cold people would come and take our Country from us."[15] Representatives from the United States reminded the Indians that the Southern states were largely responsible for their forced removal from the East.

As much as diplomatic delegations recognized and often overstated the authority of tribal councils and governments, Union and Confederate officials pitched their arguments to persuade the decision makers who governed local households. In discussions of a proposed alliance, for example, Secretary of War Leroy Pope Walker reminded slaveholding Indians that a Union victory would result in the disruption of clan-based farms, as they would "terminate in the emancipation of their slaves and the robbery of their land."[16] Households with free black Indians—often the result of intermarriage or manumission—listened attentively as Union agents promised protection and spread rumors, true and otherwise, that a Confederate victory would result in the enslavement of free blacks.[17] More important for some, the Union emphasized the duplicity of the Confederates and the not-so-veiled threat to Indian households: "The commissioners from the Confederate States have deceived you," U.S. agent Edwin Carruth stated. "They have two tongues. They wanted to get the Indians to fight, and they would rob and plunder you if they can get you into trouble."[18] Other arguments connected more explicitly to the importance of clans. In some cases, for example, they proposed eliminating differences between "half-bloods" and "full-bloods"—categories that were often imposed and used by outsiders to privilege race-based and sometimes class-based sources of authority, rather than familial sources.[19] Similarly, the United States pledged that it would treat "as a member of the said nation" any "white person who, having married a Seminole or Creek woman, resides in the said Seminole country, or . . . is permanently domiciled therein with the consent of the authorities."[20] Indian wives and households, in essence, were recognized for their ability to regulate tribal boundaries. In doing so, the United States placed decisions about immigration, citizenship, and therefore sovereignty in households rather than in councils.[21]

The enlistment of Native Americans, one of the major ambitions of both wartime governments, most explicitly addressed the centrality of households. Both the United States and the Confederacy guaranteed that Native American soldiers would not be deployed out of their own nations without first obtaining permission from tribal leaders. Part of this reticence to ship off Native soldiers had to do with apprehensions within the military about the presumed savagery and therefore unsuitability of Indian soldiers, but concerns for the Native household became equally explicit in these discussions. Native soldiers, in short, wanted to be guaranteed that they could protect their homes from intruders rather than support a generic Confederate cause. In the July 10, 1861, "Treaty of Friendship and Alliance," the Confederacy and Creek Nation agreed to a framework that tried to achieve this household-centered ambition. In addition to protecting slavery and otherwise securing the limited sovereignty of the Indian nation, the treaty privileged the importance of neighborhoods and homesteads. This concern for households—rather than Native sovereignty or what is often misattributed to a desire for home rule—emerged in a promise related to the raising of ten companies of mounted Creek soldiers. Although paid and armed "as other mounted troops in the service," the Creeks insisted and the Confederacy promised that these soldiers could "not be moved beyond the limits of the Indian country west of Arkansas without their consent."[22]

Guarantees that Native soldiers could protect Native lands did not completely satisfy constituents in Creek and Seminole country. Many men insisted that they retained the right to protect their families and households. Many local leaders worried about and exploited the distinction between the legal obligation of soldiers to protect Creek or Seminole lands and the cultural expectation and desire to protect specific Creek or Seminole lands and households. Almost immediately, rumors spread that the Confederacy intended to violate its pledge to allow Native soldiers to serve as home guards. Confederate Albert Pike, then the Confederate envoy to Native Americans, later concluded that these rumors created much of the support for Opothleyaholo's defiance and flight. "All the treaties with the Indians had also stipulated that they should not be taken out of their own country to fight without their consent," he explained. "Those who fought against us under Hopoeithleyohola were chiefly alienated by the belief, induced by that crafty old man, that we would get them to become soldiers, take them out of their own country, first into Arkansas, then into Missouri, then across the Mississippi, and when their young men were thus all gone would take and divide out their lands." Even those allied to the Confederates insisted that they should be able to protect their households, and they used "the right to refuse to leave their own country . . . as an excuse for not going [and] demanded to be paid off before they would march."[23]

Promises that they could remain in their own nation did not satisfy all of the Creeks, especially as requests for them to march elsewhere became more common. They wanted to have the physical ability to secure their "territorial rights" as nations, but they steadfastly wanted to protect their personal households from invaders. They insisted that "their country shall not be occupied or passed through by the Lincoln forces for the purpose of invading our neighbors."[24] Native soldiers frequently wanted to be stationed across the Creek Nation in a manner that allowed them to remain at either their mothers' or wives' homes. Confederate leaders faced resistance when they rejected these demands. Paskofa, a Seminole leader, expressed the widespread frustration of Creeks and Seminoles who learned that their council intended to "make a very strong law" to punish "any one who was able to fight and would not" on behalf of the Confederacy. When news of this law spread, Opothleyaholo "moved a short distance away and Camped out." Paskofa and thousands of others would independently come to a similar decision and join "Old Gauge," as they called Opothleyaholo.[25]

Households and household leaders also used treaties as opportunities to have their specific grievances heard. Wartime treaties were not just agreements between nations but rather extensions of the local and often matrilineal sources of power within the communities. Seminoles and Creeks, for example, used the treaty negotiations to address wrongs to specific families. Many of these claims dated back to the 1830s and to their forced relocation from the South. In one instance, the Confederacy promised the Apalachicola Band of Creek Indians that it would investigate the claims of heads of households who suffered "in consequence of the hurried removal west." In another instance, the Confederacy agreed to compensate the heirs of Sally Factor, a now deceased Indian slave owner, for July and Murray, two enslaved Africans who died during their impressment as interpreters by the U.S. military during the Second Seminole War (1835–42). Not surprisingly, many other Seminole or Creek women saw negotiations with the Confederacy as opportunities to address their household needs. Such was the case for Nelly Factor and Eliza Chopco, who both claimed that their fathers had been denied compensation for several dozen slaves that were wrongfully taken from them in the 1840s. The property rights, which were likely tied to their female-centered households and mothers rather than to their husbands or fathers, fell to them as members of the clan. Native households also used treaties to obtain reimbursement for horses that were stolen in the West by Comanches, Osages, or "marauding bands of Plains Indians."[26]

Households remained central to the Indians' Civil War after the treaty process divided loyalties. For example, households structured the tactics and strategies of armies from the beginning of the war. Confederate forces, for example, routinely attacked the households of "disloyal" Creeks and Seminoles. This policy began in 1861, when Confederate troops used the attacks to secure power in the hands of a few clan and national leaders. Doing so, however, made "the first concerted military action of the Civil War in Indian Territory . . . an act of warfare primarily aimed against civilians."[27] Confederate Indian soldiers, one Creek recalled, would "go over the country, burning all the houses, cabins, barns, and cribs, and carrying all the beds and chairs away, and killing or driving away the cattle." Another onlooker explained that "their houses were fired by the enemy and their horses and cattle driven off."[28] The assaults, which were designed to eliminate the ability to choose neutrality, devastated Native American households. By attacking households across Indian country, Confederate forces worked to destabilize communities that had not allied themselves to the Confederate cause. These acts often served as extensions of old animosities—as households that opposed one another in the East continued to do so in the West—but they did so in service of the Confederate war effort. As one Native American woman recalled: "The Indian did not want to fight . . . but they had to take one side or another. . . . Soldiers came and . . . simply stripped us of everything we had."[29]

Rather than a council or elite-led movement that sought to secure political advantages, the waves of refugees were formed by local decisions of "old men, women, and children, [who] had been compelled to flee for their lives from the country."[30] John Jumper, for example, explained, "We were then by our firesides, living in comparative quiet; but war came to our country and drove us from these pleasant homes; we are now wanderers and strangers."[31] Some of these citizens evacuated quickly and suffered from widespread looting; others took what moveable household property they could. They were "compelled to flee from the country with their families, leaving everything in the way of property that would impede their flight."[32] Some of the attacks occurred as the Indians were "celebrating a festival" and the "friendly Indians [were] compelled to fly with little or nothing to support life or protect themselves from the severity of the weather, and those now endeavoring to exterminate all who are loyal to the Government."[33] These refugees took flight before Opothleyaholo or anyone else could assure them of the virtues of Kansas. As historian Lela McBride explained, the refugees fled their homes before looking for assistance from local leaders. "When Opothleyaholo had taken his stand for the Union," she explains, "various Indians had begun gathering at his 2,000-acre plantation. Many, who had been threatened by the Rebel Indians, came with their ponies, cattle, hogs, chickens, and their personal possessions."[34] The household-centered evacuation of Indian country continued after the Creek refugees began moving north. Shortly after the march began, "Pro-Union refugees from the Seminole Nation . . . joined the stream of wagons, horses, and walking parties which converged on Opothleyaholo."[35] In other words, the decision to flee was made locally by families and households rather than nationally or tribally; they were made outside rather than inside the formal diplomatic process.

The march to Kansas largely appeared more like a chaotic chase of civilians and families than a traditional military engagement. Native American families included disparate clans as well as the young and old. The refugees also included African Americans and those of mixed descent who were sometimes integrated into Native communities as loved ones or occasionally enslaved. All of these refugees suffered at the hands of Confederate soldiers. Officers repeatedly bragged in their reports that they "overtook several Seminole women and children" and "took a great many women, children, and negroes prisoners."[36] In one exchange, Cooper boasted about his success in having "150 prisoners taken, mostly women and children." Another account detailed the "large number of prisoners taken, mostly women and children."[37] As the flight continued, the refugees "scattered" and "retreated to the rocky gorges amid the deep recesses of the mountains." In doing so, they lightened the load and discarded various household supplies: "Property of every description was scattered around." At one point, a Creek Confederate soldier proclaimed that they captured "60 women and children, 20 negroes, 30 wagons, 70 yoke of oxen, about 500 Indian horses, several hundred head of cattle, 100 sheep, and a great quantity of property of much value to the enemy."[38]

In short, Creek and Seminole soldiers struggled to protect their families—by birth and marriage—and otherwise fulfill the basic obligation of being Indian men. In many instances, they were simply overrun by the better-supplied Confederate soldiers. Paskofa, a Seminole leader also known as Johnson Late, explained the insult that the Indians felt as they withdrew from their homelands. "Billy Bowlegs and Opothleyaholo the two principal Chiefs did not raise their hands against [the Confederate soldiers], they tried to get out of their way, but they overtook us and Said that we were running away."[39] Paskofa may have understated the resistance that the Creek and Seminole men offered, but the resistance they offered went poorly. Confederate soldiers killed hundreds of fleeing Seminole and Creek men. One Confederate account detailed the deaths of four hundred enemy soldiers, "leaving only a few hundred men in care of the women and wounded."[40]

In Kansas, Union officials reluctantly concluded Opothleyaholo, Bowlegs, and the political leaders had followed the concerns of their households rather than led their people to safety. This recognition began as soon as the families surprised the Union officials with their arrival. Although the United States, Opothleyaholo, and other leaders had reliable communication prior to the war, Union officials were startled by the arrival of "6,000 to 8,000 under the leader of Opoth-lo-yo-ho-lo, a very aged and influential Creek." General David Hunter and other U.S. officials scrambled to provide for the sudden appearance of thousands of "loyal and destitute" refugees. They also confronted the truth that these were household units, matrilineal families that primarily consisted of women and children. Indeed, one early census of the refugees accounted for 864 men, 2,040 women, and 2,583 children who were "driven from their homes."[41]

As much as Creek and Seminole families hoped to refashion their lives in accordance to the household norms that had governed their lives in Indian Territory, sickness and a harsh winter made it nearly impossible. Their suffering made Indian households dependent on their Union hosts. Colonel Archibald B. Campbell, a trained surgeon, attempted to describe "the wretchedness of their condition." Most of the Natives' personal belongings were lost or left behind, and the clothes that they wore on the journey were threadbare. "Their only protection from the snow upon which they lie is prairie grass and from the wind and weather scraps and rags stretched upon switches. Some of them had some personal clothing; most had but shreds and rags which did not conceal their nakedness, and I saw seven varying in age from three to fifteen years without one thread upon their bodies." The distribution of blankets helped, but Campbell concluded it was insufficient. "Hogobofohyah, the second chief of the Creeks, was sick with a fever. It is time he had received from Mr. Fuller blankets enough to keep him warm, but his tent (to give it that name) was no larger than a small blanket stretched over a switch ridge pole two feet from the ground and did not reach it by a foot on either side of him."[42] Campbell was hardly the only U.S. official to worry about the widespread "destitution and terrible sufferings."[43] The refugees, countless observers concluded, were "in a most deplorable condition—men, women, and children—naked, starving, and without shelter."[44] They clustered in tent communities around extended families, tried to grow gardens, and gathered supplies from the wilderness and Union suppliers as members of extended households.

The demand for basic necessities like blankets overwhelmed Union officers in Kansas, who saw both a humanitarian crisis and a diplomatic opportunity. Many officers concluded that if they could provide the refugee households with their basic needs, the loyalties of Indian soldiers would inevitably follow. In early 1862, Mayor George Collamore insisted that the Union could either provide for households or face the prospects that they might lose their allies to the Confederacy. "To all these necessaries of life they have been accustomed. They had been told by the rebel emissaries as the chiefs informed me that they would fail to obtain these articles from their Union friends, which having turned out to be the fact has affected them with suspicion and discontent."[45] William A. Phillips, who was responsible for raising several Indian regiments in the West, repeatedly connected the basic needs of households with the ability to obtain Native enlistees. Phillips saw a relatively inexpensive solution. "I certainly think that the interests of the service and the Government could be furthered in no cheaper or better way than in clothing and feeding the Choctaws and Creeks."[46] For Phillips, "Success to a great extent depends on our clothing them neatly, feeding them, and to some extent their starving families. After all, a little goes a great way. It is cheap recruiting," he explained. "I have sent eight trains at different times into the Indian Nation this winter loaded with flour and meal I made in this country. Its effect has been most happy, in addition to its humanity."[47] Phillips discovered the connection elsewhere in Indian country where the Confederacy had used a similar policy to obtain allies. "The rebels south of the Arkansas River," he explained, "have been giving the Choctaws and Creeks corn and clothing, even, to keep them from turning over to the Government, as many of them have agreed to do in my communication with them. A small amount of means used now would save a Creek and Choctaw regiment (one of each), which we may otherwise have to fight this summer."[48]

Although blankets and flour were needed for shelter and sustenance, the wet winter put a special premium on shoes. William Dole, U.S. commissioner on Indian affairs, explained that the refugees were "naked, starving and without shelter. Numbers of them had been wounded in battle and very many being barefooted and otherwise exposed were badly frozen. The sick and feeble, the dead and dying were scattered along their route for 100 miles or more."[49] Archibald Campbell described the misery. "Many have their toes frozen off; others have feet wounded by sharp ice or branches of trees lying on the snow. But few have shoes or moccasins."[50] General David Hunter, who would later earn a reputation for bringing hard war to the civilian population of Virginia, repeatedly discussed the military importance of providing shoes to the Creek and Seminole refugees.[51] Amputations due to frostbite were commonplace in Kansas, with more than 100 Creeks and Seminoles losing one or more of their feet.[52] As a result, the list of supplies requested for the "southern refugees" went far beyond the basic needs of soldiers, as they included among dozens of other items three hundred pairs of women's shoes and twenty-eight pairs of children's shoes in 1863.[53]

The military did not provide all of the human or material resources that the refugees required. The Union employed a doctor and deployed a few soldiers to help with the relief effort, and it allocated material goods that directly met some but not all of the immediate needs.[54] The military offered little assistance in distributing the goods and repurposing the raw goods into their most effective form. Individual households, by mutual desire of Native Americans and the military, structured this operation. Raw materials were distributed to clan leaders as an efficient way to have them reach all areas of the camp. From there, Native women cooked in communal batches and sewed clothing out of the meager materials given to them. Captain Jonathan W. Turner, the commissary of subsistence, made it clear that this allotment was by design. In his requisition, he explained that "cheap unbleached sheeting could be worked up by the women into various garments for themselves and children and is much needed. The smaller children, for whom shoes could not be obtained, the women could easily make moccasins out of blankets for them. . . . Stockings might be sent down at first to supply the pressing wants of the most needy or for the women and children." Turner also requisitioned other supplies with American-style households in mind. "Of cooking utensils they are totally destitute. The ordinary soldiers' camp-kettle and mess-pan . . . would best answer the purpose. About one camp-kettle and three mess-pans would be ample for a family of six."[55] Native women, in turn, disregarded these expectations by preparing and eating the meals as members of larger extended households.

By late 1862, even before the basic needs of the Creeks and Seminoles had been met, they, along with the United States, began to plan their return home. Although the refugees would not leave Kansas until the end of the war, the desire to do so was widely shared. Indian agent George C. Snow, for example, explained that the refugees are "well fed, clothed, and their medical wants well attended to. The consequence of which is that they feel well contented, yet the early return to their homes is waited for by them with the greatest anxiety." Natives wanted to end their dependence on the United States as well as to return to the imagined comforts of homes. They are, Collamore explained, "discouraged and demoralized and remain upon the hands of the Government a burden from which their natural feeling of pride and independence would save them." Natives also wanted to escape what they feared would be a bleak future in Kansas. "I fear," Paskofa worried, "that if we stay here much longer we will all be dead." U.S. officials were equally eager, as returning the Indians would end their humanitarian responsibilities to "sustain them . . . for another year at least."[56]

The planting of corn was a centerpiece of the restoration process. The refugees cared more about restoring corn-based matrilineal households than restoring their political leader to power. In 1863, one Indian leader proclaimed that "our women and children want to get back that they may raise some corn this year."[57] Collamore similarly stated that the Indian civilians "ardently desire to return to their farms, rebuild their cabins, renew their

fences, plant the seed and obtain from the rich soil of their country a subsistence from their own industry." Commissioner Dole agreed: the Indians
were "still . . . anxious that they should immediately return to their homes
in order to plant crops in season for their support during the coming year."
The solution, Dole concluded, was "arming a home guard of Indians, who
with sufficient escort of white troops should return with these people to
their homes and protect them there while raising a crop." Once the territory was secured, the home guard could protect their households from
future depredations. The United States began recruiting for the cause, and
Dole optimistically concluded that he had "reason to consider these people
as only temporarily in Kansas and to expect from week to week that they
would be on their way home."[58]

In April 1862, Lorenzo Thomas, who was later responsible for raising
African American troops in Helena, was "authorized to raise from the loyal
Indians now in Kansas" the "First Regiment Home Guards."[59] This Indian
unit and others like it hoped to return to their homes, recapture their
homesteads, and begin the process of allowing their households to return.[60]
Although the Union home guards were unable to secure their homelands
and make them safe for refugee resettlement, some women joined them on
their campaigns. Because they were intent on "raising a crop," many Native
families joined the home guards.[61] "Part of the women and families of the
Creeks are in camp with the First Regiment."[62] Indeed, many Seminoles
followed the camps as "families," and the mostly "women and children"
expected to be self-sustaining rather shortly. These dreams were dashed,
and by 1864 fewer families were joining the campaigns as they marched
home to Indian country.[63]

As much as Union leaders shared the Creek and Seminole desire that
they return to their homes, they all recognized that Confederate tactics
in Indian Territory prevented a rapid return. Soldiers could theoretically
recapture their lands, but women were needed to clear and plant the new
crop and otherwise make Indian Territory habitable. Unfortunately, U.S. officials concluded that Indian Territory was no place for women. In 1863, for
example, William G. Coffin told Dole that guerrilla warfare made the territory inhospitable to the return of families, and the future looked bleak.[64]
William Clarke Quantrill, he explained, "said he intended to winter in
the Creek and Seminole country and fatten his horses, and make a spring
campaign in Kansas." Even if the refugees returned home safely, which
he thought to be highly unlikely, there would be nothing there to sustain
them until a new crop could be harvested. As a result, "We will inevitably

have not only to winter them the coming winter in Kansas, but summer and winter them another year outside of their homes somewhere."[65] Concern for the safety of families continued to prevent their return. In May 1864, Dole told Interior Secretary John P. Usher that returning the "mostly women and children" to "their homes, under such circumstances, would have been to consign them to almost certain annihilation, a crime against humanity too revolting to be contemplated."[66]

The Indian regiments, even as it became clear that the refugees would not return home in the near future, maintained a household-first approach. Union officers frequently overstated the loyalty of the refugees and the regiments, hoping that they could deploy them where they were best needed. Creek and Seminole men and women insisted that Native soldiers serve their households first. Returning home—rather than the desire to secure a Union victory—explicitly shaped the discourse around their behavior. Seminole leader Billy Bowlegs made this focus clear in 1863: "The South counseled us to go with them but we adhered to the old Government. We do so still. The love of the Country caused me to enlist in the U.S. Service, where I still remain. I have not set foot in my Country since but hope to do so & see some of the property I left there. My people still rejoice in that hope."[67] Other Native Americans agreed, repeatedly expressing a "desire once more to be restored to their homes."

The flight of Creeks and Seminoles from Indian Territory to Kansas reveals the centrality of households during the Civil War. By heading to Union lines in Kansas, thousands of Creek and Seminole refugees necessarily became a part of the Union war effort. Their behavior on the "Trail of Blood on Ice" is best explained through the logic of local extended families rather than that of charismatic national leaders, and it is best understood as the attempts of families to reclaim and rebuild their homes rather than as attempts to support the Union or defeat the Confederacy. Although traditional histories of this event often portray it as Chief Opothleyaholo's migration—a diplomatic overture and a march of male soldiers with their womenfolk following along—these accounts have it backward. Creeks and Seminoles used their position within the Union in order to pursue the household-centered ambitions they had when they declared their neutrality. The decisions to become refugees came from these networks of extended families. As such, they reflected the decisions of female clan leaders to provide for their families rather than to follow the dictates of town or national leaders who sought to impact the outcome of the Civil War. These Native American women were not "camp followers." They were camp leaders who guided their families to Union lines and otherwise put their concerns and ambitions at the center of the Indians' Civil War.

NOTES

1. Unless in quotations, the spelling of Native American names and words have been standardized according to contemporary norms.

2. A generation of scholars has explored how these alliances divided their Native communities even as they allowed leaders to secure local needs. Whereas early scholarship simplistically treated Indians as the supporting cast for Confederate and Union war aims, more recent scholars have persuasively emphasized how each Native community used the war to pursue diplomatic (and social) ambitions of its own. For a representative overview of this type of literature, see Bradley R. Clampitt, *Civil War and Reconstruction in Indian Territory* (Lincoln: University of Nebraska Press, 2015), especially the introduction and chap. 4. See also William McKee Evans, "Native Americans in the Civil War: Three Experiences," in *Civil War Citizens: Race, Ethnicity, and Identity in America's Bloodiest Conflict*, ed. Susannah J. Ural (New York: New York University Press, 2010), 187–212; Laurence M. Hauptman, *Between Two Fires: American Indians in the Civil War* (New York: Free Press 1995). More recent scholarship has moved beyond these divisions. For example, see Ari Kelman, *A Misplaced Massacre: Struggling over the Memory of Sand Creek* (Cambridge: Harvard University Press, 2013).

3. Anti-Confederate Southerners existed in many parts of the Confederacy and included Southerners of all races. For examples, see Victoria E. Bynum, *Free State of Jones: Mississippi's Longest War* (Chapel Hill: University of North Carolina Press, 2001); William W. Freehling, *The South vs. the South: How Anti-Confederate Southerners Shaped the Course of the Civil War* (New York: Oxford University Press, 2001); Barton A. Myers, *Rebels against the Confederacy: North Carolina's Unionists* (New York: Cambridge University Press, 2014).

4. For a summary of the interconnected Seminole and Creek wars, see William S. Belko, ed., *America's Hundred Years War: U.S. Expansion to the Gulf Coast and the Fate of the Seminole, 1763–1858* (Gainesville: University Press of Florida, 2015); Claudio Saunt, *New Order of Things: Power, Property, and the Transformation of the Creek Indians, 1733–1816* (New York: Cambridge University Press, 1999); John T. Ellisor, *The Second Creek War: Interethnic Conflict and Collusion on a Collapsing Frontier* (Lincoln: University of Nebraska Press, 2010).

5. Douglas Cooper to Judah Benjamin, January 29, 1862, in *The War of the Rebellion: A Compilation of the Official Records of the Union and Confederate Armies* (70 vols. in 128; Washington, D.C., 1880–1901), ser. 1, vol. 8, 5–14, quotation on 5 [hereafter cited as *OR*].

6. Arrell Morgan Gibson, "Native Americans and the Civil War," *American Indian Quarterly* 9 (1985): 389; William P. Dole to Caleb B. Smith, January 5, 1862, in *OR*, ser. 2, vol. 4, 2.

7. Testimony of Creek delegation, quoted in "Official Report of the Proceedings of the Council with the Indians of the West and Southwest, Held at Fort Smith, Arkansas, in September 1865," in *Annual Report of the Commissioner of Indian Affairs for 1865* (Washington, D.C.: Government Printing Office, 1865), 329 [hereafter *ARCIA*]; Hopoeithleyahola and Aluktustunuke to the President, January 28, 1862, in *OR*, ser. 1, vol. 8, 5–14.

8. George W. Collamore to William P. Dole, April 21, 1862, in *OR*, ser. 2, vol. 4, pt. 1:12.

9. Most explanations of the Creek and Seminole Civil War experience have focused on the political decisions of a handful of male leaders. See Lela J. McBride, *Opothleyaholo and the Loyal Muskogee: Their Flight to Kansas in the Civil War* (Jefferson, N.C.: McFarland, 2000), 164; Mary Jane Warde, *When the Wolf Came: The Civil War and the Indian Territory* (Little Rock: University of Arkansas Press, 2013); Mary Jane Warde, *George Washington Grayson and the Civil War, 1843–1920* (Norman: University of Oklahoma Press, 1990); Jane F. Lancaster, *Removal Aftershock: The Seminoles' Struggles to Survive in the West, 1836–1866* (Knoxville: University of Tennessee Press, 1994). This framework for understanding Native American history through the elites has a long history. For classic works on Indian Territory operations, see Annie Heloise Abel, *The American Indian in the Civil War* (1915; rpt., Lincoln: University of Nebraska Press, 1992); Wiley Britton, *The Civil War on the Border* (New York: G. P. Putnam, 1899); Wiley Britton, *The Union Indian Brigade in the Civil War* (Kansas City, Mo.: F. Hudson, 1922); "Billy Bowlegs (Holata Mico) and the Civil War: Part II," *Florida Historical Quarterly* 45 (1967): 391–402.

10. Kathryn E. Holland Braund, *Deerskins and Duffels: The Creek Indian Trade with Anglo-America* (Lincoln: University of Nebraska Press, 1996), 11–14; Richard A. Sattler, "Women's Status among the Muskogee and Cherokee," in *Women and Power in Native America*, ed. Laura Klein and Lillian Akerman (Norman: University of Oklahoma Press, 1995), 214–29; Lancaster, *Removal Aftershock*, 58–60; Jack Maurice Schultz, *The Seminole Baptist Churches of Oklahoma: Maintaining a Traditional Community* (Norman: University of Oklahoma Press, 2008), 25–28; John Reed Swanton, *Social Organization and Social Usages of the Indians of the Creek Confederacy* (Washington, D.C.: Government Printing Office, 1928), 114, 168; Susan A. Miller, *Coacoochee's Bones: A Seminole Saga* (Lawrence: University of Kansas Press, 2003), esp. 25; Rose Stremlau, *Sustaining the Cherokee Family: Kinship and the Allotment of an Indigenous Nation* (Chapel Hill: University of North Carolina Press, 2011); David A. Chang, *Color of the Land: Race, Nation, and the Politics of Landownership in Oklahoma, 1832–1929* (Chapel Hill: University of North Carolina Press, 2010); Faye Yarbrough, *Race and the Cherokee Nation: Sovereignty in the 19th Century* (Philadelphia: University of Pennsylvania Press, 2007).

11. For a discussion of the debates over centralization within Creek and Seminole society, see Saunt, *New Order of Things*; Michael Green, *The Politics of Indian Removal: Creek Government and Society in Crisis* (Lincoln: University of Nebraska Press, 1982); Christopher D. Haveman, *Rivers of Sand: Creek Indian Emigration,*

Relocation, Ethnic Cleansing in the American South (Lincoln: University of Nebraska Press, 2016).

12. Charles J. Kappler, ed., *Indian Affairs: Laws and Treaties*, 7 vols. (Washington, D.C.: Government Printing Office, 1904), 2:756–63.

13. L. Susan Work, *Seminole Nation of Oklahoma: A Legal History* (Norman: University of Oklahoma Press, 2010), 7–10.

14. Kappler, *Indian Affairs*, 2:550–52, 647, 756–63.

15. Paskofa to the President of the United States, March 10, 1864, Office of Indian Affairs, National Archives, Washington, D.C. See Kenneth W. Porter, "Billy Bowlegs (Holata Mico) in the Civil War (Part II)," *Florida Historical Quarterly* 45, no. 4 (April 1967): 393.

16. Leroy Pope Walker to David Hubbard, May 14, 1861, in *OR*, ser. 1, vol. 3, 577.

17. Kevin Mulroy, *The Seminole Freedmen: A History* (Norman: University of Oklahoma Press, 2007), 155–59; Gary Zellar, *African Creeks: Estelvste and the Creek Nation* (Norman: University of Oklahoma Press, 2007), 41–50.

18. Edwin H. Carruth to Opothleyaholo, September 10, 1861, in *OR*, ser. 1, vol. 8, 25.

19. Theda Perdue, *Mixed-Blood Indians: Racial Construction in the Early South* (Athens: University of Georgia Press, 2003).

20. Vine Deloria Jr. and Raymond J. DeMaille, eds., *Documents of American Indian Diplomacy: Treaties, Agreements, and Conventions, 1775–1979*, 2 vols. (Norman: University of Oklahoma Press, 1999), 1:620.

21. For a recent discussion of the connection between citizenship and sovereignty among southeastern Indians, see Mikaëla M. Adams, *Who Belongs? Race, Resources, and Tribal Citizenship in the Native South* (New York: Oxford University Press, 2016).

22. Deloria and DeMaille, *Documents of American Indian Diplomacy*, 1:594.

23. Albert Pike to Secretary of War, May 4, 1862, in *OR*, ser. 1, vol. 13, 819–20. See also Albert Pike to T. C. Hindman, June 8, 1862, in *OR*, ser. 1, vol. 13, 940.

24. L. P. Walker to the Military Commission of Arkansas at Little Rock, P. W. Johnson, A. Rust II., F. Thomason, W. W. Watkins, A. Garland II, May 25, 1861, in *OR*, ser. 1, vol. 3, 585.

25. Paskofa to the President, March 10, 1864, Office of Indian Affairs, National Archives.

26. Deloria and DeMaille, *Documents of American Indian Diplomacy*, 1:596, 600, 626, 642.

27. Clarissa Confer, *The Cherokee Nation in the Civil War* (Norman: University of Oklahoma Press, 2007), 103. See also Cooper to Benjamin, January 29, 1862, in *OR*, ser. 1, vol. 8, 5–14.

28. Collamore to Dole, April 21, 1862, in *ARCIA, 1862*, 156.

29. Elizabeth Watts, interview, April 27, 1937, Indian Pioneer Papers, Western History Collection, vol. 95, University of Oklahoma Libraries. See also F. G. Alex, interview, March 16, 1837, Indian Pioneers Papers, 2:6–7.

30. William P. Dole to John P. Usher, October 31, 1863, in *ARCIA*, 1863, 26.

31. John Jumper, early 1862, quoted in S. S. Scott to James Seddon, in *OR*, ser. 1, vol. 41, pt. 4:1089.

32. Dole to Smith, June 5, 1862, in *OR*, ser. 2, vol. 4, 2.

33. Archibald B. Campbell to Joseph K. Barnes, January 5, 1862, in *OR*, ser. 2, vol. 4, 6.

34. McBride, *Opothleyaholo and the Loyal Muskogee*, 164.

35. Cited in Frank Cunningham, *General Stand Waite's Confederate Indians* (1959; rpt., Norman: University of Oklahoma Press, 1998), 48.

36. Report of Col. W. C. Young, [December 1861], in *OR*, ser. 1, vol. 8, 27.

37. Cooper to Benjamin, January 29, 1862, in *OR*, ser. 1, vol. 8, 13.

38. Report of Cpt. James McIntosh, January 1, 1862, in *OR*, ser. 1, vol. 8, 23, 24.

39. Paskofa to the President, March 10, 1864, Office of Indian Affairs, National Archives.

40. Albert Pike to Secretary of War, May 4, 1862, in *OR*, ser. 1, vol. 13, 820.

41. George Cutler to William G. Coffin, September 5, 1863, in *ARCIA, 1863,* 181–82; "Report of the Commissioner of Indian Affairs," November 26, 1862, in *ARCIA,* 1863, 26.

42. Campbell to Barnes, January 5, 1862, in *OR*, ser. 2, vol. 4, 6.

43. John T. Cox to Coffin, March 18, 1864, in *ARCIA, 1864,* 477.

44. Exec. Doc. No. 132, HR, 37th Cong., 2nd sess., Relief to Indian Refugees in Southern Kansas, 1862, 2.

45. Collamore to Dole, April 21, 1862, in *OR*, ser. 2, vol. 4, pt. 1:12.

46. William A. Phillips to Samuel R. Curtis, February 26, 1863, in *OR*, ser. 1, vol. 12, pt. 2:126.

47. Phillips to James G. Blunt, March 3, 1863, in *OR*, ser. 1, vol. 12, pt. 2:140.

48. Phillips to Henry Z. Curtis, March 20, 1863, in *OR*, ser. 1, vol. 22, pt. 2:166.

49. Dole to Smith, June 5, 1862, in *OR*, ser. 2, vol. 4, 2.

50. Campbell to Barnes, January 5, 1862, in *OR*, ser. 2, vol. 4, 7.

51. Lisa Tendrich Frank, "War Comes Home: Confederate Women and Union Soldiers," in *Virginia's Civil War*, ed. Peter Wallenstein and Bertram Wyatt-Brown (Charlottesville: University of Virginia Press, 2005), 131–32.

52. Claudio Saunt, *Black, White, and Indian: Race and the Unmaking of an American Family* (New York: Oxford University Press, 2005), 95; Collamore to Dole, April 21, 1862, in *OR*, ser. 2, vol. 4, pt. 1:11–12.

53. Exec. Doc. No. 47, HR, 37th Cong., 3rd sess., Accounts of Superintendent of Indian Affairs for the Southern Superintendency (1863); Exec. Doc. No. 75, HR, 37th Cong., 3rd sess., Accounts with Creeks, Choctaws, etc. (1862), 24; Exec. Doc. No. 62, HR, 38th Cong., 2nd sess., Estimates for the Indians of the Southern Superintendency, 5; Exec. Doc. No. 132, HR, 37th Cong., 2nd sess., Relief to Indian Refugees in Southern Kansas (1862).

54. William P. Dole to Doctor [William] Kile, February 10, 1862, in *OR*, ser. 2, vol. 4, 9–10.

55. Jonathan W. Turner to William P. Dole, February 5, 1862, in *OR*, ser. 2, vol. 4, 8.

56. George C. Snow to William G. Coffin, September 4, 1863, in *ARCIA, 1863*, 185; Pas-co-va to Phillips, March 19, 1864, in *OR*, vol. 34, pt. 2:663; Collamore to Dole, April 21, 1862, in *OR* , ser. 2, vol. 4, pt. 1:13.

57. Phillips to Blunt, April 24, 1863, in *OR*, ser. 1, vol. 22, pt. 2:248; Phillips to Curtis, April 29, 1863, in *OR*, ser. 2, vol. 22, pt. 2:261.

58. Collamore to Dole, April 21, 1862, in *OR*, ser. 2, vol. 4, pt. 1:13; Dole to Smith, June 5, 1862, in *OR*, ser. 2, vol. 4, 3.

59. Lorenzo Thomas to Robert W. Furnas, April 2, 1862, in *OR*, ser. 3, vol. 2, pt. 1:2; Mark K. Christ, "'They Will Be Armed': Lorenzo Thomas Recruits Black Troops in Helena, April 6, 1863," *Arkansas Historical Quarterly* 72 (Winter 2013): 366–83.

60. Carruth to Coffin, September 6, 1863, in *ARCIA, 1863*, 186.

61. Exec. Doc. No. 132, HR, 37th Cong., 2nd sess., Relief to Indian Refuges in Southern Kansas, (1862), 2.

62. Statement of William Green, [April 13, 1864], in *OR*, ser. 1, vol. 34, pt. 3:763.

63. Report of the Commissioner on Indian Affairs, November 15, 1864, in *ARCIA, 1864*, 32.

64. Matthew M. Stith, *Extreme Civil War: Guerrilla Warfare, Environment, and Race on the Trans-Mississippi Frontier* (Baton Rouge: Louisiana State University, 2016), chap. 2.

65. Coffin to Dole, October 23, 1863, in *ARCIA, 1863*, 221.

66. Usher to Dole, May 11, 1864, in *ARCIA, 1864*, 335.

67. Billy Bowlegs to William P. Dole, May 2, 1863, Office of Indian Affairs, National Archives.

Aid and Comfort to the Enemy

Escaped Prisoners and the Home as Site of War

LORIEN FOOTE

When Major General William Tecumseh Sherman captured Atlanta on September 2, 1864, officials in charge of the Confederate prison system worried that his army would march into the heart of Georgia and liberate U.S. prisoners of war held in stockades at Macon and Andersonville. They issued orders to move the captives to Savannah and Charleston, but neither city had facilities ready to house several thousand prisoners. Because there was no single commander over Confederate prisons, there was no effective communication between officials governing prisoners of war and military officials defending the two coastal cities, for whom the unexpected arrival of trainloads of Yankee prisoners was a shocking surprise. The Confederate commander at Charleston, Major General Samuel Jones, without notifying prison authorities, sent the enlisted men to Florence in September and the officers to Columbia in early October.[1] The guards marched the Yankees from the train stations to open fields with no buildings or fences. During this transfer and in the ensuing few weeks, nearly one thousand prisoners escaped from locations in South Carolina. Another eighteen hundred absconded in February and March 1865, when officials moved the remaining prisoners to North Carolina in the wake of Sherman's invasion of the cradle of secession.[2]

The fugitives, traveling in parties of two to six men, headed toward Union army lines. The most popular route during the September–November escapes in South Carolina was northwest from Charleston or Columbia through the upcountry piedmont region that encompassed the Greenville, Anderson, Pickens, and Spartanburg districts, across the border into western North Carolina, and on to the Union lines in Knoxville, Tennessee.

Others traveled east, following the rivers that flowed into the Atlantic and that pointed them in the direction of the Federal troops occupying Hilton Head, South Carolina. Another corridor for movement was west toward Augusta, Georgia, where fugitive prisoners mistakenly believed they could link up with Sherman's invading force. Federals who escaped in February and March during the transfer to North Carolina likewise traveled to Knoxville or were scooped up by Sherman's army once it captured Columbia or made their way to the Union lines at New Bern or Wilmington, North Carolina.

Along every route, hundreds of escaped Yankees intruded in the lives of white and black Southerners living in the Confederacy. They traveled across farms, hid in outbuildings, entered the cabins of enslaved people, and knocked on doors in order to ask for food, shelter, and guidance. Homes in the Carolinas became spaces where Federal soldiers recruited active aid in their quest to return to the Union army. The successful escape of 2,800 Union soldiers from the Confederacy, numbers that amounted to a fully staffed army brigade, was possible because Southern families devoted their resources and risked their lives for that purpose. Women and children mobilized to feed, hide, guard, and guide the Yankees.[3]

When Federal prisoners absconded and fled, they traveled through several counties across the two states where an alliance of deserter households, Unionist households, and slave households waged warfare against the Confederate government and its local sympathizers. The interaction between escaped Yankee prisoners and these Southern families offers new insight into the nature of the battlefield within the Carolinas. This essay argues that thousands of Southern households made war against the Confederacy through the aid and comfort they provided to its enemies. They were the sites that empowered the movement of thousands of U.S. soldiers during the last winter of the Civil War. This aspect of the war involved the entire household; every member of the family contributed to the larger goal of funneling escaped prisoners to Union lines.

Households functioned as part of kinship networks that protected the extended family, its resources, and its local customs. By 1864, thousands of households considered the Confederacy and its war for independence a threat to all three of these. Although these households were scattered across the Carolinas, there were significant concentrations of such families in three regions where escaped prisoners traveled: South Carolina's western upcountry (Greenville, Spartanburg, and Anderson Counties); two of its northeastern counties (Horry and Darlington); and western North Carolina (Alexander, Burke, Caldwell, Cherokee, Henderson, Iredell, Madison, Watauga, and Wilkes Counties).

A significant percentage of the population in these counties had been reluctant secessionists, although the majority initially supported Confederate independence, and their commitment to the cause proved shaky when hardships endangered the household. The Confederate draft withdrew men from their families and disrupted the cycle of agricultural production. Because of a drought and a hog cholera epidemic in 1862, families had consumed the surplus food that farmers always set aside for such emergencies. There was no margin of safety for the ensuing years of war, and many soldiers' wives and children relied on inconsistent state welfare programs for food. Shortages and inflation—the price of corn increased 3,000 percent—hit many families hard, and this increased resentment of Confederate impressment, tax, and exemption policies that they believed favored wealthy slaveholders. Pervasive guerrilla violence between Unionists and rebels in western North Carolina consumed many communities and threatened the safety of all families who lived there. Dangers to the emotional, economic, and physical well-being of the family drew thousands of men from the army back to their homes in 1863 and 1864. As Victoria Bynum has pointed out, these conditions created "communities of dissent" where deserter households, allied with local African Americans, met their Confederate neighbors on the "battlefields of their own farms and woods."[4]

Deserter households defended the men evading service in the Confederate army, used force to resist local and Confederate authorities, and raided rebel sympathizers in order to obtain supplies. Military-age men were either hiding in the home or lying out in nearby woods and swamps but keeping in regular contact with their families. Thousands of deserters in both South and North Carolina joined organized bands numbering between fifty and five hundred men who drilled regularly, patrolled for and fired upon Confederate conscription officials and military units sent to find them, and robbed loyal Confederate citizens. Kristen Streater and LeeAnn Whites have pointed out that women generated the warfare that Confederate guerrillas waged against Union occupation through their role as the domestic supply line. The same was true in locations where the Confederacy occupied its dissenting counties. Wives and daughters in deserter households spawned warfare through their supply of food, clothing, and vital information about enemy locations and movements.[5]

These deserter households often worked closely with Unionist households, who conducted subversive activities in response to an aggressive military regime in both states that repressed them and denied them civil liberties. Members of secret societies in the region took solemn oaths to encourage desertion from the Confederate army, to harbor all deserters and escaped Federal prisoners of war, and to provide U.S. armies with intelligence. Unionist households in North Carolina engaged in pervasive irregular warfare, consuming thirty-two counties, that destabilized and ultimately eroded Confederate authority. Barton A. Myers has demonstrated that the Confederate and state governments effectively controlled less than 60 percent of North Carolina in early 1864. He identifies two types of irregular warfare being waged against the Confederacy. One was a "people's war of resistance and self-defense" fought by self-constituted bands of Unionists. Another was the "raiding warfare" of Union army units recruited from the dissident population in North Carolina that launched attacks from bases in East Tennessee.[6]

Households deployed violence directly against rebels in their communities and defended themselves from frequent attacks. Every member of the family had a role to play. The men cut holes between the logs composing the outer walls of their homes. When their houses were surrounded, the children bolted the door and the women handed loaded weapons to the men, who fired through the holes in the wall. "Every man, even every boy about 12 years of age is thoroughly armed," one escaped prisoner recorded in wonder. Families picketed roads to watch for raiding parties and units sent to arrest deserters. Women took the day shift; men stood guard at night.[7]

In western North Carolina, pervasive irregular warfare destabilized the Confederacy; in the South Carolina low country, slave rebellion likewise weakened the state. Enslaved men absconded whenever they had the opportunity; enslaved women slowed work and defied their masters and mistresses. Both served in the network of white and black households that supplied and harbored deserters and Unionists. By the fall of 1864, when the South Carolina government was no longer capable of quashing opposition, enslaved people increasingly utilized guerrilla tactics. Portions of the low country descended into irregular warfare, while slaves elsewhere instigated uprisings and contributed to conditions in some counties that officials described as "lawlessness" and "chaos." Slaves in St. Matthew's Parish, located in the central section of the state, organized a paramilitary company that operated against authorities.[8]

Confederate authorities waged war against the households that defied them. They recognized that without the families who hid, fed, clothed, guided, and spied for deserters, draft dodgers, and Unionist guerrillas, there would not be such widespread and effective military resistance to their regime. A vital part of their strategy on the battlefronts within the Confederacy was to crush women's activities. The Confederate government commanded military authorities to arrest without warrant citizens who harbored deserters. In the Carolinas, squads of infantry and cavalry monitored

women's movements and searched and destroyed their homes. North Carolina governor Zebulon Vance subjected women to arrest in his orders and
proclamations. The state's Guard for Home Defense, tasked with arrest-
ing disloyal citizens and deserters from the Confederate army, intimidated
and occasionally tortured women and children. South Carolina's Confederate Reserve units applied the same tactics against deserter households; in
Anderson, South Carolina, they whipped two women.[9]

The arrival of hundreds of escaped prisoners in the neighborhoods and
domestic spaces of the Carolinas added a new element to the battlefront
there. The fugitive Federals presented an opportunity to expand the warfare
taking place from the home. Forty-one-year-old Mary Estes, who lived
in Caldwell County, North Carolina, was already an enemy of the Confederate government when four fugitive prisoners crossed her path. Her
husband, William, led a gang of deserters and guerrillas who waged war
against Confederate authorities and sympathizers in their county. She and
her five children, ages six to fifteen, supplied the guerrillas with food and
clothes, carried messages between companies of deserters with information
they needed to conduct raids and ambushes, and served as guides to pilot
men through remote mountain areas. Her activities were so important that
Guard for Home Defense units watched her for days at a time, periodically
conducted searches of her house, and targeted her children. They tortured
fifteen-year-old Joseph in front of her in an attempt to discover William's
hiding place.

In late October, Joseph brought Mary the news that four men claiming
to be Confederate deserters on their way home to Kentucky were in the
family's field of sorghum grass located in a mountain ravine. Mary walked
right up to the men and asked, "What are you doing here?" When the
leader began to explain, Mary interrupted that she did not believe a word
and that she suspected they were Yankees. She informed the escaped prisoners that if she lifted her hand, the hidden men who had rifles trained
on them would open fire, and she demanded proof of their identity. When
shown a Federal officer's commission, she waved a handkerchief around
her head three times and twenty men dressed in Confederate uniforms
descended from the mountains. Mary housed the escaped prisoners for two
days, fed them, and arranged for guides to take them on the next stage of
their journey to Knoxville.[10]

The fact that Mary's decision was replicated thousands of times in both
South Carolina and North Carolina during the winter of 1864–65 alters the
scholarly picture of deserter households in these two states. Although historians are aware that deserters and their families gave aid to escaped pris-

oners traveling through the Appalachians, they have been unaware of the scale and geographic reach of prison escapes and thus the scope of household activity on this front. Reports that successful escapees made to the provost marshals of Hilton Head and Knoxville, their diaries, and their published narratives indicate that fugitive Federals uniformly received aid from deserter households, including those who were simply evading conscript officers and were not involved in deserter gangs or guerrilla bands.

Scholarship on desertion has rooted the phenomenon in the household; its dynamics and needs generally instigated and sustained desertion. This essay does not challenge that assertion. But some historians have emphasized that deserter households were not necessarily disloyal to the Confederacy even when they militarily resisted conscription. Southerners possessed multiple loyalties—to family, to God, to state, to Confederacy—that shifted in priority depending on circumstances. Loyalty to and defense of the family might momentarily supersede a continuing loyalty to the idea of Confederate independence.[11] But encounters with fugitive Yankees revealed that thousands of deserter households in South and North Carolina were willing to aid the Confederacy's enemy. They generally responded, when given the opportunity, with active assistance to the hundreds of Federals they met. Many deserters hid Yankees in their mountain caves or swampy lairs, their wives fed, provisioned, and guided the Federals, and their children were sent on errands to warn fugitives when danger approached.

Because fugitives openly expressed to deserter families their desire to escape in order to return to their regiments and fight, aiding the Federals toward that goal was a clear act of disloyalty. Indeed, the Confederate government expressly forbade such activities. In order to win the war and achieve independence, the Confederacy endeavored to restrict the movement of external and internal enemies across its borders and to control the interaction between its citizens and prisoners of war. Persons living in the Confederacy who wished to travel within or beyond its claimed boundaries had to obtain permission and a pass from military authorities. The goal, according to Secretary of War James A. Seddon, was to "preclude the passage of dangerous and disaffected persons." The Confederate Congress had authorized President Davis to suspend the writ of habeas corpus under certain specific conditions that included giving "aid and comfort" to the enemy, having communication with the enemy "without necessity and without permission of the Confederate states," and helping to "liberate prisoners of war." Davis requested and received permission to make arrests in such cases.[12]

Considering the fact that thousands of deserters, their wives, and their children "liberated" an army brigade's worth of Union prisoners, scholars must reconsider their reluctance to categorize desertion and its household support network in this region as a sign of ideological warfare against the Confederacy. Many deserter households in the Carolinas did not temporarily withdraw from state authority; during the last three months of 1864 they worked to undermine it. By the last winter of the war, deserter households in the swamps and mountains of the Carolinas made common cause with U.S. soldiers on a daily basis. This situation indicates active opposition to and open warfare against the Confederacy itself.[13]

An especially striking indicator that households were sites of warfare against the Confederacy was the mobilization of children and teenagers to aid these enemies of the state. Parents employed them as lookouts and guides and trained them to deceive representatives of the Confederacy, as Joseph did for the Estes family. Accounts of children serving these three functions are ubiquitous in escaped prisoners' diaries and published narratives. Because the home itself was the station that escaped prisoners used to resupply and hide from pursuers, the role of lookout along roads and approaches to the house was critical for success. White and black families assigned this task to children. When Willard Worcester Glazier, an escapee from Columbia, reached the outskirts of Savannah, Georgia, a slave guided him to the home of a free black family named Jones. The husband was out on a scout, but the wife volunteered the services of her eight- and six-year-old sons. Glazier posted the oldest on the road and ordered the youngest to serve as lookout for any signal from his brother. A county sheriff who used his position and his home to aid escaped prisoners trained his seven-year-old boy to protect them. He told one of the fugitives, "We have endeavored to bring him up to be a good religious, strictly honest and truthful boy, yet if anyone should come here tomorrow and ask him if there had been any strangers here, no matter what they did to him they could not get a word out of him. Isn't that a terrible way to bring up children?" Fugitive Junius Henri Browne wrote that the children he met "were unnaturally developed; their senses acute; their secretiveness perfect."[14]

Children operated on behalf of their families at long distances from the home itself. They guided escaped prisoners through the landscape and around the homes and roads that might be a danger to the Yankees. Nine- and eleven-year-old boys brought six Yankees from their home to another hiding place. "They seemed to understand perfectly the necessity of our keeping out of sight of the rebels," one of the fugitives recalled. A father sent his twelve-year-old daughter alone at night fifteen miles over the Blue Ridge Mountains to warn some prisoners he had hidden that North Carolina Guard for Home Defense units had discovered their location and were on the way.[15]

Youths performed the vital functions of guides and informants during skirmishes and armed confrontations. One group of fugitives joined famed scout Daniel Ellis and a party of seventy recruits, refugees, and other escaped prisoners he was leading through the battle zones of East Tennessee. Rebel guerrillas closed in on the expedition near Kelly's Gap in Greene County. Ellis enlisted the services of a sixteen-year-old girl who was an expert horsewoman to pilot his party out of the neighborhood. At midnight, the beautiful and graceful teenager guided the desperate men around the guerrillas' camps, the farmhouses of those who helped them, and the pickets they had posted on the road. After seven miles of stealthy movement, the young lady left the men in the woods while she rode alone over a long bridge that spanned the Nolichucky River to see if guerrillas guarded the structure and to reconnoiter the situation on the other side. She reported that the coast was clear, rode past the long line of men, and headed home alone.[16]

When households were sites of war against the Confederacy, every member contributed to that function. Historians James Marten, Anya Jabour, and Edmund Drago point out that war politicized Southern children, who engaged in patriotic activities to support it, such as little girls raising money for soldiers' aid and young men drilling in neighborhood vigilance associations. Even so, these scholars ignore children's widespread role as direct participants in the forms of warfare conducted from and in the home.[17] The parents who engaged their children in this capacity did not ignore the significance or the ramifications. They prepared their children for interrogation and torture at the hands of Confederate officials.

Another important factor in the household war against the Confederacy was the transformation of the Southern home from a domestic space to a physical site of resistance to state authority. This process began in some families with their efforts to obstruct conscription or shield deserters. In Flat Rock, North Carolina, twenty-one-year-old Martha Holinsworth, the daughter of a farmer and occasional day laborer on the estate of Treasury Secretary Christopher G. Memminger, constructed and concealed a scuttle-hole from her upstairs bedroom to a small garret after her brother Isaac deserted from the Confederate army. He hid there for more than two months, but unable to stand such close confinement, he surrendered when the governor proclaimed a general amnesty for those deserters who did so. Martha later used the garret to hide four escaped prisoners for four days and nights while she procured them a guide to Knoxville.[18]

Along the major escape routes in the Carolinas, domestic spaces became points in a network of sites stretching through cities, villages, and neigh-borhoods. As Edward Ayers and Scott Nesbit point out, studying spa-tial dimensions reveals variations in experience and makes connections between events. Fugitive movements along routes connected by collabora-tion between households provides new insight into the internal war against the Confederacy waged by deserters, Unionists, and slaves. It demonstrates that dissidents were highly organized across space and insurgents cooper-ated extensively across racial and ethnic boundaries.[19]

Households in Charleston developed a particularly intricate network of sites to hide escaped prisoners and move them from the city. When Major General Jones sent the Federal officers who had arrived in the city to Columbia, an unknown but substantial number of Yankees bolted as they were marched down King Street to the train station. Enslaved African Americans, free blacks, white Unionists, and a number of Irish and Ger-man immigrants hid the prisoners, sometimes for weeks, while they waited to escape. The citizens who aided the fugitives used Charleston's streets as pathways to transfer the Yankees from place to place when Confederates searched neighborhoods. Captain William H. Telford traveled through six locations in the city, including a shoemaker's shop on King Street, a store on Cummings Street, a bachelor's house on Calhoun Street, and a family residence near the Negro Hospital. Eventually the fugitives ended up at a city wharf, where slave pilots moved them out by boat under the cover of darkness to Union lines on Hilton Head.[20]

In the escape route that led from Columbia through the Piedmont into the Blue Ridge Mountains, the desire to aid Yankee prisoners expanded links between households mobilized against the Confederacy and extended the geographic reach of their activities. The first escaped prisoners who entered the landscape received help from enslaved African Americans acting as individuals. Those who fled weeks later found that slaves had organized across space in order to handle the volume of fugitives moving through the area. Slaves utilized key elements of the household—kin rela-tionships, a locus for activity, emotional bonds, and collective resources—to provide aid and comfort to the Confederacy's enemies. When Hanni-bal Johnson of the Third Maine escaped from Camp Sorghum in late November, enslaved people guided him between prearranged stations in northwestern South Carolina. Over eight nights in that part of his jour-ney, he was handed off to thirteen guides—one gave him the code name "birdies"—who took him to established hiding places in the woods where slave households provided food, shelter, and supplies. Johnson and his party had to travel for a couple of days without a guide but fortuitously encountered Mrs. Prince, a white Unionist in Pickens District, who piloted them to an outlier camp ten miles from her home, where they joined forty-six deserters and Unionists to travel to Knoxville.[21]

Along this route, alliances between black guides and white deserters utilized preexisting social and economic networks. Cooperation was especially effective in the Spartanburg District, which had a tradition of extralegal fraternization between whites and blacks in taverns and secret gambling venues. Despite laws against it and a penalty of forty lashes if caught, enslaved people in the village distilled and sold alcohol to neighbors of both races. Local authorities never established control over such activities, and by 1864 the deserters joined with slaves in a rampage of stealing and lawlessness and cooperated when fugitive Federals arrived in the district.[22]

Black and white households collaborated to aid three captains from the 101st Pennsylvania who had escaped from the train ferrying prisoners from Charleston to Columbia. Two weeks later, they reached the outskirts of Spartanburg and enlisted the aid of a free black, Henry Martin. That night he visited the wife of a Confederate deserter named Ray. She put her husband in contact with the escapees. Martin moved the Federals to the woods near his brother-in-law's farm while they waited for Ray to return from his hideout. He arrived in Confederate uniform and trained his rifle on the Yankees during the ensuing conversation. Only after Ray's wife arrived did the deserter agree to pilot the fugitives the next fifty miles of their journey in exchange for a silver-cased watch. Before the party left, Ray's wife begged the Federals to persuade her husband to accompany them to Union lines. By the time the party crossed the North Carolina border, Ray was convinced. He traveled all the way to Knoxville with the Federals.[23]

As was the case with Johnson and the three Pennsylvanians, it was common for escaped prisoners to add deserters to their escape parties as they crossed into the Blue Ridge. Once they reached western North Carolina, they benefited from a highly organized web of households that pooled resources to channel hundreds of Southern men to enlist in the Union army at Knoxville during the winter of 1864–65.[24] At the center of the web in Transylvania County was Robert Hamilton, the deputy sheriff and a justice of the peace. Hamilton used his position as an officer in the Guard for Home Defense to protect deserters, sending word ahead when his unit conducted patrols or raids. His squad once surrounded a house while he and three others searched it. Hamilton found the deserter hiding under a bed, but told the captain the room was empty. By November 1864, the sheriff was busy funneling to Knoxville large parties of fugitive Federals and

mountaineers. During that month, he dispatched at least two separate parties, one containing sixty men and the other twenty.[25]

The accounts of several escaped Yankees testify to interracial cooperation, to an extensive network of households that Hamilton utilized for his
operations, and to the participation of all members of the household. An
African American guide led fugitive Daniel Langworthy and his four com-
panions to Hamilton's home and called out a simple password. The sheriff hid these five in his home. At the same time, he had three veterans of
the 101st Pennsylvania in a cabin in the mountains, a location that became
known as the Pennsylvania House to later groups that stayed there. Dozens of other Yankees were stashed in households across the county waiting
for Hamilton to procure guides and establish a rendezvous date and time.[26]

A cluster of these households was located in the small community of
Brevard. Three Union officers from Maine regiments were ensconced in
the home of Jack Loftis, who kept an autograph book of all the escaped
prisoners he helped. Because rebel neighbors watched his house, he hid
the various Yankees in a small building where he kept his cider press. His
daughter gave one of the New Englanders the stockings off her feet, all she
had left after supplying so many other fugitives with footwear. Numerous
Yankee fugitives were hiding in nearby houses or other safe spots, including Lieutenant James Fales, who was kept in a cave for three days by a
shoemaker and his wife. The couple outfitted him for the journey. Eventually Fales was guided to the rendezvous point near Hamilton's house by
a twelve-year-old. All of the households who sheltered Yankees fed them
"rebel beef," provisions acquired in raids against pro-Confederate supporters in the neighborhood.[27]

Prisoners who escaped from Florence and traveled along the rivers of
low country South and North Carolina likewise found white households
that were connected to two other locations of resistance to Confederate
authority in the region: the swampy lairs of deserters and the cabins of
enslaved people. However, in this area, distances between sites were greater,
and there were no clusters of white households such as fugitives found
in Brevard, North Carolina. Instead, the more isolated white households
often relied on individual African Americans for intelligence. The experiences of John Harrold, a shoemaker enlisted in the 138th Pennsylvania,
and Sidney S. Williams, a sergeant in the Tenth Massachusetts, who separately escaped from Florence in September 1864, illustrate how Southerners living in the rural low country made war against the Confederate state
by offering aid and comfort to its enemies.

Eight days after his escape, Harrold was so feverish and weak that he collapsed in the woods and lay there alone, mentally preparing for death. James Irvin King, an elderly man who lived in the woods with his wife, picked Harrold up, placed him on a horse, and took him home. Mrs. King bathed the Federal, put clean clothes on him, and nursed him through two weeks of delirium. Once he recovered, Harrold learned that the Kings were motivated by more than just humanitarian concern for a suffering human being. They did not consider Harrold to be the enemy, they told him, because they had never supported the Confederate war effort. The couple hid the Yankee in their home for five months while he recovered from his illness and relied on information about military movements provided by a slave who lived in the neighborhood. Harrold was confident that his hiding place was known to slaves in a twenty-mile radius. "Had I been betrayed, I should have been warned in time to escape," he believed. When Sherman's invading army eventually approached the vicinity in late February 1865, a slave piloted two Federal cavalrymen to the Kings' home so they could rescue the escaped prisoner.[28]

Just as enslaved African Americans aided the King household in its quest to protect Harrold, the household that shielded Williams did so through its connection with deserters. After the Yankee and a companion escaped Florence, they traveled for several days, crossing the Pee Dee River and other streams and swamps. Hunger eventually compelled them to approach a white farmer, admit their identity, and ask for food. Abraham Moore, who lived with his widowed daughter and her children in Robeson County, North Carolina, secured a hiding place for the Federals and sent word to some deserters lying out in a swamp twenty miles away. The deserters came in to meet the Yankees. "The word deserter, as we understand it, is rather too hard to use in connection with them, as they were almost to a man earnest Union men," Williams later wrote in a sentiment that other escaped prisoners echoed. "The party that called on us was very cordial and friendly." The deserters invited the fugitives to recuperate in the swamp before continuing the journey to Union lines at New Bern, North Carolina. They spent five weeks in the fortified position the deserters had constructed, which included a log cabin with six bunks. The fugitives' "new friends" had their wives and sweethearts provide a suit of clothes and stockings for each Yankee. The deserters made the escapees new shoes out of leather stolen from a tanner. Slaves who lived nearby provided meal and salt in exchange for parts of wild cattle the deserters shot in the swamp. In the underworld that defied Confederate authority, homes, swamps, and cabins were connected in a world of exchange, provision, and aid to the enemy.[29]

A complete map of Civil War battlefields would mark the households, both enslaved and free, that lay along escaped prisoners' routes through the Carolinas. From those households, men and women shot at their neighbors and launched supply raids against pro-Confederate supporters. Out of those households came the supplies that enabled thousands of men to fight and defeat state and Confederate military units that operated against them. Moving between households, children piloted thousands of Union soldiers to safety. Slave cabins and yeoman farmhouses joined together in a network of sites that ultimately channeled thousands of Southern white men out of the Carolinas, who returned as raiders wearing the uniform of the United States. The war in the Carolinas must be situated in the household as well as in the fortifications defending Charleston and Wilmington.

NOTES

1. Samuel Cooper to John H. Winder, September 5, 1864, U.S. War Department, *The War of the Rebellion: A Compilation of the Official Records of the Union and Confederate Armies* (Washington, D.C.: Government Printing Office, 1880–1901; hereafter *OR*), ser. 2, vol. 7, 773; Samuel Jones to James Seddon, September 12, 1864, *OR*, ser. 2, vol. 7, 817; Winder to Cooper, December 6, 1864, Jones to Cooper, September 29, 1864, William J. Hardee to Milledge Bonham, October 7, 1864, David Urquhart to Cooper and endorsements, October 26, 1864, *OR*, ser. 2, vol. 7, 1196, 894, 930, 1046.

2. Lorien Foote, "Fugitive Federals Database." This database contains the names of 3,010 individuals who escaped from Confederate prison camps and successfully reached the lines of the Union army. It includes the following information, if available: rank and regiment, when and where captured, when and where escaped, and when and where the person reported to Union lines. The database is a compilation of records found in the National Archives. "Register of Federal Prisoners of War Who Escaped from Confederate Authorities," RG 249, entry 31, no. 45; "Memorandum of Escaped Prisoners from the Hands of the Rebels," RG 249, entry 32, box 1; "List of Federal Prisoners of War Who Escaped from Confederate Authorities," RG 249, entry 109; "Union Prisoners of War—Escaped from Confederate Authorities," RG 393, Part 1, entry 4318; "Rolls and Reports of Federal Prisoners of War Who Escaped from Confederate Prisons," RG 249, entry 32, box 1; "Statements of Escaped Union Prisoners, Refugees, and Rebel Deserters," RG 393, part 1, entries 4294 and 4295; "Lists of Escaped Prisoners, Deserters, and Refugees," RG 249, entry 107, box 11, roll 979; "Letters Received Relating to Union Naval POWs: Reports from Officers and Seamen of the U.S. Navy Who Were Prisoner of War in the South," RG 45, entry 56.

3. A few scholars have studied escaped prisoners of war in the region, without recognizing the scale of escapes, as examples of personal narratives or as windows

into Northern views of Appalachian culture. See John C. Inscoe, "'Moving through Deserter Country,'" in *The Civil War in Appalachia: Collected Essays*, ed. Kenneth W. Noe and Shannon H. Wilson (Knoxville: University of Tennessee Press, 1997); Jonathan Dean Sarris, *A Separate Civil War: Communities in Conflict in the Mountain South* (Charlottesville: University of Virginia Press, 2006); Ann Fabian, *The Unvarnished Truth: Personal Narratives in Nineteenth-Century America* (Berkeley: University of California Press, 2000).

4. Victoria E. Bynum, *The Long Shadow of the Civil War: Southern Dissent and Its Legacies* (Chapel Hill: University of North Carolina Press, 2010), 5–8, 41; John C. Inscoe and Gordon B. McKinney, eds. *The Heart of Confederate Appalachia: Western North Carolina in the Civil War* (Chapel Hill: University of North Carolina Press, 2000), 75–84, 114–15, 126–28, 145, 167–75; Archie Vernon Huff Jr., *Greenville: The History of the City and County in the South Carolina Piedmont* (Columbia: University of South Carolina Press, 1995), 112–15, 128–43; Charles Edward Cauthen, *South Carolina Goes to War, 1860–1865* (Chapel Hill: University of North Carolina Press, 1950), 4–12, 27–28, 150.

5. Ashmore to Jordan, March 26, 1864, Simkins to Boylston, May 7, 1864, and Feiden to Ashmore, June 4, 1864, *OR*, ser. 1, vol. 35, pt. 2:376, 478, 521; Cauthen, *South Carolina Goes to War*, 27–28, 150; LeeAnn Whites and Alecia P. Long, eds., *Occupied Women: Gender, Military Occupation, and the American Civil War* (Baton Rouge: Louisiana State University Press, 2009), 7, and Kristen Streater's essay in that volume, "'She-Rebels' on the Supply Line: Gender Conventions in Civil War Kentucky," 56–78. Whites's article on the subject is "Forty Shirts and a Wagonload of Wheat: Women, the Domestic Supply Line, and the Civil War on the Western Border," *Journal of the Civil War Era* 1 (March 2011): 56–78.

6. Vance to Secretary of War Seddon, July 25, 1863, *OR*, ser. 4, vol. 2, 674; Lay to Preston, September 2, 1863, *OR*, ser. 4, vol. 2, 783–86; Andrew M. Benson, "Prison Life and Escape," *First Maine Bugle* 3 (April 1893): 8; Walter to Bragg, May 8, 1864, *OR*, ser. 4, vol. 3, 393–96; Barton A. Myers, *Rebels against the Confederacy: North Carolina's Unionists* (New York: Cambridge University Press, 2014), 4–13, 124, 137, 244–45.

7. Philip N. Racine, ed., *Unspoiled Heart: The Journal of Charles Mattocks of the 17th Maine* (Knoxville: University of Tennessee Press, 1994), 236–40; "An Account of Captain Conley's Escape from Prison," 23, Manuscript Division, Library of Congress, Washington, D.C.; James M. Fales, *Prison Life of Lieut. James M. Fales* (Providence: N. B. Williams, 1882), 57.

8. James Chesnut Jr. to Andrew G. Magrath, December 21, 1864, Magrath to Green, December 21, 1864, Magrath to Frederick, December 21, 1864, Magrath Order Book, 1864–65, South Carolina Department of Archives and History, Columbia; Leslie A. Schwalm, *A Hard Fight for We: Women's Transition from Slavery to Freedom in South Carolina* (Urbana: University of Illinois Press, 1997), 4–5, 79–107; Walter Edgar, *South Carolina: A History* (Columbia: University of South Carolina Press, 1998), 367; Stephanie McCurry, *Confederate Reckoning: Power and Politics in*

the Civil War South (Cambridge: Harvard University Press, 2010), 256–61; Marli F. Weiner, *Mistresses and Slaves: Plantation Women in South Carolina, 1830–1880* (Urbana: University of Illinois Press, 1998), 170–79.

9. GO 31, March 10, 1864, *OR*, ser. 4, vol. 3, 203; An Act to Prevent Desertion from Confederate or State Military Service, and Evasion of Conscription, September 30, 1863, no. 4666, *Published Laws of South Carolina*, SCDAH; Cauthen, *South Carolina Goes to War*, 176; McCurry, *Confederate Reckoning*, 126–30; James Chesnut Jr. to F. E. Harrison, October 15, 1864, Military Letterbook, SCDAH; Settle to Vance, October 4, 1864, Thomas Settle Jr. Letters, NCSA; Myers, *Rebels against the Confederacy*, 124–27, 137, 244–45; Bynum, *Long Shadow of the Civil War*, 3.

10. J. Madison Drake, *Narrative of the Capture, Imprisonment, and Escape of J. Madison Drake, Captain Ninth New Jersey Volunteers* (1866), 41–46, Rare Books and Manuscripts Division, Huntington Library, San Marino, Calif.; Linda M. Staley and John O. Hawkins, *The 1860 Census of Caldwell County, North Carolina* (Lenoir, N.C.: Caldwell County Genealogical Society, 1983).

11. Judkin Browning, *Shifting Loyalties: The Union Occupation of Eastern North Carolina* (Chapel Hill: University of North Carolina Press, 2011), 4; Scott King-Owen, "Conditional Confederates: Absenteeism among Western North Carolina Soldiers, 1861–1865," *Civil War History* 57, no. 4 (2011): 349–79; Aaron Sheehan-Dean, *Why Confederates Fought: Family and Nation in Civil War Virginia* (Chapel Hill: University of North Carolina Press, 2007), 10; Aaron W. Marrs, "Desertion and Loyalty in the South Carolina Infantry," *Civil War History* 50, no. 1 (March 2004): 47–65.

12. James A. Seddon to Jefferson Davis, January 11, 1865, *OR*, ser. 4, vol. 3, 1015; Amy Murrell Taylor, *The Divided Family in Civil War America* (Chapel Hill: University of North Carolina Press, 2005), 93; Seddon to Davis, November 8, 1864, *OR*, ser. 4, vol. 3, 802–16; Davis to Senate and House of Representatives, November 9, 1864, *OR*, ser. 4, vol. 3, 819–20; Davis to Senate and House of Representatives, February 3, 1864, *OR*, ser. 4, vol. 3, 67–70; General Order 31, March 10, 1864, Adj. and Insp. General's Office, *OR*, ser. 4, vol. 3, 203.

13. Patrick J. Doyle, "Understanding the Desertion of South Carolinian Soldiers during the Final Years of the Confederacy," *Historical Journal* 56 (September 2013): 657–79. Doyle's study of deserters listed in the "Federal Register of Confederate Deserters Who Took the Oath of Allegiance" supports the conclusion presented here regarding deserters. Deserters from South Carolina who took the oath tended to be from locations in South Carolina where the community supported deserters who formed armed criminal bands that indicate such deserters were alienated from the state.

14. Willard Worcester Glazier, *The Capture, the Prison Pen, and the Escape* (New York: R. H. Ferguson, 1870), 264–87; Daniel Avery Langworthy, *Reminiscences of a Prisoner of War and His Escape* (Minneapolis: Byron, 1915), 57–58; Junius Henri Browne, *Four Years in Secessia: Adventures within and beyond the Union Lines* (Hartford, Conn.: O. D. Case, 1865), 379.

15. W. H. Newlin, *An Account of the Escape of Six Federal Soldiers from Prison at Danville, Va.: Their Travels by Night through the Enemy's Country to the Union Picket at Gauley Bridge, West Virginia, in the Winter of 1863–64* (Cincinnati, Ohio: Western Methodist Book Concern Print, 1881), 99; Albert D. Richardson, *The Secret Service, the Field, the Dungeon, and the Escape* (Hartford, Conn.: American, 1865), 473–74.

16. Richardson, *Secret Service*, 501–2; Browne, *Four Years in Secessia*, 421–23.

17. James Marten, *The Children's Civil War* (Chapel Hill: University of North Carolina Press, 1998), 3–5, 102, 149; Anya Jabour, *Topsy-Turvy: How the Civil War Turned the World Upside Down for Southern Children* (Chicago: Ivan R. Dee, 2010), 10, 77; Edmund L. Drago, *Confederate Phoenix: Rebel Children and Their Families in South Carolina* (New York: Fordham University Press, 2008), 2–6.

18. John V. Hadley, *Seven Months a Prisoner; or, Thirty-Six Days in the Woods* (Indianapolis: J. M. & F. J. Meikel, 1868), 133–40; Christopher G. Memminger Account Book, box 1, folder 9, SHC 502, Southern Historical Collection, Wilson Library, University of North Carolina, Chapel Hill; Lois T. Dorsey, *United States Census 1850 Henderson County, North Carolina* (Hendersonville, N.C.: Genealogy, 1983), 38, 106; Joe A. Cowart, *Cowart's 1850 Census Henderson Co., NC with Analysis and Index* (Hendersonville, N.C.: J. A. Cowart, 2003), 271A.

19. Edward L. Ayers and Scott Nesbit, "Seeing Emancipation: Scale and Freedom in the American South," *Journal of the Civil War Era* 1 (March 2011): 3–24. Historian Stephanie M. H. Camp argues that whites entered slaves' "rival geography" in significant numbers for the first time during the Civil War and she notes that Confederate deserters and Union soldiers joined with Southern whites who had traded illegally with slaves before the war. Camp, *Closer to Freedom: Enslaved Women and Everyday Resistance in the Plantation South* (Chapel Hill: University of North Carolina Press, 2004), 135–36. Victoria E. Bynum also found increasing cross-racial communication between blacks and disaffected Southern whites. Bynum, *Long Shadow of the Civil War*, 3.

20. "Statement of Cpt. Telford, N.D.," RBPMG, Hilton Head, S.C., RG 393, entry 4295, NA.

21. Hannibal A. Johnson, "The Sword of Honor from Captivity to Freedom," *Personal Narratives of Events in the War of the Rebellion, Being Papers Read before the Rhode Island Soldiers and Sailors Historical Society* (Providence: Published by the Society, 1903), 28–38. See also M. A. Cochran, "Reminiscences of Life in Rebel Prisons (Concluded)," in *Sketches of War History, 1861–1865: Papers Prepared for the Commandery of the State of Ohio, Military Order of the Loyal Legion of the United States* (Cincinnati: Robert Clarke, 1903), 5:51–53.

22. Philip N. Racine, *Living a Big War in a Small Place: Spartanburg, South Carolina, during the Confederacy* (Columbia: University of South Carolina Press, 2013), 13–14, 47, 55, 81.

23. "Account of Captain Conley's Escape from Prison," 15–18.

24. Myers, *Rebels against the Confederacy*, 128, 149; Richard Nelson Current, *Lincoln's Loyalists: Union Soldiers from the Confederacy* (Boston: Northeastern Univer-

sity Press, 1992), 48–49, 71; Samuel W. Scott and Samuel P. Angel, *History of the Thirteenth Regiment Tennessee Volunteer Cavalry, U.S.A.* (Philadelphia: P. W. Ziegler, 1903), 136, 141, 394, 423–36; Ron V. Killian, *A History of the North Carolina Third Mounted Infantry Volunteers, USA. March, 1864 . . . August 1865* (Bowie, Md.: Heritage Books, 2000), 1–3, 150–52; Matthew Bumgarner, *Kirk's Raiders: A Notorious Band of Scoundrels and Thieves* (Hickory, N.C.: Tarheel Press, 2000), 15–18, 145.

25. Governor's Office, Lists of Justices of the Peace, 1865, North Carolina State Archives, Raleigh; "Robert Hamilton" in Grace Turner and Miles Philbeck, *Transylvania County North Carolina Will Abstracts, 1861–1910* (N.p.: privately published, 1991).

26. Langworthy, *Reminiscences of a Prisoner of War*, 57–58; "Account of Captain Conley," 21–23. Capt. Isaiah Conley, Cpt. F. B. Dawson, and 1st Lt. W. C. Davidson, all of the 101st Pennsylvania, escaped on October 5. When they arrived at Hamilton's house, five fugitives were hiding at the house: Capt. Chauncy S. Aldrich, Capt. Daniel Avery Langworthy, and 1st Lt. J. E. Twillinger, all of the 85th New York, 1st Lt. G. S. Hastings of the 2nd N.Y. Ind Batt, and Capt. G. H. Starr of the 104th New York, who had escaped from Columbia in early October. These eight men belonged to a Union garrison at Plymouth that was surrounded and surrendered en masse on April 20, 1864. Two other officers from the Plymouth garrison, Captain Cady of the Twenty-Fourth N.Y. and Lieutenant Masters of the Second North Carolina, who also escaped from the train, were hiding in the Pennsylvania House. October 27–30, C. S. Aldrich Civil War Diary, SMI, folder 1, Chauncy S. Aldrich Collection, PMM.

27. Racine, *Unspoiled Heart*, 236–40; Charles O. Hunt, "Our Escape from Camp Sorghum. By Lieutenant Charles O. Hunt. Read December 3, 1890," *War Papers Read before the Commandery of the State of Maine, Military Order of the Loyal Legion of the United States*, vol. 1 (Portland, Maine: Thurston Print, 1898), 106–13; Fales, *Prison Life of Fales*, 56–58.

28. John Harrold, *Libby, Andersonville, Florence: The Capture, Imprisonment, Escape, and Rescue of John Harrold, a Union Soldier in the War of the Rebellion* (Philadelphia: Wm. B. Selheimer, 1870), 88–106.

29. Sidney S. Williams, "From Spotsylvania to Wilmington, N.C., by Way of Andersonville and Florence," *Personal Narratives of Events in the War of the Rebellion, Being Papers Read before the Rhode Island Soldiers and Sailors Historical Society*, 5th ser., no. 10 (Providence: Published by the Society, 1899), 17–29.

PART 4

Reconstructing the Household

Disordered Households

Reconstruction, Klan Terror, and the Law

VICTORIA E. BYNUM

Perhaps no one homefront can be termed "typical," but that of Orange County, North Carolina, presented a combination of factors that help us understand the connections between the Civil War, Southern homefronts, emancipation, and Reconstruction households. Orange County's diverse population featured mostly yeoman farmers interspersed with planters, business entrepreneurs, professors, lawyers, enslaved African Americans, poor whites, and free people of color. Long before the Civil War, a lively interracial subculture with complex social and kinship ties had emerged that contradicted the dominant Southern ideal of white families and enslaved African Americans governed by benevolent white patriarchs in a system decreed by the Great Almighty. The core principles of this so-called organic society were completely upended by households composed of non-slaveholding whites and free people of color. Within these lower-class interracial homes, one encountered black patriarchs, sexually active unmarried women, and free children of color; absent was the authority of white masters, as most were headed either by women or men of color.[1]

In its effort to prevent or dismantle such households, the state empowered court magistrates to prosecute behavior defined as illicit, including attempted marriages across the color line, between free and enslaved people, and fornication in general. With a sizeable cohort of people forbidden to marry, significant numbers of children were born to single mothers, who were then hauled before the courts on bastardy charges. These efforts at social control reinforced the well-entrenched institution of slavery and the accompanying fiction of separate and distinct races. Bolstering such efforts were state laws, ordinances, and practices that kept poor whites as well as free people of color land-poor, badly paid for labor, and subject to public whippings and incarceration. Just as black people were deemed by temperament and intelligence to be fit only for enslavement, so also were poor white and free interracial families dismissed as degraded and immoral. Their presence was tolerated so long as they remained illiterate, disorganized, and politically mute.[2]

Despite Southern leaders' image of an ideal society in which people were separated by race, status, and therefore kinship, in fact, antebellum slave-holding households were themselves interracial and frequently included mixed-race children. White men's sexual exploitation of enslaved women contributed to a large population of light-skinned African Americans who inherited their mothers' status and racial identity, which made the identities of their white fathers easy to conceal. In contrast, white women could not easily conceal the birth of mixed-race children, exposing by their behavior the myth of slaveholders' fantasy of a pure white race existing apart from enslaved blacks. Not only did the mixing of white women and black men threaten social and legal constructions of whiteness, it also contributed to increasing numbers of free people of color.[3]

The Confederacy's Civil War defeat, followed by the nation's emancipation of slaves, magnified the threats presented by racial mixing among the lower classes. Dynastic slaveholding families that had long trafficked in plantation crops and human misery were suddenly faced with the loss of servants, cooks, and field workers. As former slaveholders scrambled to reclaim the labor of former slaves, freedpeople struggled to regain lost children, marry, establish households, and move about as they chose, perhaps to distant places that offered better wages and landownership.[4]

In Orange County, as throughout the defeated Confederacy, the ensuing crisis was at once political, economic, and personal. Who would determine the political course of the postwar South? The fate of the Southern plantation economy? The status of former masters and mistresses among former slaves possibly elevated to positions—they shuddered to imagine—of equality? As throughout the South, the struggle over political power immediately erupted in the public arenas of statehouse and press, but the crises over households and labor now centered on Orange County's 5,000-plus freedpeople, alongside prewar interracial couples and their mixed-race descendants, who looked toward gaining the citizenship denied to all people of color in 1857 by the U.S. Supreme Court.[5]

The outbreak of the Civil War had strained relations of class and race, especially as the underground trade in illicit goods between slaves, poor whites, and free people of color expanded to include deserters and Unionists. Early on, local leaders cracked down hard on Orange County citizens who openly opposed secession. In Chapel Hill, William Lloyd, Cannon Bowers, and Joseph Ivey were said to be the only men in their neighborhood who dared vote against secession. In nearby Durham, even wealthy, slaveholding Unionist William W. Guess faced harassment from Confederates, who organized a boycott of his grain mill. Just to the west, heavily Unionist Quaker Belt counties erupted in inner civil wars.[6]

If open dissent against the Confederacy was dangerous for nonslaveholding white farmers, it was potentially deadly for African Americans. Nelly Stroud of Chapel Hill remembered that "colored people" like her did not discuss the politics of the war, at least not publicly: "A still tongue made a wise head." As a washerwoman, Stroud's livelihood depended upon the willingness of whites to hire her; she dared not shoot off her mouth about politically charged issues. Even her friend Nancy Brewer, an economically independent woman of color who owned her own home and had purchased her husband out of slavery, agreed with Stroud that people of color generally kept quiet. She felt compelled to add, however, that they always sympathized with the Union cause, believing it was "God's will for the colored race to be free." Despite the dangers of expressing such sentiments in public, during the final two years of war, open dissent resurged, particularly in neighborhoods where farmers and laborers faced economic disaster. The domestic and political turmoil that followed would set the stage for showdowns during Reconstruction over which political party would prevail in the wake of Confederate defeat.[7]

The U.S. victory over the Confederacy in 1865 should have been a time of jubilant celebration for pro-Union Southerners and newly freed slaves. And so it was, at least initially. In class terms, President Andrew Johnson's appointment of the powerful newspaper editor and peace Democrat William Woods Holden—a politician of humble roots, born illegitimately to a poor white woman—boded well for a pro-Union yeomanry anxious to politically bury the state's old aristocracy. For freedpeople, the news was not so good. In keeping with President Johnson's notorious support for coercive state "black codes," Governor Holden supported neither universal suffrage nor land distribution to formerly enslaved people. Nevertheless, the old guard despised Holden for his wartime leadership of North Carolina's peace movement, and they immediately revolted against his appointment. Violent attacks against former Unionists accordingly increased, and in the heavily pro-Union Randolph County area, those Unionists fought back. Holden's movement toward greater white democracy was soon short-circuited, however, by his gubernatorial defeat in 1866 by the antisecessionist but politically elitist Jonathan Worth. There would be no democratic revolution in North Carolina.[8]

Freedpeople faced a dark time under President Johnson's leadership in 1865 and 1866. Like Johnson himself, whites of all classes had long been socialized to revile blacks, and the notion that formerly enslaved people might be elevated to equal status with even the poorest of whites appalled many if not most of them. In 1866, the best most freedpeople could hope for was that more paternalistic planters might allow them to build a cabin on their land in exchange for their labor. Clearly, however, in the aftermath of emancipation, people of color could protect neither their dependents, their homes, nor themselves. The words of Colonel Samuel Thomas, assistant commissioner of Mississippi's Freedmen's Bureau, resonated throughout the post–Civil War South. White people, wrote Thomas in September 1865, "still have the ingrained feeling that black people at large belong to the whites at large." He digressed: "To kill a negro they do not deem murder, to debauch a negro woman they do not think fornication, to take property away from a negro they do not consider robbery."[9]

As provisional governor, William Holden followed the conservative path, stressing that nothing beyond marriage and employment were crucial to freedpeople's successful transition to freedom. By 1866, white politicians were united in their belief that marriage was a right as well as a duty—and would help stabilize black communities. What they initially failed to consider was the extent to which marriage might also afford black men greater personal and economic self-sufficiency within households in which they, not white men, reaped the benefits of their wives' and children's labor.[10]

North Carolina legislators may also have initially misread the implications of charging former slave women with bastardy after the Thirteenth Amendment to the Constitution (1865) abolished slavery. After generations of being denied marriage and custody of their children, freedwomen were now expected to confine motherhood to marriage, just as freedmen were now expected to support financially their children. In theory, such expectations neatly dovetailed with their newly legal marriages, but in practice such laws ignored the long-standing sexual prerogatives of white men. Before the war, white men might treat slave quarters as brothels in which women's services were free of cost and without social consequences. Now the same women were called to court should they become pregnant and commanded to name their child's father. Suddenly Southern white men faced a degree of public scrutiny unfamiliar to many of them.[11]

The bastardy case of Orange County's Pattie Ruffin, formerly enslaved by North Carolina chief justice Thomas Ruffin, is instructive. Seventeen-year-old Pattie became pregnant the year following slavery's abolition and was accordingly summoned to appear in court to identify the father of her child. Her predicament was complicated by the fact that her child's father was a white man who wished not to be identified as her sexual partner or as the father of a mixed-race child. No doubt from a prominent family, he soon received critical intervention from prominent state politician and lawyer John W. Graham. On August 19, 1866, Graham explained in a letter to Colonel Hugh B. Guthrie that "negro testimony is rather inconvenient to some who have been prowling around too promiscuously." He directed Guthrie to inform Pattie that she had a "right" to refuse to name the father as long as she paid the court five dollars and posted bond pledging that her illegitimate child would never become a burden on the county. In closing, Graham expressed his hope that "we might let the young fellows go for what was done before negroes were allowed to testify" against white people.[12]

Graham clearly thought nothing of coercing a teenaged black domestic servant into forgoing support payments for her child in order to protect the identity of a young scion from an elite family. Adhering to the maxim "boys will be boys," Graham personally intervened on behalf of the "young friend of mine" who was "quite uneasy" about the prospect of being charged as the "Papa" of Pattie Ruffin's baby. For her part, Pattie did as she was told. On August 21, 1866, she refused to name her child's father in court. She was left to raise her child alone, with only her biological kin to assist her.

Freedom revealed that thousands of children existed whose fathers were even less easily identified and whose networks of kin were fractured by generations of enslavement. For them, the courts turned to county apprenticeship systems. Apprenticeship laws had been drawn up for North Carolina during the seventeenth century as a means to support indigent, illegitimate children. Under this system, children were bound by contract to work for propertied adults of the county, who in turn fed and clothed them. Apprenticeship not only supported indigent children but it also supplemented slavery by providing state control over the labor of mixed-race children. Particularly in counties such as Orange, with high numbers of free people of color, the courts focused primarily on free children of African ancestry, whether born to white or African American mothers. In the 1850s, 61 percent of Orange County's apprenticed children were designated "black" or "mulatto," although free women of color made up only 9 percent of female-headed households. Application of the "one drop rule" of race accounted for the seeming discrepancy. Many, if not most, apprenticed mixed-race children had white mothers and light-skinned fathers. In the biracial world created by slaveholding lawmakers, any known degree of African ancestry dictated that one be labeled "colored"—no matter how light one's skin. How else to keep the white race "pure"?[13]

Apprenticeship was about labor as well as racial control. To deny to parents the custody of their own children not only broke bonds of love, affection, and culture but also prevented parents from creating viable household economies. In the struggle to achieve independence, rural male heads of households relied on their wives' and children's labor as well as on their own. However, under the apprenticeship system, their children's labor benefited the household economy of a distant "master."[14] Small wonder that former slaveholders latched on to apprenticeship in the wake of emancipation—here was an immediate answer to their loss of slave labor. Both labor contracts and apprenticeship bonds with former slaves and their children were administered by the Freedmen's Bureau, allowing many former slaveholders to replicate their old plantation labor force.[15] Planters seemed not to consider (or care), however, that freedpeople who willingly signed work contracts with former slave masters felt differently about handing over custody of their children to them. Early on, freedpeople defied the apprenticeship system. Remembering the days following emancipation, Sarah Debro of Orange County recalled how her mother refused to let "Miss Polly" keep her, telling the former mistress that she and her daughter would be "slaves no more to nobody."[16]

On the other hand, freedpeople unable to provide adequate labor to planters were often turned out of plantations and left with no viable source of income. Dependent, helpless former slaves were a particular concern for bureau authorities. On Christmas Day 1865, Lieutenant E. A. Harris of the Freedmen's Bureau of Morgantown wondered what was to be done with "very young orphans, blind and infirm—totally dependent Negroes." Not only were former masters loath to care for crippled and sickly freedpeople, he wrote, but there were many children "so young that no one will take them for any consideration. . . . Masters wish them removed from their plantations at once."[17]

For newly freed men, gaining custody over children, including the right to reap the benefits of their labor, was essential to claiming authority over their household, a basic male prerogative denied them under slavery. At the same time, continued poverty, despite back-breaking "free" labor, nurtured in many a desire to seek fresher fields of opportunity. Orange County's black men tended to marry women from outside their neighborhood and also to leave the county in greater numbers than their white counterparts. In June 1866, Benjamin Markham of Orange County received a let-

ter from his brother, G. R. Markham, expressing fears of a labor shortage on account of so many freedmen moving west and leaving women and
children behind, "strowling about" the streets. "I think that some of them is
bound to starve," he wrote, "but they are free."[18]

"Free," of course, was a relative term. Freedwomen, especially those with
children, sometimes begged former slaveholders to hire them rather than
join the wandering poor described by G. R. Markham. Extreme poverty
among poor whites and blacks was reported throughout the state, and
Freedmen's Bureau agents received reports of women and children who
died from lack of food and medical care. Even labor contracts did not
ensure their security. In early 1867, Charles Yarbro, of Lexington, bluntly
informed bureau agent W. F. Henderson that he would no longer supply
"vittles & clothing" to Harriet, his former slave, now that she was pregnant
with her second child. Yarbro ordered Harriet to seek new employment and
a new home, which she did. But she soon returned to his plantation after
being denied work at a nearby factory. "If she don't get a place by Monday
I shall set her out in the road," Yarbro warned agent Henderson. Henderson advised him that breaking his contract with Harriet was "against civil
law," but there is no evidence that he prevented Harriet's expulsion.[19]

Clearly, in North Carolina and throughout the South, leaders from the
old Confederacy had regained power in state legislatures and passed coercive laws that made a mockery of black freedom. In response, in 1867 congressional radicals and Northern black activists pushed for and won federal
and military control over Reconstruction of the South. Former governor
William Holden quickly responded by organizing a Republican Party in
North Carolina. Violence soon erupted, as state leaders raged against their
threatened loss of political authority and racial dominance. Radical Reconstruction threatened to turn their world upside down, and most did not
doubt that their diminished power signaled the destruction of civilized
society. However, more than political and racial dominance were at stake.
At its most fundamental, day-to-day level, slaveholding men's right to dom-
inate households—their own and those of their laborers—was also challenged. Their defense of that right soon put the lives of freedpeople, members of interracial communities, and politically active Republicans at risk.[20]

With shrill warnings about "black Republicanism" and help from the Ku
Klux Klan, North Carolina's Conservative Union Party (a coalition of anti-
Republican Whigs and Democrats) pushed back hard against the state's
new Republican Party. In the eastern portion of North Carolina, however,
blacks were too numerous and too necessary a labor force to be cowed into
submission. In the western mountain counties, where few blacks lived and

where Unionists had flourished during the war, poor white farmers joined the Republican Party in droves. Two strongholds of Republicanism, then, eastern blacks and western white voters, were not easily swayed before 1875 by white supremacist threats or rhetoric. The situation was quite different in the state's Piedmont region, where both whites and blacks joined the Republican Party in substantial numbers. With former governor Holden as their leader, the North Carolina Republican Party endorsed Congress's Reconstruction Acts, pledging its support for military supervision of the South's reentry into the United States. It agreed as well to hold a convention at which a new state constitution would be framed that ratified the Fourteenth Amendment and conferred rights of citizenship upon African Americans. By mid-1867, a new day seemed to be dawning.[21]

In 1868, Holden won his race to once again be governor of North Carolina. However, as powerful as the state's Republican coalition was, the Conservative Party had a trump card that it did not hesitate to play: the deeply ingrained disdain that most whites felt for blacks, especially newly empowered blacks. Klan violence soon erupted in response to ratification of the state constitution of 1868, which provided for free public schooling for black and white children as well as universal male suffrage. Conservatives railed against the inevitable mixing of races they predicted would follow, blasting the biracial Republican Union Leagues as proof that blacks intended to rule the South.[22]

It was not enough for Conservatives to merely drive black men out of politics; *all* blacks must be returned to their previous servile condition. Klan terror soon raged throughout the North Carolina piedmont but had less traction in some counties than in others. Randolph, Moore, and Montgomery Counties, with their large pro-Union yeoman populations and a small but devout community of Wesleyan Methodists, were less responsive to white supremacist tactics. This region, considered the "heart" of the Quaker Belt, remained more strongly attached to the Republican Party throughout Reconstruction than the counties of Alamance, Caswell, Orange, and Granville, where Klan terrorists mounted a culture of intimidation. In these counties, wartime Unionism was more effectively muted, while larger populations of freedpeople made it easier to inflame white fears of empowered blacks and racial amalgamation. Such convictions lasted well into the twentieth century. In March 1961, North Carolina's *Slate* magazine still insisted that the Ku Klux Klan "became active" during Reconstruction in response to "roaming ex-slaves" who "robbed, raped and killed." Many Southern white editors simply took at face value the words of white supremacists, many of them Klan members themselves, from almost a century earlier.[23]

Superior court judge and Klan member David Schenck, for example, claimed in his diary that "a negro was made to be governed with severity— and nothing else will answer the purpose," after witnessing ex-slaves cele- brating the Christmas season of 1868 with a lavish use of alcohol. Schenck embodied the white upper-class assumption that formerly enslaved people, and black people in general, must not wield power and could not direct their own households. His complaints about "drunkenness, theft, cheating, and lewdness" ignored the inevitability of celebrations of freedom and even excessive lawbreaking among people who experienced freedom for the first time in their lives and expected more than continued impoverishment.[24]

A long, devastating war followed by the sudden end of slavery had upended Southern society and thrown its communities into chaos. Court records between 1865 and 1868 are filled with accounts of thefts, affrays, and drunkenness among both whites and blacks, testimony to the pro- found disorder and threat of starvation that accompanied political turmoil. Although Conservatives like Schenck used this turmoil to insist that "dis- solute" blacks must be forcibly controlled for the protection of society and white womanhood, they and the Klan were after far more than criminals during Reconstruction; people of color were to defer to and depend upon whites in freedom as they had in slavery.

In this racially divided and class-bound society, not all violence was perpetrated by the Klan or necessarily premeditated. The Klan, after all, emerged from the common assumption of many whites that it was their duty and right to police blacks in both the public and private spheres of society. The 1867 killing of Bill Fuller, a freedman, is a case in point. Fuller attended a corn shucking at the home of another freedman, Bill Faucett, where a group gathered both to work and to play music and sing songs. Faucett's home was located on the land of his employer, sixty-year-old for- mer slaveholder Catlett Tinnin, who soon became infuriated by the fes- tive sights and sounds emanating from his tenant's house. Perhaps Tinnin was irritated by revelers enjoying their freedom, or perhaps the noise just got to him. Whatever the case, he angrily entered Bill Faucett's home and confronted the men, threatening to "blow out their brains." The men, who dared not take lightly such threats from a white man, quickly scattered. Tinnin then walked to a window and fired his gun. Bill Fuller, who had just exited the same window, took the bullet in his leg.[25]

The injured man was not discovered for almost an hour, and he died from his wound. During the court's investigation, witnesses seemed to agree that Tinnin did not intend to kill Fuller, but had fired indiscriminately through the window without seeing him. Tinnin's feelings, they pointed out, were

"very much hurt" when he discovered what he had done and he had immediately called for a doctor. Perhaps Tinnin was innocent of premeditated
murder as he and his witnesses claimed, or perhaps the freedmen who testified in his defense were too scared to say otherwise. Either way, Bill Fuller
died because of the right claimed by white men to patrol the households of
freedpeople. Significantly, Tinnin told Bill Faucett that had he known Faucett was hosting a corn shucking rather than an ordinary frolic, he would
not have interfered. As during slavery, white men would "allow" black men
who gathered together to work white men's land rather than simply to revel
in freedom, to engage in a bit of merriment along the way. In this manner, both the labor and social life of freedmen remained the property of
white men.[26]

By 1868, the local courts of Orange and neighboring counties were too
overwhelmed and intimidated to adequately punish Klan crimes. Writing
in 1915, as the movie *Birth of a Nation* romanticized and helped to revive
a dormant Klan, Jacob Alson Long, former lawyer and "chief" of the Alamance County Order of White Brotherhood, attributed Klan terrorism
during Reconstruction to black voters' support for Scalawag candidates
(former Unionists who ran as Republicans) for office through the vehicle of
the Union Leagues. Long soon shifted, however, to telling an iconic story
about a freedman who sought to marry the "blooming" teenaged daughter of his former enslaver and had threatened her with death to achieve
his end. When the freedman's plot was uncovered, Long wrote, the "lifting" (lynching) of this "serpent" was secretly executed by white men in the
"wilderness"—and on the Sabbath Day, no less. "The Anglo Saxon never in
all ages appears the inferior race," Long proudly concluded. So there it was:
white fears that black men wanted nothing less than white brides. According to Long, political power alone would not satisfy the "serpents" who
intended to adorn their bedrooms with the virginal bodies of white men's
daughters.[27]

Court records and contemporary reports of Klan outrages from Orange
and surrounding counties tell a very different story. Under siege by Klansmen in 1868 and 1869, one group of men from a prominent mixed-race community of neighboring Granville County twice petitioned Governor Holden
for aid. Of Native American, African, and white descent, the group's leaders had been free long before the Civil War, and they described themselves
as an alliance of "the Colored race and labering class of white people." Having joined their local Republican Union League alongside freedmen and
white Unionists, they informed the governor that "On Saturday night last,
the Ku Klux were raging in Oxford and Tally Ho. They first formed them-

selves in line in front of the Colored School Room, thinking the League's men were at lodge there. And failing to find them, went off to other places and don the same, tho as it happen the Leagues had adjo[urned] before they came out and they watched them. . . . And they now say they intend to brake up the Leagues before the Election."[28]

To accomplish this goal, the Klan wreaked domestic terrorism upon the households of black and mixed-race citizens. For the rest of their lives, former slaves Mandy Coverson and Martha Allen would remember the Klan's special hatred of "Free Issues" (antebellum free-born people of color). Coverson believed the Klan took their spite out on free mixed-race people because they feared their "great influence" on newly freed blacks. Martha Allen described how Klansmen visited "free issue" houses, where they stripped family members of their clothes, whipped the old folks, and danced with "pretty yaller gals" that they took to "bed" (raped).[29]

The memories of Coverson and Allen are distant echoes of Reconstruction records. Granville's petitioners detailed three separate raids in which "colored" couples were beaten and ejected from their homes. The rape of one wife was strongly suggested in their description of how the Klan had "cut her dress open and tied her to a tree." In another raid, a Klansman shot the wife of a black man as she fled. Petitioners noted that she "now lies in a low state of health." These allegations were corroborated by white citizens of Granville who described these and other Klan outrages in a separate letter.[30]

Klan attacks on the homes of black couples and its abuse of wives were likewise common in Orange County. Sampson Atwater's wife suffered a gash to her forehead after being knocked to the ground for begging the Klan to spare her husband's life. In another case, the wives of two men who shared a household were beaten up by Klan members looking for their husbands. The wife of black Republican activist Henry Jones was "abused and cursed" for a similar reason: Jones was not at home when they came looking for him. Many white male laborers and farmers, convinced that black equality threatened their own status, joined wealthier men who had organized the Klan in becoming Klansmen. Still, as in Granville County, hatred of the old Confederacy united some whites and people of color, if only on political terms. The Klan reportedly threatened and whipped several white men of Orange County who spoke out against Klan violence. Nathaniel King, described as an "old man," left the county after being beaten up because of his political views. When the wife of white farmer Neverson Cates openly declared that Klansmen should be arrested after harassing her, she was hushed by her husband who warned her that the Klan was too strong. Other white laborers and farmers, convinced that black equality threatened their own status, instead became Klansmen.[31]

Again and again, victims and witnesses attested to the Klan's campaign of terror. In March 1869, Squire Alston, a fifty-year-old black laborer, described about a dozen masked men who had broken into his home two days earlier. The story was horrifyingly similar: armed Klansmen rousted him and his wife from their bed, ordered them from their home, and proceeded to torch the house, fire off guns, and throw rocks at Alston as he struggled to extinguish the flames.[32]

By September 1869, the Klan's war on black and mixed-race neighborhoods included several grisly murders. From Hillsboro, S. B. Williams, a black pastor and schoolteacher, reported the murders of two black men to Governor Holden. One man had been forcibly removed from jail and shot. The other was found with his tongue cut out and his throat slashed. Williams, afraid for his and others' lives, asked the governor to provide either a police force or arms for the citizens. That same month, four masked men with pistols seized black laborer Wright Malone from a coal kiln and hanged him. Concerned whites, especially Republicans, soon joined African Americans in reporting cold-blooded murders to Governor Holden. Prominent lawyer James B. Mason described five Klan raids in Chapel Hill alone in the space of two weeks. Klansmen, he told the governor, were "rowdying up & down" the streets late at night. Mason asked that his name not be revealed.[33]

Governor Holden did not ignore the desperate pleas of his constituents. Under the Shofner Act of 1870, Holden imposed martial law on the piedmont counties of Alamance and Caswell, declaring each to be in a state of insurrection and ordering state troops into both under the direction of U.S. officer George W. Kirk. But his letter of July 19, 1870, to North Carolina chief justice Richmond Pearson was a wrenching confession of failure: "I have invoked public opinion to aid me in suppressing this treason! I have issued proclamation after proclamation to the people of the state to break up these unlawful combinations . . . all in vain!" And, finally, his recognition that "The civil courts are no longer a protection to life, liberty, and property; assassinations and outrage go unpunished, and the civil magistrates are intimidated & are afraid to perform their functions."[34] For his efforts, Holden became entangled in the "Kirk-Holden War." Local leaders, many of them members of the Conservative Party and often of the Klan as well, whipped up support among the local populace by denouncing Holden's suspension of civil rights and waving the bloody shirt in their denouncements of a U.S. officer appointed to head the intrusion into their counties.

Although more than one hundred arrests were made during Holden's war on the Klan, its controversial nature led President Ulysses S. Grant to deny federal support for the governor's crackdown. Emboldened by federal timidity and popular opposition to marshal law, the North Carolina Assembly impeached Holden in December 1870, and in March 1871 he was convicted. At the behest of beleaguered Republicans and African Americans, Holden had risked his political capital and lost. Again and again, racism and a sense of outrage at an intrusive government would lead white North Carolinians to privilege white supremacy and local autonomy over efforts to protect African Americans and white Republicans from terror and outright murder.[35]

Orange County freedmen who kept their heads down may have saved their own lives, but they made little economic progress during Reconstruction. Only 14.1 percent of black male household heads owned real estate in 1870, and the average size of their farms was only one-quarter that of white farms. By 1880, three-fourths of the county's black farmers, compared to one-fourth of white farmers, would be sharecroppers. Meanwhile, planters and former slaveholders continued to enjoy wealth despite their loss of capital in enslaved property.[36]

Radical Reconstruction nonetheless benefited freedpeople. In 1868, ratification of the Fourteenth Amendment to the Constitution gave black parents the tools to fight apprenticeship contracts. In Montgomery County in 1869, Lila McDonald successfully regained custody of her children after her Republican lawyer filed a petition citing apprenticeship of former slaves as "contrary to the provisions of the Fourteenth article of the United States [Constitution and] ... the spirit of the Reconstruction Acts of Congress." Such challenges occurred throughout the state after 1868, contributing to the eventual demise of the apprenticeship system. Most parents who sought to rescind apprenticeships appealed to provost marshals or agents of the Freedmen's Bureau; others, like Lila McDonald, initiated court suits. During these few years in which men of color briefly wielded political power, just the threat of appealing to authorities worked for one mother. Former slave Viney Baker remembered with pride how her mother combined subterfuge with threat to regain custody of her. After "Miss Allen" allowed Viney's mother to take her for a weekend "visit," the mother refused to return her daughter and threatened to take her case to the "Carpetbaggers" if the Allens objected.[37]

Despite Republican judges' sympathy for freedpeople's civil rights, they did not always rule in favor of those seeking custody of their formerly enslaved children. The difficulty of proving paternity cases was particularly complicated, as enslaved fathers often could not live near their children or form permanent, stable relationships with their mothers. Allen Compton's lawyer took full advantage of such factors in 1871 when the former slaveholder's right to custody of fourteen-year-old Green Compton was challenged by Alexander Corbin, who claimed to be the boy's biological father. Compton's lawyers emphasized that Corbin himself admitted that he barely knew the boy he now called "son" and that he had not sought custody of him in the immediate aftermath of the war. Nor had Corbin challenged the apprenticeship of Green to Compton back in 1866. The lawyer also took an easy shot at the character of Green's deceased enslaved mother, Minerva, calling it "very bad," since "most of her children" had different fathers, making it impossible to know if Corbin was one of those fathers.[38]

Judge George Laws ruled against Alexander Corbin in probate court. Corbin's lawyer, Republican Isaac R. Strayhorn, appealed Judge Law's decision to the Seventh District Superior Court. Citing testimony from witnesses who claimed that Minerva and her master, Allen Compton, had casually stated on separate occasions that Corbin was Green's father, Strayhorn also reminded the court that under slavery, Minerva could not have married any of her children's fathers. Superior court justice Albion Tourgee, although a Republican and courageous defender of freedpeople's laws, nevertheless upheld Judge Law's decision.[39]

Two pieces of evidence may have compelled Tourgee to rule against Corbin. First, certain testimony indicated that Minerva had a free black husband, although her marriage would not have been legally valid, from around 1857–58 until the time of her death in 1861, and that this husband had recognized Green as his son. Second, Corbin's failure to seek custody of Green before 1871 raised suspicions. Was it merely coincidental that Green was by then a strong teenage boy, capable of contributing valuable labor to a household? As we have seen, in the rural setting of the nineteenth-century South, where family labor undergirded the independence of nonslaveholding farmers long before the Civil War, struggles over children were simultaneously struggles over labor.[40]

Freedman Ben Harris protested his children's apprenticeship contracts with a plea to Colonel John R. Edie of the Freedmen's Bureau that "surly the Law doe Not Call for Children to be bond out when their peapel is Abel to keep them!" His former master countered that Harris only wanted his children's earnings and would keep them in "rags and half-starved" if granted custody. Of course, freedpeople did desire such earnings, which were essential to postwar household economies, but they also wanted the company of their children. Certainly, most former slaveholders were not primarily concerned with the welfare of freedchildren when they sought apprenticeship contracts. Most were interested in employing and apprenticing strong, able-bodied laborers. Even the paternalistic concerns that D. C. Parrish of Orange County expressed for his former slave John could not mask his economic interest in regaining the teenaged boy's labor. While pulling corn in Parrish's cornfield, John "was carried off " by a freedman claiming to be his father. "I call it stealing," complained Parrish to Freedmen's Bureau officer Isaac Porter. John, he explained, was a "favourite boy" whom he had even sent to Sunday school. After admitting that John was not much interested in Bible study, however, Parrish got to the point: the boy's father wanted him now that "I have raised him to be larger enough to be of good service to me."[41]

Racism, prevailing norms of gender behavior, and political ideology all influenced Reconstruction court decisions crucial to successful petitions by freedpeople. One might expect judges to be more sympathetic to mothers seeking custody than to fathers, but Lila McDonald's ability to win her apprenticeship suit was also enhanced by living in the heavily Unionist—and therefore Republican—section of Montgomery County that stretched into the heart of the North Carolina Quaker Belt. Her lawyer, a local Republican of Quaker heritage, had opposed Southern secession. Pattie Ruffin of Orange County, on the other hand, entered a courthouse in which magistrates were predisposed to judge her harshly. In the eyes of the law, giving birth to an illegitimate child was both illegal and immoral, of course, but there was more to it than that. Pattie had entered into an interracial affair with a well-connected member of Orange County's substantial slaveholding class, one who might call on a prominent political leader for aid. And that leader, John W. Graham, was no friend to freedpeople. A member of the Conservative Party by 1868, Graham introduced the bill in the General Assembly, passed by the state senate in January 1873, that granted amnesty to members of the Ku Klux Klan.[42]

Marriage, Republicans agreed, was the true and proper place for freedwomen—the perfect antidote to the sexual exploitation they had long suffered under slavery—as well as the vehicle for building stable, loving households. Unfortunately, some women escaped abuse by their white enslavers only to encounter the same from newly empowered black husbands. Many freedwomen reported abuse and neglect by husbands as well as employers to underfunded and paternalistic Freedmen's bureaus. J. Cowles, of Hamptonville, referred the case of Clary, a freedwoman, to the bureau after she requested protection from her husband, freedman Rufus Blackburn, who, she claimed, had violently forced her from their home, taken up with another woman, and kept the furniture, pots, and quilts left to her by her master. Clary wanted the bureau to intercede and force Blackburn to return her goods. Similarly, Dillie, a field hand described by W. H. Worden as "an industrious woman," complained to the bureau that she and her six children were being turned out of their home by her husband.[43]

Some women sought refuge from husbands who viewed them as their property now that slavery was abolished. Having been denied access to wives and households under slavery, black men were understandably eager to assume authority over both in freedom. An exaggerated sense of ownership, however, offended those freedwomen who objected to trading the bondage of slavery for the bonds of marriage. After Alfred Gray's wife refused to live with him in their High Point home, he showed up at her new home, claiming that "she was my wife and I had a right to her." When Mrs. Gray refused to go home, the two came to blows. She then told agent Dilworth that she intended to divorce her "cruel and unkind" husband. But Mr. Gray reiterated rights of ownership: "I consider her my property and thus I have a right to her." Within a month, he had reportedly convinced his wife of his "written authority" to take possession of her, and she returned home with him.[44]

Although the Freedmen's Bureau mediated domestic disputes between husbands and wives and at times provided immediate relief or advice, it had neither the funding nor the power to change the societal conditions that produced ongoing personal crises. Sometimes the bureau was forced to mediate conflicts in which both the plaintiff and the defendant were ultimately victims. This was certainly the case when Linda McQueen, a freedwoman of Montgomery County, named freedman Harry Butler as the father of her infant after allegedly being coerced into hiding the identity of the child's white father.[45] Butler's Republican attorney, Benjamin F. Simmons, argued that Butler, who had fathered two of McQueen's previous children, was, like McQueen, a "pure-blooded African" and therefore too dark to be the father of her light-skinned infant. But a jury found Butler guilty and ordered him to pay $75 child support in three installments over a year's time. That, and additional court costs, forced Butler to indenture himself to Spencer Haltom, a white man, for three years in exchange for Haltom paying his debts.[46]

Butler was rescued from his dismal fate by his lawyer's appeal to the Freedmen's Bureau. Responding to Simmons's claim that his client's apprenticeship amounted to "secondary slavery," the bureau granted him a new trial, and Butler was soon acquitted. That decision was clearly a victory for the black community, ten members (male and female) of whom testified on Butler's behalf. The witnesses on behalf of McQueen were all white, suggesting, indeed, that certain white members of the community had coerced her into concealing the identity of her child's true father. But if we assume that McQueen falsely named Harry Butler as charged, we may also assume she had no good choice in the matter. What is certain is that, like Pattie Ruffin and countless other freedwomen, Linda McQueen was left to support her child as best she could after suffering a humiliating trial. Untouched was the child's alleged white father, who was never identified in court.[47]

Before the Civil War, Southern lawmakers had discouraged interracial liaisons between white women and men of color, while tolerating the relatively few interracial unions that endured over time. After 1870, however, white attacks on interracial relationships, including marriages, intensified; neither social nor sexual congress between black men and white women was to be tolerated. "Every night or two some negro gets a flogging," David Schenck wrote approvingly in his diary, "or some white man or woman who are miscegenating together."[48]

In 1883, former governor Holden would assure the Raleigh *News and Observer* that he had left the Republican Party in part because "Negro equality is a great and threatening evil." Citing racially mixed schools as "but another name for equality," Holden reminded the press that Republicans had opposed integrated schools in 1868. So desperate had the quest for racial purity become among white North Carolina lawmakers that in 1884 Dicey McQueen Williams, a white woman, was forced to file a deed in county court swearing that her daughter, Mary Ann McQueen, was "purely white and clear of any African blood whatsoever," despite the fact that Mary Ann's father, Calvin McQueen (who had died during the Civil War), was also considered white.[49]

Since no one had questioned that Calvin and Dicey were white, why were there suspicions that their daughter might have "African blood"? The reason was simple: shortly before the war began, the McQueens' marriage had ended. Dicey subsequently entered into an interracial union that was accepted in Montgomery County during the 1860s as a legal marriage. Dicey and her second husband, light-skinned Wilson Williams, had several children together, meaning that Mary Ann McQueen, a white child, lived among "black" siblings, no matter how light their skin. Her own whiteness would be forever suspect.[50]

In this environment of heightened white supremacy and growing calls for racial segregation, several members of the Hopkins family of Granville County initiated a property suit against Ann Bowers Boothe of Orange

County, the widow of their uncle, Nash Boothe. Citing rumors that Ann Boothe was part black, the Hopkinses challenged her right to inherit her husband's land. Lawyers for the Hopkinses noted Ann's immersion in an interracial subculture as evidence for their claims. Ann's Durham neighborhood included white yeoman farmers, many of whom were Unionists during the war, laborers, a few former slaveholders, and many people of color. She herself lived on the land of John Johnston and next door to Madison Nunn, men of color who had been harassed by the Klan in 1869. Her roots were in Orange County's large yeoman class. Like most of her Bowers kinfolk, including her mother, she farmed a small plot of land.[51]

Ann and her mother, Lydia, who was not a typical yeoman farmwife, hailed from the very underclass persecuted by the Klan during the early days of Reconstruction. Lydia had been brought before court magistrates on bastardy charges several times before the war, and there's no evidence that she ever married at all. She was not alone; pregnant white women from yeoman families were regularly shamed by the courts, compromising their chances for prosperous marriages. These unmarried mothers typically took jobs as domestics or field workers and lived quiet, obscure lives. Others, like Lydia, became locally renowned "public women," not necessarily prostitutes but members of an interracial subculture in which drinking, gambling, and informal exchanges of favors took place. Thus her daughter Ann was raised in an interracial world of farmers, laborers, and enslaved people, many of whom rooted for the U.S. army during the war.[52]

Ann Bowers was barely out of her teens when she took up with Nash Boothe, a well-known womanizer and brawler who had previously been her mother's boyfriend. Between 1870 and 1872, Nash cohabited with Lydia Bowers in her Durham home, where Ann also lived. In 1872, shortly after Lydia and Nash were charged by the courts with fornication, Lydia died. Nash, in spite of his subsequent marriage to "Mary Jane," soon became involved with Ann, prompting his wife to divorce him on grounds of adultery and abandonment. Ann told the court that she and Nash subsequently married on May 30, 1876.[53]

Nash Boothe was well known for his escapades in the town of Durham. In 1854, he and Dr. Bartlett Durham, for whom the town was named, were separately charged with assaulting and battering one another. Similar charges against Boothe are scattered throughout Orange County's criminal action papers. Jailed in 1870 for another assault and battery, he petitioned the court to release him early because he had a family to feed and a crop on hand. Katy Carroll, a defense witness for Ann Boothe, described Nash as a "bad, hard drinking, fussy man." And Katy Carroll would know. The

Esther Carroll who lived with her in 1870 was likely the same Esther Carroll named as Nash Boothe's partner in adultery in his wife's 1873 divorce suit.[54]

Like Nash, Ann's mother, Lydia, had a reputation for misbehavior in the town of Durham. Rumors that daughter Ann had "black blood" had swirled from the time of her birth. Neighborhood gossip held that Lewis "Red" Pratt, a former slave, was Ann's true father. Lewis Pratt was a light-skinned man with kinky red hair (hence his nickname "Red") who belonged to Durham's interracial enclave in which blacks and whites, enslaved and free, interacted on a regular if unequal basis. Lewis worked as a blacksmith for his enslaver, William N. Pratt, who was one of the richest slaveholders in Orange County. Sometime before the war, Pratt freed Lewis in return for his "meritorious" service. Strong evidence supported the claim that Lewis Pratt had been intimate with Lydia Bowers. According to his own brother, he had once described Lydia as a "fine sweetheart" who was hard to break away from. Still, no one seemed able to prove that Lewis Pratt was Ann Boothe's father.[55]

Defense witnesses claimed that Lydia Bowers had sworn in court that Alexander Copley, a white man, was the father of her bastard daughter and that Copley had paid the requisite court fine and visited with Ann over the years. Katy Carroll testified that she once heard Copley say that "he intended to take the child home and make it work for him when big enough." Plaintiff witnesses countered that Copley had been furious at Lydia for swearing a Negro child to him and that her friends had locked her away to keep Copley from whipping her. There was no documentation for either version of Ann's entry into the world. She testified that her mother had always told her that Copley was her father and denied that Copley had ever tried to whip her mother. Ann also claimed never to have seen Lewis Pratt face to face.[56]

Katy Carroll's deposition on behalf of Ann demonstrated the absurdity of the court's discussion of racial categorization. Carroll, age fifty-six, had long known Lydia and Ann, and she knew them both as white women. A poor white woman from their same neighborhood, she also understood the lives of single and married women who worked for their living. Ann, she pointed out, worked hard "ploughing, hoeing, and doing other outdoor work," so of course her skin was dark. Lewis Pratt, Nash Boothe, and Alex Copley, she added, were all about the same color (although only one of them was "black"), and Ann's skin was "brighter than any one of the three."[57]

Mixed-race women and women who socially or sexually crossed the color line demonstrated the intimate connections between women's personal lives and the politics of race and class before, during, and after the Civil War. In the end, it was not Ann's paternity, which was based on hearsay, but her frequent associations with people of color that sufficed to convict her of being black and thereby deprive her of her property. In pleading their case, plaintiff lawyers were quick to note that Ann currently lived on land owned by a black man. Ann Boothe was decreed, by reputation and association, to be a "low, dissolute, colored woman" who had no right to inherit a white man's property.

It was no mere coincidence that the attorney who prosecuted the case against Ann Bowers Boothe was John W. Graham, the same lawyer who prevented freedwoman Pattie Ruffin in 1866 from either identifying or collecting child support from the white father of her child and the same lawyer who in 1873 won blanket amnesty for Klansmen convicted of crimes. This was, after all, where Conservative leaders had been headed since 1865, when the previously quoted Colonel Samuel Thomas remarked of them: "To debauch a negro woman they do not think fornication, to take property away from a negro they do not consider robbery."[58]

During Reconstruction, Southern white politicians, the Ku Klux Klan, and lawmakers rose up against the social and political revolution that confronted them in 1867, wreaking incalculable damage on the lives and households of ordinary people. Defeated Confederates were determined that no matter what level of violence it took, or what changes in the law, men of color must not become the equals of white men, either as statesmen or patriarchs of independent households. Nor were women of color to assert their sexual autonomy or think that they, like white women, might claim the prerogatives of domestic security. Simply being white was never enough. Poor whites were to keep their place, politically, socially, and sexually, or risk being equated, as Ann Bowers Boothe would be for the rest of her life, with the degraded black race.[59]

NOTES

1. On the class and racial composition of Civil War era Orange County, see Robert C. Kenzer, *Kinship and Neighborhood in a Southern Community: Orange County, North Carolina, 1849–1881* (Knoxville: University of Tennessee Press, 1987), 6–51. For an economic analysis, see Charles C. Bolton, *Poor Whites of the Antebellum South: Tenants and Laborers in Central North Carolina and Northeast Mississippi* (Durham, N.C.: Duke University Press, 1994), 11–41. On Orange County's interracial subculture, see Victoria Bynum, *Unruly Women: The Politics of Social and Sexual Control in the Old South* (Chapel Hill: University of North Carolina Press, 1992), 88–110. For the classic contemporary defense of slavery as an "organic" institution

that existed for the greater good of society, see George Fitzhugh, *Sociology of the South; or, The Failure of Free Society* (1854; rpt., Sydney, Australia: Wentworth Press, 2016). For the history of racist ideas used to justify slavery, see Ibram X. Kendi, *Stamped from the Beginning: The Definitive History of Racist Ideas in America* (New York: Nation Books, 2016).

2. Keri Leigh Merritt, *Masterless Men: Poor Whites and Slavery in the Antebellum South* (New York: Cambridge University Press, 2017), 114–78, 253–57; Nancy Isenberg, *White Trash: The 400-Year Untold Story of Class in America* (New York: Viking Press, 2016); Jeff Forret, *Race Relations at the Margins: Slaves and Poor Whites in the Antebellum Southern Countryside* (Baton Rouge: Louisiana State University Press, 2006), 22–23, 115–31; Charles C. Bolton, "Edward Isham and Poor White Labor in the Old South," in *The Confessions of Edward Isham: A Poor White Life of the Old South*, ed. Charles C. Bolton and Scott P. Culclasure (Athens: University of Georgia Press, 1998), 19–31; Bolton, *Poor Whites of the Antebellum South*, 42–65.

3. On enslaved women in the American South, see Deborah Gray White, *Ar'n't I a Woman? Female Slaves in the Plantation South* (New York: Norton, 1985, 1999); Stephanie M. H. Camp, *Closer to Freedom: Enslaved Women and Everyday Resistance in the Slave South* (Chapel Hill: University of North Carolina Press, 2004). On slave masters' sexual abuse of enslaved women, see Brenda Stevenson, *Life in Black and White: Family and Community in the Slave South* (New York: Oxford University Press, 1997), 137–39, 223, 236; Loren Schweninger, *Families in Crisis in the Old South: Divorce, Slavery, and the Law* (Chapel Hill: University of North Carolina Press, 2012), 98–114; Bynum, *Unruly Women*, 35–45. For personal accounts of sexual abuse by white masters, see esp. Harriet A. Jacobs, *Life of a Slave Girl, Written by Herself* (Cambridge: Harvard University Press, 1987) and Pauli Murray, *Proud Shoes: The Story of an American Family* (1956; rpt., New York: Harper and Row, 1978).

4. On the part played by slave mistresses in creating this misery, see Thavolia Glymph, *Out of the House of Bondage: The Transformation of the Plantation Household* (New York: Cambridge University Press, 2006). On freedpeople and households, see Laura Edwards, *Gendered Strife and Confusion: The Political Culture of Reconstruction* (Urbana: University of Illinois Press, 1997), 24–65.

5. The struggle over black democracy during Reconstruction has been amply documented and analyzed by historians. Most recently, see David Williams, *I Freed Myself: African American Self-Emancipation in the Civil War Era* (New York: Cambridge University Press, 2014), 208–43; and Steven Hahn, *A Nation under Our Feet: Black Political Struggles in the Rural South from Slavery to the Great Migration* (Cambridge: Harvard University Press, 2005), 178–235. Number of slaves in Orange County from Kenzer, *Kinship and Neighborhood*, 193n57. For the Supreme Court's 1857 decision (written by Chief Justice Roger Taney) that neither slaves nor free Americans of African ancestry qualified for citizenship, see *Dred Scott v. Sandford*, 60 U.S. 393 (1857).

6. On heightened class conflict during the war, see Bruce Levine, *The House of Dixie: The Civil War and the Social Revolution That Transformed the South* (New York: Random House, 2013), 209–17, and David Williams, *Bitterly Divided: The South's*

Inner Civil War (New York: New Press, 2008). The history of class-based Unionism in the Quaker Belt is detailed by William T. Auman, *Civil War in the North Carolina Quaker Belt: The Confederate Campaign against Peace Agitators, Deserters, and Draft Dodgers* (Jefferson, N.C.: McFarland, 2014). See also David Brown and Patrick Doyle, "Violence, Conflict, and Loyalty in the Carolina Piedmont," in *The Civil War Guerrilla: Unfolding the Black Flag in History, Memory, and Myth*, ed. Joseph Beilein Jr. and Matthew C. Hulbert (Lexington: University Press of Kentucky, 2015), 71–98. On conflict in Orange County, see Kenzer, *Kinship and Neighborhood*, 66–70. Descriptions of Orange County Unionists are from testimonies of William Lloyd Sr. in Joseph Ivey Claim #37087, March 24, 1875, and Wm. W. Guess, John Cole Claim #12789, and Samuel Cole Claim, #12790, Orange County, N.C., scc-na.

7. Kenzer, *Kinship and Neighborhood*, 86–91. Nancy Brewer purchased her husband, Green Brewer, a slave, sometime before 1858, when she bought a home and lot in the town of Chapel Hill. Quoted from Nancy Brewer Claim #11545, Orange County, scc-na.

8. Paul D. Escott, *Many Excellent People: Power and Privilege in North Carolina, 1850–1900* (Chapel Hill: University of North Carolina Press, 1985), 85–112; Hahn, *A Nation under Our Feet*, 235; Williams, *I Freed Myself*, 216.

9. Col. Samuel Thomas to [?], September 1865, Records of the Assistant Commissioner for the State of Mississippi, Freedman's Bureau Papers, m826, reel 1. The historiography that documents Thomas's charges is voluminous. On North Carolina, see especially Edwards, *Gendered Strife and Confusion*.

10. Escott, *Many Excellent People*, 94–95; Edwards, *Gendered Strife and Confusion*, 28–32.

11. Edwards, *Gendered Strife and Confusion*, 35.

12. Graham's use of plural nouns indicated that he did not think that the favor would be extended only to his "young friend." John W. Graham, Hillsboro, N.C., to Col. H. B. Guthrie, Chapel Hill, N.C., August 19, 1866. I found Graham's letter lying loose among the Bastardy Bonds, Orange County, ncdah.

13. On the antebellum apprenticeship system, see Bynum, *Unruly Women*, 88–91, and Karen Zipf, *Labor of Innocents: Forced Apprenticeship in North Carolina, 1715–1906* (Baton Rouge: Louisiana State University Press, 2005). On the increasing whiteness of free "black" people due to race mixing, see Merritt, *Masterless Men*, 256–66.

14. On yeoman households and the crucial labor of dependents, see Stephanie McCurry, *Masters of Small Worlds: Yeoman Households, Gender Relations, and the Antebellum South Carolina Low Country* (New York: Oxford University Press, 1995), 6, 59.

15. On Reconstruction policies concerning apprenticeship of former slaves, see Indentures of Apprenticeship, September 1865–December 1866, ser. 2489, and Register of Indentured Apprentices, November 1865–June 1866, ser. 2488, Freedmen's Bureau Papers.

16. Zipf, *Labor of Innocents*, 47; Escott, *Many Excellent People*, 123–25; George P. Rawick, ed., *The American Slave: A Composite Autobiography* (Westport, Conn.:

Greenwood Press, 1972), vol. 14, pt. 1, pp. 248–50. As odious as sharecropping became, it originally appears to have been preferred by freedpeople over planters' preference for a wage labor system in which whites would directly supervise their work. Considered alongside freedpeople's rejection of apprenticeship, it appears they fought for a labor system that least resembled the old slaveholding power structure. See Eric Foner, *Reconstruction: American's Unfinished Revolution, 1863–1877* (Baton Rouge: Louisiana State University Press, 1988), 93.

17. Some former slaveholders wanted nothing to do with freedpeople at all. See Escott, *Many Excellent People*, 120–21; E. A. Harris, Lt. and Assistant Superintendent, December 25, 1865, to Col. C. A. Cilley, Letters Received, ser. 2837, Freedmen's Bureau Papers, NARA; and Zipf, *Labor of Innocents*, 47.

18. G. R. Markham to Benjamin Markham, June 11, 1866, Benjamin Markham Papers, Manuscripts Department, Duke University, Durham, N.C. On marriage and mobility among black men of Orange County, see Kenzer, *Kinship and Neighborhood*, 108. On black men and issues of masculinity, see Daniel P. Black, *Dismantling Black Manhood: An Historical and Literary Analysis of the Legacy of Slavery* (New York: Routledge, 1997); Darlene Clark Hine, ed., *19th Century: From Emancipation to Jim Crow*, vol. 2 of *A Question of Manhood: A Reader in U.S. Black Men's History and Masculinity* (Bloomington: Indiana University Press, 2001). For a feminist and sociological commentary on freed black men, see bell hooks's essay "Plantation Patriarchy," in her *We Real Cool: Black Men and Masculinity* (New York: Routledge, 2003), 1–14.

19. Chas. Yarbro to Mr. Henderson, February 8, 1867, and W. J. Henderson to J. R. Edie, February 7, 1867, Letters Received, ser. 2837, Freedman's Bureau Papers, NARA.

20. Hahn, *A Nation under Our Feet*, 190–203; Escott, *Many Excellent People*, 150–55; Gordon McKinney, *Southern Mountain Republicans: Politics and the Southern Appalachian Community* (1978; rpt. Nashville: University of Tennessee Press, 1998); Karen L. Zipf, "'The Whites Shall Rule the Land or Die': Gender, Race, and Class in North Carolina Reconstruction Politics," *Journal of Southern History* 65, no. 3 (August 1999): 499–534; Edwards, *Gendered Strife and Confusion*.

21. Marc Kruman, *Parties and Politics in North Carolina, 1834–1865* (Baton Rouge: Louisiana State University Press, 1983), 230–32; McKinney, *Southern Mountain Republicans*; Zipf, "'Whites Shall Rule the Land or Die,'" 503–4; Jeffrey Crow, "Thomas Settle Jr. and the Memory of the Civil War," *Journal of Southern History* 62, no. 4 (November 1996): 701–6.

22. Zipf, "'Whites Shall Rule the Land or Die,'" 524–25, 534; Escott, *Many Excellent People*, 152–67.

23. Escott, *Many Excellent People*, 158, 160; Bess Beatty, *Alamance: The Holt Family and Industrialization in a Southern County, 1837–1900* (Baton Rouge: Louisiana State University Press, 1999), 110–17. For an account of Orange County Reconstruction from the perspective of a local multiracial family, see Murray, *Proud Shoes*, 166–228.

24. David Schenck Diary, December 1868, David Schenck Books, SHC.

25. Tinnin, born around 1800, owned fourteen slaves in 1860. The men attending the corn shucking may all have been his former slaves (U.S. Bureau of the Census, Population and Slave Schedules, 1850, 1860, 1870, Orange County, N.C.). Details of Fuller's death are from *State v. Catlett C. Tinnin*, Superior Court, spring 1867, Criminal Action Papers, 1866–67, Orange County, NCDAH.

26. *State v. Catlett C. Tinnin*.

27. Recollections of Jacob Alson Long, #2282, SHC. Emboldened by *Birth of a Nation's* 1915 romantic image of the Klan, Long freely admitted to many of its Reconstruction acts of terrorism.

28. Petition to Gov. Wm W. Holden from Silas L. Curtis et al., Tally Ho, Granville County, N.C. Governors' Papers, Holden, October 11, 1868. The description of the men as belonging to the "colored race" and laboring class of white men is from their second petition of August 11, 1869. On the national and grassroots origins of the Union Leagues, see Hahn, *A Nation at Our Feet*, 203. On the origins of the Tally Ho mixed-race community, see Victoria Bynum, *Renegade South*, "Free People of Color in Slaveholding North Carolina: The Andersons of Granville County," https://renegadesouth.wordpress.com/2017/04/01/free-people-of-color -in-slaveholding-north-carolina-the-andersons-of-granville-county/. For names and fuller details regarding this community's two petitions, see Victoria Bynum, "A North Carolina Community in Crisis," *Renegade South*, https://renegadesouth .wordpress.com/2014/07/28/a-north-carolina-community-in-crisis-1868-1869/.

29. Mandy Coverson was from Union County; Martha Allen from Craven. Both narratives are from Rawick, *The American Slave*, North Carolina, vol. 14, pt. 1, 15, 181.

30. Petition to Gov. Wm W. Holden from Silas L. Curtis et al., Tally Ho, Granville County, N.C. Governors' Papers, Holden, October 11, 1868. In regard to KKK outrages in Granville County, see also letter of Moses M. Hester, Joseph Coley, and Jacob Winston to Gov. Holden, n.d., Governors' Papers, 1869.

31. Report of KKK Outrages in Orange County by James B. Mason, Andrew J. King, and Turner King to Gov. Holden, January 10, 1871, William Woods Holden Collection, Duke University, Durham, N.C. On upper-class leadership and broad white membership in the Klan with notable exceptions, see Escott, *Many Excellent People*, 154–60, and Edwards, *Gendered Strife and Confusion*, 33.

32. Testimony of Squire Alston, Criminal Action Papers, 1868–69, Criminal Action Papers, Orange County, NCDAH. Although Alston identified three of his attackers, the accused men never appeared in court to answer charges of assault and battery.

33. S. B. Williams to Gov. Holden, September 16, 1869; James B. Mason to Gov. Holden, September 22, 1869, both in Governors' Papers, Holden, NCDAH. The murder of Wright Malone is from Coroner's Report, September 1869, Orange County, NCDAH.

34. Gov. Wm W. Holden to Chief Justice Richmond Pearson, July 19, 1870, No. 386, Governors' Letter Books, Holden.

35. Escott, *Many Excellent People*, 162; Bess Beatty, *Alamance*, 110–11. Despite Governor Holden's impeachment ordeal, Republicans continued their struggle to gain control over the Klan. In January 1871, in preparation for federal investigations of the Klan, James B. Mason coauthored a lengthy report of Klan outrages, which provided names, political affiliations, and details of abuses.

36. Kenzer, *Kinship and Neighborhood*, 133–41.

37. Petition of Lila McDonald, Civil Action Papers, April 12, 1869, Montgomery County, N.C., NCDAH; Rawick, *American Slave*, vol. 14, pt. 1, p. 72.

38. Petition of Alex Corbin, Probate Court, May 13, 1871, Civil Action Papers, Orange County, N.C., NCDAH.

39. Appeal in the matter of the Petition of Alex Corbin from Probate Court, Superior Court, 7th Judicial District, Albion Tourgee, Judge, Civil Action Papers, Orange County, N.C., NCDAH. Political affiliation of Isaac Strayhorn from Kenzer, *Kinship and Neighborhood*, 138. On Tourgee's career as a Klan-fighting Republican judge, see Otto Olsen, *Carpetbagger's Crusade: The Life of Albion Winegar Tourgee* (Baltimore: Johns Hopkins University Press, 1965).

40. McCurry, *Masters of Small World*, 61.

41. Ben Harris to Mr. W. L. Miller, agent, January 15, 1867, and Wm. Andrews to Col. Jno R. Edie, Superintendent, February 15, 1867, both in Letters Received, Freedmen's Bureau Papers; D. C. Parrish to Lt. Isaac Porter, Assistant Superintendent, Sub-district of Orange and Alamance Counties, September 14, 1867, Letters Received, May 1866–December 1868, ser. 2686, Freedmen's Bureau Papers.

42. For a fuller comparison of women's Civil War–era behavior in planter-dominated Orange County versus the heavily Unionist Quaker Belt, see Victoria Bynum, "Occupied at Home: Women Confront Confederate Forces in North Carolina's Quaker Belt," in *Occupied Women: Gender, Military Occupation, and the American Civil War*, ed. LeeAnn Whites and Alecia P. Long (Baton Rouge: Louisiana State University Press, 2009), 155–70.

43. J. Cowles to Capt. William Jones, subdivision of Statesville, July 23, 1867, and W. H. Worden to Col. Edie, August 27, 1866, Freedmen's Bureau Papers, NARA. On the financial and paternalistic limits of the Freedmen's Bureau, see especially William S. McFeeley, *Yankee Stepfather: General O. O. Howard and the Freedman* (New York: W. W. Norton, 1994).

44. Alfred Gray to Gen. Sickels, Commander, Military District #2, April 12, 1867, and A. Dilworth, Agent, Col. Edie, May 15, 1867, Freedmen's Bureau Papers, NARA. On freedwomen's insistence on rights within marriage, see Edwards, *Gendered Strife and Confusion*, 57–59, and Victoria Bynum, "Reshaping the Bonds of Womanhood: Divorce in Reconstruction North Carolina," in *Divided Houses: Gender and the Civil War*, ed. Catherine Clinton and Nina Silber (New York: Oxford University Press, 1992), 320–33.

45. McFeeley, *Yankee Stepfather*, 317; *State v. Scinthia Mary McQuin* [Linda Mary McQueen], woman of color, for concealing the birth of a child, August 28, 1867, Minute Docket of the Superior Court, Montgomery County, NCDAH.

46. *State (Linder McQueen) v. Harry Butler*, March 1867, Criminal Action Papers, Montgomery County, N.C., NCDAH; *Scinday Mary McQueen* [Linda Mary McQueen] *v. Harry Butler*, August 28, 1867, Minute Dockets of the Superior Court, Montgomery County, N.C., NCDAH.

47. *Scinday Mary McQueen* [Linda Mary McQueen] *v. Harry Butler*, September 11, 1867, Criminal Action Papers, Montgomery County, N.C., NCDAH; Attorney B. F. Simmons, to Brevet Maj. Gen. Nelson A. Miles, Commissioner, Freedmen's Bureau of N.C., and Wm. McFarland, Agent, Freedmen's Bureau, to Col. M. Cogswell, Sub Assistant Commissioner, October 10, 1867, Letters Received, Freedman's Bureau Papers, NARA.

48. Bynum, *Unruly Women*, 124–25; Schenck Diary, June 10, 1870, Schenck Books, SHC. On postwar changes in the law in Southern states in regard to race relations, see Peter Bardaglio, *Reconstructing the Household: Sex and the Law in the Nineteenth-Century South* (Chapel Hill: University of North Carolina Press, 1995).

49. William W. Holden to Raleigh *News & Observer*, August 31, 1883, copy from Holden Collection, Special Collections, Duke University. Deed of Diza Ann Williams, sworn before I. M. Deaton, Registrar of Deeds, February 6, 1884, Miscellaneous Books 3, folder 25, Montgomery County, N.C., NCDAH.

50. Evidence that Wilson and Dicey Williams's marriage was treated as legal is in Wilson's application for an exemption from military service during the Civil War: T. H. Houghton recommended that Wilson be exempted even "though his wife [is] a white woman." Letter Book of Chief Enrolling Office, Seventh Congressional District, Lexington, N.C., 1864, Confederate Conscript Papers, SHC; Federal Manuscript Census, Population Schedule, 1860, Montgomery County, N.C., NCDAH. In the 1880 census of same, Wilson Williams was noted as divorced.

51. *John Hopkins, Alexander Hopkins, Sally Hopkins (by Alexander Hopkins), Robert Daniel and wife Emma Daniel, Thomas Adcock and wife Larcena, Jordan Nance and wife Sally v. Ann (Bowers) Boothe and daughters Eliza and Nannie (Bowers) Boothe*, Superior Court, 1888–92, Estate Records, Orange County, N.C., NCDAH. Reports of Klan harassment of the Johnstons and Madison Nunn are from Report of KKK Outrages in Orange County by James B. Mason et al., William Woods Holden Collection, Manuscripts Department, Duke University, Durham, N.C. Ann's Unionist kinsman, Cannon Bowers, was a prosperous nonslaveholding Durham farmer (Federal Manuscript Census, Population Schedules, 1860, 1870, Orange County, NCDAH).

52. Bynum, *Unruly Women*, 104–10.

53. Mary Jane Boothe charged Nash Boothe with marrying her and then abandoning her and their child in 1873. She charged him with committing adultery with Easter Carroll and also Ann Bowers; Ann's name was later crossed out. In 1870, Lydia Bowers, age 38, headed a household that included George Bowers, 21, Ann Eliza Bowers, 16, Nash Boothe, 38, and Annie Dollar, 30. Ann claimed she and Nash were married in Wake County on May 30, 1876, but I've not found the record. Lydia Bowers disappears from the records after 1872. *Mary Jane Boothe v.*

Nash Boothe, Superior Court, fall 1875, Divorce Records, Orange County; U. S. Bureau of the Census, Federal Manuscript Census, Population Schedule, 1870, Orange County, N.C.; *State v. Lydia Bowers and Nash Boothe*, fornication, Superior Court, 1872, Criminal Action Papers, Orange County, N.C., all in NCDAH.

54. *State v. Dr. Bartlett L. Durham*, A&B [assault and battery] on Nash Boothe, and *State v. Nash Boothe*, A&B on Bartlett Durham, both in May 1854; *State v. Nash Boothe*, A&B on George Trice, fall 1866; Peace Warrant against Nash Boothe by Cate and Victoria Dezerne and Tapley Patterson, August 1871: all in Criminal Action Papers, Orange County, N.C., NCDAH. Petition of Nash Boothe and seventeen signatories to Gov. Holden, June 17, 1870, Governors' Papers, Holden, NCDAH; Deposition of Katy Carroll [aka Katy Gilbert], *Hopkins et al. v. Boothe et al.*, NCDAH. Forty years old in 1870, Katy Carroll shared a household headed by eighty-seven-year-old Archy Carroll (perhaps her father) and Esther Carroll, age twenty-two (perhaps her daughter), and Betsy Rue, age thirty-seven (Federal Manuscript Censuses, Population Schedules, 1870, Orange County, N.C.).

55. *Hopkins et al. v. Boothe et al.*, NCDAH. Quote from Lewis Pratt's half-brother, Louis Jenkins.

56. *Hopkins et al. v. Boothe et al.*

57. Archy Carroll, with whom Katy and three other women lived, was a modest farmer before the war, claiming a personal estate valued at $300 in 1860. In 1870, neither he nor any of the women claimed estates of any sort. Federal Manuscript Censuses, Population Schedules, 1850, 1860, 1870, Orange County, N.C.

58. *Hopkins et al. v. Boothe et al.* Quoted passage from Colonel Samuel Thomas, September 1865, Letters Received, Freedmen's Bureau Papers, NARA.

59. In a classic example of the social and political construction of racial identity, Ann Boothe's racial designation went from "white" to "black" as a result of this trial. The 1870 Federal Manuscript Census listed her as Ann Eliza Bowers, "white," living in Durham township, while the 1900 census listed an "Annie Boothe," age forty (according to the 1870 census, Ann would have been forty-six) as "black" and living in nearby Chapel Hill. "Annie Boothe" is listed as having given birth seven times, twice since the trial, which is consistent with Ann's statement that she and Nash Boothe had five children together. In this Annie's household is a daughter named Nannie, also consistent with court records that identified Ann Bowers Boothe's children by name.

Dead Husband, Dead Son

Widows, Mothers-in-Law, and Mourning in the Confederacy

Angela Esco Elder

Between 1861 and 1865, approximately 750,000 men died in the American Civil War, leaving behind some 200,000 widows and many more grieving mothers and sisters. The Civil War unleashed both a staggering amount of grief and a staggering display of it. "There were so many ladies there, all dressed in deep mourning," Lucy Breckinridge said of a Virginia party in December 1862, "that we felt as if we were at a convent and formed a sisterhood." As Breckinridge implied, women were often brought closer by grief. Death deepened their common bond and highlighted the peculiar burdens of their sex. However, the pressures of grieving, piled upon the pressures of the war itself, could also exacerbate tensions. This essay examines one of the most historically contentious household relationships, that between mothers and daughters-in-law, during one of its most fraught points—the moment when two women came together to mourn a man they loved, to their minds, uniquely. By sentiment and practice, a household was a network of social support and social insurance, especially during difficult times. But when widows and bereaved mothers clashed, grief exacerbated their differences. Looking at Reconstruction at the national level obscures the incredible amount of cultural work and conflict that went into reconstructing households at the most intimate of levels. Given the number of deaths, this household struggle was, in fact, one of the biggest projects to come out of the war. Studying white households at their pressure points and along their fault lines exposes the central role of death and mourning in the reconstruction of many Confederate households.[1]

Together, a mother and her daughter-in-law kissed their soldier goodbye, awaited news of his death, and when he didn't march home, turned to reconstructing a household without him—a process at once intimate and fraught with the potential for conflict. As other scholars of female Southern honor have suggested, nineteenth-century white women typically avoided dueling and engaging in drunken fistfights, but they had their own competitive codes of conduct that governed the social slights, punishments, and penances they doled out on each other. Much research has been published on the vast economic, political, and cultural work that women performed during the Civil War, from their roles as nurses and in armament manufactories to their critical importance overseeing the command and control centers, their homes, during the guerrilla conflict, as well as to their dominating presence in the Ladies' Memorial Associations and ultimately the United Daughters of the Confederacy. Less attention has been paid to the degree to which, in all of these roles, they often fought *with each other*. No social work gets done without friction; all human beings have their own, sometimes prickly sense of the way things ought to be. This friction was no less present in the work of mourning, in which wives and mothers were both united in grief and divided over decisions about mourning, (grand)children, and the degree to which the widow remained tied to her dead husband's household.[2]

The emotional work of reconstructing white families in mourning did not begin with the end of the war but with the end of a life. The death of a man triggered immediate and pressing decisions. Families discussed and debated who would retrieve the body, where the body should be buried, where his widow should live both during the war and after, who, wife or mother, should go through his earthly possessions, who would have what say in the raising of his children, and in some situations, who had the greater claim to grief. When death took away the man who had brought them together in the first place, grieving mothers and widows had to renegotiate who they would be to each other, now and in the future. Their household was as much a psychological space as a physical one.[3]

There existed a set of nuclear family connections and expectations within the household that evolved as a younger generation rose, married, and left the house, and an older one helped gradually to set up independent households for their children even as their own influence waned. The Civil War was a massive disruption to this process, killing large numbers of relatively young men and turning wives into widows by the thousands. In the antebellum period, widows were often older women, grandmothered into a status as comparatively independent white women who could own property and be heads of households. Civil War widows' experiences varied from the antebellum experiences, in part because it was a time of war, in part because many were in their sexual and childbearing prime, and in part because there were so many of them. In such great numbers, with their brothers, uncles, fathers, and male cousins often still away at war, Confederate widows seemed to their contemporaries relatively manless and unmoored, and in need of counsel. Their mothers-in-law could reach out to comfort or control them, depending on the emotional needs of the moment.

It is difficult to understand the impact of a soldier's death on the relationship between his wife and mother without first understanding what that female relationship looked like before he died, a relationship that was often very new in 1861. This essay explores both the experiences of couples who had been married for a number of years prior to the war as well as the experiences of those couples swept up in the unprecedented flurry of wartime weddings. Because the Civil War had unleashed such a torrent of marriages, it was sometimes the case that a man's mother and his wife did not know each other well, nor did they have the time to establish household dynamics before the soldier left for war, breeding resentment and tension as they negotiated their relationships with one another. In Virginia, Judith McGuire described "a perfect mania on the subject of matrimony" during the war. "Some of the churches may be seen open and lighted almost every night for bridals," she noted, "and wherever I turn I hear of marriages in prospect." Take Frank Schaller, for example, who on July 2, 1861, wrote his "dearest Sophy" about a conversation he had with a reverend, who encouraged him to "make a strong effort to get a wife." Frank would rise to colonel in the Twenty-Second Mississippi Infantry. "Every day I feel more reluctant to go into an uncertain life without having the consciousness of being yours entirely," he reflected. "Should I fall, you could have at least the satisfaction to be a soldier's widow who I trust will only die in honor. Besides, though I know you do not want me to tell you this, some pension would insure you the prospect of a humble but honorable existence." They wed on July 22, 1863. Frank was later wounded, but he ultimately survived the war. As much as men loved their mothers, sisters, and family members, they also craved the reassurance of wives awaiting their return as they marched toward an undecided future, an emotion that hastened them down the aisle.[4]

Frank was hardly alone in his urgency to wed. "You cannot imagine, my dear Miss Georgia, how sad, how—very sad I felt at our parting," wrote William Duncan Smith to his sweetheart, nor "how profoundly I love you. But you do love me, do you not?" Though they had only been courting three months, William wanted desperately to be married. "A war is fast approaching. Oh Let me claim you as my own! Let me have the right to

protect you, and shield you by my earnest love," he begged. Georgia, however, was a dutiful daughter so dedicated to family and tradition that her
mother had praised her as "an old fashioned little thing." Even so, amid the
temper of the times, Georgia suddenly felt a little like seceding from her
own family. "[I am] so sick of living in this lonely place with so many cares
& so few pleasures," she confessed to her father. And so, in July 1861, she
consented to marry a man she hardly knew. "The hour has come," she wrote
her brother, "the man who . . . I have consented to marry . . . is about to
leave for war [and] I have at length after weight of prayer—after tears and
with earnest faith in God's direction—determined to marry him before he
goes to Virginia—and follow him there in a few weeks." She continued,
"I feared that you all might not approve, but my heart relented." Wedding
ceremonies, typically small and attended by close family and friends, did
not require extensive planning. Most often, young couples rushed nuptials,
but they were not out of the blue. Similarly, many men married women
within their communities, joining two families who were at least familiar with one another. Even so, the relationship of a mother sharing her
son, her family, and her household, even if the new wife did not move into
it physically, brought a higher level of intimacy into these multigenera-
tional female relationships. Because of the rush of marriages that came at
the onset of war, some grieving mothers would find themselves mourning
with widowed daughters-in-law whom they hardly knew and had hardly
approved of in the first place.[5]

What is odd about these wartime marriages, when compared with traditional antebellum marriages, was not only how many there were and how
relatively quickly such matches were made, but also the fact that the men
in question were always immediately gone, leaving behind multigenera-
tional households and kinship networks composed of women who were
still uneasy with each other even as they were thrown into common cultural work—sewing for the armies, sending care packages, scanning the
wounded lists, and constantly paying attention to what the latest gossip and
rumor might mean for their menfolk. Bound by the schedules of marching armies, a new couple often did not have the time to form a clearly
defined, independent physical household separate from extended families.
When a new wife took her husband's last name, she was immediately met
with another woman who already had it. Together, a mother and daughter-
in-law may have sent a soldier to war and begun the work of supporting
him, even if they hardly knew one another. Some wives appreciated the
fresh start a marriage brought, not having or not liking their own birth
families, choosing instead to fully embrace their husbands' families. Others

had harder transitions. But either way, with her husband away, a new wife was left alone to negotiate her place within this physical and psychological household, a household often containing sisters, brothers, a mother, and a father who knew her husband far better than she did, a fact that had the potential to be a source of discord when he died.

When their husbands left for war, many wives chose to move in with, or at least move closer to, their extended families to combat the loneliness, anxiety, and fear that came with being a soldier's wife. When the war began, Jorantha Semmes moved in with her husband's cousins in Canton, Mississippi. Even though she had been a member of the family for quite some time, Jorantha believed she and her five children were an unwelcome "nuisance" to the household. Further, she became furious when her host whipped her children alongside his own. Wives of younger ages and shorter marriages struggled in decisions between their birth families and their husbands' families. Emma Crutcher moved to Vicksburg to live with her in-laws soon after her husband enlisted. When her own parents rented a large house in a remote area to avoid the troops, she doubted her decision. Ultimately her desire to be near a railroad or post office, in order to communicate with her husband, won out, so she remained in Vicksburg with her in-laws. Not all wives moved near or in with their husbands' families; this decision was a complicated one for many families. These mixed households often resulted from economic necessity, from wartime decisions related to safety, and from a desire for emotional and social support.[6]

From their camps, soldiers complained, celebrated, and shared their wartime experiences with these two major women in their lives. The young and recently married sons were also caught between households or enmeshed in two, imperfectly broken from the homes of their youth and not yet established in the homes of their new families. Early in the war, the situation was rather ideal as men had two women to write for, perform to, and be adored by. As long as they were in the field, they developed their relationships entirely on paper. Certainly they saved their raptures for their sweethearts. "My deare wife," began one soldier in January 1862, "my heart is fild with greef and my eyes with tears to think that we ar so far apart that I cannot See you and my Sweet little Children." He died in 1863. Stephen Dodson Ramseur was even more effusive, calling his betrothed "My Sweetest Darling, My Heart's Queen, my Best beloved, My beautiful little wife," and stressing "how earnestly, increasingly I long to be with you." He died in 1864, a week shy of his first wedding anniversary. However, soldiers' mothers were a mainstay, too, and a source of potentially deeper motivation to be good and to be worthy. "Mother's health is delicate," a sister wrote to her brother. "She pines to see her boy, her eldest, her hope stay and comfort, although she bears the separation from you with Christian resignation and fortitude.... [She also] says, don't forget to read your bible." Just as a new husband took on many of the duties formally tasked to a father, a new wife replaced a man's mother in many ways. Nathaniel Dawson admitted to his fiancée that he hoped to marry her to fill a void left by his deceased mother. "It is ten years this morning since my good mother died," he told her, "and I have been thinking of her virtues.... I was devoted to my mother and when she died, I felt all alone and yearned for the love of someone to supply her place." They married in 1862. Soldiers clung to their female relations as they knew them, less concerned in sorting out their mothers and their wives from afar, instead enjoying their support and affection in the mail.[7]

Together, mothers, wives, and sisters were bound up in the common work of fearing and anticipating the loss of these men. Minerva McClatchey believed she worried ceaselessly because "we hear thousands of rumors—but nothing reliable." Rosa Delony, a future widow, told her husband, "Faith and hope and every thing else nearly dies out of my fearful heart in view of the monstrous fact of our indefinite separation." She felt "as restive and impatient as a young unbroken colt," aching for news of her husband and for the day when he could finally return home. As it was for many women, for Rosa "constant anxiety" seemed to be "tearing out" her very spirit. Husbands and sons tried to comfort their worried loved ones. "Now you need not bee uneasy about me if I get killed," wrote one soldier to his wife, anticipating a battle, "just say I dyed in a good cause ould abe lincon and his cabinet could not daunt me now." Despite reassurances like this, mothers and their daughters-in-law quietly braced themselves for bad news. Though they may not have loved one another, they loved the same man.[8]

Mothers and wives were equally at the mercy of inconsistent casualty reporting, many struggling to maintain their composure in daily activities. "Well tomorrow is Williams birth day," wrote one soon-to-be widow. "O if we could only know if he be living or dead, if we knew he was still among the living we should hope some time to see him. And if we knew him to be dead than we should give up the last hope, and suspense would be at an end." The arrival of a rumpled envelope addressed with unfamiliar handwriting might contain a message from a man like William Fields, who wrote "as you in all probability have not heard of the death of your husband and as I was a witness to his death I consider it my duty to write you although I am a stranger to you." Inconsistent casualty reports printed in Confederate newspapers often contained false information, making a personal letter all the more important in confirming a death. Wounded between the first and second button of his shirt, William Lee would be one of 387 Confederate soldiers killed in the first Battle of Manassas. As he lay suffering, William's mind remained focused on his wife, Lillie, and his mother, a detail not lost on his cousin Eddie. "I prayed for him, for his wife and child, for his Mother," Edwin wrote to his aunt, "that all of us might bow with humble hearts to the will of that God whose every act is full of love." Though William was in pain and "still forbidden to talk," Edwin explained, "he beckoned me to him and said, in a low whisper, 'Eddie, write to Lil and Mother.'" This note would be an invaluable message, invaluable confirmation, for his anxious mother and wife.[9]

Preparing for the possibility of a soldier's death was not only an emotional task but also an economic and physical endeavor. As they readied their household to survive a man's temporary, and possibly permanent, absence, women often sought the counsel of their soldier. C. D. Epps, a Georgia farmer who directed his wife's farming practices through his letters, wrote, "You wrote to me to write to you about managing. You know best now. Do the best you can to make something to eat." Likewise, Edwin Fay told his wife, "You ask me what I think of the trade of the house for the negroes. I don't know what to say to you except that I want you to act just as if you were a widow in your own right. You know I place implicit confidence in your judgement." In his absence, he trusted her decisions over their household and needed her to direct the household as a widow would, making independent decisions. Similarly, E. P. Petty of Texas told his wife, "I approve anything you do. . . . I am not now the head of the family and dont pretend to dictate," while another soldier reflected, "Dear me, why should I advise an experienced farmer like yourself?" In these roles, women gained experience in running households, preparing them for the possible new realities. One Florida war widow, who did not embrace these additional responsibilities during the war, struggled to manage after her husband's death. She recalled in a letter to her brother, "Oh how often Winston has told me that I ought not be so dependent on him, but to learn how to manage." She had married her husband about eighteen months before the war. Younger wives who had depended on the directions of their husbands were more likely to turn to their extended families for help after the deaths of husbands.[10]

For thousands of families, a mother and her daughter-in-law had their worst fears realized when they learned their soldier had died. The feelings of shock and sorrow seized them both, often uniting these women, binding them together in their grief. Mary Patrick captured the emotions of many mothers in her journal entry after the death of her son in May 1862.

"Hush poor heart! Beat not so wildly, stop let me tell it on this quiet page," she noted. "My Son. Oh my Son. Beautiful, noble, generous, Mother loving boy! Solace of my widowed years. . . . I would willingly die before the day goes out. Father forgive me." Her entry included a poem dedicated to a "mother's ceaseless moan" and the memories of teaching a young boy to walk, talk, and pray. For many mothers, the unnaturalness of outliving a child in full bloom continually haunted them with a pain that demanded release—and a sympathetic hearing. Who better for such things than the only other person on the planet who might be expected to love as she had loved, with the fullness of a woman's heart. "My son, my son, my first born, my pride, my hope," wrote one grieving mother to her daughter-in-law. "Oh this wicked war of oppression—I know he died gloriously fighting for the freedom of his country but I can not feel that. . . . The loss of my child, my darling son, how can I out live him?"[11]

Often wives felt the same way as these grieving mothers, and a surprising number of women frantically dug up graves to confirm the face within, collapsed on floors, lamented bitterly, clutched bodies of dead men, and demanded proof. Widows and mothers alike became "wild with grief" and made buildings ring with their "bitter lamentations." One widow felt so utterly disoriented by her new role that she wrote to her brother, "I know not how to write I am so bewildered" and "I can not realize the whole truth, it seems dark and mysterious." For others, shock brought silence, such as the widow who appeared "unnaturally calm and has not shed a tear . . . poor girl, I fear the reaction when his body arrives—she had a sad and heavy responsibility left upon her and so young." Although some women quietly celebrated widowhood as a release from unhappy or hasty marriages, most found themselves emotionally and physically traumatized. Drained by food shortages, housework, marching armies, and fears for the future, Confederate women often learned of their loved ones' deaths at a precarious time in their own lives—while they were pregnant or insecure financially or emotionally. The news led some women to act uncharacteristically for a few days, some for a few weeks, and left others permanently damaged.[12]

The degree to which a widow mourned did not necessarily correlate with the length of her marriage. Some young and recently married women struggled tremendously with the deaths of their husbands, as heartbroken as widows who had been married for decades. Some older women appeared to grieve less, seamlessly replacing their central identity of wife with mother, doting and devoting themselves to their children, motherhood providing daily purpose and direction. Wives without children were unable to lean on an identity in motherhood, feeling lost in their orientation and seemingly prolonging their grief. When "Richmond's belle" Hetty Cary walked down the aisle and married a Confederate colonel, John Pegram, on Thursday, January 19, 1865, she did not know the war was almost over, nor did she know that her new husband was about to die. In spite of the war, "all was bright and beautiful" at their wedding, which took place in Saint Paul's Episcopal Church. John soon returned to duty and on February 5, he received a shot above his lower rib and died almost instantly in the snow. Exactly three weeks from the date of her wedding, Hetty found herself in the same church, with the same people, and the same minister, walking down the same aisle for the funeral. One female diarist wrote, "Again has St. Paul's, his own beloved church receive[d] the soldier and his bride—the one coffined for a hero's grave, the other, pale and trembling, though still by his side, in widow's garb." Twenty-nine-year-old Hetty "was like a flower broken in the stalk," so heartbroken that earlier she had to be torn from the body "almost by force." Three weeks a wife, Hetty would remain a widow for more than fifteen years.[13]

For others, a short marriage seemed to lessen the grief of becoming a widow. In December 1863 or January 1864, twenty-year-old Fannie Franklin Hargrave married James N. Carson. A Union soldier shot and killed James on July 3, 1864. When Fannie left for Tennessee in November 1865 to wed her late husband's business partner, Fannie's sister was "tormented" by Fannie's admirers back in Georgia. Her sister complained that "every time I go out, or see anybody 'have you heard from Miss Carson' is dinged in my ears." She explained to Fannie, "I have been questioned by some of your admirers until I have grown almost tired." To pacify one eager suitor, Fannie's sister promised a lock of Fannie's hair, but instead "clipped a tress from old yellow oxen tail, perfumed it highly and sent it to him with the request that he should wear it next to his heart and not expose it to the vulgar gaze of anyone. The last time I saw him he drew it out of his breast pocket and pressed it tenderly to his lips." On the subject of Fannie's new marriage, which took place when she was still supposed to be mourning her first husband, Fannie wrote her friends, "Now don't go scolding because I didn't tell in my other letter for I didn't think then it would come off so soon." Fannie's sister responded, "I can hardly help from hating Mr. Brannan for stealing you from us. Poor Jule cried for three days and nights after you left." Her friend Molly remarked, "I was quite surprised when I heard you were going to marry." Another flatly told her, "O I wish you were not married." In a fleeting moment of introspection, even Fannie doubted her decision, writing, "I hope I made my choice with considerable deliberation."[14]

After a death, other soldiers often wrote both wives and mothers to inform them and set into motion a household's mourning rituals. William Delony's fellow soldiers, for instance, took it upon themselves to inform his wife and mother that William had died as a result of his battle wound. Rosa, who was eight months into her fifth pregnancy at the time, learned of her husband's death not from the hospital or newspaper but from local friends. William Church, a sergeant in Will's Georgia Troopers, informed Mrs. Pleasant Stovall of Will's death in a hastily written telegram. "On account of her condition break the news to Mrs. Delony as best you can. . . . William Gaston Delony . . . died on Friday afternoon from the effects of gunshot wounds he received on the left leg. His funeral took place on Saturday afternoon about four o'clock at Stanton Hospital where he died," he informed Stovall, who worked with Rosa in the Ladies' Aid Society. Church was a dear friend of the Delony family. They knew that with the arrival of this slip of paper, Rosa's life would change. However, as worried as Will's friends were about informing Rosa, they also were sure to get the news to his mother, who lived in another state. As one chaplain informed Rosa, "Col. Delony's mother was written to," and she arrived "soon after his death and burial. She received as a memento of her son the gold pencil case which he brought with him to the hospital." Rosa was unable to travel, due to her pregnancy, but her mother-in-law would not miss the opportunity to visit the men who were with her son in life and death, see his grave, and receive a keepsake.[15]

The sudden, dramatic, and faraway nature of wartime deaths forced female members of households to reassess and alter their antebellum death practices. Family members were expected to sit beside a bed, hold the loved one's hand, and witness his passing, fulfilling the antebellum "Good Death." However, during war, wives and mothers would wait together far from the death scene for detailed letters. Using these notes, which contained all the particulars of a soldier's death, a mother and wife could imagine herself beside him. Other mothers and wives, after learning of a soldier's illness or wound, would desperately try to reach him. Women traveled with or without a companion for protection through enemy lines without money and with little rest in hopes that they could nurse their husbands or sons to health or at least see them one last time. One soldier, like many others, described "a poor woman" who came "from Alamance County to see her husband who she supposed was in [the] hospital." It was March 1862. "Poor creature, she came to find that he had been buried four or five days," the soldier explained to his wife. "She spent her last cent to get here. She walked out here from town—two miles—through the rain and mud to see his Captain. I sent her back in the ambulance and gave her $5." Seemingly reflecting more to himself than his wife, he added, "Wasn't her case a hard one. Many is the poor heart that will be broken by this war. May God spare yours is my daily prayer." His own wife's heart would not be spared; he was killed in 1863.[16]

After absorbing the difficult news that their soldier was dead, a mother and her daughter-in-law had a series of decisions to make about the future of their household, but often the most immediate desire was to get the body home. Mothers and daughters-in-law agreed that their loved ones should not rest among strangers, and they went to great lengths to bring the body home to rest in the church cemetery or family plot. Before the war, Mary Gray often prayed in cemeteries, reflecting, "I often feel as if it would be a privilege to live near the graves of buried love, 'tis a good & proper place for meditation." Similarly, Frances Bestor grew to appreciate her mother's grave, writing "'Tis a very sad place to visit—yet it always makes me feel so very near to Mother, I feel when I leave it as tho' I had seen her." If a Confederate woman could manage to determine the location of her husband or son's body, she should "seek a grave for the dead" at home, "close by those he loved, among kindred and friends in the fair sunny land he died to defend." A graveyard, slightly set apart from daily life, offered a convenient place where the living went to reflect on and commune with the dead. At the dedication of one in 1831, an orator shared his belief that after spending time by a gravesite, "we return to the world, and we feel ourselves purer and better and wiser from this communion with the dead," for "what is a grave, to us, but a thin barrier dividing time from eternity and earth from heaven?" Widows and mothers, then, wanted their loved one in this type of resting place close to home not simply out of ritualistic obligation but for healing.[17]

The reinterment of sons and husbands close to home also fulfilled the request of recently deceased soldiers who had wanted nothing more than to be near their families in death. This desire was universal; soldiers on both sides of the war wanted to be buried at home, usually in the cemeteries tied to their fathers' families, but not always. The war divided families, challenged them, and stretched the bonds of kinship, heaping even more pressure on the women who remained. Even so, men did not want to be forgotten by loved ones. William F. Vermilion, of the Thirty-Sixth Iowa, wrote his wife, "You have often asked what I want you to do if I should not get home." He had come to a conclusion. "Get me home if you can," he penned, "bury me on some nice loyal spot of ground, plant flowers over the grave." Most important, "don't forget to go to that spot Dollie. I don't want to sleep in the land of traitors," he explained. "I couldn't rest well." Similarly, a South Carolinian wrote, "some how I have a horror of being thrown out in a neglected place or bee trampled on as I have seen a number of graves here." During the war, a woman could not control how her husband or son died, nor would she most likely have the opportunity to be present at his burial. But by gathering up bits of information about his gravesite in letters from family, friends, and soldiers, she could piece together a plan to get his body home to her, to bury him nearby, to visit, and to mourn. By the time the first Ladies' Memorial Associations formed in 1865, widows and their mothers-in-law had often been at the work of interment and memorialization for many months, projecting their rages and resentments, even for each other, into their work of burying the dead and onto the North.[18]

In addition to their common grief and desire to bring their loved one's body home, mourning mothers and wives were also united by dress, following the same gendered expectations for loved ones in mourning. By tradition, mothers were to mourn their sons for a minimum of one year. Widows were to wear mourning clothing for two and a half years. As one 1856 etiquette book put it, "Dress has its language, which is, or may be, read and understood by all. . . . There should be a harmony between your dress and your circumstances." Thus, in the first year of mourning, "the bereaved wore solid black wool garments," a "simple crape bonnet—never a hat—and a long, thick, black crape veil." Throughout the mourning period, a woman would progress to shorter veil, lighter materials, and eventually garments of gray or violet. The veil, especially, separated the widow from the world, while the costume as a whole signaled to her community the role she now played. In addition to etiquette books, condolence letters would also urge women to mourn in a particular way. Wartime letters urged a new widow to resign herself to God's will, focus on her children, model her actions on older widows, and attempt to get her husband's body home for burial. During the war, American society became increasingly convinced that it was essential for war widows and mothers to remember their late loved ones both honorably and often. Condolence letters would refer to the man not as a "late husband" but rather as a "brave, gallant husband." Soldiering men didn't just die, but died "whilst gallantly fighting for his country." Letters placed an emphasis on remembrance, writing messages like "Bless God that you had such a husband whose memory is honored and whose children will feel proud." Fulfilling these expectations were key pieces to the proper "performance" of Confederate womanhood.[19]

Although some elements of initial grief and mourning rituals would unite mothers and daughters-in-law, deepening their relationships in the wake of their loved ones' deaths, the pressures of reconstructing house-

holds without their sons and husbands could also create tremendous conflict within the household, especially when it came to the topic of location. After the death, a desire to be close to the widow—to comfort, mourn
with, care for, and direct—increased for many in-laws, for they sought to
cement their son's wife as a member of their household, even though he
no longer lived. The death of a husband damaged a household structure,
but it also offered the opportunity for a new kind of household to emerge.
Although a mother would have to rebuild her household without a son,
she expected it to include her son's wife and his children. No longer able
to mother their own sons, mothers-in-law often turned to their daughters-
in-law and their sons' children, direct links and reminders of the boys
they had raised. When one mother's only son was mortally wounded, the
woman who delivered the news recorded, "A sad task it was, but the poor
bereaved old mother seemed to smother her own grief to comfort the poor
crushed wife." The author remained struck by the mother's desire to place
her daughter-in-law's needs before her own grief, to comfort and care for
the wife as one would a child. In August 1864, Maria Delony desperately
wanted to get to her daughter-in-law, who had been married to her son
nine years before his death. "I have written to a lady friend who sent me
word she thought she could get me a permit but I have little hope of getting to you before winter. May then be able to get permission. . . . Oh how
I wish I could get to you now without waiting. I am sick at heart," Maria
explained. She believed she could be of assistance in a variety of ways, both
physical and emotional. Similarly, after the death of her husband, Emma
Garnett received a letter from her sister-in-law sharing, "Mother will go to
you very soon. She loved you as her own child, and will do all she can to
give you comfort." A soldier's death turned a wife into a widow, but left no
clear transformational label for a grieving mother. Within the ideal household, a married woman was a mother, a label that both directed her daily
duties and defined her identity. When a son married, his mother shared
this role with his new wife, continuing to advise and emotionally support him as needed. A mother expected her son to outlive her, but when
he predeceased her, his death forced her to redefine her identity and role
within the household. Mothering her daughter-in-law and her grandchil-
dren allowed her to retain her identity as a mother and adapt her skills to
the situation before her. Living with, or close to, her son's family assisted
with this transition.[20]

Some mothers traveled to be with their daughters-in-law, but for others
the solution was for the daughter-in-law to come to her, to assuage her
own great grief over her son's death. "My poor child," began Lucinda Helm

to Emilie, "my heart has yearned over you and Hardin's orphaned children." Lucinda lived in Kentucky. Emilie had been married to her son for seven years. When Benjamin Hardin Helm left for war, Emilie went with him, traveling with her husband's regiment. She was in Georgia when Benjamin received a mortal wound at Chickamauga, and she became a twenty-six-year-old widowed mother of three children under the age of six. "I feel that the blow is more than I can bear. . . . Come home to us Emilie," Lucinda begged from Kentucky. She assured her daughter-in-law that if she came back, "I will furnish you with a nurse soon as you get here." More important, in Kentucky, Emilie would "be as a daughter and his children my children." Just to be sure her message came through clearly, Lucinda added, "Oh Emilie I wish for you and your children every day," and she signed the note "your affectionate Mother." Emilie would return to Kentucky, but she would not remain there permanently.[21]

As for the desires of widows, not surprisingly they varied, from those who desperately desired familial support in their time of grief to those who wanted to be completely alone. Certainly, this matter was an economic one as well as an emotional one. Some widows confided in their mothers-in-law, like Mattie Morgan, feeling as though few others would understand their great grief. "The dark waters of sorrow have overwhelmed me, and I can scarcely realize that I live, for has not the light and joy from life gone from me? In the midst of my happiness, my most tranquil happiness, this terrible affliction came to crush me," she shared with her mother-in-law in October 1864. She had married Henrietta's son in December 1862. Other widows, like Etta Kosnegary of Tennessee, did not know how to feel, beginning a letter, "I think sometimes if I could be . . . with some body that loved him [her husband] as well as I did I would feel better," but ending it with "company does me no good I had rather be alone."[22]

Mothers-in-law tried to step into the role of advisor for widows like Etta, counseling daughters-in-law as their sons once had, using the mail to create a consistent household connection that spanned the miles. "We were thankful to see your hand writing," began one mother before chiding her daughter-in-law for not writing more. Another wrote, "Do write often for we seldom receive more than 1 out of 10." Beyond sentimental desires, the difficulty of running a family without a husband worried many mothers-in-law. "You must not give up to your feelings my dear child, but think of those precious ones whose sole dependence is upon you. Strive to cheer up," encouraged Maria Delony to her daughter-in-law. "I know it must have been hard for you to keep up & take that interest in your duties which your children & domestic cares call for, & I don't wonder that you yielded to these feelings [of grief]" reflected another. Alice Harrison's mother-in-law advised her to let her brother take care of her affairs after her husband's death. She explained, "Oh you know not enough of human nature to have such to deal with, and your life will become more and more labourious and miserable." No longer guided by their husbands, daughters-in-law often found themselves inundated by letters filled with advice from their mothers-in-law.[23]

To be sure, some relationships between mothers and daughters-in-law, already terse, worsened as a result of the war and its pressures. On May 25, 1859, Ann Marie Stewart Turner married a man in Texas. When he left to fight for the Confederacy, Ann packed up her children and moved, living with his family in North Carolina during the war. Once there, she penned pages upon pages of complaints to her mother, back in Texas, about her mother-in-law's "unhappy temper" and "unruly tongue." The mother-in-law was not simply upset that Ann married her only son but also accused Ann of making moves on her own husband. The mother-in-law "said I had fondled around her husband till he cared more for me than any man might for any woman but his wife," Ann wrote, and "that he had a passion for me [which] I encouraged by combing his hair." The addition of Ann to the physical household was a disruptive one, highlighting the potential difficulties of physically combining families. Ann's hardships increased in 1864, when a ball struck and killed her husband at the Battle of the Crater. "For your sake and my dear little ones I try to bear my loss as well as I can," Ann wrote her mother and sister, but she couldn't help but feel that the death was some divine retribution on her and her mother-in-law for failing to get along. "I have often wished to revenge myself" on her, Ann wrote, "and I feel now that I have been punished for this, for now a hand stronger than mine has struck her a blow which falls heavy on us both." While this situation was not common in the war, disagreements between mothers and their daughters-in-law certainly had the potential to heighten under stress, especially if the women were living in close quarters. Reconstructing the household and the relationship between widows and mothers-in-law became even more difficult in situations where their personalities clashed.[24]

Examining the relationships between mothers and their daughters-in-law reveals the ways households reconstituted themselves in the wake of wartime death. In a letter to the secretary of state in October 1865, Clara Barton called for a record of the dead, arguing that "the wife released her husband and the mother sent forth her son," but "neither agreed that for the destruction of her treasures no account should be rendered her." Certainly, widows and mothers wanted their soldiers counted, but the death of a soldier destroyed more than a treasured life; it had the potential to destroy a treasured household. For some families, soldier deaths united mothers with their daughters-in-law, creating tightly intertwined households of mutual grief, support, and love. Other households, already cracked by wartime stress and personality conflicts, shattered. Examining these varied relationships between mothers and daughters-in-law, at points of unity and discord, sheds light on reconstruction at an intimate level, a familial level, and exposes the centrality of death in many postwar households.[25]

NOTES

1. This essay keeps all spelling and phrasing quoted from documents in its original form, except on occasions when punctuation has been converted to modern-day notations for clarity. The number of women widowed by the Civil War is difficult to determine. J. David Hacker provides the most recent number, suggesting that approximately 750,000 men lost their lives in the Civil War, and that if 28 percent of the men who died in the war were married at the time of their death, 200,000 widows would be created. There are no statistics currently available on Confederate/Union/African American widowhood percentages. Similarly, the precise number of mothers who lost sons is unknown, as some mothers would have predeceased their sons, and some lost more than one son to the war. J. David Hacker, "A Census-Based Count of the Civil War Dead," *Civil War History* 57, no. 4 (2011): 311; Lucy Breckinridge, December 18, 1862, *Lucy Breckinridge of Grove Hill: The Journal of a Virginia Girl, 1862–1864*, ed. Mary D. Robertson (Columbia: University of South Carolina Press, 1994), 88–89.

2. Scholars are increasingly exploring women, honor, and the South. See Lisa Tendrich Frank, "'Between Death and Dishonor': Defending Confederate Womanhood during Sherman's March," in *Southern Character: Essays in Honor of Bertram Wyatt-Brown*, ed. Lisa Tendrich Frank and Daniel Kilbride (Gainesville: University Press of Florida, 2011), 116–27.

3. Just as I argue household reconstruction began at the end of a life, not the end of the war, historian Eric Foner argues that emancipation began the process of reconstruction before the war was over. Foner, *Reconstruction: America's Unfinished Revolution, 1863–1877* (New York: HarperCollins, 1989).

4. Certainly, not all women sought marriage during the war. Historian Anya Jabour persuasively argued that many young women used the war to actively delay marriage. Anya Jabour, *Scarlett's Sisters: Young Women in the Old South* (Chapel Hill: University of North Carolina Press, 2007). The shortage of marriageable men offered them an acceptable alternative to marriage and an excuse to remain single. Judith W. McGuire, January 8, 1865, *Diary of a Southern Refugee during the War by a Lady of Virginia* (Lincoln: University of Nebraska Press, 1995), 329; Frank Schaller, *Soldiering for Glory: The Civil War Letters of Colonel Frank Schaller, Twenty-Second*

Mississippi Infantry, ed. Mary W. Schaller and Martin N. Schaller (Columbia: University of South Carolina Press, 2007), 44, 124.

5. For more about the King family, see Stephen Berry, "More Alluring at a Distance: Absentee Patriarchy and the Thomas Butler King Family," *Georgia Historical Quarterly* 81, no. 4 (Winter 1997): 863–96. See also William Duncan Smith, Savannah, to Georgia Page King, St. Simons, April 10, 1861; Anna Page King to Thomas Butler King, August 15, 1842; Georgia Page King to Thomas Butler King, April 18, 1861; William Duncan Smith to Georgia Page King, April 19, 1861; Georgia Page King to Henry Lord Page King, July 1, 1861; and Georgia Page King to John Floyd King, July 8, 1861, all stored in the King and Wilder Family Papers, 1817–1946, Georgia Historical Society, Savannah.

6. Drew Gilpin Faust, *Mothers of Invention: Women of the Slaveholding South in the American Civil War* (New York: Vintage, 1996), 33; Jorantha Semmes, Benedict Joseph Semmes Papers, Southern Historical Collection, University of North Carolina, as quoted in Faust, 37; Emma Crutcher to Will Crutcher, March 1, 1862, Crutcher-Shannon Papers, Center for American History, University of Texas, as quoted in Faust, 36–37.

7. Ebenezer B. Coggin, a farmer with only $100 in personal estate in 1860, joined the Forty-Seventh Alabama Infantry in 1862. He wrote a steady stream of letters to his wife, Ann, until his death in October 1863. U.S. Bureau of the Census, 1860 U.S. Federal Census Population Schedule of Northern Division, Chambers, Alabama, ancestry.com; Ebenezer B Coggin to Ann E. Coggin, January 20, 1862, Ebenezer B. Coggin Papers, 1862–89, Alabama Department of Archives and History, Montgomery; Stephen Dodson Ramseur, *The Bravest of the Brave: The Correspondence of Stephen Dodson Ramseur*, ed. George G. Kundahl (Chapel Hill: University of North Carolina Press, 2010), 261. Sam was imprisoned near Gettysburg. Marion Dewoody Nelson to Sam Dewoody, December 4, 1864, Dewoody Family Collection, Arkansas State Archives; Nathaniel Dawson to Elodie Todd, June 6, 1861, Dawson Papers, Southern Historical Collection, University of North Carolina at Chapel Hill.

8. Minerva Leah Rowles McClatchey, "A Georgia Woman's Civil War Diary: The Journal of Minerva Leah Rowles McClatchey," ed. T. Conn Bryan, *Georgia Historical Quarterly* 51, no. 2 (1967): 212–13; Rosa Delony to Will Delony, June 15, 1862, William Gaston Deloney Papers, Hargrett Rare Book and Manuscript Library, University of Georgia, Athens (henceforth referred to as Deloney Papers, UGA). Rosa Delony to Will Delony, August 2, 1863, Deloney Papers, UGA; John Cotton to Mariah Hindsman Cotton, August 1, 1862, in *Yours Till Death: Civil War Letters of John W. Cotton*, ed. Lucille Griffith (Birmingham: University of Alabama Press, 1951), 13.

9. Eunice Richardson Stone Connolly to Lois Davis, March 8, 1863, as quoted in Martha Hodes, *The Sea Captain's Wife: A True Story of Love, Race, and War in the Nineteenth Century* (New York: W. W. Norton, 2006), 145; William Fields to Mrs. Fitzpatrick, June 8, 1865, Maria Clopton Papers, Medical and Hospital Collection,

Eleanor S. Brockenbrough Library, Museum of the Confederacy, Richmond, Va., as quoted in Drew Gilpin Faust, *This Republic of Suffering: Death and the American Civil War* (New York: Random House, 2008), 15. "Eddie" is Edwin J. Lee, aide-de-camp of Stonewall Jackson, and William F. Lee is a young cousin of Robert E. Lee. Edwin J. Lee to Aunt, November 18, 1861, William Fitzhugh Lee Papers, State Historical Society of Missouri.

10. In the case of this Florida widow, she relied heavily on her brothers for support. Commodore Decatur Epps to Catherine Epps, August 3, 1862, C. D. Epps Papers, 1862–1915, Southern Historical Collection, Wilson Library, University of North Carolina, Chapel Hill [hereafter SHC]; Edwin H. Fay to wife, November 13, 1863, as quoted in *This Infernal War: The Confederate Letters of Edwin H. Fay*, ed. Bell Irvin Wiley with the assistance of Lucy E. Fay (Austin: University of Texas Press, 1958), 359; Elijah P. Petty, *Journey to Pleasant Hill: The Civil War Letters of Captain Elijah P. Petty, Walker's Texas Division, CSA* (Austin: University of Texas Press, 1982), 103; Morgan Callaway to Leila Callaway, August 28 and December 20, 1863, Morgan Callaway Papers, Emory University, as quoted in Faust, *Mothers of Invention*, 123; Octavia Stephens to Davis Bryant, June 11, 1864, Stephens-Bryant Family Papers, George A. Smathers Special and Area Studies Collections, University of Florida, Gainesville.

11. Mary S. Patrick, May 22, 1862, Mary S. Patrick Diary, Arkansas History Commission; Lucinda Helm to Emilie Todd Helm, October 21, 1863, Helm Papers, Kentucky Historical Society [henceforth referred to as Helm Papers, KHS].

12. McGuire, October 28, 1865, *Diary of a Southern Refugee*, 310–13; Jane Cary to Mr. Riccards, as quoted in Walter S. Griggs Jr., *General John Pegram, C.S.A.* (Lynchburg, Va.: H. E. Howard, 1993), 118; Octavia Stephens to Davis Bryant, April 4, 1864, in *Rose Cottage Chronicles: Civil War Letter of the Bryant-Stephens Families of North Florida*, ed. Arch Fredric Blakey, Ann Smith Lainhart, and Winston Bryant Stephens Jr. (Gainesville: University Press of Florida, 1998), 334; Emma Holmes, July 4, 1862, in *The Diary of Miss Emma Holmes 1861–1866*, ed. John F. Marszalek (Baton Rouge: Louisiana State University Press, 1979), 179.

13. Hetty's mother-in-law, Virginia Johnson Pegram, was a similarly strong woman. When Virginia's husband died in 1844, she ran a school in Richmond until 1866 and never remarried. Henry Kyd Douglas, *I Rode with Stonewall: The War Experiences of the Youngest Member of Jackson's Staff* (Chapel Hill: University of North Carolina Press, 1940), 271, 325; McGuire, March 12, 1865, 341; Burton Harrison, *Recollections Grave and Gay* (New York: Charles Scribner's Sons, 1911), 203, 205; Jane Cary to Mr. Riccards, as quoted in Griggs, *General John Pegram*, 118.

14. Unfortunately, the historical record does not reveal how Fannie's mother-in-law felt about Fannie's actions. In a case study of Virginia, historian Robert Kenzer compiled statistical data suggesting that the younger a widow was, the greater the likelihood that she would remarry. Through an analysis of pension records and census data, Kenzer determined that 1866 was the most common year for remarriage and that widows who remarried had a median age of twenty-four

years in 1860. Urban widows also appeared to have greater opportunities for new marriages. Kenzer concluded that "given the tremendous shortage of men after the conflict, the opportunity to remarry was quite restricted except for the youngest and wealthiest southern women." This shortage helps to explain why some young widows, when presented with an opportunity for marriage, refused to wait out the customary two and a half years of mourning. Robert Kenzer, "The Uncertainty of Life: A Profile of Virginia's Civil War Widows," in *The War Was You and Me: Civilians in the American Civil War*, ed. Joan E. Cashin (Princeton, N.J.: Princeton University Press, 2002), 125. An unnamed sister to Fannie Hargrave Carson Brannan, November 4, 1865; Mollie to Fannie Hargrave Carson Brannan, no date; Bessie Lowe to Fannie Hargrave Carson Brannan, no date. All letters are in the Hargrave Family Papers, Annie Belle Weaver Special Collections, Ingram Library, University of West Georgia.

15. The Southern Telegraphy Company, telegram from W. L. Church to Pleasant Stovall, October 6, 1863, Deloney Papers, UGA; John F. Stegeman, *These Men She Gave: Civil War Diary of Athens, Georgia* (Athens: University of Georgia Press, 1964), 99, 149–50; W. H. Channing to Rosa Delony, November 28, 1863, Deloney Papers, UGA.

16. William Pender to Fanny, March 30, 1862, in *The General to His Lady: The Civil War Letters of William Dorsey Pender to Fanny Pender*, ed. William W. Hassler (Chapel Hill: University of North Carolina Press, 1962), 129–30.

17. For more on Union families' attempts to bring home their husbands' bodies during and after the Civil War, see Judith Giesberg, "The Work That Remains," *Civil War Monitor Magazine* 1, no. 1 (Fall 2011): 39–45; Mary Douglass Gray to Frances Douglass, October 7, 1840, Douglass Correspondence, Duke University; Frances Jane Bestor Robertson Journal, September 17, 1854, in American Women's Diaries, segment 2, Southern Women microfilm, reel 2, as quoted in Scott Stephan, *Redeeming the Southern Family: Evangelical Women and Domestic Devotion in the Antebellum South* (Athens: University of Georgia Press, 2008), 215; McGuire, October 28, 1864, *Diary of a Southern Refugee*, 310–13; Joseph Story, *An Address Delivered on the Dedication of the Cemetery at Mount Auburn* (Boston: Joseph T. Edwin Buckingham, 1831), 13, 7, 11, as quoted in Gary Wills, *Lincoln at Gettysburg: The Words That Remade America* (New York: Simon & Schuster, 1992), 65.

18. For more on the burying of dead in the Civil War, see Faust, *Republic of Suffering*, chap. 3. William Vermilion to Mary Vermilion, June 30, 1863 in *Love amid the Turmoil: The Civil War Letters of William and Mary Vermilion*, ed. Donald C. Elder III (Iowa City: Iowa Press, 2005), 150; Daniel E. Sutherland, *Seasons of War: The Ordeal of a Confederate Community, 1861–1865* (New York: Free Press, 1995), 274; LeeAnn Whites, *Gender Matters: Civil War, Reconstruction, and the Making of the New South* (New York: Palgrave Macmillan, 2005), 88.

19. All female kin played a role in mourning, including sisters who lost their brothers to war, many of whom went on to play leading roles in the Ladies' Memorial Association and United Daughters of the Confederacy and were arguably

a larger population than widows. *How to Behave: A Pocket Manual of Republican Etiquette, and Guide to Correct Personal Habits* (New York: Fowler and Wells, 1856); Margaret M. Coffin, *Death in Early America: The History and Folklore of Customs and Superstitions of Early Medicine, Funerals, Burials, and Mourning* (New York: Thomas Nelson, 1976), 197–98; Lizzie Torrey, *The Ideal of Womanhood; or, Words to the Women of America* (Boston: Wentworth, Hewes, 1859), 130–32; Martha D. D., October 13, 1863; Martha D. Duncan, January 14, 1864, Deloney Papers, UGA.

20. In some ways, this idea is what Charles Frazier's *Cold Mountain* gets right— that women fought their own wars at home, against each other, with each other, condensing new households that would endure after the man that brought them together was gone. Frazier, *Cold Mountain* (New York: Vintage, 1997); Cornelia Peake McDonald, *A Woman's Civil War: A Diary with Reminiscences of the War, from March 1862*, ed. Minrose C. Gwin (Madison: University of Wisconsin Press, 1992), 211; Maria Delony to Rosa Delony, August 11, 1864, Deloney Papers, UGA; Letter to Emma S. Garnett, May 20, 1863, Garnett Family Letters, Library of Virginia.

21. Contemporaries of the Civil War commonly took this view of children as "orphaned" when their father died, even though their mother lived. Even Abraham Lincoln, in his Second Inaugural Address, called for the nation to care "for his widow and his orphan" of deceased soldiers. Lucinda Helm to Emilie Todd Helm, October 21, 1863, Helm Papers, KHS.

22. Mattie R. Morgan to Henrietta Morgan, October 31, 1864, Hunt-Morgan-Hill Family Collection, American Civil War Museum; Etta Kosnegary to Family, November 12, 1862, Etta Kosnegary Letter, Louisiana State University.

23. Unfortunately, it is difficult to determine many of the widows' reactions to advice from their mothers-in-law. Letter collections often contain letters to the widow, but the letters she sent off to her family members in response are not included. Lucinda Helm to Emilie Todd Helm, October 21, 1863, Helm Papers, KHS; Maria Delony to Rosa Delony, August 11, 1864, Deloney Papers, UGA; May Louise Comfort to Charlotte Comfort, December 22, 1873, Comfort Family Papers, 1848–1900, Virginia Historical Society, Richmond; Janett Harrison to Alice Harrison, January 27, 1862, Harrison Family Papers, Virginia Historical Society.

24. Ann Marie Stewart Turner to My Dear Mother, September 29, October 17, and December 12, 1864, Anne Marie Stewart Turner Collection, Woodson Research Center, Fondren Library, Rice University, Houston (accessible online).

25. Clara Barton to Edwin Stanton, Secretary of War, October 1865, Clara Barton Papers, Library of Congress.

Stand by Your Manhood

The United Confederate Veterans and the
Rehabilitation of the Southern Household

BRIAN CRAIG MILLER

> You boys whip the Yankees and go home to your sweethearts, and if there
> is one here that has not a sweetheart, if he will give me his name, I will
> have the Legislature provide one.
>
> —Governor Zebulon Vance of North Carolina

One Southern veteran recalled, "They [Southern soldiers] kissed their
loved ones goodbye and marched forth in all the grandeur and splendor of
southern youth and manhood."[1] The very act of marching off to war and
leaving their households and families provided Southern men a prime opportunity to cement their masculine status among their family members,
their peers, and their community. Southern men used the war to aggres-
sively defend their manhood. Marching into battle, standing shoulder to
shoulder with a fellow man, and fighting in an honorable manner (which
excluded running away or a cowardly capture) emerged as routine opportunities for thousands of Confederate men to externally show their honorable worth. Southern society had structured the patriarchal household
in a manner where men needed to showcase their worth not only to their
spouses and family members but also to their community peers. A strong
Southern household, at least in how it would be evaluated by Southern society, demanded a strong male head of household. Prior to the Civil War,
Southern men asserted their manhood through mastery or control of their
wives, children, and enslaved workers. Other men externally validated their
honorable sense of self-worth by behaving and looking like a man and
through appropriate dress and a strong male physique. Men needed to embody their own patriarchal position within the family and the brotherhood

of men through acts and rituals from dueling to electioneering. The ante-bellum parameters of manhood were put to the test with the onset of the Civil War, as men expected a victorious and thus honorable outcome to the conflict that would solidify their masculine status as head of household.[2]

This article will explore the questions surrounding masculinity as they were framed within the Southern household at the conclusion of the Civil War and reflected in the activities of the United Confederate Veterans. Upon their return from the battlefield, Southern men expected to reassume their prewar positions within the household. However, the burden of defeat, combined with the independence experienced by Southern women, evaporated traditional notions and expectations of gender identity and roles inside the household. Veterans sought economic opportunities to reassert their place at the head of the household; however, disability and debilitating pains and wounds that never seemed to completely heal damaged not only the household but also its ability to return to its antebellum position. Disillusioned and damaged men returned to the household as emotional and economic burdens, especially if they could no longer serve in the traditional male role. Thus, as time progressed, an aging class of veterans, sapped of their strength and ability to work, lost the ability to maintain their position as head of household. Veterans turned to the pension, a steady but meager flow of cash, to help acquire a level of self-sufficiency and an important marker of postwar masculinity. In the midst of economic struggles to maintain the vitality of the household, Southern veterans also coped with the burden of a potentially dishonorable defeat that shattered some elements of manhood. After all, Southern men marched off to war to defend the household order and solidify their position among their family and peers. The return proved difficult, as the Southern landscape was littered with broken homesteads, broken families, and the presence of victorious Union soldiers. Some men had nowhere to turn and looked to their fellow veterans to reconstruct a newly forged household of peers. Thus the rhetoric of the Lost Cause had the potential to reconstruct a new household, where honor and glory had been victorious even when armies had failed. The United Confederate Veterans (UCV), the largest veteran organization in the South devoted to Lost Cause politics, utilized publications and reunions to spout a deeply masculine rhetoric that had a twin purpose: to solidify the position of the male head of household and, if that failed, to forge an entirely new Southern household, one that had not been shattered by the war. In other words, the UCV worked to clear the clouds of defeat that made it difficult for Southern men to define themselves as men and stood in as the ersatz patriarch.

In a world where masculine identity was purposefully tied to performance in war, the outcome of the Civil War shattered the very ideals of Southern manhood and, by connection, the ideals of the Southern household. The crisis in gender produced by the Civil War allowed the household to emerge as the pivotal location for men and women to understand the larger ramifications of their wartime experience. However, the Southern household had collapsed under the weight of the war, and the remnants now faced the reality of a large number of damaged and disillusioned veterans thrown back into an arena where questions of dependency and disability now consumed old notions of manhood and womanhood.[3] The newly dependent position of white men within the household, which flipped traditional female dependency on its head, actually started long before Confederate men returned home, as they found themselves sick or wounded and dependent on the care of volunteer nurses.[4] Debilitating wounds created a new class of men who remained dependent on a spouse or other family members and friends to help them navigate through the challenges brought on by their newfound disability. Confederate women understood the vital role they played in mending the broken household by healing both the broken bodies and the broken expectations of secession and war.

John Herbert Claiborne, a Confederate veteran, reflected on the final moments of the Civil War after he had firsthand experience in dealing with the challenges that men and women faced inside a household altered by conflict. He thought about the landscape, which had been littered with "a great number of muskets stuck in the ground by the bayonets, whose owners, heart-sick and fainting of hunger and fatigue, had thrown them away, and gone, none knew whither." Southern men, who defined themselves through their military service and saw the war as an avenue to solidifying their position as head of household, now simply threw away the symbolic materials of war by tossing aside their muskets. Southern soldiers succumbed after "four years of peril and fatigue and fighting" to "gaunt hunger" that overcame their manly ability to sustain additional days in military service.[5] The end of the war produced much uncertainty for men who did not know what awaited them upon their return, from the status of their relationship to the condition of their homestead and potential economic prospects. Others worried about how the reunited nation would react to their military service, especially if they were not welcomed back as prodigal sons and, instead, faced prosecution as traitors. At Appomattox, one Confederate officer noted that "some of the Confederates were so depressed in spirit, so filled with apprehensions as to the policy to be adopted by the civil authorities at Washington, that the future seemed to them shrouded in gloom." A cloud of gloom and uncertainty settled in the minds of many men who journeyed home and trickled into small towns and rural farmhouses unsure of how their households had fared. In some locations, civilians emerged from their doorsteps to say to the veterans, "God Bless you all; we are just as proud of you, and thank you just as much as if it had turned out differently."[6]

The failure of the war only compounded the misery veterans faced when they returned with little to no economic capital and no means to support their households. Thus veterans routinely sent letters to governors across the South begging for financial assistance that could help heal the broken household in the form of a pension. Men asked to be dependent on the state in order to ensure they could once again care for their own familial dependents. Hundreds of veterans found themselves forced to violate household norms by begging for money on the streets of major American cities; thousands more filled out paperwork, traveled to a warehouse or courthouse, or went through exhaustive measures to prove that they had honorably served and departed the Civil War in order to garner a prosthetic device, a land grant, or a pension. Prior to the establishment of a pension system in Louisiana, the city of New Orleans was forced to crack down on the large number of individuals, many of whom were damaged veterans, begging for change in the French Quarter. One newspaper reported, "The whole community is shocked, disgusted, and sickened that these maimed beggars may secure a few nickels." Thus the city held an event known as "Corralling the Cripples," where city officials rounded up the beggars and placed them in a local almshouse. Southern veterans who lacked a household now found themselves swept up and placed into the almshouse, a poor substitute particularly as it only served as a temporary residence and the city of New Orleans only allowed veterans to return to the streets to beg. Limited manual labor job opportunities for injured men plus a bounty of lackadaisical state legislatures that waited years to issue pensions created poverty that had the potential to permanently damage the Southern household.[7]

The Confederate veterans who faced a lack of job prospects and the specter of poverty knocking at their door also faced a diminished masculine identity. They tried to go back into their previous professions. Men who failed to find employment ended up encapsulated in idleness and dependency on their wives or other family members, which forced them to be just a part of a household rather than its head. A newly forged dependency of veterans on other members of the household for medical care or even for the bare essentials of survival meant that the men lost a very important part of their identity. After all, the daily grind of hammering nails or harvesting corn allowed men to feel as if they belonged among their neighbors and peers. The financial rewards of work allowed men to maintain their masculine status inside the household. Men feared that unemployment had the potential to diminish their stature, and it even threatened any glory gained from military service.[8] Thus, as one Southern writer noted, Confederate veterans emerged from the army "ragged and poor, some of them crippled for life, with no Government pension to depend upon." Granted, the money paid by a pension represented only a fraction of the amount necessary to maintain a household. However, it would have been better than nothing at all, especially for the men who physically could no longer farm or mine to survive. Pensioners may have even felt a tinge of masculinity stripped away because they had to be reliant on the government to care for their household, but they also must have realized the consequences of being unable to maintain the health and welfare of their spouses and children. Pensions were necessary, but veterans preferred work, and once they acquired it, "their labors have not gone unrewarded."[9] One former Confederate admitted a year after the war, "I am never before so entirely devoted to any occupation or business as I am now to the improvement and cultivation of my farm."[10]

Many amputees and chronically ill veterans who had limited work opportunities remained entirely dependent on their wives. For example, Charles Klem, who lost his leg at Dallas, Georgia, on May 28, 1864, had no property or income and relied on his wife, who had an estate worth $350. Sarah Jane Klem earned the only income for the family at a rate of $50 to $60 per year from some sewing work. Her husband remained in a miserable condition as he succumbed to glaucoma, which blinded him in both eyes, and he endured searing pain in his lungs from a gunshot wound sustained at the Battle of Stones River. Although Klem eventually secured a pension from the state of Kentucky, he died a few months after his application had been approved. His wife then found herself forced to apply for a widow's pension, and she worked as a clerk in a local store in order to support herself and their daughter.[11]

Economic opportunities acquired or missed were only the first challenge facing veterans in their quest to normalize their manhood and regain their status in their households. In some instances, the Southern household had been violently shaken to the point where its very foundation had been permanently shattered. Soldiers returned home to find their marriages in shambles, as time, distance, and the challenges fostered by the war diminished romantic bonds. One historian explains that "rumors of infidelity filtered back to wartime encampments," prompting soldiers to "confront incontrovertible evidence of faithlessness" as they returned home.

Although men headed to war to help solidify their position in the household, when they returned home with little to show for their participation
in the war other than years of heartache and difficulty, a broken marriage
or a fractured relationship further intensified the difficulty of reintegrat-
ing into civilian society. Many men assumed that they needed a household,
a relationship with a woman, and a family to support in order to define
themselves in the postwar period. If those elements never materialized or
were permanently damaged by the war, men needed to find new avenues
to define themselves as men. The memorial efforts of the Lost Cause that
formed all over the former Confederacy served that purpose.[12]

As historian Wayne Wei-Siang Hsieh argues, veterans turned inward
and constructed an "emotional community" that allowed them to express
their experiences pertaining to combat while adjusting to their position
within the household. A man who had served in combat tried to return
to business as usual as head of household, but he could not often express
his anguish or sorrow or lash out at the physical and emotional pain that
engulfed his very existence. After all, the contours of Southern honor
within the household dictated that white men internalize rather than exter-
nalize their emotions. Thus veterans utilized the memory of the Civil War
as a means to highlight the manly qualities of Confederate soldiers and
officers that replaced the traditional role of men in the now altered or even
broken household. A community of veterans, constructed through the
bonds of memory, would forge a new Southern household, one that continually supported and fostered the ideals of Southern manhood.[13]

Various veteran organizations popped up across the South to serve as an
arena where men could remind themselves and each other of their masculine worth that may have been diminished in the Southern household. The
Confederate Survivors Association, formally organized in 1878 in Augusta,
Georgia, emerged as a temporary household for those who wanted to cul-
tivate friendships among the various branches of the military of the former
Confederacy. The group hoped to serve as an outlet where veterans received
encouragement, practiced "manly virtues," exhibited a loyalty to the Confederate past, and utilized charitable endeavors to help one another in this
family of veterans.[14] In 1888, veterans in the city of Louisville constructed a
similar group with the formation of the Confederate Association of Kentucky. The organization served as a gathering place where veterans recognized honorable service, created an appropriate and honorable memory of
their departed colleagues, fostered "the fraternal ties of comradeship," and
participated in charitable endeavors to maintain the health and welfare of
those still living.[15]

These local organizations were limited and disjointed in their ability to create a new overarching household of veterans, and in 1889 they merged to form the United Confederate Veterans. The idea of a national Confederate veteran organization had been bandied about from time to time throughout the late 1880s but had never received much serious consideration. Historians have speculated as to why the Confederate veterans did not quickly coalesce around the idea of a national group that could create a temporary household forged in the bonds of brotherhood. Perhaps the scars fostered by the war had proven too deep for men to quickly put aside the reasons for military failure. Or maybe the politics of Reconstruction, coupled with political and social gains for African Americans, weakened the desire for veterans to relive the meaning of the conflict. The fractured state of the Confederacy at the close of the war, coupled with diminished Confederate nationalism, may have made a quick road to a larger group simply untenable.[16]

The UCV emerged out of a concerted effort by veterans who felt the need to address the efforts of outside forces to permanently alter their masculine status, not only within the Southern household but also in society at large. Confederate veterans worried that the Northern textbooks starting to appear in Southern classrooms would alter the way that children viewed the sacrifices of their fathers and thus held the potential to further diminish the status of the male head of household. The failure of state governments to provide sufficient financial support for the ever aging veteran population as well as for Confederate widows and orphaned children contributed to mounting pressure for a more concerted charitable endeavor to mend what the war and years of neglect continued to create.

Thus the men who organized the UCV came up with their slogan "Social, Literary, Historical and Benevolent" in order to describe the activities of the organization. Membership would be open only to the true men of the Confederacy who had "honorably served" in the army or navy until the end of the war "unless discharged for real and physical disability, or honorably released from service." The men who made up the household within the UCV would have "an unimpeachable war record" and welcome the chance to foster friendship among veterans. In order to achieve that goal, veterans would be encouraged to write their history of the war and share their stories, memoirs, and even artifacts and relics of the war with their local camp and the national organization. UCV members also raised funds to honor the men who had passed on by providing "suitable headstones" for the graves of the dead and building monuments "to our great leaders and heroic soldiers, sailors, and people." Finally, the organization saw itself as an avenue for benevolence through caring for the disabled veterans, needy widows, and the orphaned children of the South. Efforts to raise funds for veteran homes or charitable groups would ensure that the UCV maintained a legacy of rebuilding or at least reaffirming the Southern household.[17]

The United Confederate Veterans valued the benevolent aspects of their organization. In 1902, when someone raised the question of whether or not the group should endorse specific political candidates for office, the head of the UCV, John B. Gordon, issued a circular letter that noted, "It is then, the duty and honor demands, that the members of the UCV Association shall see that its benevolent features are not tarnished in any manner, nor diverted in any way from the pure, noble and philanthropic purposes which its founders intended."[18] Although the leadership of the UCV expected the organization to remain purely philanthropic and care for those inside the Southern household who needed it, members could not stop themselves from diving into disagreements over the contested meaning of the Civil War. Textbooks and monuments, which had the ability to diminish the masculine reputation of a veteran, towered above caring for the actual veterans, which may explain why few seriously injured Confederates joined the organization. After five years of existence, the UCV only reported 270 disabled members out of a total membership of nearly 25,000.[19]

Confederate veterans approved of being part of this new household of men because they believed that they had a completely different set of life experiences than their civilian counterparts. Maintaining a specific memory of the war and upholding the honorable reputation of fathers, brothers, and sons on the battlefield took precedence over caring for the still living members of the household if they were veterans. Despite the plethora of pages written on the war that anyone could peruse at their leisure, many veterans believed that the "true" story of the war, the one rooted in the Confederate side of the experience, remained absent from the historical narrative that preserved the honor of a generation of Southern men. Only the men who marched and battled could truly understand and thus properly convey the experiences of war. Some veterans expressed concern when the activities of commemoration and memory suddenly were overrun by civilian spectators and participants. The veterans started to turn inward as the UCV created a new household where they found themselves better able to relate to one another about what the war had truly done to their existence. Duke Goodman wrote, "I find in many portions of the state that the UCV camps are amalgamating with the masses and holding reunions; the masses are fast overshadowing these camps. The day is not far distant when, if this is kept up, these camps will lose their identity." The mere presence of men who did not wear the uniform potentially damaged the newly forged household of veterans constructed in order to affirm the legacy of the war.[20]

The identity and relationships forged among veterans in ucv camps quickly emerged as a preeminent way to reaffirm the masculinity of the defeated Confederate veterans that many could not find in their own civilian households. The veterans constructed what was essentially a new household within the ranks of the ucv where they delivered a heap of praise toward one another that solidified their masculine identity due to their military service. One speaker to a group of Confederate veterans wholeheartedly believed that the former comrade stood "worthy of the most exalted praise and even adoration" because he stood "covered with glory, both civil and military, reaped in the harvest field of life by the scytheblade of true manhood in the strong hands of energy and intelligence."[21] The battlefields across the American landscape served as the storybook for the tale of Southern manhood. The battles that raged across pristine farmland, along the banks of mighty streams, in forested nooks, and on piles of giant rocks, like at Gettysburg, stood as the places where the blood spilled allowed for Southern soldiers to use their own blood to construct a new household where their masculine status was never called into question.[22]

Many of the speakers recognized the importance that a gathering of veterans played in reaffirming the honor and sacrifices of the men seated in the audience. One speaker at a reunion in Birmingham, Alabama, concluded his address by thanking everyone who worked on the gathering. The organizers who provided entertainment, comfort, and provisions had created an occasion when countless orators could offer "beautiful expression[s] both in words and acts, of the estimate you have so generously and kindly put upon our manhood, courage, and valor as soldiers, and of our lives as citizens."[23] In 1895, the president of the ucv reflected on the veterans who had passed away and asserted that "they had proven their true manhood in the days when men were sorely and severely tried." The ucv president wanted to maintain the bonds within the ucv household, despite the passing of some members. Inside the local ucv camps, former soldiers had created a fictive family household that had been buttressed by military sacrifice and honored through recognition of strong friendships. A continual process of remembering the deeds of departed comrades emerged as the best possible means for reconstructing the bonds of love and friendship between former soldiers that evaporated due to the passage of time and the stigma of defeat.[24]

As the aging crowd of Confederate veterans made their yearly pilgrimage to attend the reunions, the speakers participating in the festivities routinely reminded the audience that their manhood, and that of their deceased comrades, should never be called into question. Memorialization efforts required that each subsequent generation of Southerners understand their role in crafting the memory of the conflict. Randolph Harrison McKim, who addressed a reunion in Nashville, told the audience that the freshly constructed monuments that dotted the South were not "intended to perpetuate the angry passions of the Civil War, or to foster or keep alive any feeling of hostility to our brethren of other parts of the Union." Rather, the monuments served as mini arenas where men could loyally worship "at the shrine of the splendid manhood of our heroic soldiers, and the even more splendid womanhood, whose fortitude and whose endurance have challenged the admiration of the world." Commemorations and monuments that honored the prime facets of Southern manhood and womanhood fostered an environment, according to McKim, where future generations would feel compelled to enter into military service in the same manner as their fathers and grandfathers did during the 1860s. The tenets of Southern manhood were required for the next generation of citizen soldiers to "gird the Stars and Stripes with an impenetrable rampart of steel."[25]

In his lengthy address, McKim reminded the crowd of veterans that their manhood remained intact because they did not have to deal with financial dependency in the form of a pension. He declared, "You are not pensioners on the bounty of the Union, thank God! Your manhood is not sapped by eating the bread of dependence." McKim noted that many of the veterans faced conditions of poverty as "bravely as you faced the cannon's mouth." The impoverished veteran now stood as the newly reconstructed "aristocracy of the South." McKim delivered his remarks to a largely physically intact audience. The veterans who sacrificed limbs or suffered on a daily basis from gunshot wounds that never quite healed or could not emotionally cope with the rigors of war remained at home. The damaged men did not have the financial capital or mobility, let alone the desire, to travel a great distance to be part of the memorial proceedings. Instead, they stayed home, where they remained dependent on a pension or prosthetic limb from the state government or reliant on the kindness of family members or strangers to help them survive another day. Despite the calls for the bonds of friendship among veterans, the absence of damaged and dependent veterans limited the construction of a replacement household, as some veterans were physically unable to leave their current homestead.[26]

Throughout the years of reunion after reunion, speakers stepped onto the podium to remind the ever-aging audience that their manhood remained solidified within the household of veterans, at least in the mind of the speaker and those who valued commemorative efforts. Don Halsey, at a reunion in 1924, reminisced that the men who fought for the Confederacy sacrificed "their souls and the blood of their bodies" during "the best years of their manhood." Reverend M. Ashby Jones, who took to the podium after Halsey, spent his rhetorical moments noting that men are not necessarily defined by their professional trade or occupation. "The possibilities of manhood are infinitely greater than any profession, and whenever a life can be defined in terms of a special task it means the life has been narrowed and limited by that task," explained Jones. He saw manhood as "something too rich and deep to find its full and complete expression in the forms of any particular work." Instead, the men needed to realize that their own self-worth should be defined by how they acted as head of a household within the traditional Southern family and how they acted among their peers inside the UCV. If any of the veterans needed a model man to emulate, they could look to Robert E. Lee, who, according to Jones, "was a soldier, but he was infinitely more, he was a man."[27]

The ticking hands of the clock forced many speakers before the group of veterans to acknowledge that time remained of the essence to ensure that the masculine virtues of the previous generation of soldiers would be preserved. In 1908, General Bennett H. Young told a group of veterans in Kentucky, "The average age of the Confederate soldier is now 72 years, and it seems almost impossible that the boys who were with us in the march and on the battlefield are now men of more than three score years." Despite the passage of time, the Confederate veterans did not harbor resentment against their former foe nor did they lash out at society and their fellow man. Rather, they remained "brave and constant" in civilian life as they had done in the ranks of the army. The "heroes of fifteen hundred battles in which they engaged were marked by the highest characteristics of true and superb manhood and exalted citizenship." Although many veterans in the audience would soon have to admit that death moved toward them with "a busy and relentless hand," they needed to stand strong and know that they possessed the entire requisite masculine honor to accept death with a gracious bow. "Comrades, we shall meet him with the sublime courage," declared Young, "born of the highest and truest manhood, and when at last the inevitable must come we will face it as we faced the enemy on the battlefield during the four years of unparalleled conflict."[28]

The death of any prominent Confederate officer prompted a speaker to step forward and affirm that they had not died in vain. Robert E. Lee, the epitome of Southern manhood, never had his masculinity called into question. As one writer noted, "Whatever conclusions may be reached as to his plans in that battle, no one can question the superb character of his manhood."[29] When the chief of staff to J. E. B. Stuart died, the veterans of Virginia wished to express their "love for his manhood."[30] When Confederate veteran William Smith died, an unknown author wrote, "What a noble old man. What a living spring there was in him of virtue and manhood." The writer concluded that anytime someone wanted a lesson in courage, virtue, or manhood, they could simply turn to the life story of Smith.[31] Josiah Gorgas, the man responsible for Confederate ordnance during the war, received similar masculine accolades upon his death. One writer said, "How, by precept, but more by example, he elevated the standard of morals and a true manhood among the corps of cadets."[32] During a tribute to General F. S. Ferguson, J. K. Barton noted, "The outlines of worth and manhood—truth and fidelity—courage and conviction stand out in bold relief." In a tribute to Robert Dandridge Jackson, a local ucv camp in Birmingham, Alabama, described Jackson as someone who "came to manhood, fully equipped, a character sound and rounded, a typical young Southerner, ready to do a man's part in the world." Jackson, who served as a surgeon during the war, returned to Alabama "as poor as the poorest of us" and tried to practice medicine "amid the impoverished people of his old home."[33]

The waxing of masculine postludes did not always need a visit from the grim reaper. After Confederate general Joseph Wheeler spoke before a gathering of veterans, one man noted, "He demonstrated in his own life that manhood and purity are above riches, that they are higher than titles."[34] Another Southern writer, when discussing Confederate Henry Stone, noted that he remained alive, "vigorous in body, keen in mind, always ready to fight, and fight hard, for a good cause, an ornament to the bar, and a splendid specimen of that splendid manhood that the soldiers of the Confederacy furnished a reunited country."[35]

Many within the veteran household believed that future generations of men held some responsibility in honoring the sacrifices of the Civil War generation. In a way, the next several generations would garner at least a portion of their masculine status from how they recognized the sacrifices of their fathers and grandfathers. Joseph Martin, at a gathering of veterans, declared that Southerners never needed to apologize or "beg pardon for our manhood in the past." Rather, it would be up to the next generations of sons to "be true" to their fathers and always stand ready to defend their manhood by remaining "loyal to their memory."[36] J. Harvey Mathes, in a published volume of the reminiscences of Confederate veterans from Memphis, Tennessee, noted that Southerners had long cast aside the cloud of "humiliation and defeat" and remained "cheerful, industrious, loyal citizens." Nonetheless, they still deserved a heightened level of respect for the "deeds and sacrifices of the men who wore the gray, whose names will be honored as long as American valor and true manhood endure"[37]

A personal assessment of their military service prompted some veterans to look back on their wartime years as a positive experience that did not serve as a harbinger to defining their manhood. In 1895, Felix Robertson wrote a letter to another veteran in Texas in order to assess his wartime experience. Robertson stated, "When I look back on our experience in the army, I am glad to say that I have, to a great extent, lost the memory of the things that were most disagreeable in that life; and I often recall, with increased pulse and filling eyes, incidents of unselfishness and heroism that we were accustomed to see every day in that service." Robertson had undergone an erasure of the negative elements in combat and camp in order to find personal emotional satisfaction with his military service. He concluded, "And not withstanding all the bitterness that still comes when I think of our defeat, I rejoice and am glad that I was a member of that noble band." Robertson had not completely shelved any anger over the failure of the Confederacy; rather, he found a way to compartmentalize it into a mostly positive set of memories that allowed him to function on a daily basis.[38]

The rhetoric of lifting up Confederate manhood also appeared in the speeches offered by Union officials who attended the 1917 UCV reunion held in Washington, D.C. General Ell Torrance, a previous commander of the Grand Army of the Republic (the Union version of the UCV), told the crowd, "Our material prosperity is not the most important thing. It is manhood and womanhood; it is justice and fairness; a square deal for every man, woman and child, not only in America, but in the world." When the crowd later gathered around the United Daughters of the Confederacy monument in Arlington Cemetery, Torrance of Minneapolis explained, "Arlington is beautiful beyond compare—beautiful for situation and nationally sacred because of its memories. These memories are of a most inspiring and refining nature. They are interwoven with chivalric manhood and noble womanhood." Bishop Collins Denny echoed the rhetoric of manhood offered by Torrance but also enhanced deeper discussion of reconciliation. He declared, "We cannot, as we ought not, to forget you old veterans, nor your comrades who sleep in our soil. Heroes all, we hail you." Collins described the blood spilled as having the ability to write "the epic of your manhood and no true man would now obliterate one word. Indelible is your record and the climb of the centuries will but brighten your deeds." The gathering in the nation's capital, a fitting location given a program so heavy in reconciliation rhetoric in the midst of World War I, prompted Collins to call for a perseverance of the memory that the UCV had worked to secure. He concluded, "Never can we become so ungrateful as to forget how in your youth the South stripped herself to very nakedness, gave exhaustingly her last resources, gave the lives of her dearest and her best, gave all save honor."[39]

Throughout their extensive memorial efforts, the United Confederate Veterans took on an important but often overlooked role on the frontlines of reconstructing the Southern household by creating a space for men to reaffirm their masculine status in society. Confederate defeat dictated that Southern men needed to take more concerted efforts to show that any masculine status stripped away by war's failure could be rebuilt through employment, a strong relationship where the man prominently emerged as the head of household, or the memorial efforts of various veteran groups. The premier Confederate veteran group asserted themselves through monument construction, textbook writing, and numerous speeches at meetings and reunions as an important catalyst in rehabilitating the masculine identity of many Southern men who questioned their self-worth in the face of injury, diminished economic prospects, or the loss of a romantic partner. As Southern memorial efforts sought to construct a dignified and honorable army of marble men in town squares across the South, the living monuments had their honorable, manly participation in the Civil War reaffirmed time and time again through a brotherhood rededicated to the defeat of the shadows cast by Union victory.

NOTES

1. United Daughters of the Confederacy, Arkansas Division, Confederate Veterans' Documents, w.0034, box 2, folder 10 Tomlinson, and box 3, folder 15 Vaughn, Amelia Gorgas Library, University of Alabama.

2. Clyde Griffen, "Reconstructing Masculinity from the Evangelical Revival to the Waning of Progressivism: A Speculative Synthesis," in *Meanings for Manhood: Constructions of Masculinity in Victorian America*, ed. Mark C. Carnes and Clyde Griffen (Chicago: University of Chicago Press, 1990), 191; LeeAnn Whites, *The Civil War as a Crisis in Gender: Augusta, Georgia, 1860–1890* (Athens: University of Georgia Press, 1995), 11; Lorri Glover, *Southern Sons: Becoming Men in the New Nation* (Baltimore: Johns Hopkins University Press, 2007), 3, 91, 97, 101; Craig Thompson Friend and Lorri Glover, "Rethinking Southern Masculinity: An Introduction," in *Southern Manhood: Perspectives on Masculinity in the Old South*, ed. Craig Thompson Friend and Lorri Glover (Athens: University of Georgia Press, 2004), x, xi; Bertram Wyatt-Brown, *Southern Honor: Ethics and Behavior in the Old South* (New York: Oxford University Press, 1982), 14; Laura F. Edwards, "The Problem of De-

pendency: African Americans, Labor Relations, and the Law in the Nineteenth-Century South," *Agricultural History* 72, no. 2 (Spring 1998): 315; Jane Dailey, *Before Jim Crow: The Politics of Race in Postemancipation Virginia* (Chapel Hill: University of North Carolina Press, 2000), 90–95; Stephen W. Berry II, *All That Makes a Man: Love and Ambition in the Civil War South* (New York: Oxford University Press, 2003), 12, 20–21. For an antebellum account of the origins of manhood, see Stephanie McCurry, *Masters of Small Worlds: Yeoman Households, Gender Relations, and the Political Culture of the Antebellum South Carolina Low Country* (New York: Oxford University Press, 1995). For more on how the image of the whole man equated manhood, see Kenneth S. Greenberg, *Honor & Slavery: Lies, Duels, Noses, Masks, Dressing as a Woman, Gifts, Strangers, Humanitarianism, Death, Slave Rebellions, the Proslavery Argument, Baseball, Hunting, and Gambling in the Old South* (Princeton: Princeton University Press, 1996); Gail Benderman, *Manliness and Civilization: A Cultural History of Gender and Race in the United States, 1880–1917* (Chicago: University of Chicago Press, 1995); E. Anthony Rotundo, *American Manhood: Transformations in Masculinity from the Revolution to the Modern Era* (New York: Basic Books, 1993); Christina S. Jarvis, *The Male Body at War: American Masculinity during World War II* (DeKalb: Northern Illinois University Press, 2004). For more on honor and Southern manhood, see Wyatt-Brown, *Southern Honor*, 34–36, 133–34, 144–59, 164–70; W. J. Cash, *The Mind of the South* (New York: Vintage, 1991); Kenneth S. Greenberg, *Masters and Statesmen: The Political Culture of Slavery* (Baltimore: Johns Hopkins University Press, 1985); Steven M. Stowe, *Intimacy and Power in the Old South* (Baltimore: Johns Hopkins University Press, 1987); Joanne B. Freeman, *Affairs of Honor: National Politics in the New Republic* (New Haven: Yale University Press, 2001); Edward L. Ayers, *Vengeance and Justice: Crime and Punishment in the Nineteenth-Century South* (New York: Oxford University Press, 1984). For more on gender notions in the antebellum and wartime South, as well as ways men defined themselves in the period, see Kathleen M. Brown, *Good Wives, Nasty Wenches, and Anxious Patriarchs: Gender, Race, and Power in Colonial Virginia* (Chapel Hill: University of North Carolina Press, 1996); Laura Edwards, *Scarlett Doesn't Live Here Anymore: Women in the Civil War Era* (Urbana: University of Illinois Press, 2000); John Mayfield, "'The Soul of a Man!' William Gilmore Simms and the Myths of Southern Manhood," *Journal of the Early Republic* 15 (1995): 477–500; Janet Moore Lindman, "Acting the Manly Christian: White Evangelical Masculinity in Revolutionary Virginia," *William and Mary Quarterly* 57 (2000): 393–416; and Anya Jabour, "Male Friendship and Masculinity in the Early National South: William Wirt and His Friends," *Journal of the Early Republic* 20 (2000): 83–111. For more on how young Confederates perceived the war as a solidification of manhood, see Peter S. Carmichael, *The Last Generation: Young Virginians in Peace, War, and Reunion* (Chapel Hill: University of North Carolina Press, 2005), especially 162–64; and Mark V. Wetherington, *Plain Folk's Fight: The Civil War and Reconstruction in Piney Woods Georgia* (Chapel Hill: University of North Carolina Press, 2005), especially 81–111.

3. For more on notions of manhood and womanhood, see Whites, *The Civil War as a Crisis in Gender*; Anya Jabour, *Scarlett's Sisters: Young Women in the Old South* (Chapel Hill: University of North Carolina Press, 2007); Victoria E. Ott, *Confederate Daughters: Coming of Age during the Civil War* (Carbondale: Southern Illinois University Press, 2008); Glover, *Southern Sons*; Laura F. Edwards, *Gendered Strife and Confusion: The Political Culture of Reconstruction* (Urbana: University of Illinois Press, 1997); Edwards, *Scarlett Doesn't Live Here Anymore*. For more on the experience of Confederate women during and after the war, see Anne Sarah Rubin, *A Shattered Nation: The Rise and Fall of the Confederacy, 1861–1868* (Chapel Hill: University of North Carolina Press, 2005), 54–77; Lisa Tendrich Frank, *The Civilian War: Confederate Women and Union Soldiers during Sherman's March* (Baton Rouge: Louisiana State University Press, 2015); Brian Craig Miller, *Empty Sleeves: Amputation in the Civil War South* (Athens: University of Georgia Press, 2015), especially chap. 3; Jane Turner Censer, *The Reconstruction of White Southern Womanhood, 1865–1890* (Baton Rouge: Louisiana State University Press, 2003); Edmund L. Drago, *Confederate Phoenix: Rebel Children and Their Families in South Carolina* (New York: Fordham University Press, 2008); Drew Gilpin Faust, *Mothers of Invention: Women of the Slaveholding South in the American Civil War* (New York: Vintage Books, 1996); Catherine Clinton and Nina Silber, eds., *Battle Scars: Gender and Sexuality in the American Civil War* (New York: Oxford University Press, 2006); Catherine Clinton and Nina Silber, eds., *Divided Houses: Gender and the Civil War* (New York: Oxford University Press, 1992); Alecia P. Long, *The Great Southern Babylon: Sex, Race, and Respectability in New Orleans, 1865–1920* (Baton Rouge: Louisiana State University Press, 2004); LeeAnn Whites, *Gender Matters: Civil War, Reconstruction, and the Making of the New South* (New York: Palgrave Macmillan, 2005); LeeAnn Whites and Alecia P. Long, eds., *Occupied Women: Gender, Military Occupation, and the American Civil War* (Baton Rouge: Louisiana State University Press, 2009); and Berry, *All That Makes a Man*, 95–111.

4. Faust, *Mothers of Invention*, 238–44. For more on the burdens of nursing, see Lisa A. Long, *Rehabilitating Bodies: Health, History, and the American Civil War* (Philadelphia: University of Pennsylvania Press, 2003), 180–209; Libra R. Hilde, *Worth a Dozen Men: Women and Nursing in the Civil War South* (Charlottesville: University of Virginia Press, 2012); Jane E. Schultz, *Women at the Front: Hospital Workers in Civil War America* (Chapel Hill: University of North Carolina Press, 2007).

5. George S. Bernard, ed., *War Talks of Confederate Veterans* (Petersburg, Va.: Fenn and Owen, 1892), 256, accessed at Kentucky Historical Society, Frankfort (KYHS).

6. Paul A. Cimbala, *Veterans North and South: The Transition from Soldier to Civilian after the American Civil War* (Santa Barbara, Calif.: Praeger, 2015), 13, 31.

7. See Wayne Wei-Siang Hsieh, "'Go to Your Gawd Like a Soldier': Transnational Reflections on Veteranhood," *Journal of the Civil War Era* 5, no. 4 (December 2015): 565. Hsieh noted that "Confederate veterans did not normally suffer from the utter destitution associated with British veterans." For ample examples of impoverished conditions, see Miller, *Empty Sleeves*, 134–35.

8. John A. Casey Jr., *New Men: Reconstructing the Image of the Veteran in Late-Nineteenth-Century American Literature and Culture* (New York: Fordham University Press, 2015), 12, 29, 49–50, 61.

9. *Morgan's Men: A Narrative of Personal Experiences by Henry Lane Stone George B Eastin Camp, No 803 UCV at the Free Public Library, Louisville, Ky., April 8, 1919*, KYHS.

10. Cimbala, *Veterans North and South*, 72.

11. Confederate Pension Files #450 and #2697, State of Kentucky Archives, Frankfort.

12. Cimbala, *Veterans North and South*, 60–61.

13. Hsieh, "'Go to Your Gawd Like a Soldier,'" 553.

14. "An Address Delivered before the Confederate Survivors' Association, in Augusta, Georgia, 1879, April 26, 1879," Charles C. Jones Jr. Papers, Virginia Historical Society, Richmond (VHS).

15. "Constitution and By-Laws of the Confederate Association of Kentucky Organized 2 April 1888 at Louisville, Ky.," Bartlett Family: Papers, 1858–1930, folder 24, Filson Historical Society, Louisville.

16. William W. White, *The Confederate Veteran* (Tuscaloosa, Ala.: Confederate, 1962), 11.

17. "National Constitution Adopted April 1892—Third Annual Meeting in New Orleans," Louisiana Historical Association Papers 55-o box 1, folder 1, Howard-Tilton Memorial Library, Tulane University (TU). For more on the UCV, see Cimbala, *Veterans North and South*; Edward Ayers, *The Promise of the New South: Life after Reconstruction* (New York: Oxford University Press, 1992); W. Fitzhugh Brundage, *The Southern Past: A Clash of Race and Memory* (Cambridge: Harvard University Press, 2005); David W. Blight, *Race and Reunion: The Civil War in American Memory* (Cambridge: Harvard University Press, 2002); Caroline E. Janney, *Remembering the Civil War: Reunion and the Limits of Reconciliation* (Chapel Hill: University of North Carolina Press, 2013); and Gaines Foster, *Ghosts of the Confederacy: Defeat, the Lost Cause, and the Emergence of the New South, 1865–1913* (New York: Oxford University Press, 1988).

18. "Circular Letter from John B. Gordon, December 6, 1902," Louisiana Historical Association Papers 55-o box 1, folder 6, TU.

19. "1893 UCV Report," Joseph Jones Papers, Special Collections, Louisiana State University Library (LSU).

20. Casey, *New Men*, 9, 113.

21. "United Daughters of the Confederacy, Arkansas Division," Confederate Veterans' Documents, W.0034, folder 13, James Williams, Amelia Gorgas Library, University of Alabama at Tuscaloosa.

22. *Speech of General Bennett H. Young: Delivered at Birmingham, June 16, 1916 Reunion*, Filson Historical Society, Louisville.

23. *Speech of General Bennett H. Young.*

24. "Annual Report of the President Confederate Veterans Association, 1895," VHS.

25. *The Motives and Aims of the Soldiers of the South in the Civil War: An Oration Delivered before the United Confederate Veterans at Their Fourteenth Annual Reunion at Nashville, Tennessee, June 14, 1904, by Randolph Harrison McKim*, VHS.

26. *The Motives and Aims of the Soldiers.*

27. *Thirty-Seventh Reunion Grand Camp, UCV and 29th Reunion, SCV*, 1924, VHS..

28. *Confederate Home Messenger*, Pewee Valley, Ky., November 1908, KYHS.

29. "United Daughters of the Confederacy, Amelia Gayle Gorgas Chapter Records," MSS 1469, Scrapbook, 1953–54, 1469.015, University Libraries Division of Special Collections, University of Alabama (UA).

30. *Proceedings of the Eighth Annual Meeting of the Grand Camp Confederate Veterans 1895*, VHS.

31. "Grand Camp Confederate Veterans," R. E. Lee Camp No. 1, box 30, folder Portrait Subjects S, VHS.

32. "United Daughters of the Confederacy, Amelia Gayle Gorgas Chapter Records," MSS 1469, Scrapbooks, 1942, 1949–59, 1455, UA.

33. "United Confederate Veterans Camp W. J. Hardee, N. 39. Birmingham, AL, Records," w.0048, UA.

34. "United Daughters of the Confederacy, Alabama Division Records," box 1401, folder 36, MSS 1472, UA.

35. *Morgan's Men: A Narrative of Personal Experiences by Henry Lane Stone George B Eastin Camp, No 803 UCV at the Free Public Library, Louisville, Ky., April 8, 1919*, KYHS.

36. "United Daughters of the Confederacy, Alabama Division Records," box 1400, folder 1, MSS 1472, UA.

37. J. Harvey Mathes, *The Old Guard in Gray: Researches in the Annals of the Confederate Historical Association. Sketches of Memphis Veterans Who Upheld Her Standards in the War, and of Other Confederate Worthies* (Memphis, Tenn.: Press of S. C. Toof, 1897), 18.

38. Cimbala, *Veterans North and South*, 121

39. *Thomas Osborne Scrapbook, 1917*, Filson Historical Society, Louisville.

From Household to Personhood in America

STEPHEN BERRY

The first-ever U.S. census, taken in 1790, only lists the names of heads of households, most of whom were men, with their dependents enumerated but unnamed below them. The 1850 census lists every free man, woman, and child in America; the enslaved are counted but remain nameless on a separate schedule. The 1870 census is an expansive list of Americans; there is only one schedule and all persons are named.[1]

State bureaucracy can care about people for right and wrong reasons. Hitler's Germany was ruthlessly precise about who was who. However, this simple snapshot of the census—of how a state "sees"—is telling. In 1790, we were a nation of households. In 1850 we were a nation that recognized whites as people and blacks as (mostly) things. In 1870, most of us had a line; we were all people, all a datum in the brain of the state.[2]

The Civil War was the critical point in this transformation of who "counts" as a person in America. This volume is a meditation on who counts: Should the Civil War be written as a history of (mostly) white men and their guns, or should it be written as the history of every man, woman, and child who had a stake in, and an influence upon, the outcome of a "global event"? And, if the latter, what theoretical framework do we have to contain it all?

In 1860, Americans lived in houses, not homes. Homes came later, after the transition from a household economy to an industrial one and after the rise of the middle class. A home was presided over by a woman who created a sanctuary for her husband and then for herself and her children. For a hundred years after she first created a "home," her labor did not count in the same way as did her husband's or in the same way as it had in the preindustrial period. She was remunerated by something else—her "fulfill-ment" as a "True Woman" in the "Cult of Domesticity."[3]

In 1860, most Americans still lived in houses, irreducible loci of produc-tion and reproduction, economic units as much as familial ones. The word "husband" comes from the Old Norse *hús* (house) coupled to *bóndi* (tiller of the soil). In its very etymology, "husband" is the center of the house, and the house is the center of economic activity. The etymology of "wife" is very different—it simply means "woman." Such etymological explorations bring context to the term "household." It was created precisely to encompass a husband, a wife, and the children and servants that a husband's *hús* pro-tected and exploited. The word "hold," like the word "keep," implied a place of physical protection, the penumbra of safety around an (ostensibly) pow-erful male. "Hold" had other, equally relevant meanings: "to have or keep in the hand; keep fast; grasp; to keep in a specified state or relation." A "house-hold" system was a system that subsumed, not a system that liberated.[4]

When Lincoln invoked the "House Divided," his listeners knew pre-cisely where he was coming from: "And Jesus knew their thoughts, and said unto them, Every kingdom divided against itself is brought to desola-tion, and every city or house divided against itself shall not stand." Before the twentieth century, house/city/kingdom were the nesting dolls of the patriarchal order. To invoke a house falling was to conjure an image not of walls collapsing but of masculine obliteration in an assault on the house-hold itself—the Fall of the House of Usher.[5]

For Confederates, the Civil War represented a colossal threat to houses and households. Dwellings, barns, smokehouses, outbuildings, fences, crops, and livestock destroyed, cities occupied and put to the torch, wives threatened, families scattered, "servants" liberated, sons murdered . . . noth-ing to pass down, no one to pass it down to anyway—the Fall of the House of Dixie—patriarchal obliteration. Such destruction was not *incidental* to the conflict, as this book shows, but central to how the Civil War was pros-ecuted and won.[6]

The conflict was a household war on the federal side, too. Yes, a political sensibility—Union—sent men sprinting into a cannon's mouth, but it was no mere abstraction. In seeking a word to describe a collective of states, the word "union" had been chosen precisely because it borrowed against its familial and marital meanings. By 1860, Union had become the Federals' paternity, their inheritance, their *house*—everything that had to be trans-mitted from Founding Fathers to freedom-loving sons. The Slave Pow-er's plot to nationalize slavery—to take enslaved African Americans every-where—was equally threatening to the households of Northern white abolitionists and Northern white racists. For abolitionists, slavery's great perversion was what it did to the black household, emasculating Christian men and raping Christian women. For the North's white supremacists, the nationalization of slavery threatened to place blacks in their neighborhoods, shop floors, and schools, and how could any household be sacrosanct with such people so near? David Wilmot highlighted precisely this fear in attempting to bar slavery from the territories "won" from Mexico: "I have no squeamish sensitiveness on the subject of slavery—no morbid sympathy for the slave," he said. "I would preserve for free white labor a fair country, a rich inheritance, where the sons of toil, of my own race and own color, can live without the disgrace which association with negro slavery brings upon free labor." The Wilmots of the North fought for blood and (free) soil—for (white) households.[7]

For the enslaved, enslavement had always been a household war; the Civil War only intensified the conflict. For generations, enslaved people had carved out their own cultural and social spaces in staggering acts of imagination and will. Still they had neither wives nor children who couldn't be threatened with rape or sale, no sons who could be sent out into the world to carry on the family name. No wonder then that as Washington politicians wrangled about the language of the Thirteenth, Fourteenth, and Fifteenth Amendments, freedpeople went to work erecting *houses*, reuniting their families, pulling their women from the field, and sending their children to school. They too sought to protect human dignity as they knew it, including its cornerstone: the (black) patriarchal household.[8]

To understand the Civil War as a "household war" is to escape, finally, the homefront/battlefront binary. Buffs may continue to understand the Civil War as the narrow work of men and guns, but since the 1990s, scholars working on guerrilla warfare, contraband camps, occupation studies, Confederate politics, and Civil War refugees have proven that, even in a narrow military sense, the Civil War cannot be understood as a sequence of battles, and Civil War battles cannot be physically separated from the homefront. What *Household War* offers is an analytical framework to contain the insights of everyone—the military historians on the one side and the historians of race, labor, and gender on the other.[9]

Ironically, the household itself, as defined here, did not long survive the Civil War. In Paul E. Johnson's classic *A Shopkeeper's Millennium*, the early national "household" is portrayed deftly as an extended economic unit as much as a familial one. A man who made wagon wheels, for instance, went out to his barn in the morning with his apprentice and they drank from the same flask and told the same jokes as they made and sold wagon wheels to local men they knew and drank and told jokes with until the apprentice took over the business. Their wives raised children and chickens and made butter and bread in a household where everyone worked tirelessly for each other and the local market. The Southern version of this household was equally organic and more disturbing. The enslaved were, in an illusionary sense, part of a working family, black and white, even if the beatings were more calculated because everyone had to do "their part." At the nucleus of the household in both cases was a (usually white) man, the force of his prerogatives, positive and negative, keeping everything and everyone orbiting around him and all in their proper sphere.[10]

Before and especially after the Civil War, modernization, a word that means everything and nothing, split the atom, broke the household apart: no more handmade wagon wheels, no more apprentices, no more sales mediated by handshakes and smiles and inquiries about Aunt Edna's gallstones. The wheels were now made on an assembly line. The manager made bank selling bulk to strangers; the linemen got drunk and told their own (dirtier) jokes; middle-class women quit "working" in one sense to start "working" in another, reforming the hard edges of the world that capitalism had wrought, presiding over homes, not houses, the new centers of the consumer economy and oases from the industrial one.[11]

Splitting the atom, however, made it possible for all to have an individual relationship to themselves and the market. A modern understanding of personhood would be erected on the ruin of the premodern understanding of household. Here the Civil War played an enormous role. When ratified in 1868, the Fourteenth Amendment defined, for the first time, American citizenship and the rights thereunto appertaining, beginning a process of enshrining in law the world's first great postulation of personhood: "We hold these truths to be self-evident . . ."[12]

No war is the sum of its means; every war is the sum of its consequences. Fought by and upon American households, the Civil War ironically struck a devastating blow to the household as the constituent unit of American life. The full process would be a slow one, winding through Klan rallies, spousal beatings, and failed Equal Rights Amendments on a circuitous road to a Universal Declaration of Human Rights. But the Civil War did much to place the sanctity of the individual (as a legal entity) ahead of the sanctity of the household (as an "organic" economic and patriarchal entity). Both systems have their value and values; only one has a future.

NOTES

1. The history of Native Americans and the census is even more complicated. In establishing the census, Article 1, Section 2 of the Constitution explicitly excluded "Indians not taxed," meaning those living beyond U.S. authority or living on reservations. The first census to count Native Americans in significant numbers (forty thousand) was 1860; instructions to marshals noted: "The families of Indians who have renounced tribal rule, and who under state or territory laws exercise the rights of citizens, are to be enumerated." These instructions were further revised in 1870: "Indians not in tribal relations, whether full-bloods or half-breeds, who are found mingled with the white population, residing in white families, engaged as servants or laborers, or living in huts or wigwams on the outskirts of towns or settlements are to be regarded as a part of the ordinary population of the country . . . and are to be embraced in enumeration." Even so the estimated proportion of Native Americans who officially "counted" that year was 8 percent. See James P. Collins, "Native Americans in the Census, 1860–1890," *Prologue Magazine* 38, no. 2 (Summer 2006), https://www.archives.gov/publications/prologue/2006/summer/indian-census.html. For a broader social history of the census, see Margo J. Anderson, *The American Census: A Social History* (New Haven: Yale University Press, 1988).

2. James C. Scott, *Seeing Like a State: How Certain Schemes to Improve the Human Condition Have Failed* (New Haven: Yale University Press, 1998).

3. Barbara Welter, "The Cult of True Womanhood: 1820–1860," *American Quarterly* 18, no. 2 (Summer 1966): 151–74. See also Mary P. Ryan, *Cradle of the Middle Class: The Family in Oneida County, New York, 1790–1865* (New York: Cambridge University Press, 1983).

4. Carole Shammas, *A History of Household Government in America* (Charlottesville: University of Virginia Press, 2002), xiii. As Shammas notes: "The disintegration of household powers during the mid-nineteenth century—the household's 'civil war'—is much more central to what makes that period seem modern than industrialization or urbanization."

5. Gospel of Matthew 12:25, KJV.

6. Bruce Levine, *The Fall of the House of Dixie: The Civil War and the Social Revolution That Transformed the South* (New York: Random House, 2014).

7. David Wilmot, *Congressional Globe*, 29th Cong., 2nd sess., 1847.

8. On black women's labor in multiple senses in the colonial period, see Jennifer L. Morgan, *Laboring Women: Reproduction and Gender in New World Slavery* (Philadelphia: University of Pennsylvania Press, 2004). For the Civil War era, see Thavolia Glymph, *Out of the House of Bondage: The Transformation of the Plantation Household* (New York: Cambridge University Press, 2008).

9. LeeAnn Whites, *The Civil War as a Crisis in Gender: Augusta, Georgia, 1860–1890* (Athens: University of Georgia Press, 1995); LeeAnn Whites and Alecia P. Long, eds., *Occupied Women: Gender, Military Occupation, and the American Civil*

War (Baton Rouge: Louisiana State University Press, 2009); Chandra Manning, *Troubled Refuge: Struggling for Freedom in the Civil War* (New York: Random House, 2016); Lisa Tendrich Frank, *The Civilian War: Confederate Women and Union Soldiers during Sherman's March* (Baton Rouge: Louisiana State University Press, 2015); Joseph M. Beilein Jr., *Bushwhackers: Guerrilla Warfare, Manhood, and the Household in Civil War Missouri* (Kent, Ohio: Kent State University Press, 2016); Stephanie McCurry, *Confederate Reckoning: Power and Politics in the Civil War South* (Cambridge: Harvard University Press, 2010); Daniel E. Sutherland, *A Savage Conflict: The Decisive Role of Guerrillas in the American Civil War* (Chapel Hill: University of North Carolina Press, 2009); Victoria E. Bynum, *The Free State of Jones: Mississippi's Longest Civil War* (Chapel Hill: University of North Carolina Press, 2005). See also Lorien Foote, "Rethinking the Confederate Homefront," *Journal of the Civil War Era* 7, no. 3 (September 2017): 446–65.

10. Paul E. Johnson, *A Shopkeeper's Millennium: Society and Revivals in Rochester, New York, 1815–1837* (New York: Hill and Wang, 1994).

11. Modernization theory traces back to Max Weber but remains controversial. See Wolfgang Knobi, "Theories That Won't Pass Away: The Never-ending Story," in *Handbook of Historical Sociology*, ed. Gerard Delanty and Engin F. Isin (London: SAGE, 2003), 96–107. For a nuanced portrait of low-wage labor and its relationship to market transitions in early America, see Seth Rockman, *Scraping By: Wage Labor, Slavery, and Survival in Early Baltimore* (Baltimore: Johns Hopkins University Press, 2009).

12. Amy Dru Stanley makes the point that the transition to personhood was made possible by the advent of the contract, especially for wage labor and marriage. See Amy Dru Stanley, *From Bondage to Contract: Wage Labor, Marriage, and the Market in the Age of Slave Emancipation* (New York: Cambridge University Press, 1998).

CONTRIBUTORS

Joseph M. Beilein Jr. is the author of *Bushwhackers: Guerrilla Warfare, Manhood, and the Household in Civil War Missouri* (2016) and coeditor of *The Civil War Guerrilla: Unfolding the Black Flag in History, Memory, and Myth* (2015). He has also published numerous essays on the history of guerrilla warfare and gender in the Civil War. He is an associate professor of history at Penn State Erie, the Behrend College.

Stephen Berry is Gregory Professor of the Civil War Era at the University of Georgia, where he specializes in the history of the nineteenth-century American South. The author or editor of six books, Berry also oversees the web project CSI: Dixie. Berry's work has been supported by the National Endowment for the Humanities, the Mellon Foundation, and the American Council of Learned Societies, among others. He is currently working on *The Black Prince: The Emancipated Life of Prince Rivers of South Carolina*.

Victoria E. Bynum is Distinguished Professor Emeritus of History at Texas State University, San Marcos. A scholar of class, gender, and race relations in the Civil War era South, she is an award-winning author and a National Endowment of the Humanities Fellow. Her book *The Free State of Jones* (2001) inspired the 2016 movie *The Free State of Jones*.

Joan E. Cashin received her doctorate at Harvard University, and is a professor of history at Ohio State University. She is the author most recently of *War Stuff: The Struggle for Human and Environmental Resources in the American Civil War* (2018) and the editor of *War Matters: Material Culture in the Civil War Era* (2018).

Angela Esco Elder is an assistant professor of history at Converse College. She earned her doctorate at the University of Georgia, and she was the 2016–17 Virginia Center for Civil War Studies postdoctoral fellow at Virginia Tech. Her research explores gender, emotion, family, and trauma in the Civil War era South. She is the coeditor of *Practical Strangers: The Courtship Correspondence of Nathaniel Dawson and Elodie Todd, Sister of Mary Todd Lincoln* (2017).

Lorien Foote is the Patricia and Bookman Peters Professor in History at Texas A&M University and the director of graduate studies. She is the author of four books, including *The Yankee Plague: Escaped Union Prisoners and the Collapse of the Confederacy* (2016). Her digital humanities project visualizes the escape of three thousand Union prisoners of war and includes contributions from undergraduate researchers at three universities: www.ehistory.org/projects/fugitive-federals.html.

Andrew K. Frank is the Allen Morris Professor at Florida State University. He is the author of numerous books and articles on Native American history. His books include *Before the Pioneers: Indians, Settlers, Slaves, and the Founding of Miami* (2017) and *Creeks and Southerners: Biculturalism on the Early American Frontier* (2005). He is writing a history of the Seminoles and other indigenous Floridians. He received his PhD from the University of Florida.

Lisa Tendrich Frank is the author of *The Civilian War: Confederate Women and Union Soldiers during Sherman's March* (2015). She has also published five edited collections and a dozen articles and book chapters on women's history and the Civil War. She is writing a book on the forced evacuation of Atlanta's civilians in 1864. She received her PhD from the University of Florida.

Brian Craig Miller is dean of humanities, social science, and fine arts at Mission College in Santa Clara, California. He also serves as the editor of the journal *Civil War History* and is a series coeditor for *The Civil War Era in the South*. His most recent book is *Empty Sleeves: Amputation in the Civil War South* (2015).

Julie A. Mujic is a visiting assistant professor in global commerce at Denison University and owns Paramount Historical Consulting, LLC. Her forthcoming book, *Why They Stayed: The Mind of Northern Men in the Civil War Midwest*, will be published by Fordham University Press.

Brooks D. Simpson is ASU Foundation Professor of History at Arizona State University. He is the author, editor, or coeditor of several books on the Civil War and Reconstruction era. He is best known for *Ulysses S. Grant: Triumph over Adversity, 1822–1865* (2000), *The Reconstruction Presidents* (1998), and *Reconstruction: Voices from America's First Great Struggle for Racial Equality* (2018).

Margaret Storey is professor of history and associate dean of the College of Liberal Arts and Social Sciences at DePaul University in Chicago. She is the author of *Loyalty and Loss: Alabama's Unionists in the Civil War and Reconstruction* (2004); editor of the memoir of a Tennessee Union cavalryman, *Tried Men and True; or, Union Life in Dixie* (2011); and coauthor, with Nicolas Proctor, of *Kentucky 1861: Loyalty, State, and Nation* (2017), part of the W. W. Norton series Reacting to the Past.

Jonathan W. White is associate professor of American studies at Christopher Newport University. He is the author or editor of nine books and more than one hundred articles, essays, and reviews. He serves as vice chair of the Lincoln Forum, chair of the board of the Abraham Lincoln Institute, on the boards of the Abraham Lincoln Association and the John L. Nau III Center for Civil War History at the University of Virginia, and on the Ford's Theatre Advisory Council.

LeeAnn Whites is Professor Emerita of History at the University of Missouri. She is the author of many books and articles on the Civil War era and women in the nineteenth-century South; her works include *The Civil War as a Crisis in Gender: Augusta, Georgia, 1860–1890* (1995); *Gender Matters: Civil War, Reconstruction, and the Making of the New South* (2005); and *Occupied Women: Gender, Military Occupation, and the American Civil War* (2009).

INDEX

UnCivil Wars